References for the Rest of Us

COMPUTER BOOK SERIES FROM IDG

Are you intimidated and confused by computers? Do you find that traditional manuals are overloaded with technical details you'll never use? Do your friends and family always call you to fix simple problems on their PCs? Then the *. . . For Dummies*™ computer book series from IDG is for you.

. . . For Dummies books are written for those frustrated computer users who know they aren't really dumb but find that PC hardware, software, and indeed the unique vocabulary of computing make them feel helpless. *. . . For Dummies* books use a lighthearted approach, a down-to-earth style, and even cartoons and humorous icons to diffuse computer novices' fears and build their confidence. Lighthearted but not lightweight, these books are a perfect survival guide for anyone forced to use a computer.

"I like my copy so much I told friends; now they bought copies."

Irene C., Orwell, Ohio

"Quick, concise, nontechnical, and humorous."

Jay A., Elburn, Illinois

"Thanks, I needed this book. Now I can sleep at night."

Robin F., British Columbia, Canada

Already, hundreds of thousands of satisfied readers agree. They have made *. . . For Dummies* books the #1 introductory level computer book series and have written asking for more. So, if you're looking for the most fun and easy way to learn about computers, look to *. . . For Dummies* books to give you a helping hand.

MORE WINDOWS™ FOR DUMMIES®

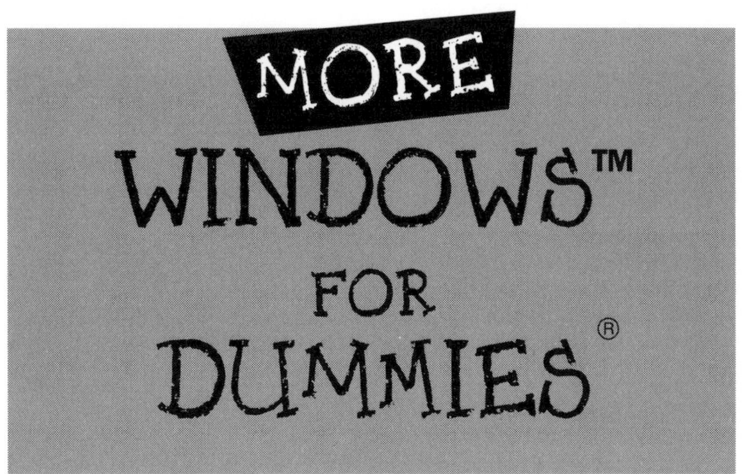

by Andy Rathbone

IDG Books Worldwide, Inc.
An International Data Group Company

Foster City, CA ♦ Chicago, IL ♦ Indianapolis, IN ♦ Braintree, MA ♦ Dallas, TX

More Windows™ For Dummies®

Published by
IDG Books Worldwide, Inc.
An International Data Group Company
919 E. Hillsdale Blvd.
Suite 400
Foster City, CA 94404

Library of Congress Catalog Card No.: 93-80351

ISBN: 1-56884-048-9

Printed in the United States of America

10 9 8 7

1B/RX/QT/ZV

Distributed in the United States by IDG Books Worldwide, Inc.

Distributed by Macmillan Canada for Canada; by Computer and Technical Books for the Caribbean Basin; by Contemporanea de Ediciones for Venezuela; by Distribuidora Cuspide for Argentina; by CITEC for Brazil; by Ediciones ZETA S.C.R. Ltda. for Peru; by Editorial Limusa SA for Mexico; by Transworld Publishers Limited in the United Kingdom and Europe; by Al-Maiman Publishers & Distributors for Saudi Arabia; by Simron Pty. Ltd. for South Africa; by IDG Communications (HK) Ltd. for Hong Kong; by Toppan Company Ltd. for Japan; by Addison Wesley Publishing Company for Korea; by Longman Singapore Publishers Ltd. for Singapore, Malaysia, Thailand and Indonesia; by Unalis Corporation for Taiwan; by WS Computer Publishing Company, Inc. for the Philippines; by WoodsLane Pty. Ltd. for Australia; by WoodsLane Enterprises Ltd. for New Zealand.

For general information on IDG Books in the U.S., including information on discounts and premiums, contact IDG Books at 800-434-3422 or 415-655-3000.

For information on where to purchase IDG Books outside the U.S., contact IDG Books International at 415-655-3021 or fax 415-655-3295.

For information on translations, contact Marc Jeffrey Mikulich, Director, Foreign & Subsidiary Rights, at IDG Books Worldwide, 415-655-3018 or fax 415-655-3295.

For sales inquiries and special prices for bulk quantities, write to the address above or call IDG Books Worldwide at 415-655-3000.

For information on using IDG Books in the classroom, or ordering examination copies, contact Jim Kelly at 800-434-2086.

About the Author

Andy Rathbone

Andy Rathbone started geeking around with computers in 1985 when he bought a boxy CP/M Kaypro 2X with lime-green letters. Like other budding nerds, he soon began playing with null-modem adapters, dialing up computer bulletin boards, and working part time at Radio Shack.

In between playing computer games, he served as editor of the *Daily Aztec* newspaper at San Diego State University. After graduating with a comparative literature degree, he went to work for a bizarre underground coffee-table magazine that sort of disappeared.

Andy began combining his two interests, words and computers, by selling articles to a local computer magazine. During the next few years, Rathbone started ghostwriting computer books for more-famous computer authors, as well as writing several hundred articles about computers for technoid publications like *Supercomputing Review*, *CompuServe*, *ID Systems*, *DataPro,* and *Shareware.*

In 1992, Andy and *DOS For Dummies* author/legend Dan Gookin teamed up to write *PCs For Dummies*, which was a runner-up in the Computer Press Association's 1993 awards. Andy subsequently wrote *Windows For Dummies*, *OS/2 For Dummies*, and *Upgrading and Fixing PCs For Dummies.*

Andy is currently writing *Multimedia For Dummies*, as well as contributing regularly to *CompuServe*, a magazine mailed monthly to CompuServe members. (Feel free to drop him a line at 75300,1565.)

Andy lives with his most-excellent wife, Tina, and their cat in San Diego, California. When not writing, Rathbone fiddles with his MIDI synthesizer and tries to keep the cat off both keyboards.

Welcome to the world of IDG Books Worldwide.

IDG Books Worldwide, Inc., is a subsidiary of International Data Group, the world's largest publisher of computer-related information and the leading global provider of information services on information technology. IDG was founded more than 25 years ago and now employs more than 7,200 people worldwide. IDG publishes more than 233 computer publications in 65 countries (see listing below). More than sixty million people read one or more IDG publications each month.

Launched in 1990, IDG Books Worldwide is today the #1 publisher of best-selling computer books in the United States. We are proud to have received 3 awards from the Computer Press Association in recognition of editorial excellence, and our best-selling *...For Dummies*™ series has more than 12 million copies in print with translations in 25 languages. IDG Books, through a recent joint venture with IDG's Hi-Tech Beijing, became the first U.S. publisher to publish a computer book in the People's Republic of China. In record time, IDG Books has become the first choice for millions of readers around the world who want to learn how to better manage their businesses.

Our mission is simple: Every IDG book is designed to bring extra value and skill-building instructions to the reader. Our books are written by experts who understand and care about our readers. The knowledge base of our editorial staff comes from years of experience in publishing, education, and journalism — experience which we use to produce books for the '90s. In short, we care about books, so we attract the best people. We devote special attention to details such as audience, interior design, use of icons, and illustrations. And because we use an efficient process of authoring, editing, and desktop publishing our books electronically, we can spend more time ensuring superior content and spend less time on the technicalities of making books.

You can count on our commitment to deliver high-quality books at competitive prices on topics consumers want to read about. At IDG, we value quality, and we have been delivering quality for more than 25 years. You'll find no better book on a subject than an IDG book.

John Kilcullen
President and CEO
IDG Books Worldwide, Inc.

IDG Books Worldwide, Inc., is a subsidiary of International Data Group, the world's largest publisher of computer-related information and the leading global provider of information services on information technology. International Data Group publishes over 220 computer publications in 65 countries. More than fifty million people read one or more International Data Group publications each month. The officers are Patrick J. McGovern, Founder and Board Chairman; Kelly Conlin, President; Jim Casella, Chief Operating Officer. International Data Group's publications include: **ARGENTINA'S** Computerworld Argentina, Infoworld Argentina; **AUSTRALIA'S** Computerworld Australia, Computer Living, Australian PC World, Australian Macworld, Network World, Mobile Business Australia, Publish!, Reseller, IDG Sources; **AUSTRIA'S** Computerwelt Oesterreich, PC Test; **BELGIUM'S** Data News (CW); **BOLIVIA'S** Computerworld; **BRAZIL'S** Computerworld, Connections, Game Power, Mundo Unix, PC World, Publish, Super Game; **BULGARIA'S** Computerworld Bulgaria, PC & Mac World Bulgaria, Network World Bulgaria; **CANADA'S** CIO Canada, Computerworld Canada, InfoCanada, Network World Canada, Reseller; **CHILE'S** Computerworld Chile, Informatica; **COLOMBIA'S** Computerworld Colombia, PC World; **COSTA RICA'S** PC World; **CZECH REPUBLIC'S** Computerworld, Elektronika, PC World; **DENMARK'S** Communications World, Computerworld Danmark, Computerworld Focus, Macintosh Produktkatalog, Macworld Danmark, PC World Danmark, PC Produktguide, Tech World, Windows World; **ECUADOR'S** PC World Ecuador; **EGYPT'S** Computerworld (CW) Middle East, PC World Middle East; **FINLAND'S** MikroPC, Tietoviikko, Tietoverkko; **FRANCE'S** Distributique, GOLDEN MAC, InfoPC, Le Guide du Monde Informatique, Le Monde Informatique, Telecoms & Reseaux; **GERMANY'S** Computerwoche, Computerwoche Focus, Computerwoche Extra, Electronic Entertainment, Gamepro, Information Management, Macwelt, Netzwelt, PC Welt, Publish, Publish; **GREECE'S** Publish & Macworld; **HONG KONG'S** Computerworld Hong Kong, PC World Hong Kong; **HUNGARY'S** Computerworld SZT, PC World; **INDIA'S** Computers & Communications; **INDONESIA'S** Info Komputer; **IRELAND'S** ComputerScope; **ISRAEL'S** Beyond Windows, Computerworld Israel, Multimedia, PC World Israel; **ITALY'S** Computerworld Italia, Lotus Magazine, Macworld Italia, Networking Italia, PC Shopping Italy, PC World Italia; **JAPAN'S** Computerworld Today, Information Systems World, Macworld Japan, Nikkei Personal Computing, SunWorld Japan, Windows World; **KENYA'S** East African Computer News; **KOREA'S** Computerworld Korea, Macworld Korea, PC World Korea; **LATIN AMERICA'S** GamePro; **MALAYSIA'S** Computerworld Malaysia, PC World Malaysia; **MEXICO'S** Compu Edicion, Compu Manufactura, Computacion/Punto de Venta, Computerworld Mexico, MacWorld, Mundo Unix, PC World, Windows; **THE NETHERLANDS'** Computer! Totaal, Computable (CW), LAN Magazine, Lotus Magazine, MacWorld; **NEW ZEALAND'S** Computer Buyer, Computerworld New Zealand, Network World, New Zealand PC World; **NIGERIA'S** PC World Africa; **NORWAY'S** Computerworld Norge, Lotusworld Norge, Macworld Norge, Maxi Data, Networld, PC World Ekspress, PC World Nettverk, PC World Norge, PC World's Produktguide, Publish& Multimedia World, Student Data, Unix World, Windowsworld; **PAKISTAN'S** PC World Pakistan; **PANAMA'S** PC World Panama; **PERU'S** Computerworld Peru, PC World; **PEOPLE'S REPUBLIC OF CHINA'S** China Computerworld, China Infoworld, China PC Info Magazine, Computer Fan, PC World China, Electronics International, Electronics Today/Multimedia World, Electronic Product World, China Network World, Software World Magazine, Telecom Product World; **PHILIPPINES'** Computerworld Philippines, PC Digest (PCW); **POLAND'S** Computerworld Poland, Computerworld Special Report, Networld, PC World/Komputer, Sunworld; **PORTUGAL'S** Cerebro/PC World, Correio Informatico/Computerworld, MacIn; **ROMANIA'S** Computerworld, PC World, Telecom Romania; **RUSSIA'S** Computerworld-Moscow, Mir - PK (PCW), Sety (Networks); **SINGAPORE'S** Computerworld Southeast Asia, PC World Singapore; **SLOVENIA'S** Monitor Magazine; **SOUTH AFRICA'S** Computer Mail (CIO),Computing S.A.,Network World S.A., Software World; **SPAIN'S** Advanced Systems, Amiga World, Computerworld Espana, Communicaciones World, Macworld Espana, NeXTWORLD, Super Juegos Magazine (GamePro), PC World Espana, Publish; **SWEDEN'S** Attack, ComputerSweden, Corporate Computing, Macworld, Mikrodatorn, Natverk & Kommunikation, PC World, CAP & Design, Datalngenjoren, Maxi Data,Windows World; **SWITZERLAND'S** Computerworld Schweiz, Macworld Schweiz, PC Tip; **TAIWAN'S** Computerworld Taiwan, PC World Taiwan; **THAILAND'S** Thai Computerworld; **TURKEY'S** Computerworld Monitor, Macworld Turkiye, PC World Turkiye; **UKRAINE'S** Computerworld, Computers+Software Magazine; **UNITED KINGDOM'S** Computing /Computerworld, Connexion/Network World, Lotus Magazine, Macworld, Open Computing/Sunworld; **UNITED STATES'** Advanced Systems, AmigaWorld, Cable in the Classroom, CD Review, CIO, Computerworld, Computerworld Client/Server Journal, Digital Video, DOS World, Electronic Entertainment Magazine (E2), Federal Computer Week, Game Hits, GamePro, IDG Books, Infoworld, Laser Event, Macworld, Maximize, Multimedia World, Network World, PC Letter, PC World, Publish, SWATPro, Video Event; **URUGUAY'S** PC World Uruguay; **VENEZUELA'S** Computerworld Venezuela, PC World; **VIETNAM'S** PC World Vietnam. 02/28/95

WINNER
Eighth Annual Computer Press Awards 1992

WINNER
Ninth Annual Computer Press Awards 1993

IDG
BOOKS

Dedication

To Windows users around the world.

Credits

Executive Vice President, Strategic Product Planning and Research
David Solomon

Editorial Director
Diane Graves Steele

Acquisitions Editor
Megg Bonar

Brand Manager
Judith A. Taylor

Editorial Managers
Tracy L. Barr
Sandra Blackthorn
Kristin A. Cocks

Editorial Assistants
Tamara S. Castleman
Stacey Holden Prince
Kevin Spencer

Acquisitions Assistant
Suki Gear

Production Director
Beth Jenkins

Supervisor of Project Coordination
Cindy L. Phipps

Pre-Press Coordinator
Steve Peake

Associate Pre-Press Coordinator
Tony Augsburger

Project Editor
H. Leigh Davis

Editors
Jodi Jensen
Barbara L. Potter
Pat Seiler

Technical Reviewer
Ron Dippold,
Senior Engineer,
Qualcomm Incorporated

Production Staff
Paul Belcastro
Valery Bourke
Mary Breidenbach
Sherry Gomoll
Drew R. Moore
Laura Puranen
Patricia R. Reynolds
Theresa Sánchez-Baker
Gina Scott

Proofreader
Sandy Grieshop

Indexer
Sherry Massey

Cover Design
Kavish + Kavish

Acknowledgments

Special thanks to Leigh Davis, Tina Rathbone, Ron Dippold, Matt Wagner, Dan and Sandy Gookin, John Kilcullen, Barb Potter, and Kristin Cocks.

(The publisher would like to give special thanks to Patrick J. McGovern, without whom this book would not have been possible.)

Contents at a Glance

Cartoons at a Glance

By Rich Tennant

page 267

page 217

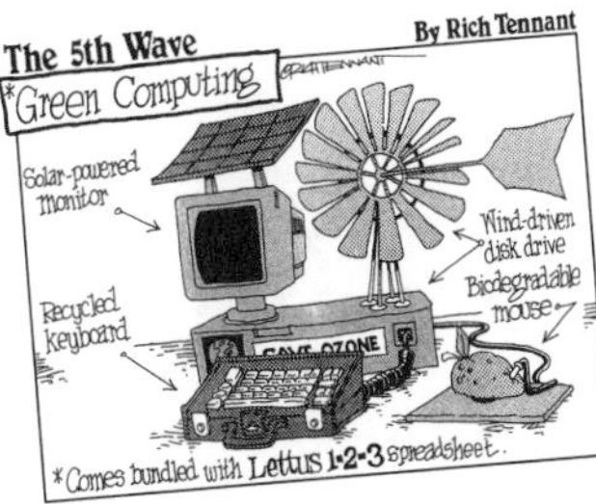

page 339

page 116

page 216

page 178

page 82

page 325

page 7

page 93

Table of Contents

Introduction

Welcome to *More Windows For Dummies*, the book for people who find themselves doing more with Windows than they ever wanted to.

The Windows *point-and-click* lifestyle never retires. No matter how long Windows has lived on your computer, it still tosses out fresh bits of confusion at regular intervals. You constantly find yourself needing to make Windows do just a little bit more than it did before. . . .

That's where this book comes in. Don't worry — it doesn't try to turn you into a card-carrying Windows wizard. No, this book merely dishes out the information that you need to make Windows do your bidding. And — if possible — to make Windows do it a little more quickly than before.

About This Book

Windows isn't *new* anymore. Just like anything that's exposed to the weather, Windows occasionally needs a little touching up. How do you make Windows deal with your latest new programs, for example? And how do you get those programs off the floppy disks and onto the Program Manager?

Or perhaps you want to spark up a newsletter or report with a fun new *font*. How? Or maybe you upgraded your computer to make Windows run faster and smoother — but now, unfortunately, Windows refuses to work at all. What do you do?

This book helps you tackle Windows chores such as these:

- Installing a new program
- *Un*installing an old program
- Using those new DOS 6 Windows utilities
- Making the mouse work right
- Deciding which Windows files you can get rid of
- Using Windows on a laptop
- Calling other computers with Terminal
- Figuring out what all those other Windows versions do

The information in this book is in easy-to-read packets that are just like the notes you got from that smart kid in math class with the big front teeth.

How to Use This Book

This book doesn't force you to *learn* anything about Windows. Save your brain cells for the important things in life. Instead, treat this book as your favorite reference. When you find yourself facing a particularly odious new Windows chore, find that subject in the Index or Table of Contents. Flip to the appropriate page and follow the step-by-step instructions. Done? Then close the book and finish your Windows work, most likely a little more quickly than before.

In the back of this book, you'll find the usual Index you might expect, which lists all the tasks and topics in this book. But, the Index *also* refers you to the original book, *Windows For Dummies*, whenever appropriate.

You — Yes, You

Chances are, you've been using Windows for a little while — maybe a month or two. You've figured out how to make Windows do *some* things. It may take all day, but you can usually convince Windows to do more or less what you want. But you're getting a little less tolerant of how Windows keeps tossing new obstacles in your path.

If *everything* about Windows looks new and confusing, check out this book's parent, *Windows For Dummies.* It explains how to start moving around in Windows without breaking anything.

But if you're looking to solve those *new* problems that Windows keeps bringing up, this book is for you.

How This Book Is Organized

Everything is easier to find when it's stored in its own well-marked bin, and the information in this book is no exception. This book contains five main parts, and each part is divided into several chapters. You don't have to read Chapters 1 through 4, however, before you can figure out what's going on in Chapter 5.

No, treat this book like the candy bins at the grocery store. Just reach straight in and grab the piece of information you want when you want it. You don't need to taste *everything* before you reach for the candy in the middle bin. In fact, the guy at the deli counter will yell if you even try.

Instead, just look up your particular problem and find the answer: a self-contained nugget that explains your particular situation and, what's more important, its particular solution.

Here are the book's main parts.

Part I: More on Everyday Stuff

Here you can find answers to those Windows questions that pop up every day. Part I is stuffed with the information you didn't know you needed to know — until you'd been using Windows for a while.

First-timers may want to check out Chapter 1, the *basics* chapter. It explains how to start Windows, push its menus around, and shut it down for the day. Chapter 1 is also a handy reference for Windows users who suddenly realize that they need to know the difference between the Save command and the Save As command.

Part II: Making Windows Do More

Sooner or later, you'll need to make Windows do something new. For example, what's all that new Backup and Anti-Virus stuff that came in DOS 6? How do you make Windows work with that expensive new sound card? Can bulky old Windows *really* fit on your new laptop? Part II answers these questions.

Plus, it tells you how to make Terminal do more than simply sound depressing.

Part III: Getting More Out of Windows

Believe it or not, normal, everyday people like you have tricked Windows into doing what they want it to do. Here you find Windows desktops that were arranged by Windows users. You see how they set up Windows to solve their problems and learn what buttons you can push to make Windows just as helpful to you.

Plus, you find clear-cut instructions on how to keep the mouse — and the rest of the computer — rolling down the right path.

Part IV: More Advanced Ugly Tasks Explained Carefully

Windows eventually asks you to do something you'd just as soon not do. This part of the book tackles the most tortuous Windows tasks and turns them into simple, step-by-step procedures. Large signposts carefully mark all the areas that are most likely to collapse first.

Part V: More Shortcuts and Tips Galore

Finally, there's no sense in working harder than necessary. This part of the book explains the easiest ways to make Windows do the most work — all with the least amount of effort on your part.

Icons Used in This Book

A picture is worth a thousand words. I'm being paid by the word for this book, so it has lots of *icons* — pictures that say "Look here!" Here's what the icons are saying:

This icon indicates a task or technique explained in step format.

Swerve past these signposts and don't bother slowing down. These icons point out boring pieces of extraneous technical information. (In fact, this technical stuff is only in the book so that your kids will have something to read.)

Keep an eye out for these icons. They point out a quick way of doing something. It's the kind of information that belongs on a sticky note next to the monitor — if there's any room left.

When you need a friendly reminder to do something, you see this icon.

When you need a cautious tap on the shoulder to warn you not to do something, this icon is nearby.

This books covers the latest versions of DOS: 6.0 and 6.2. However, when the text refers to DOS 6, it includes DOS 6.0 *and* 6.2. When you see the DOS 6.2 icon in the margin, however, the text refers to something that pertains to 6.2 *only*.

Where to Go from Here

If you're looking for the most base-level Windows information, head for Chapter 1. If you're still stumped, head back to the book store for *Windows For Dummies.*

But if you're looking for a just a little more information to get you through the day, you've got the right book right now. Grab it with both hands, and you're ready to start striking back with full force. Good luck!

Part I

More on Everyday Stuff

In This Part . . .

This part of the book covers the stuff Windows tosses at you every day: bunches of boxes that pile up on the screen like junk mail after a vacation. The first chapter explains how to shovel those boxes around so you can find the good stuff.

The next few chapters talk about how to renovate the aging World of Windows. You find out how to install new programs, add wallpaper, change fonts, install new screen savers, switch to new icons, record sounds, and use those other Windows goodies that are flooding the market.

Finally, you learn the answer to that burning question: What the heck are all those other Windows versions supposed to do? Do you need Windows 3.1, Windows for Workgroups, Windows NT, or Windows with a View?

Chapter 1

A Bit o' the Basics

In This Chapter

- Understanding the Windows routine
- Starting Windows
- Starting a program
- Opening a file
- Saving a file
- Printing a file
- Using a mouse
- Moving windows
- Exiting a program
- Exiting Windows

New to Windows or need a refresher? Then you're ready for this chapter. Here, you find out how to get some work done, despite the fancy *window* metaphor. You figure out how all those little menus are supposed to work and how you can make that little mouse arrow jump to the right places at the right times.

Finally, this chapter makes sure that *you* have the last word: You find out how to shoo Windows off the screen when you've had enough pointing and clicking for one day.

The Windows Computing Routine

Like government bureaucrats, computer users soon learn to follow the same steps over and over. That's the only way to make computers do your bidding.

Windows expects — demands, in fact — that you complete each of the steps in the following list to accomplish just about anything. The rest of this chapter covers each of these steps in full gory detail.

1. **Start Windows.**

   After you flip the computer's on switch, you need to call Windows onto the computer screen. This task is called *starting, running,* or *loading* Windows.

2. **Start a program.**

   After Windows appears on-screen, you can call one of its little helpers, which are also known as *programs,* to the screen too. These programs are ready to add your numbers, organize your words, deal your playing cards, or help you perform any other computing chores. (Programs are often called *software* or *applications* in order to confuse their users.)

3. **Load a file.**

   After the program appears on-screen, it expects you to *load a file* into it. In other words, it wants you to pour existing numbers or words into it so you can start stirring them around. Or, if you don't have any existing data, you can start entering new stuff — which is known as *creating* a file. (Oh, the computer uses the word *data* to describe all the stuff you create.)

4. **Save the file.**

   Done diddling with your data? Then tell the program to *save* your newly mingled mixture of numbers or words so you can play with them another day. The program saves them in a container called a *file.*

5. **Exit the program.**

   When you finish using a particular program, close it down. That process is called *exiting* a program. (It's different from *exciting* a program, which appeals only to a few eccentric programmers.)

6. **Exit Windows**

   Finally, when you're done with Windows, you can make it leave — *exit* — the screen.

Don't just flip the computer's off-switch when you're done working in Windows. You need to use the Exit Windows command so that Windows has time to pack its bags before you shut down the computer.

That's it! The rest of this chapter shows you how to perform those same six steps over and over again. Welcome to computers!

Start Here

Although some people claim that Windows is easy to use, Windows isn't listening. No, Windows listens to only two things: the mouse and the keyboard. You can boss Windows around by moving the mouse across your desk and pushing those little buttons on the mouse's back.

Or, if you're not quite ready to get *that* friendly with a mouse, use the keyboard. In fact, using the keyboard is the only way to make Windows first come to life, as described in the following section.

Starting Windows

To start Windows, head for the *DOS prompt*, a little computing wisp that looks like this:

```
C:\>
```

The DOS prompt usually appears on-screen when you first turn on the computer. To start Windows, type **WIN** at the DOS prompt and press Enter:

```
C:\> WIN
```

The little `C:\>` thing disappears, and Windows begins its slow migration to the screen.

Depending on the computer's speed (which is roughly equivalent to its price tag) Windows can take anywhere from 3 to 30 seconds to show up for work.

- Sometimes, computers don't toss a DOS prompt on-screen when they first wake up. Instead, they gently deposit their owners at a *menu shell* — a list of numbered options on-screen. If you see a number next to the word *Windows*, press that number. Windows should head for the screen.

- Want to make Windows load itself in a certain way — with your favorite programs already set up and running, for example? Then head for Chapter 17. It's loaded with ways to make Windows start doing your bidding the instant it hits the screen. In fact, you can make Windows start up automatically whenever you turn on your computer. Imagine!

- A little advertisement for Windows appears on-screen when you first start Windows up. To avoid that blurb, type the following at the DOS prompt:

```
C:\> WIN :
```

That is, type **WIN,** a space, and a colon. Windows doesn't load any faster, but you get to stare at a black screen rather than a Windows ad.

Starting a program

You do all of your Windows work in *programs.* Windows itself merely gives the programs a stage to dance on.

The words *load, launch, start,* and *run* all describe the same thing: making a program come to the screen so that you can get some work done.

Windows offers several ways to start a program, and the following sections describe all of them.

Starting a program from the Program Manager

The easiest way to start a program is by launching it from the *Program Manager,* a button-filled bunch of boxes that looks similar to what you see in Figure 1-1. When Windows first steps onto the screen, it brings the Program Manager along with it. See the little picture buttons — *icons* — that live inside the Program Manager? Each icon stands for a program.

When you push an icon-button with the mouse, you start a program. The process works like this:

1. **Slide the mouse across your desk until the little arrow points at your favorite program's icon.**
2. **Got the arrow hunkered down in the right place? Then double-click the left mouse button, keeping the arrow hovering over the icon the whole time.**

The program dutifully hops to the front of the screen.

- If this mouse *arrow* and *double-click* stuff sounds a little confusing, head for the "Mouse Mechanics," section, later in this chapter.
- If this *basics* chapter seems like old hat, however, then skip it. All of the new stuff is in the other chapters.
- Want to put an icon for a new program onto the Program Manager? Then forge ahead to Chapter 2. It explains how to install a Windows or DOS program — even if the program didn't come with a quick 'n' easy installation program.

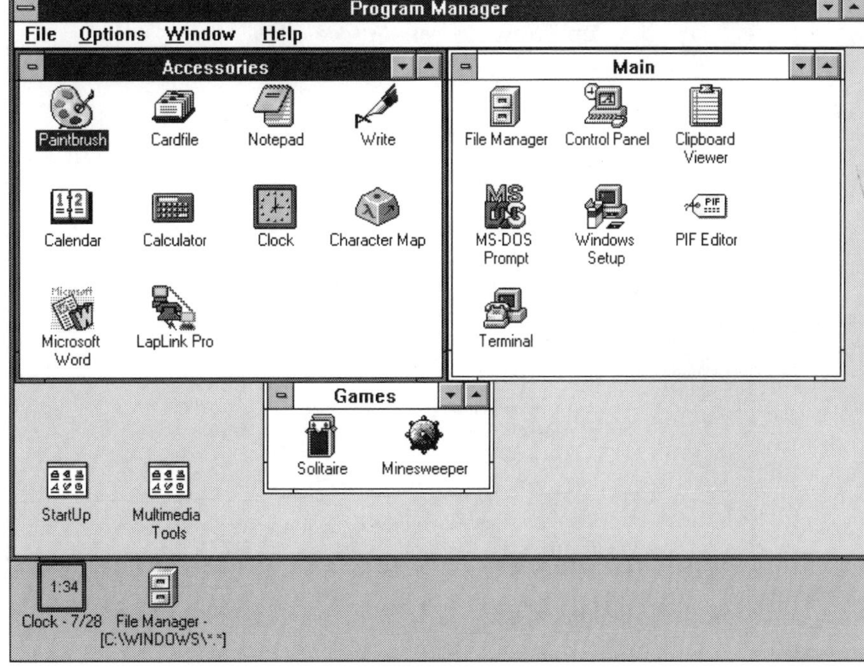

Figure 1-1: When you double-click on an icon in the Program Manager, that program hops to the screen.

Starting a program from the File Manager

Some folks don't like the Program Manager's panel of picture buttons. They prefer the grim File Manager. The File Manager does away with the programs' little pictures, leaving just their labels.

In this case, those labels are the programs' filenames, plus a few other technical details, as seen in Figure 1-2.

You start a program in the File Manager the same way that you start one in the Program Manager.

1. **Slide the mouse around on your desk until the little arrow points to the filename of the program that you want to bring to the screen.**

   A program's filename almost always ends with the letters *.EXE.* A few ornery DOS programs end in the letters *.COM,* however.

2. **While pointing at the program's name, double-click the left mouse button.**

   The program rises to the front of the screen, ready for action.

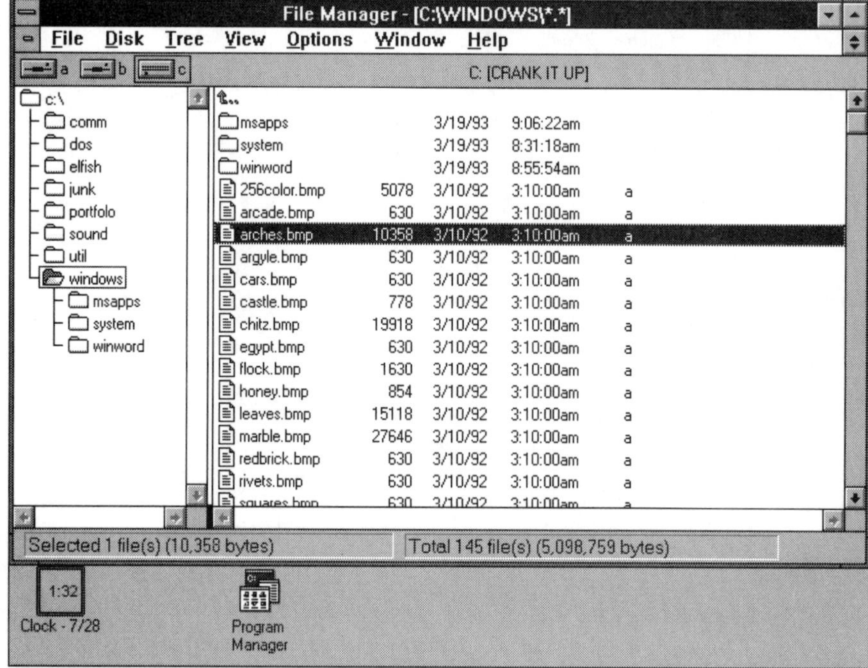

Figure 1-2: The File Manager shows a file's name, size, birth date, and other biological details.

- Unlike the Program Manager, where every icon stands for a program, the File Manager shows all of the files on the hard drive — not just programs. What are all those other files? Chapter 16 contains a handy chart to help you identify them.
- The File Manager can do much more than load programs. For example, you can use it to move files around on the hard drive. Chapter 2 describes this chore.
- Also, try pointing the mouse arrow at one of the filenames and clicking once. The filename darkens. Now, click on File in the File Manager's *menu bar* — that strip of official-looking words along its top. A menu drops down, listing all the things you can do to that file: change its name, make a copy of it, delete it, or perform other computer-like activities.

- Confused about the File Manager? Then press the key labeled F1. (It's usually located near the keyboard's upper-left corner.) The Windows Help program appears, ready to answer your questions. In fact, press F1 anytime Windows leaves you rubbing your elbows in exasperation. The Help program will pop up, usually bringing helpful information that pertains to your current dilemma.

Opening a File

A file is a computer's container for holding *data* — bits of important information — on disk. So whether you're trying to create something on a computer or touch up something that was created earlier, you need to snap open its container. That little chore is called *opening the file*.

Opening a file in a program

In a refreshing change of pace, all Windows programs let you open a file by following the same steps:

1. **Click on File in the program's menu bar, as shown in Figure 1-3.**

Figure 1-3: Click on File to expose a menu with file-oriented choices.

2. **When the menu falls down, click on Open, as shown in Figure 1-4.**

   The Open box appears, as shown in Figure 1-5. By clicking on the words in this box, you can search for files in different locations.

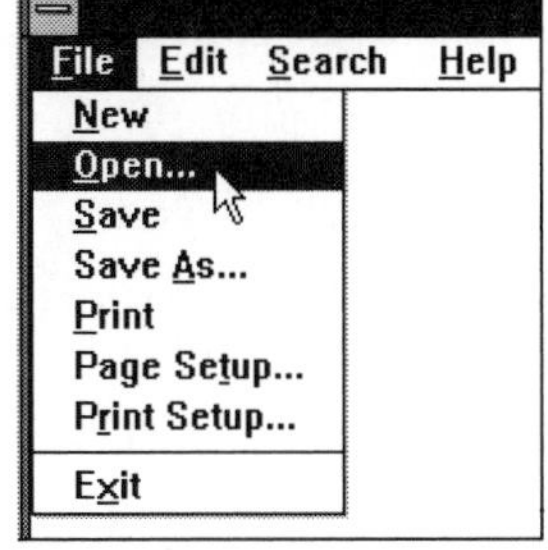

Figure 1-4: Click on Open to choose the file that you want to open.

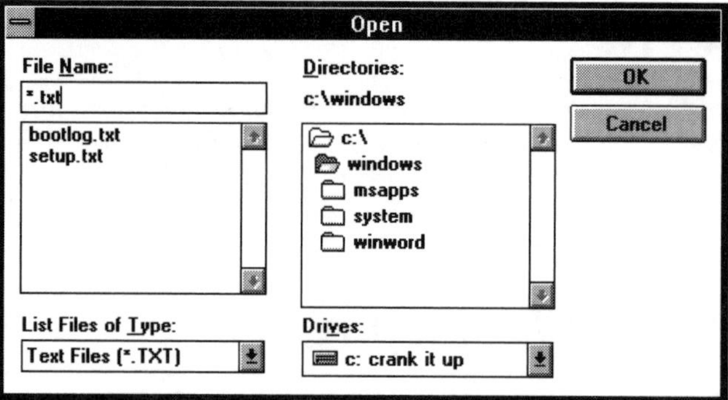

Figure 1-5: You use the Open box to find a file and call it into the program.

3. **If you see the name of the file you're after in the File Name box, double-click on it.**

   The program immediately opens that file. If you don't see your file right off the bat, though, you have to do a little hunting, as described in the next section.

Opening a file in a different directory

See the little folders in Figure 1-5? Each little yellow folder in the Directories box represents a different directory on the disk. To look for a file in a different directory, double-click on a different folder. The files that live in that directory suddenly appear in the File Name box.

Is your file listed now? Then double-click on it, and the program will load it.

Opening a file on a different disk drive

See the Drives box in Figure 1-5? Click in it to see a menu of the computer's disk drives. After you click on any of the listed drives, the Directories box suddenly shows the directories that live on that drive.

- Click on A: or B: to see the directories on the floppy drives.

  If there is no disk in the drive, Windows asks you to make sure a good disk is in the drive.

  For example, if you put the floppy disk in drive A:, double-click on the little picture of the drive labeled *a*.

- Click on any of the other letters to start spelunking on the hard drives that lurk inside the computer.

Viewing different types of files

Sometimes the File Name box doesn't display all the files in a directory. For example, the List Files of Type box in Figure 1-5 says that the File Name box is currently displaying all Text Files (files ending in .TXT).

To see other types of files, click on the downward-pointing arrow in the List Files of Type box. Then use the menu that drops down to choose a different type of file — or even all the files — in that directory.

- By looking in different directories and on different disk drives in the Open box, you'll eventually stumble across the file you're after.
- The List Files of Type box normally displays the types of files you're interested in. For example, when you try to open a file in Notepad, the box displays Text files. In Paintbrush, the box displays Paintbrush files. Paintbrush files end in .BMP for bitmap.
- This Files of Type stuff can be a little dizzying at first. To find out which Windows program creates which type of file, head for Chapter 16.
- Still can't find your file? Chapter 19 shows how to make the File Manager search for files.

- See how some words in a menu have an underlined letter, like the F in File and the O in Open? That letter is a shortcut. You can press and release the Alt key and then press that underlined letter to trigger that menu item. For example, you press Alt, F, and O, to make the File Open box pop up without any urging from the mouse.

Opening a file in the File Manager

Finally, something easy: The File Manager can open a file the same way that it loads a program. You just double-click on the name of the file that you're hungry for, and that file pops to the screen. It works like this:

1. **Find the name of the file that you want to open.**
2. **Move the mouse until the little arrow points at the filename.**
3. **Without moving the arrow away, double-click the mouse button.**

That's it. The File Manager first loads the program that created the file. Then it loads the file into that program. For example, if you double-click on a file that you created in Windows Notepad, the File Manager first loads Notepad, and then it loads the file into Notepad, leaving them both on-screen.

Opening a file in the File Manager is easier than making a sandwich — especially if the mustard lid has dried closed.

Saving a File

Talk about lack of foresight. Even after you spend all morning painstakingly calculating the corporate cash flow, Windows thinks you've been goofing around.

You see, computer programs don't know that you want to *save* your work. Unless you specifically tell the program to save it, the program just dumps it. And you can never retrieve unsaved files, not even with reinforced tongs.

To make a program save a file, do this:

1. **Click on File from the program's menu bar.**

   A menu of file-oriented chores appears, as shown in Figure 1-3.

2. **After the menu falls down, click on Save.**

   A box pops up, looking much like the one in Figure 1-5.

3. **Type in a name for the newly created file.**

   If Windows freaks out over the newly created file's name, you're probably trying to use one of the Forbidden Filename Characters that are described in Chapter 2.

4. **Click on the folders in the Directories window until you open the directory where you want to store the file.**

5. **Press Enter.**

The program saves the file in that directory.

- After you save a file for the first time, you won't have to repeat Steps 3-5. Instead, the program just saves the file, using the same name and directory. Kind of anticlimactic, actually.
- If you want to use a different name or location to save a file, then choose the Save As option. That option comes in handy when you want to open a file, change a few numbers or paragraphs, and save the file under a new name or directory.

- The easiest way to save a file in any Windows program is to press these three keys, one after the other: Alt,F,S. The little light on the hard drive blinks, and the program saves the file. Quick and easy, as long as you can remember Alt,F,S.

Printing a File

Printing a file works the same way as opening or saving one. Click on the right spots and grab the piece of paper as it slides out of the printer. If the printer is turned on and plugged in and the paper doesn't jam, you print a file this way:

1. **Click on File from the program's menu bar.**

   Once again, a menu of file-oriented chores appears, just as you see in Figure 1-3.

2. **After the menu falls down, click on Print.**

The program dutifully sends the information to the printer.

- Some programs toss a Print box in your face, asking for more information. For example, Paintbrush asks how many copies you want to print, and Word for Windows asks whether you want to print all the pages or just a select few.

  Notepad, on the other hand, merely whisks the text straight to the printer. Whoosh! No stopping that program.

- People with more than one printer can choose the Print Setup option instead. That option lets them choose which printer they want the information routed to. Then choose the program's Print command.

- The quickest way to tell a program to print something is to press Alt,F,P. That method is faster than fumbling around with menus.

Mouse Mechanics

Nine out of ten German philosophers agree: Windows prefers computers that are equipped with a mouse. Unlike the whiskered variety, a computer mouse looks like a little plastic bar of soap with a tail that plugs into the back of the computer.

When you nudge the mouse across your desk, Windows responds by nudging a tiny arrow — a mouse *pointer* — across the screen.

When the mouse's arrow points to a button on-screen, push one of the buttons on the mouse's back — the left one — to magically push the on-screen button.

- Don't pick up the mouse and point it at the screen. The little on-screen arrow won't budge, not even if you make spaceship noises. The mouse's belly needs to rub around on your desk.
- In fact, the mouse works best when it rolls around on a *mouse pad,* a flat piece of rubber that looks like a child's place mat.
- If the mouse has reached the end of its rope and the arrow *still* isn't pointing at the right spot, lift the mouse off the desk. Then set it back down again, giving the cord some slack before nudging it around your desk again. In fact, picking up and repositioning a mouse is a major form of exercise for many computer aficionados.
- Sometimes, unfortunately, moving the mouse doesn't move the arrow. This heartbreaking predicament is solved in Chapter 10.

- A mouse has its own mouse language; the major terms are demystified in the following sections.

What's a click?

Pushing a button on the back of a mouse makes a clicking noise. So the engineers behind mouse movements dubbed the press of a button as a *click.*

- You perform a click by pushing and quickly *releasing* the mouse button just as you use a button on a telephone. Pushing and *holding down* the mouse button is a completely different procedure. Computers and their mice take everything very literally.
- You'll find yourself clicking on lots of things in Windows — buttons, icons, words, edges of squares — even prairie dogs in some of the latest Windows games.

What's a double-click?

You perform a double-click by pushing and releasing the mouse button twice to make two clicks. But there's a catch to double-clicking: You have to press the mouse button *twice in rapid succession.*

If your clicks aren't fast enough, Windows thinks you're just fooling around and making two single clicks, not a bona fide double-click.

- After a little practice, you'll be able to double-click or click in the right place at the right time. After all, finding reverse gear the first time took a little practice too.
- If Windows has trouble telling the difference between your clicks and double-clicks, head for Chapter 10. That chapter shows how to fine-tune the Windows *mouse click recognition* areas.

Which mouse button do I use?

Most mice have two buttons. Some have three, and some real chunky NASA models have a dozen or more. Nevertheless, Windows listens to one mouse button — the one on the left.

- You can click the other mouse buttons as much as you like. They won't do anything, though.
- Actually, although Windows itself uses only the left button, some Windows programs listen to the right button as well. Paintbrush and Microsoft Word for Windows, for example, both add some sneaky right-button commands. However, 99 percent of Windows mouse clicks come from the left button.

- In fact, whenever you see the nonspecific phrase, "click the mouse," click the left mouse button to remain safely above the high-water mark.
- If your right mouse button works and your left doesn't, then see Chapter 10. Some left-hander must have swapped your mouse buttons.

What's a drag 'n' drop?

The *point and click* concept stunned computer scientists with its inherent simplicity. So they took a vote and decided to complicate matters by adding the *drag and drop*.

Here's how it looks on the dance floor:

1. **Nudge the mouse on your desk until the on-screen arrow points at something on-screen that you want to move — an icon in Program Manager, for example.**
2. **Hold down the mouse button and *don't* release it. Then, while still holding down the button, subtly move the mouse.**

   The object you pointed at glues itself to the mouse pointer. As you move the mouse, the pointer moves and *drags* the object along with it.
3. **Drag the object to a new position — a different window in the Program Manager, for example — and release the mouse button.**

The pointer subsequently lets go of the object and *drops* it in its new location.

- Dragging and dropping can be a quick way to move stuff around on the screen. If you're not using a mouse with Windows, however, you're left out — no dragging and dropping for you.
- Windows doesn't tell you which things you can drag and drop. Some items drag willingly, but others hold on for dear life.
- You can drag most of the icons in the Program Manager, and in the File Manager you can drag around all the filenames and little folder directories.
- In Microsoft Word for Windows, you can drag around words, paragraphs, and large chunks of text.

Window Mechanics

The designers of Windows had to know they were asking for trouble. How could anybody possibly work on a monitor-sized desktop that's smaller than one square foot?

When you work in Windows, everything piles up on top of everything else. You're not doing anything wrong — it's supposed to pile up. So this section explains how to move extraneous windows out of the way and make the important ones rise to the top.

You also learn how to find that window that was there just a second ago. . . .

Finding a misplaced window

Windows offers as many ways to retrieve windows as it does ways to lose them. To extract your favorite window from the on-screen pile, try these methods until one of 'em works:

- Can you see any part of the window you're after? Then click on any part of it.

  The window instantly rises to the top. Whew!

- If the window is completely hidden, hold down Ctrl and press Esc.

  A little window called the Task List pops up, as shown in Figure 1-6. Does the Task List show the name of the window you're after? Then double-click on it to make it rise to the top.

Figure 1-6: Double-click on any window in the Task List to bring it back to the top.

- Hold down Alt and press Tab.

  A little box hops to the center of the screen, listing one of the windows. If you want that window, let go of the Alt key, and the window hops to the top.

  Not the right one? Then keep holding down Alt and press Tab again and again. Sooner or later, Windows lists the window you're after. Leggo of Alt, and that window pops to the forefront.

If pressing Alt+Tab doesn't bring the names of windows to the front of the screen, double-click on the Control Panel icon from the Program Manager. Then double-click on the Desktop icon in the Control Panel. When a complicated form comes up on-screen, click in the Fast "Alt+Tab" Switching box until an *X* appears. That *X* lets the Alt+Tab trick out of the cage.

- Press Ctrl+Esc to bring up the Task List. Then click on the Tile button.

  Windows *tiles* all the open windows across the desktop, like tiles on a patio. They're too small to get much use out of, but, hey, at least you've found them all. If you click on the Cascade button instead of Tile, Windows deals all the open windows across the screen like playing cards.

Almost any of the preceding techniques can round up and lasso runaway windows.

Changing a window's size or location

Open windows rarely appear on-screen in just the right size. Either they're too big and cover up everything else, or they're too small to play with.

To change a window's size, try any of the following tricks:

Double-click on the title bar

See the bar running across the top of the window in Figure 1-7? A window's title appears in that bar, which is why it's called the *title bar*.

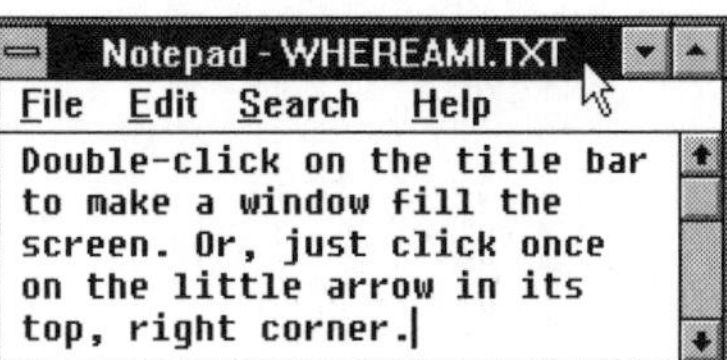

Figure 1-7: Double-click on the title to toggle a window's size.

Double-click on the title bar and the window will grow as big as it can. Or if the window *already* is as big as it can get, a deft double-click on the title bar shrinks it back down to normal size.

To move a window around on the screen, drag its title bar. The window turns into a little outline as you drag it around the screen with the mouse. When you like the window's new location, let go of the mouse button to drop the window in the new spot.

Drag its borders

For pinpoint accuracy in changing a window's size, drag its *borders* — the window's edges — in or out and drop them in their new location. The trick works like this:

1. **Move the mouse arrow until it points at the side or corner of a window, as shown in Figure 1-8.**

Figure 1-8: A double-headed arrow shows the directions you can drag.

2. **While holding down the mouse button, nudge the mouse to move the window inward or outward (see Figure 1-9).**

Figure 1-9: As you move the mouse, you move the border.

3. **When the window is the size you want, release the mouse button.**

   The window snaps to fit its new size, as shown in Figure 1-10.

You can change a window's size by dragging either its borders or its corners.

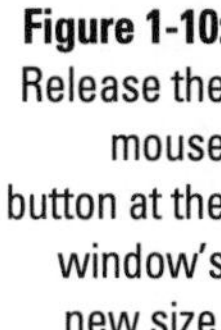

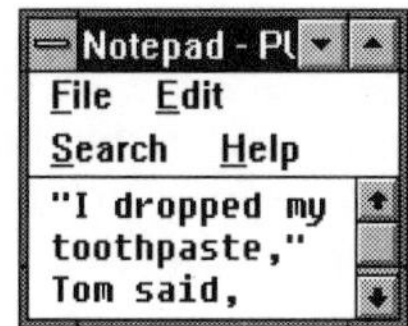

Figure 1-10: Release the mouse button at the window's new size.

Click on the little corner arrows

You can shrink or expand a window by clicking on the little arrows in its upper-right corner (see Figure 1-11).

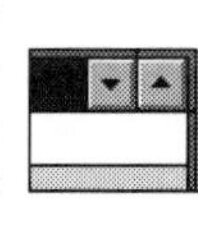

Figure 1-11: The upward-pointing arrow fills the entire screen.

After you click on the upward-pointing arrow, the window will grow as big as it can and cover up anything in its path.

- The little upward-pointing arrow that was in the upper-right corner turns into a two-headed arrow, with one arrow pointing up and another one pointing down. Click on the two-headed arrow to toggle back to the window's regular size.
- To shrink a window — turn it into a little icon at the bottom of the screen — click on the little downward-pointing arrow.
- Double-clicking on the window's title bar does the same thing as clicking on the upward-pointing arrow and the two-headed arrow — toggles the window between full-screen and normal-sized.

Done for the Day

When you've finished working, you haven't *really* finished working. No, the computer still demands a little more of your time. Before you can turn off the computer, you need to follow the steps described in the rest of this section.

Don't simply turn off the computer when Windows is on-screen, no matter how frustrated you are. You must save your work and exit Windows the right way. Doing anything else can cause problems.

Save your work

As described in "Saving a File," earlier in this chapter, you save your work by telling the program to save it in a file so that you can return to it another day.

Exit any running DOS programs

Are you running any DOS programs? You need to exit them before Windows will let you leave. If you're running a DOS prompt (that little `C:\>` thing) in a window, type **EXIT** and press Enter:

```
C:\> EXIT
```

Some DOS programs make you press several keys before they'll disappear. Try pressing F10 and Alt+X or, if you're really stumped, check the program's manual. When you press the correct keys, the program shrivels up, disappears from the screen, and leaves you back at Windows.

Exit any Windows programs

Unlike DOS programs, Windows programs shut themselves down automatically when you shut down Windows. They even ask whether you want to save your work. Still, you can use one of these methods to exit a Windows program:

- Double-click on the little box in the program's upper-left corner, as shown in Figure 1-12.

  The program disappears. If you haven't saved your work first, however, the program cautiously asks if you're *sure* you don't want to save your work.

- This trick doesn't work for DOS programs that are running in Windows.

Figure 1-12: Double-click on this little box to close a Windows program.

- Hold down Alt and press F4 (known in Windows parlance as pressing Alt+F4).
- Click on File in the menu bar and then click on Exit from the little menu that pops down.
- Press Alt,F,X, one after the other. That sequence quickly calls up the little File menu and presses the Exit button, all without the help of a mouse.

Exiting a program isn't a four-step procedure. You can use any of these methods to shut down a program.

Windows offers bunches of ways to do the same thing. Some folks say that the alternatives offered by Windows make it easier to use. Others say they just complicate matters.

Exit Windows

Windows is mystically tied to the Program Manager. When you exit the Program Manager, you automatically exit Windows. So, to exit Windows, apply any of the four methods described in the preceding section to the Program Manager.

- If any DOS programs are still running, however, Windows will tell you to close them down first.

- One quick way to shut down Windows is to press Ctrl+Esc. When the Task List pops up, click on the line that says Program Manager and then click on the End Task button. Windows stops whatever else it's thinking about and asks whether you're *sure* you want to exit Windows.

Chapter 2

How to Install New Software

In This Chapter

- Installing Windows and DOS programs
- Using installation programs
- Working without installation programs
- Copying files by using the File Manager
- Creating directories in the File Manager
- Adding program icons to the Program Manager

Imagine buying a toothbrush, opening the package, and finding a packet of loose little bristles, plus instructions on fastening them to the brush's plastic handle. And you just wanted to brush your teeth!

A new Windows program can bring similar complications. You don't always find the new program's icon waiting for you in the Program Manager. Instead, you find a floppy disk with a bunch of strange files on it. Which file does what? Where do they go?

Some programs come with an installation program that simplifies the whole process. Other programs leave it all up to you. To keep things simple, this chapter shows how to pry a program off a floppy disk, stick it on the hard drive, and put its icon in the Program Manager, where it belongs.

The Installation Headache

Programs are merely little bits of instructions for the computer, telling it to do different things at different times.

Unfortunately, most programs don't store those instructions in a single, easy-to-handle file. Instead, they're often spread out over several files — sometimes spread out over several floppy disks.

Regardless of what program you're installing, the basic idea behind installation is the same. You copy the program's files from the floppy disk onto the computer's hard drive. Then you place the program's start-me button — its icon — onto the Program Manager so that you can start using the program with a simple double-click.

- Programs come in two main types: DOS programs and Windows programs. Windows programs cause the fewest problems because they are designed to run under Windows. They're pretty much *plug 'n' play.*
- DOS programs, on the other hand, don't know anything about Windows. They're as helpless as a tourist who is visiting Disneyland on Labor Day and trying to find a bathroom without using a map.
- To help care for these confused DOS programs, Windows prefers that you make a *PIF (Program Information File).* A PIF is like a chart at the foot of a hospital patient's bed. It tells Windows what that DOS program needs so that it can run: memory limits, video expectations, and more trivia.
- Some DOS programs can run without a PIF. Other DOS programs come with a PIF included, making things easier. If DOS programs are causing problems, Chapter 14 holds all the PIF tips.
- Windows programs never need a PIF. They can automatically find the things that programs hold dear — sound cards, video cards, hard drives, and other treats.

What's an Installation Program?

Installing a program can be a long, tortuous process. So, programmers handled the chore the best way they could. They wrote a second program designed specifically to install the first program.

Known as an *installation program,* it handles the chores of copying the program to the computer's innards and making sure that it gets along with Windows.

- Most programs sold in software stores come with an installation program.
- Some programmers were lazy, however, and didn't write an installation program. As a result, the installation chores are squarely in your hands.
- Most shareware programs don't come with an installation program, so you have to tackle their installation yourself.

- The secret to a successful marriage is to know when to nod your head earnestly and say, "Gosh, you may be right, dear."

What's shareware?

In the early 1980s, an iconoclastic programmer named Jim Button startled the software industry by simply giving away his database program, PC-File. The catch? Button asked any satisfied PC-File users to mail him a check.

Much to the surprise of everybody, Button included, this honor system has since grossed Button a million dollars each year. The shareware concept has matured into a healthy business.

By simply giving away their wares, shareware programmers can avoid the high costs of advertising, marketing, packaging, and distributing their products. They give away their programs on a trial basis, however. Users who discover a program, install it, and find it useful are obligated to mail the programmer a registration fee — usually somewhere between $5 and $30.

The price may be low, but the quality level usually is high. Only programs that really do the job convince new users to mail back that registration check.

How to Install a Program

The steps that are described from here to the end of the chapter transform a bundle of disks into a program that actually runs on your computer.

By following all of these steps, you'll install your new program, whether you like it or not. (And if you *don't* like it, head for Chapter 13 for instructions on how to *un*install it.)

If you're stumped by only a few installation procedures — putting a new program's icon on the Program Manager, for example — then jump ahead to that particular step. Pogo sticks are allowed here.

Finally, installing a program isn't as hard as it looks. This chapter describes every step in clinical detail — down to the last toe muscle twitch. After you install a program or two, you'll find that it's as easy as walking and chewing gum at the same time.

If you only need a handrail while installing a new program, follow these steps:

1. **Find the program's disk.**
2. **Put the disk in the disk drive.**
3. **View the disk's contents in the File Manager.**
4. **Read any README files.**
5. **Find and load the installation program.**

   No installation program? Then keep going:

6. **Create a new directory on the hard drive.**
7. **Copy the program's files to the new directory.**
8. **Put the program's icon in the Program Manager.**

Finding the installation disk

If your software came in a big box, start rooting around for the floppy disks. Look for one that's labeled *Disk 1*, *Setup*, *Installation*, or something similar.

While you're rummaging, look for a cheat sheet. Some companies offer a quick, one-page set of installation instructions. (Others hide the installation tips in the middle of the inch-thick manual.)

- If the software comes on a single disk, use that disk. The label doesn't matter.
- If you find a cheat sheet, give it a quick ogle. It may have some handy tips or pertinent warnings.
- If you find a registration card inside the box, fill it out and mail it in. Some companies make you register the program before they'll give you any technical support on the telephone. Other companies just put you on a mailing list.

Sliding a disk into the disk drive

If the disk doesn't fit in your disk drives, troop back to the software store and ask to exchange your software for the *other* size of disk.

- Floppy disks slide into the drive with their label facing up. These disks have either a shiny metal edge or a small oval window — either way, slide that edge in first.
- Some disk drives make you slide down a little lever to hold the disk in place. Other drives swallow the disk with no special urging.

Viewing a disk's contents in the File Manager

Before working with a floppy disk, look at the files that live on it:

1. **Load the File Manager by double-clicking on its little file cabinet icon in the Program Manager.**

2. **Find the little pictures of disk drives along the File Manager's top edge.**

3. **Click on the little picture of the floppy drive.**

   For example, if you put the floppy disk in drive A:, click on the little picture of the drive labeled *a*.

   Or, if you put the disk in drive B:, click on the little drive labeled *b*.

   Either way, the File Manager shows the disk's contents (see Figure 2-1).

Clicking on a disk drive icon in the File Manager puts a view of that disk's contents in the currently open window.

Double-clicking, in contrast, doesn't change the view of the currently open window. Instead, it brings to the screen a second window that shows the contents of the newly clicked upon drive.

If the File Manager's window is too small for easy viewing, try this trick. Shrink all the open windows except for the File Manager into icons. Then press Ctrl+Esc to call up the Windows Task List, a box that lists all the open windows. Click on the Task List's Tile button to have the Task List neatly align the File Manager window on-screen, as shown in Figure 2-1.

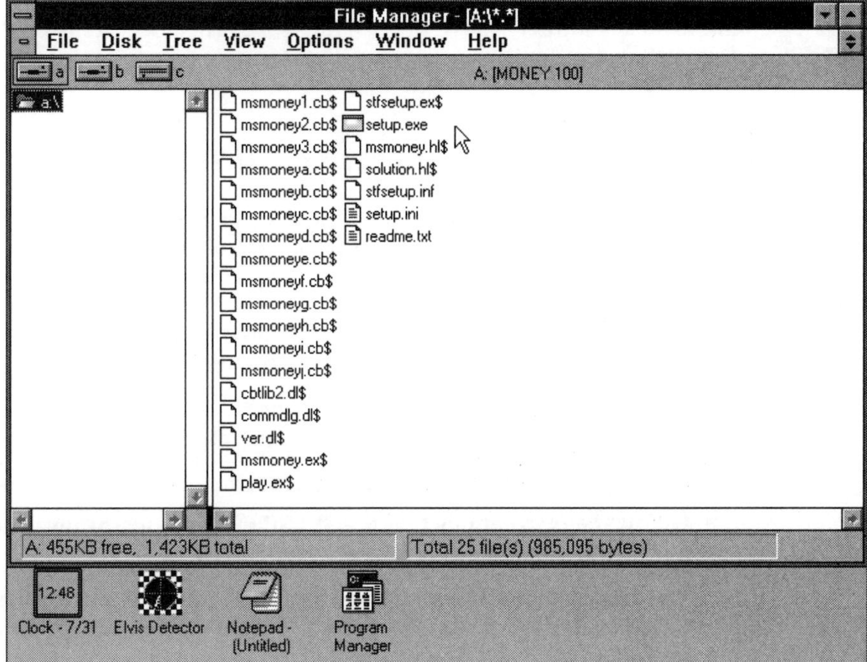

Figure 2-1: The File Manager, displaying filenames on the Microsoft Money disk in drive A.

Reading README files

When programmers notice a goof in the software manual, they don't grab the White-Out. Instead, they type a list of all the corrections and store them in a file called README.TXT, README, README.DOC or something similar.

In fact, Figure 2-1 shows a file called README.TXT. To view that file, double-click on its name. The Windows Notepad text editor pops up to show the README.TXT file's contents, and you learn which parts of the manual may trip you up.

Also, some README files contain quick, stick-to-the-point instructions on how the program expects you to install it. They're always worth at least a casual browse before you give up and move on.

Sometimes a disgruntled programmer names the README file README!.DOG or something even more obtuse. Because the file doesn't end in .TXT, double-clicking on it doesn't automatically bring up Notepad. So minimize Notepad to an icon along the bottom of the screen, just as it appears in Figure 2-1. Then drag the README!.DOG file from the File Manager and drop it on the Notepad icon. Double-click on the Notepad icon to make Notepad come to the screen and show you what's inside README!.DOG. (This drag-and-drop stuff is covered in Chapter 1.)

Feel free to double-click on a file named README.WRI. Files ending in .WRI automatically attract the Windows Write word processor; Write comes to the screen, showing the file for your reading pleasure.

Finding a program's installation program

If you're lucky, your program came with an customized installation program that automatically handles the awkward migration from floppy disk to Program Manager. Here's how to tell for sure:

1. **While the File Manager displays the disk's contents, look for a file named INSTALL.EXE, SETUP.EXE, or something similar.**

   See anything that looks like the SETUP.EXE program listed in Figure 2-1? If so, you've found the installation program.

2. **Double-click on that particular filename.**

3. **Follow the instructions that the SETUP program tosses onto the screen, and you're home free.**

   The program copies itself to the hard drive and sticks a little icon in the Program Manager. Chances are, it even creates a new *Program Group* — its own separate little box — in the Program Manager.

Finding no installation program, however, means bad news: You have to handle all the grunt work yourself. So practice grunting earnestly a few times before you move to the next section.

Viewing a floppy disk and a hard drive in the File Manager

If the lazy programmers didn't write an installation program for you, you have to install the program yourself.

So, what's on the floppy disk? And where should it live on the hard drive? Here's how to see drive A: and drive C: in the File Manager at the same time.

1. **Make sure your File Manager has a window open for drive A and drive C.**

   The beginning of this chapter tells you how to view a disk's contents.

2. **While you are in the File Manager, hold down Shift and press F4.**

   That's it. The File Manager tiles the two windows across the screen, as shown in Figure 2-2. Then you can see the contents of both drives at the same time.

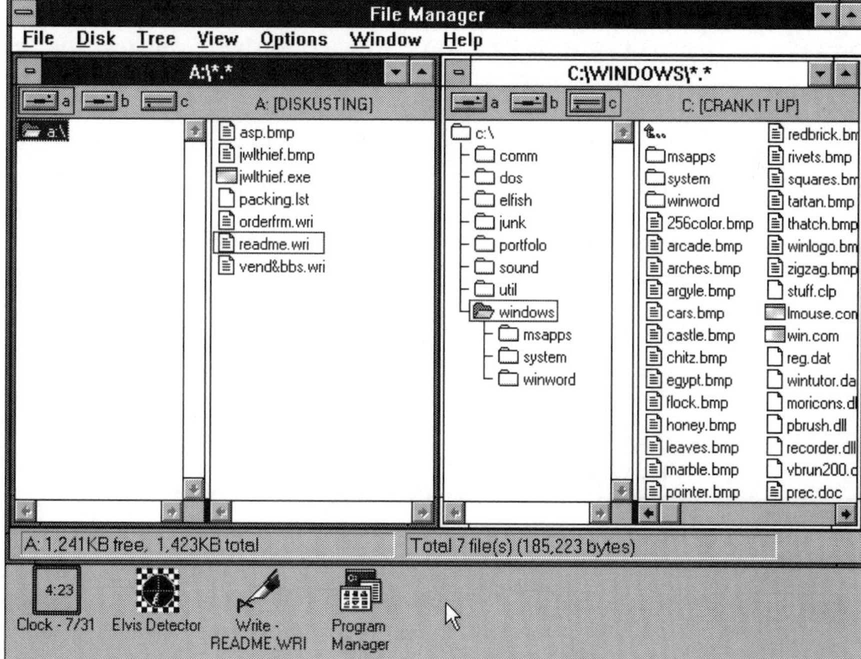

Figure 2-2: Pressing Shift+F4 in the File Manager aligns the open windows neatly across the screen.

The new program — the one without an installation program — is in the drive A: window. That program's upcoming home, drive C:, is in the other window.

- The File Manager looks pretty crowded with more than two windows in it. If the File Manager shows you more than two windows, you can get rid of the windows you don't need. Just double-click in the little box in the upper-left corner of each window that you don't want to see anymore. When you're through, press Shift+F4 to make the File Manager retile the remaining windows.
- Or, if only one window appears on-screen, double-click on the missing drive's icon from along the top of the File Manager. Then press Shift+F4.

Creating a new directory on the hard drive

Programs live in little folders that are called *directories*. The hard drive is full of 'em. Each little manila folder in the File Manager stands for a different directory.

To keep your new program easy to find, put it in its own little directory. Nestle its new folder — its new directory — in the Windows directory.

Here's how to create a new directory in the Windows directory:

1. **Highlight the WINDOWS folder in the drive C: window.**

   Simply click once on WINDOWS in the drive C: window. The little WINDOWS folder turns a different color — becomes highlighted — to indicate that you've selected it for further adventures.

2. **Click on File in the File Manager's main menu.**

   A new menu drops down, as shown in Figure 2-3.

3. **Click on Create Directory from the File Manager's File menu.**

   A box appears, as shown in Figure 2-4.

4. **Type in a short name for the new directory and press Enter.**

   Type in a descriptive eight-letter name for the new directory and press Enter. For example, to install a program called Jewel Thief, name the directory THIEF or something similar.

   After you press Enter, the new THIEF folder appears below the WINDOWS folder on the File Manager, just as in Figure 2-5.

You can actually use upper- or lowercase letters when naming a file in Windows. This book uses uppercase letters so it's easier for you to see what to type.

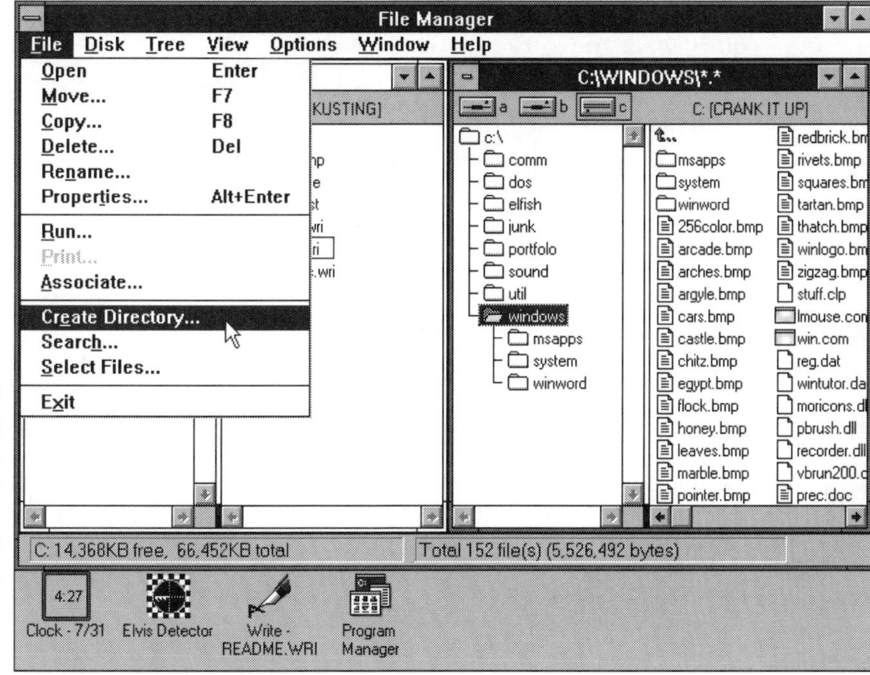

Figure 2-3: Click on Create Directory to create a new home for the new program.

Create Directory

Current Directory: C:\WINDOWS

Name: thief

OK

Cancel

Help

Figure 2-4: Type in a name for the new directory.

Windows can't digest these filenames

Windows squirms uncomfortably if you try to use more than eight letters or numbers in a filename or directory. Windows also gets bad cramps if you try to use a space. No can do. Don't use any of these forbidden characters, either:

. " / \ [ ] : * | < > + = ; , ?

Nothing *really* weird happens if you try to feed Windows something it can't handle. In fact, if you try to create a directory named BALD EAGLE, Windows simply shortens the directory's name to BALD and creates it anyway. But if you try to use one of the forbidden characters, Windows issues some bizarre complaints.

The moral? Limit the names of files and directories to simple letters or numbers with no spaces in between them.

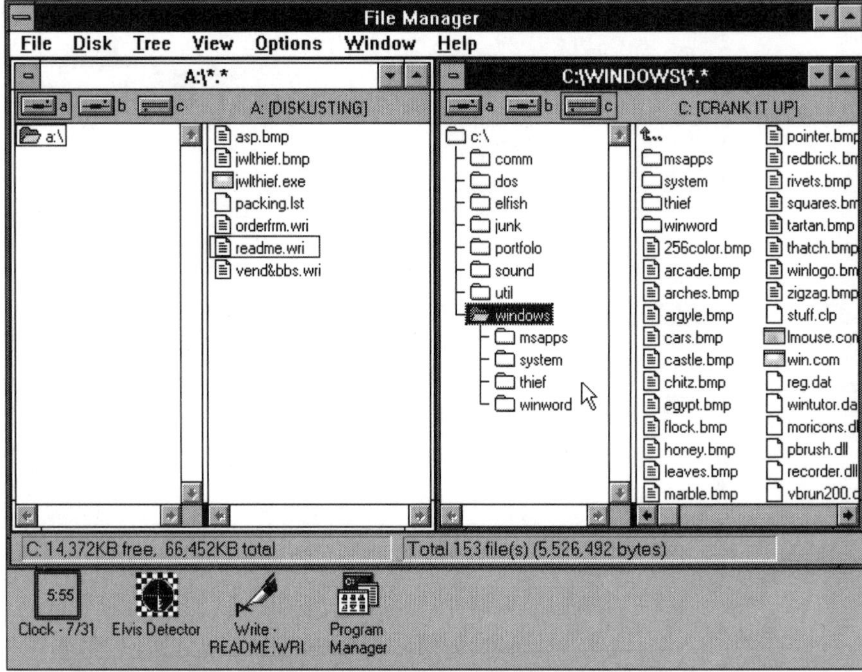

Figure 2-5: The new THIEF folder for the Jewel Thief program branches from the WINDOWS folder.

Selecting files in the File Manager

Before the File Manager can copy files, it needs to know what files to copy. You need to select the files this way:

1. **Click on the first file that you want to select from the list.**

   In the list for drive A: in Figure 2-5, ASP.BMP is the first file, so click on its filename.

2. **Hold down Shift and click on the last file that you want to select from the list.**

   In this case, click on VEND&BBS.WRI. Because your index finger obediently held down Shift, the File Manager selects the first file, the last file, and all the files in between, as shown in Figure 2-6.

   - If the program has only one file, then just click on it. The File Manager selects that file automatically.
   - The Shift trick selects consecutive chunks of files. If you don't want to select a file that's in the middle of a list, try the Ctrl trick. Use Shift to highlight all the files. Then, while holding down Ctrl, click on the filenames that you don't want to be selected. The File Manager deselects them, leaving the other files still selected.
   - When peeling a clove of garlic, give it a deft twist with both hands to break the tough outer covering and make the skin easier to remove.

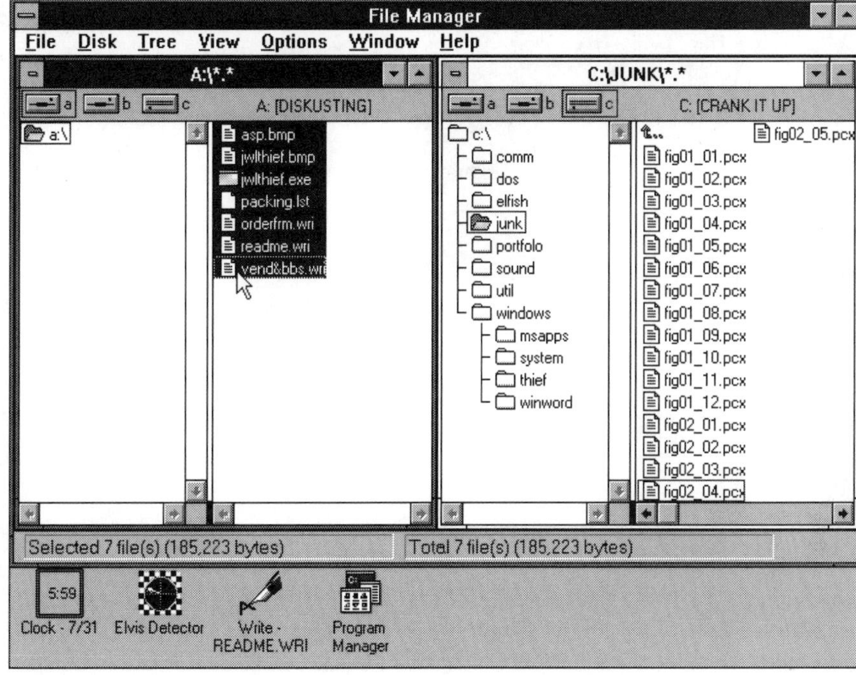

Figure 2-6: To select all the files in a window, click on the first file and then hold down Shift while you click on the last file.

Copying files from a floppy disk to the hard drive

Copying files from a floppy disk to the hard drive calls for a drag and drop. If *drag and drop* still sounds like a Mafia move, flip to Chapter 1 for a refresher. Drag and drop is simply a terrifying nickname for a simple mouse maneuver.

If you have already selected the files that you want, as described in the preceding section, follow these steps to start copying:

1. **Move the pointer over the selected files.**

   Nudge the mouse until the little arrow hovers over the selected — highlighted — files. (If your files aren't selected, back up to the preceding section.)

2. **Hold down the mouse button and then point at the destination folder on drive C:.**

   The key here is to point at one of the selected files and *hold down* the mouse button. Then, while still holding down the button, move the mouse until the arrow points at the destination folder — the THIEF folder — in the adjacent window. See how a little pile of papers appears beneath the pointer, as shown in Figure 2-7? The pile of papers tells you that you're dragging those files to that directory.

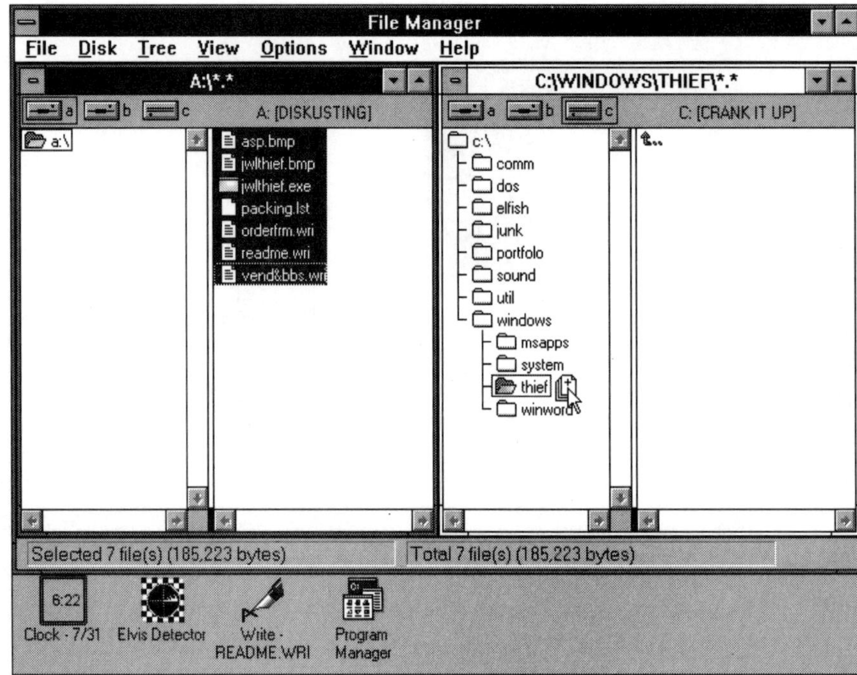

Figure 2-7: A little pile of papers appears beneath the mouse pointer as you drag the files from drive A to the directory on drive C.

3. **Release the mouse button.**

   When the arrow hovers over the destination folder — the THIEF folder, in this case — release the mouse button to drop the files into that folder.

   You have copied the files to the new directory on the hard drive.

4. **Click on the Yes button**

   Sometimes, the File Manager tosses a box like the one in Figure 2-8 in your face and asks whether you're sure you want to copy those files. When you click on the Yes button, the File Manager starts copying the files to their new home.

The hard drive whirs for a few moments as the File Manager goes to work. Eager to win your approval, the File Manager lists the name of each file as it copies it to the hard drive. After a minute or so, the File Manager lists the new programs in their new directory, as shown in Figure 2-9.

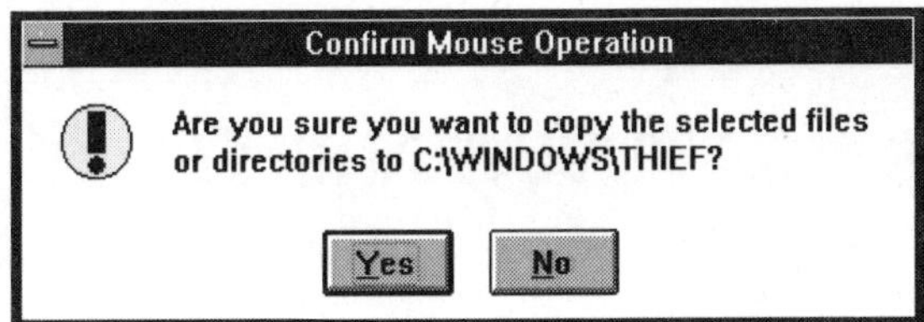

Figure 2-8: Click on the Yes button if you want to copy the files.

- When you're copying files, the File Manager takes the process literally: It creates a copy of the files on the floppy drive. The original files stay on the disk for safekeeping.
- To copy files from the hard drive to a floppy disk, just reverse this process. Drag the files to the floppy drive handy when you make backup copies of important files.

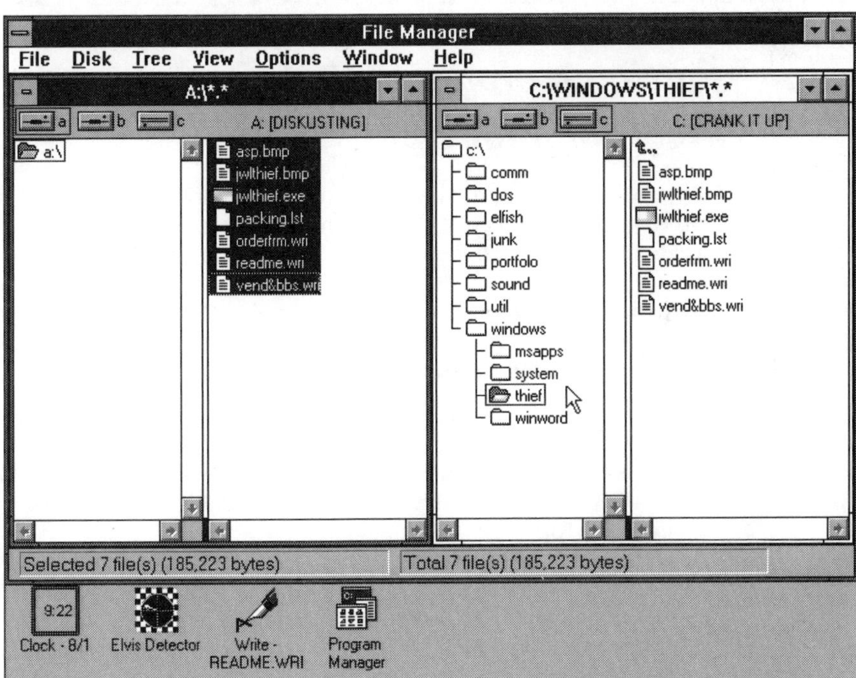

Figure 2-9: The files now appear in the THIEF directory on the hard drive.

What is C:\WINDOWS\THIEF?

When the File Manager asks for approval, as seen in Figure 2-8, the little on-screen box says that you're copying files into `C:\WINDOWS\THIEF`. Those words are computer code for the following:

- The `C:` part stands for drive C:, the hard drive. DOS likes to see colons after letters when it's talking about hard drives.
- The `\WINDOWS` part stands for the WINDOWS folder — or directory — on the hard drive. DOS likes to put a \, commonly called a *backslash*, between directories and between hard drive letters and directories.
- The `\THIEF` part stands for the newly created THIEF folder, complete with the mandatory backslash.

This complicated DOS structural stuff pops up in Windows every once in a while. It's there to remind you that Windows is merely a layer of flesh riding uncomfortably over some particularly sharp DOS bones.

Putting a program's icon in the Program Manager

After a Windows program moves onto the hard drive, it's ready to get its button — icon — placed in the Program Manager. Windows offers a bunch of ways to stick a new program's icon in the Program Manager.

Here's the easiest way:

1. **Open the Program Manager on-screen.**

   If the Program Manager is an icon at the bottom of the screen, double-click on it to make it rise to the surface. Can't find the Program Manager icon? Press Ctrl+Esc. The ever-handy Windows Task List pops up. Double-click on the Program Manager's name on the list to make the Program Manager fly to the top.

2. **Hold down Alt and double-click in a group window.**

   Figure out which of the Program Manager's windows should get the program's icon. Then, while holding down Alt, double-click in a bare spot in that window. Any corner will do fine. The Program Item Properties box pops up, with a little form for you to fill out (see Figure 2-10).

3. **Fill out the Description box and press Enter.**

   Type in the name of the program that you're installing. The Program Manager sticks the name beneath the icon as its *title* — those descriptive words that ride beneath the icon.

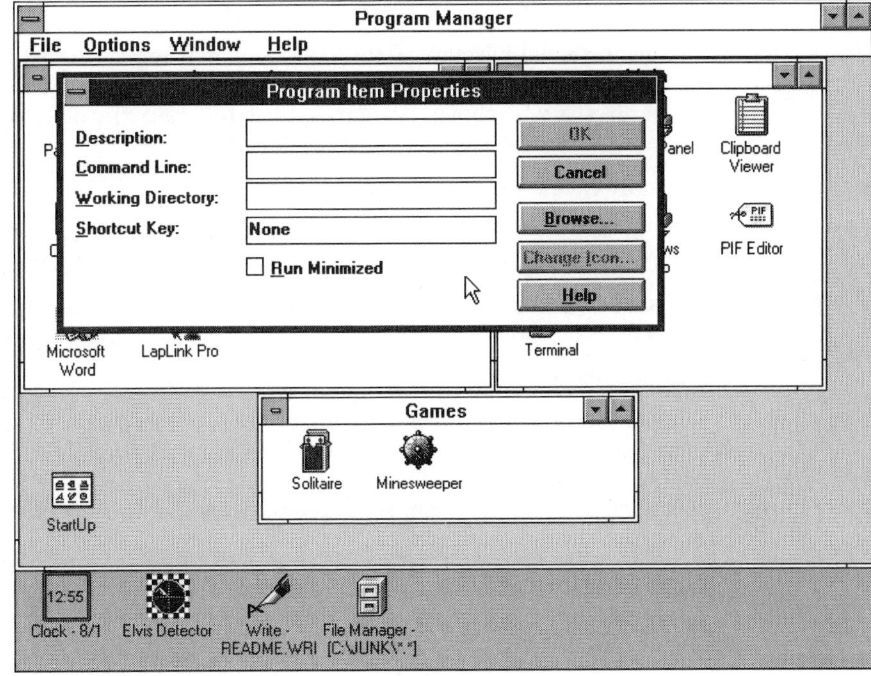

Figure 2-10: The Program Manager makes you fill out this form to add a program's icon.

Although Windows offers plenty of room for the description, keep it as short as you can. Long icon titles bump into each other like fancy feathered hats in elevators.

4. **Click in the Command Line box and then click the Browse button.**

   A Browse box pops up, as shown in Figure 2-11. It should look vaguely familiar because it's almost identical to the box that you use to open files from within programs. (Look at Figure 1-5 in Chapter 1, if you're skeptical.)

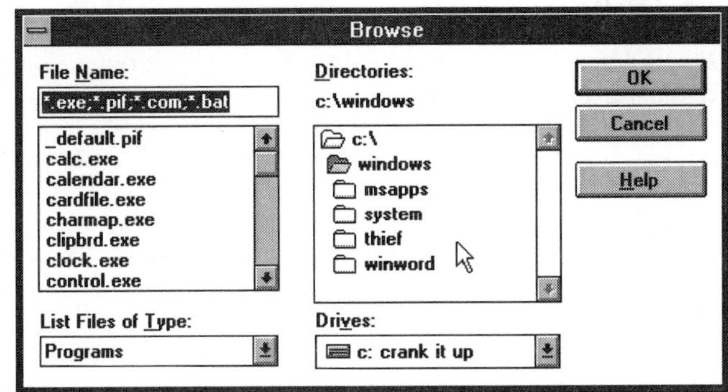

Figure 2-11: The Browse box can show the name of any program in any directory.

5. **Double-click on the new program's directory.**

   In this case, double-click on the THIEF folder — that's where the new program is living. The Browse box immediately lists all the programs in that directory, as shown in Figure 2-12. In this case, the directory has only one program, and its name is JWLTHIEF.EXE.

6. **Double-click on the program's filename.**

   In this case, you double-click on the filename JWLTHIEF.EXE. The Browse box disappears, leaving the Program Item Properties box in its place.

   TIP: If you've installed a DOS program, look in the directory for a file that ends in .PIF. If you find one, double-click on the PIF file, not on the program's name.

7. **Click the OK button.**

   That's it! The last box disappears, and the program's icon appears on the Program Manager, ready to leap to life with a quick double-click.

Of course, you may run into some of the problems that the next section tackles.

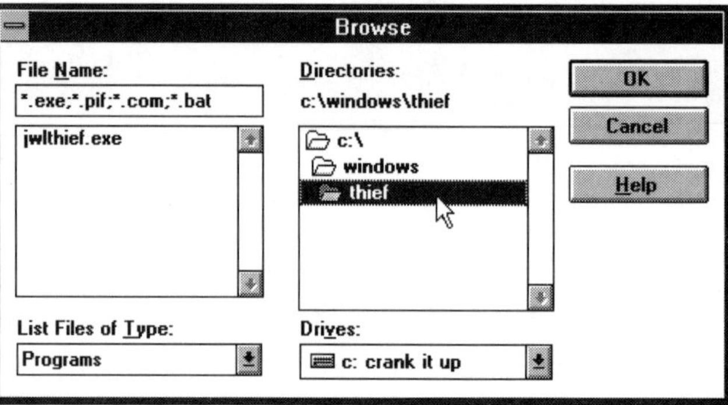

Figure 2-12: This Browse box shows all the programs in the THIEF directory.

It won't install right!

Occasionally, a widget falls into the wrong gear of the gatzoid, bringing everything to a resounding halt. Here are some of the more common problems that you can encounter while installing programs.

It's one big file ending in .ZIP!

If your file ends in .ZIP, like PICK.ZIP, you're holding a file that has been *zipped.* I'm not kidding.

The file has been compressed — shrunken like a dry sponge. You need an *unzipping* program to put water back into the sponge and turn the program into something you can use.

That unzipping program is called PKUNZIP, and it's shareware. You can find a description of shareware earlier in this chapter, and Chapter 12 tells you how to unzip a file.

It keeps asking for some VBRUN thing!

Like ungracious dinner guests, some Windows programs keep shouting for *more*. Some of them start asking for a file called VBRUN100.DLL or something with a similarly vague name.

The solution? Find that VBRUN.DLL file. It doesn't come with Windows, however. Instead, you can *download* it — copy it onto your computer — from most computer bulletin boards or on-line services, such as CompuServe.

After you download it, copy it to the \WINDOWS directory and ignore it. The program will shut up and run.

- The program may ask for VBRUN100.DLL, VBRUN200.DLL, VBRUN300.DLL — you get the idea. The different numbers stand for different version numbers. Make sure that you download the same version that the program asks for.
- You need the specific version of VBRUN that the program asks for. You can't just get VBRUN300.DLL and expect is to satisfy older programs that ask for the earlier versions of VBRUN.

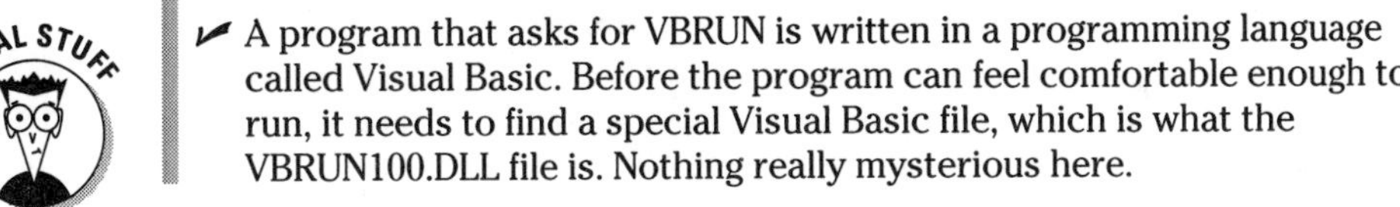

- A program that asks for VBRUN is written in a programming language called Visual Basic. Before the program can feel comfortable enough to run, it needs to find a special Visual Basic file, which is what the VBRUN100.DLL file is. Nothing really mysterious here.

My DOS program doesn't work!

DOS programs never expected to run under Windows. Some of them simply can't stand the lifestyle change.

It's as if somebody dropped you onto an ice-skating rink, and you were wearing slippery tennis shoes. You'd need ice skates to function normally.

A DOS program's *ice skates* come in the form of a Program Information File, known as a PIF.

When you create a PIF for a DOS program, Windows knows how to treat it better, and it performs better.

Unfortunately, creating a PIF can be even harder than learning how to ice skate, so PIFs get their own chapter — Chapter 14.

There's no room on the hard disk!

Sometimes, Windows stops copying files from the floppy disk to the hard disk because there's no room in the inn. The hard drive is full of files, with no room left for the stragglers.

You can install a bigger hard drive quickly. Or you can delete some of the files on the hard drive that you don't need. In fact, you can even delete some Windows files that are on a hit list in Chapter 16.

Chapter 3

Wallowing in Wallpaper, Screen Savers, Icons, Fonts, Sounds, and Drivers

In This Chapter

- Wallpaper
- Screen savers
- Icons
- Fonts
- Sounds
- Drivers

You've probably seen a wild new screen saver on a coworker's computer. Whenever she steps away from her computer for a few minutes, the screen turns black, and the little Grateful Dead Bear starts kicking across the screen.

Or how about that guy down the street who uses all those weird fonts when he makes wild party fliers? Plus, he just upped his icon collection to 763 with that new Bart Simpson icon he found last week.

Or how about that guy whose computer lets loose with a different-sounding burp whenever he loads or exits Windows?

You can sprinkle hundreds of these little spices on the Windows pie. Screen savers, icons, and sounds merely add new flavors. But the latest device drivers add necessary nourishment; Windows probably can't work without them.

This chapter shows how to keep Windows up to date by adding the new stuff and trimming off the old.

Where Can You Get These Things?

Windows comes with a few screen savers, fonts, sounds, and icons. But where are people getting all their new goodies? Chances are, they're pulling them from some of the following pots.

Off the shelf

Most software stores carry boxes of Windows add-ons. Look in the Windows software section for packages of fonts, sounds, screen savers, icons — even movies.

- ***Good news:*** The stuff you can buy in the software store usually comes with an installation program, making it simpler to set up and put to work.
- ***Bad news:*** The stuff costs money; but software purchased by mail-order can sometimes be a tad cheaper. (Keep reading — you can grab some of these goodies for free. . . .)

From the manufacturer

Sooner or later you'll need a new *driver* — software that enables Windows to hold an intelligible conversation with a mouse, sound card, video card, or other gadget.

Windows comes with drivers for many computer parts. However, all of the drivers are more than a year old. Your best bet for a new, custom-written driver is to go straight to the company that made the gadget. You can sometimes get new drivers by calling Microsoft at 1-800-426-9400 and forking over about $20.

If Windows isn't working well with your sound or video card, try calling the tech support number of the company that made the card. Ask the techie who answers to send you the card's latest driver on a floppy disk. Some companies charge shipping costs, and others mail the drivers free of charge. Still other companies offer a third route: They let you grab the files through the phone lines.

Through the phone lines

This method may sound kind of wacky at first, but I'm not making it up. Some companies hook up a computer to their telephone lines. Then you connect your computer to your phone lines by using a *modem*.

With the help of the modem and the Windows Terminal program (or any other modem program), you can dial up the company's computer and get copies of the latest Windows goodies. In fact, Microsoft's BBS (bulletin board system) has the latest drivers for a huge assortment of printers, sound cards, video cards, and other toys.

Best yet, all that stuff is free for the taking (except for the long-distance charges that will show up on your phone bill).

Some people call up CompuServe — a huge computer that's connected to a huge number of phone lines and charges huge fees. Well, actually it costs between $6 and $20 an hour, depending on how fast you're grabbing stuff. CompuServe carries bunches of icons, screen savers, wallpaper, and drivers and zillions of other software programs — all ready for the taking.

If you've bought a modem and want to put Terminal to work, hop ahead to Chapter 7.

User groups

Some folks can't stop talking about their computers. So, their spouses send them to local *user groups*. A user group is simply a club, just like a Saturday Sewing Club or '67 Corvette Lovers' club.

The members all meet, usually on a weekend or evening, and swap talk about the joy of computing. If you're having trouble with Windows or locating some of its parts, ask your local computer store where the local Windows User Group meets.

Chances are, one of the folks at the meeting will come up with the Windows goodie you're after.

From friends

Some charity-minded programmers give away their work for free (*freeware*). Knowing that people around the world are using their *flying eyeball* screen saver makes them feel all warm inside. Other programmers offer their programs as *shareware,* which is described in Chapter 2. You can try shareware programs for free; if you like them, you're obligated to mail the programmer a registration fee.

Many people swap these freeware and shareware programs with each other. If you're worried about viruses, check out Chapter 6. It describes how to use the Windows Anti-Virus program in DOS 6 and DOS 6.2.

- You can find plenty of shareware on CompuServe.

- Shareware and freeware are in a different legal realm than that of the boxed software that is sold in stores. That boxed software is known as *commercial* software, and giving copies of commercial software to friends can cause some big legal problems.
- In fact, making a copy of Windows and giving it to a friend is illegal.
- Feel free to give away, or even sell, old copies of commercial software. Just be sure to include the manual and don't keep a copy of the software for yourself.

Wallowing in Wallpaper

Windows *wallpaper* is the pretty pictures that you can stick to the back of the screen. When you first install Windows, it looks pretty forlorn, with a boring gray backdrop. Windows comes with several sheets of wallpaper to spruce things up, but those offerings can get pretty old, fast.

So, people start adding their own wallpaper, like the stuff in Figure 3-1.

Adding wallpaper is the easiest way to make Windows reflect your own personal computer style.

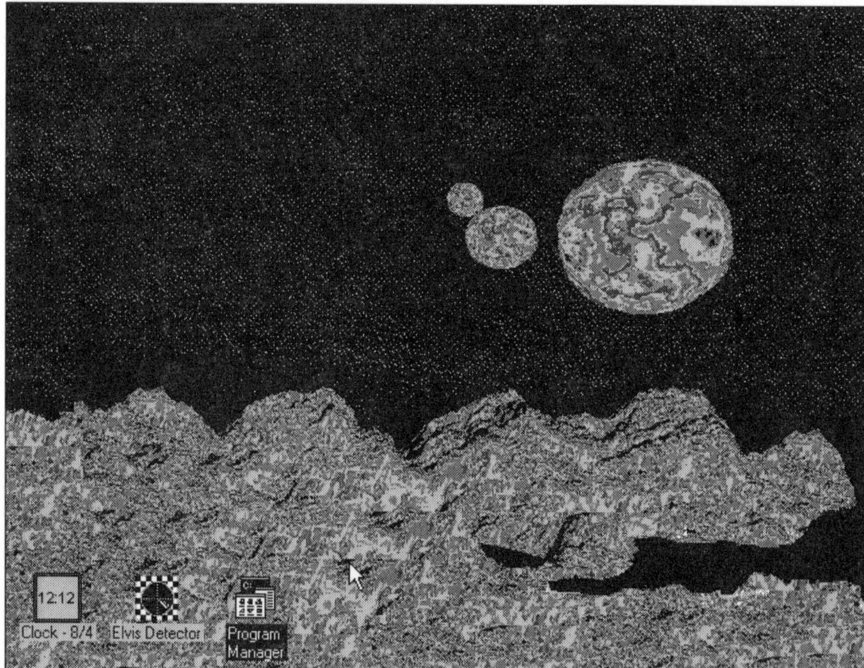

Figure 3-1: Wallpaper is the backdrop for all the icons and open windows.

What are wallpaper files?

Wallpaper is a picture that is stored in a special format known as a *bitmap* file. For easy identification, bitmap files end with .BMP. For example, 256COLOR.BMP, MARBLE.BMP, and LEAVES.BMP are some of the wallpaper files that are included with Windows.

If you're tired of the wallpaper Windows came with, create your own. You can use anything you draw in Windows Paintbrush as wallpaper.

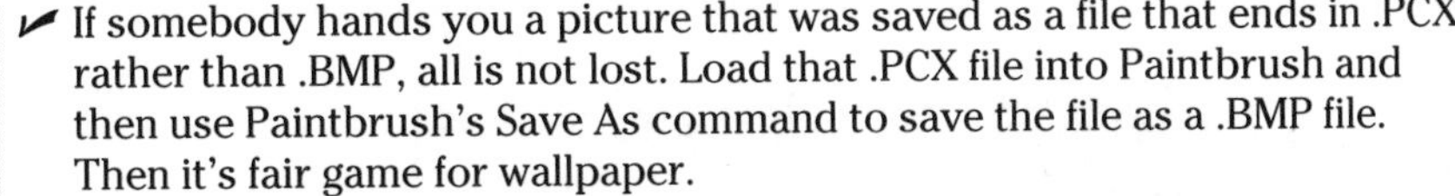

- If somebody hands you a picture that was saved as a file that ends in .PCX rather than .BMP, all is not lost. Load that .PCX file into Paintbrush and then use Paintbrush's Save As command to save the file as a .BMP file. Then it's fair game for wallpaper.

- Windows Paintbrush has severe problems with large images that contain lots of colors. Don't be surprised if Paintbrush saves your deluxe, 256-color picture as a completely black file. It's not your fault; one of the Windows programmers blew it.

Where to put wallpaper

Windows looks for its wallpaper — bitmap files — in only one place: the computer's \WINDOWS directory. So if you have some wallpaper named WALLY.BMP on the floppy disk in drive A:, copy the files from drive A: into the hard drive's \WINDOWS directory. (Chapter 2 covers copying files from a floppy drive to a hard drive.)

How to display wallpaper

Follow these steps to display your new wallpaper (or any other wallpaper, for that matter):

1. **From within the Program Manager, double-click on the Control Panel icon.**

   The Control Panel window leaps to the screen, as shown in Figure 3-2.

2. **Double-click on the Control Panel's Desktop icon.**

   The Windows Desktop box appears, ready for you to start fiddling.

3. **Click on the downward-pointing arrow next to File in the Wallpaper section.**

   A little menu drops down, listing all the bitmap files in the \WINDOWS directory. Those files are the current wallpaper choices, and the list looks somewhat like the list in Figure 3-3.

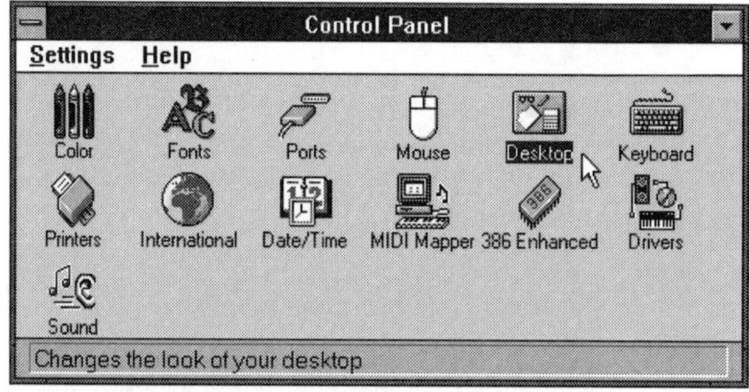

Figure 3-2: Double-click on the Control Panel's Desktop icon.

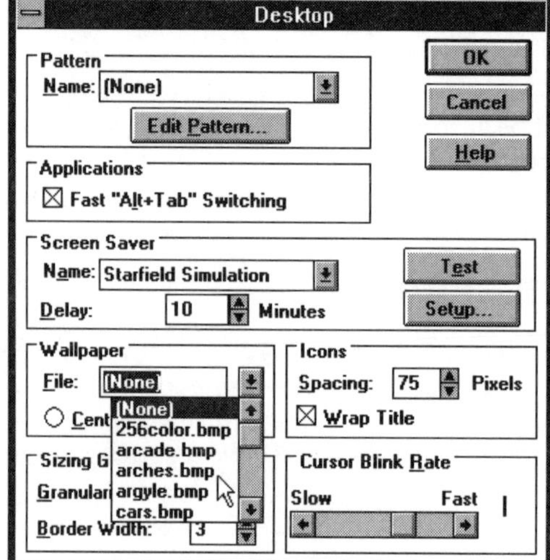

Figure 3-3: Click on the wallpaper that you want as a backdrop on your screen.

If a wallpaper file isn't stored in the \WINDOWS directory, it doesn't show up as an option in the list.

OK, you *can* open wallpaper that lives in a different directory. Just type the path name along with the wallpaper. To use the COOLPAPR.BMP file in your C:\GRAPHICS directory, type **C:\GRAPHICS\COOLPAPR.BMP** in the wallpaper's File box.

4. **Click on your choice for wallpaper and then click the OK button.**

   If you don't see the wallpaper file that you want right away, try *scrolling* down the list. Press the keyboard's PgDn key to move down the list one page at a time, press the down-arrow key to move down the list one name at a time, or click on the arrows above and below the *scroll bar* to see files listed farther down the list. See the one you want? Then click on it.

If you have a small piece of wallpaper, click on the Tile button to tile the art across the screen, over and over. Click on the Center button to display a huge piece of wallpaper; Windows centers the image on the screen.

5. **Done? Click on the OK button to make the Control Panel disappear, leaving the new wallpaper plastered across the back of the screen.**

How to get rid of wallpaper

Bitmap files consume a great deal of space on the hard drive, so excess wallpaper can fill up a hard disk fast.

To get rid of old wallpaper, follow these steps:

1. **Click on the File Manager icon in the Program Manager.**

File Manager

   The File Manager leaps to the screen.

2. **Click on View from the File Manager's menu. Then, when the menu drops down, make sure that the Sort by Type option is selected.**

   Now, your .BMP files will line up like the files in Figure 3-4.

3. **Click on the \WINDOWS directory and scroll to the files that end in .BMP.**

   Click in the scroll bar along the bottom of the File Manager to change your view of the files. Eventually, you see the .BMP files, as shown in Figure 3-4.

   To see how big those .BMP files are, click on View from the File Manager's menu bar. Then, when the menu drops down, make sure that the All File Details option is selected. The number listed closest to the file's name is the file's size, and the bigger the number, the more space that file is hogging up.

4. **Hold down Ctrl and click on the .BMP files that you don't want anymore.**

   The filenames darken to indicate that you have selected them for further action.

5. **Release Ctrl and press Del; then click the OK button.**

   The File Manager erases those files from the hard drive. (If it asks permission first, click on the Yes button.)

What's the hard part?

Changing wallpaper or adding new wallpaper is pretty easy. You shouldn't go wild, though, for two reasons.

Figure 3-4: Click in the scroll bar along the bottom of the File Manager to see more files.

- First, huge, ornate wallpaper files take up a lotta memory, which can slow Windows down. If Windows starts running sluggishly, stick with the boring gray backdrop. Or use a tiny piece of wallpaper and tile it across the screen.
- Second, huge wallpaper files take up a lotta space on a hard drive. Don't fill up the hard drive with frivolous wallpaper that you'll never use. When bitmaps get boring, delete them or copy them to a floppy disk to trade with friends.

- If you can't remember what a bitmap file looks like, double-click on the file's name from within the File Manager. Paintbrush open up and display the picture.

Adding or Changing a Screen Saver

If you've seen a dusty old monitor peering from the shelves at the Salvation Army store, you've probably seen WordPerfect too. The popular word processor's faint outline still appears on many old monitors, even when they're turned off.

In the old days, frequently used programs burned an image of themselves onto the monitor's face. So, to save the screens, a programmer invented a *screen saver*. When the computer's keyboard hasn't been touched for a few minutes, the screen saver kicks in and turns the screen black to give the monitor a rest.

Burn-in isn't really a problem with today's color monitors, but screen savers persist — mainly because they're fun. Plus, turning on a screen saver when you go to get a cup of coffee keeps other people from seeing what you're really doing on the computer.

What are screen saver files?

Screen savers aren't as simple as the files you use for wallpaper. You need to be a programmer to build a Windows screen saver. It's a little of program of sorts that's stored in a file that ends with .SCR. For example, two of the screen savers that are included with Windows are called SSFLYWIN.SCR and SSMARQUE.SCR.

Where to put screen savers

Just like wallpaper files, screen savers have to live in the \WINDOWS directory. So if you have a screen saver named DBEAR.SCR on the floppy disk in drive A:, copy DBEAR.SCR from drive A: onto the hard drive's \WINDOWS directory. Chapter 2 covers copying files from a floppy drive to the hard drive.

How to use screen savers

To try out a new screen saver, follow these steps:

1. **From within the Program Manager, double-click on the Control Panel icon.**

2. **Double-click on the Control Panel's Desktop icon, which is shown in Figure 3-5.**

   The Control Panel's Desktop window pops up, offering bunches of options to change.

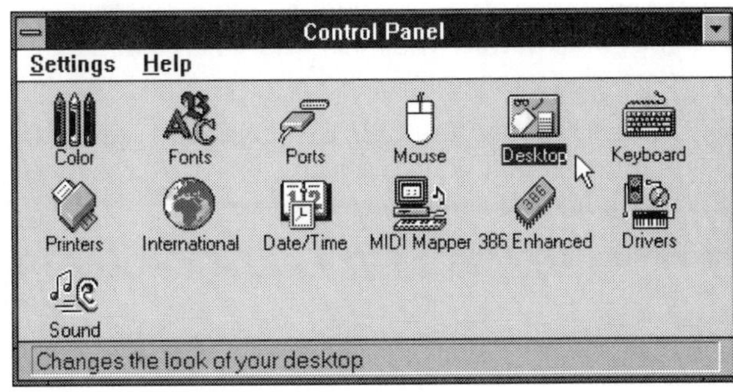

Figure 3-5: Double-click on the Desktop icon.

3. **Click on the downward-pointing arrow next to Name in the Screen Saver section.**

   A little menu pops down, listing the current screen saver choices, as shown in Figure 3-6.

   Windows lists wallpaper files by their filenames, but it lists screen savers by their titles. In Figure 3-6, for example, Windows lists the file DBEAR.SCR as Dancin' Bear.

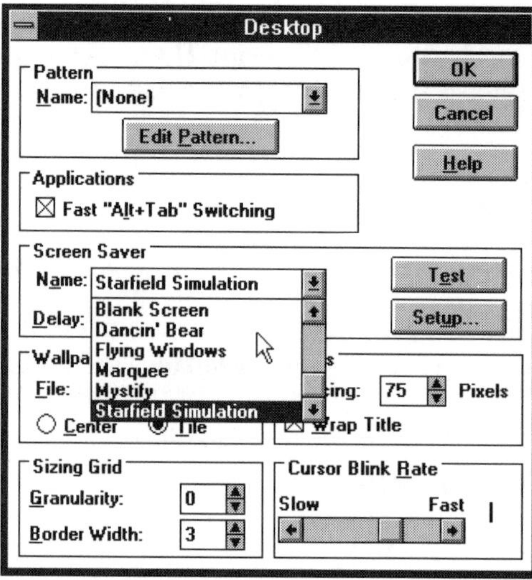

Figure 3-6: Choose the screen saver that you want to have kick in when you haven't touched the keyboard for a while.

If a screen saver file isn't stored in the \WINDOWS directory, it doesn't show up as an option.

4. **Click on your choice for a screen saver and click on the Test button.**

   The screen saver should whir into action. Satisfied? Then jostle the mouse or press a key to bring Windows back to the forefront.

   To fiddle with the screen saver, click on the Setup button. For example, you click on the Setup button when you want to adjust the dancing bear's dancin' speed or set a password.

   Click on the arrows next to Minutes in the box to the right of Delay to set the number of minutes that Windows waits for you to touch the mouse or keyboard before it has the screen saver kick in.

5. **When you are satisfied with the screen saver, click on the OK button to return to work.**

How to get rid of screen savers

When you're sick of the same old screen savers, delete the old ones to keep the hard drive from filling up.

To get rid of old screen savers, follow these steps:

1. **Click on the File Manager icon in the Program Manager.**

   The File Manager leaps to the screen.

2. **Click on View from the File Manager's menu. Then, when the menu drops down, make sure that the Sort by Type option is selected.**

   Now, your .SCR files line up like the files in Figure 3-7.

3. **Click on the \WINDOWS directory and scroll to the files that end in .SCR.**

   Click in the scroll bar along the bottom of the File Manager to change your view of the files. Eventually, you see the screen saver files, as shown in Figure 3-7.

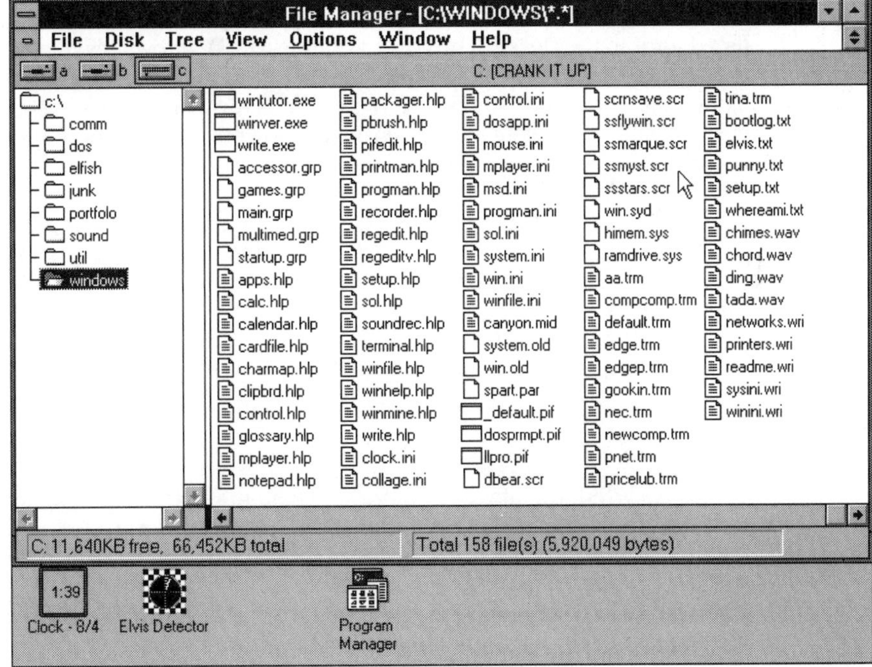

Figure 3-7: Click in the scroll bar along the bottom of the File Manager to see more files.

To see how big those .SCR files are, click on View from the File Manager's menu bar. Then, when the menu drops down, make sure that the All File Details option is selected. The number listed closest to the file's name is the file's size, and the bigger the number, the more space that file is hogging up.

4. **Hold down Ctrl and click on the .SCR files that you don't want anymore.**

   The filenames darken to indicate that you have selected them for further action.

5. **Done? Release Ctrl and press Del; then click the OK button.**

   The File Manager erases the selected .SCR files from the hard drive. (If it asks permission first, click on the Yes button.)

What's the hard part?

Don't let too many screen savers pile up in your Windows directory; they hog up space, just as wallpaper does.

Also, a screen saver's filename can be completely different from the name that's listed for it in the Desktop box. For example, the Windows Mystify screen saver is called SSMYST.SCR. The discrepancy between the filename and the way it's listed makes it hard to know which file stands for which screen saver. Be careful when you delete old screen savers so you don't delete the wrong one by accident.

Finally, finding good screen savers can be hard, because creating them takes so much work. A programmer needs to sit down and create one, preferably while in a good mood. Expect to find a lot more wallpaper and icons floating around than screen savers.

All About Icons

Soon after Windows hits a computer, the icon urge sets in. Face it, icons are cute. Pointing and clicking at a little picture of Mona Lisa is a lot more fun than typing C:\UTILITY\PAINT\ART.EXE and pressing Enter.

If you've ever collected anything — stamps, seashells, bubble-gum wrappers — you'll be tempted to start adding "just a few more" icons to your current crop.

What are icon files?

Icons — those little pictures you point at and click on — come embedded inside every Windows program. The Program Manager reaches inside the program, grabs its embedded icon, and sticks the icon on the menu.

But DOS programs are too boring to come with any embedded icons. So Windows uses the same generic MS-DOS icon to represent all DOS programs.

A Boring Icon

Luckily, you can use the Program Manager to jazz things up. You can assign any icon to any program, whether its ancestry is DOS or Windows.

A single icon comes packaged in a small file that ends in .ICO, such as BART.ICO or FLAVOR.ICO. A group of icons also can come packaged as a program — a file ending in .EXE. Some files ending in .DLL also contain icons.

The Program Manager can assign any of those icons to any program — if you tickle the Program Manager in the right place.

Oh, and although wallpaper files and icon files both contain pictures, the two types of files aren't interchangeable. Their goods are stored in completely different formats.

Where to put icons

Although Windows is picky about the location of its wallpaper and screen savers, icons can live anywhere on the hard drive. To stay organized, however, try to keep all the icon files in their own directory.

For example, create an \ICONS directory that's nestled in the \WINDOWS directory by following the instructions in Chapter 2. Then, when you come across any new icons, copy their files into the new \ICONS directory. (Chapter 2 also contains instructions for copying files onto a hard disk.)

How to change an icon in the Program Manager

To change a program icon, follow these steps:

1. **Call the Program Manager to the forefront.**

   Can't find the Program Manager? Press Ctrl+Esc to usher the Windows Task List to the screen. After you double-click on the Program Manager's name from the list, the Program Manager rises from the dead.

2. **Hold down Alt and double-click on the icon that you're sick of.**

   The Program Manager tosses a little window in your face, like the one in Figure 3-8.

   The program's current icon appears in the box's lower-left corner.

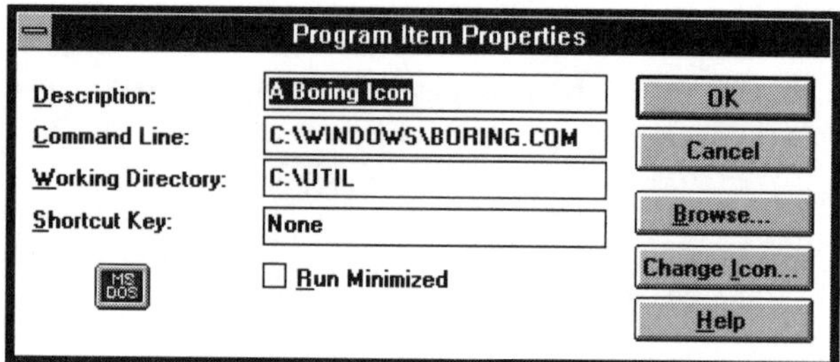

Figure 3-8: Use this box to change the icon Program Manager uses for a program.

3. **Click on the Change Icon button.**

   If you're trying to change a Windows program icon, the Program Manager then reaches inside the Windows program and shows the current choice of icons. For the File Manager, for example, you see the box in Figure 3-9.

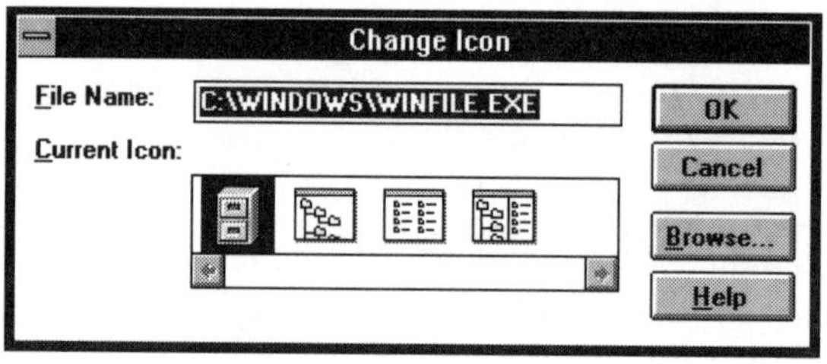

Figure 3-9: These four icons live inside the File Manager.

   If you're trying to change that boring, generic DOS icon, however, a frustrated Program Manager tosses out a box like the one in Figure 3-10.

   DOS programs don't have embedded icons, so Windows does the next best thing. It lets you choose from the icons that live inside the Program Manager (see Figure 3-11).

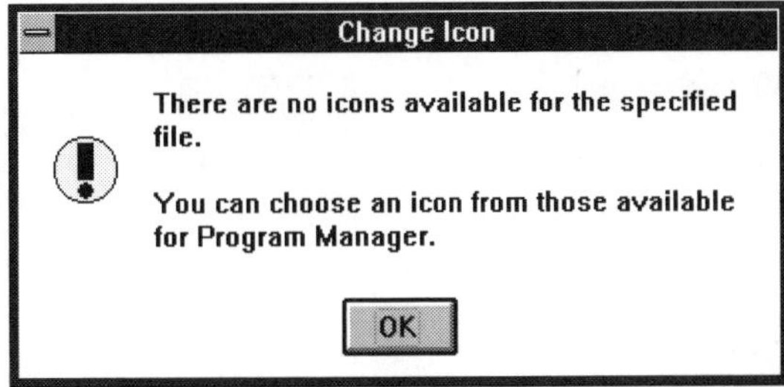

Figure 3-10: Program Manager can't find any icons inside a DOS program.

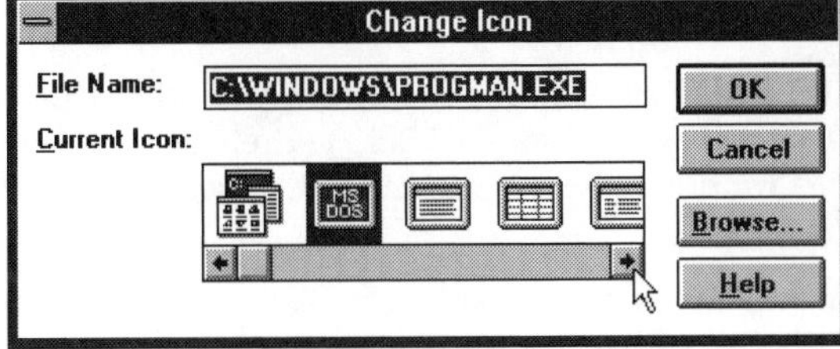

Figure 3-11: Windows gives you a choice of DOS icons inside the Program Manager.

Some programs — Program Manager, for example — come with more icons than can fit in that little Current Icon box. To see more icons, click on the arrows on the scroll bar that's directly beneath the icons.

If you see an icon that you like, double-click on it and click on the OK button on the next box. The new icon appears in the Program Manager, and you're through.

If the current choice of icons still look lame, however, move on to Step 4.

4. **Click on the Browse button to select different icons.**

   A click on the Browse button opens a box like the one in Figure 3-12.

   You can choose icons in three different ways:

   - Assign an icon from one program to any other program. In fact, several programs can share the same icon without slapping each other. Program files end in .EXE.
   - Take an icon from a packaged collection of icons; those files usually end in .DLL.

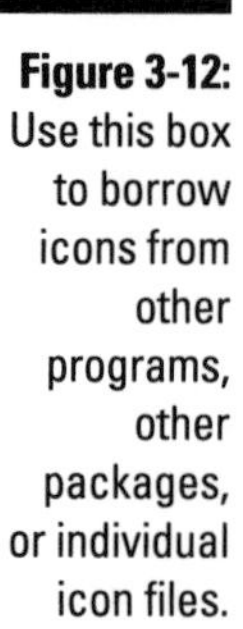

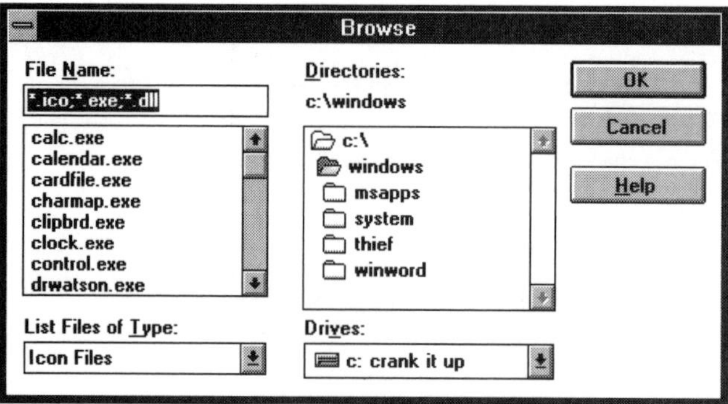

Figure 3-12: Use this box to borrow icons from other programs, other packages, or individual icon files.

- If you come across some .ICO files, which were described earlier in this discussion of icons, double-click on their directory in the Directories window. The names of the .ICO files appear in the File Name box.

Windows comes with a hidden package of icons that is stored in a file called MORICONS.DLL. It lives in the Windows directory and comes with icons for many popular DOS programs. Click on the name MORICONS.DLL in the File Name box to see the icons inside. You might find some icons hidden inside files ending with .SCR and .DRV, as well. (For example, check out VGA.DRV, hidden in your \WINDOWS\SYSTEM directory.)

Click on the little folders in the Directories box to look at files that live in other directories; Chapter 1 carries more detailed instructions for ferreting through folders such as these.

5. **Double-click on the name of the icon file that you want.**

   The box shown in Figure 3-9 reappears, showing the new icon choice. Still don't like it? Head back to Step 4 and keep trying new icons.

   When you finally find a good icon, click on the OK button. Then click on the next screen's OK button to get back to the Program Manager, where the new, jazzy icon has replaced that old, boring icon.

How to get rid of dorky icons

After you start collecting icons, the little guys come on fast and furiously. Finding them packaged in groups of thousands is not uncommon.

When you find yourself with icons coming out of your ears, delete the yucky ones this way:

1. **Decide which icons to delete.**

   Open the Program Manager, locate the dorky icon files, and write down their filenames. (If you need help in finding the files, see the instructions in the preceding section.)

2. **Open the File Manager.**

   Double-click on the File Manager icon in the Program Manager.

3. **Delete the files.**

   Click on the name of a dorky file, press the Del key, and click on the OK button. Repeat these steps for each icon that you want to delete.

- Yes, it's laborious. If all of the icon files are in a single directory, however, the File Manager can wipe out the entire directory at once.

- Be careful when you delete files. To stay on high ground, just delete files that end in .ICO. If you're deleting a file that ends in .DLL, make sure that it's the file that contains the icons you want to get rid of. Many other programs use .DLL files — they don't all contain icons.
- Dozens of shareware packages make creating icons, deleting icons, and assigning icons to programs easy. Check out Brian Livingston's *Windows Gizmos* for some of the programs. CompuServe and computer bulletin boards, which are discussed in Chapter 7, also have icon programs.

What's the hard part?

Icons get tricky in two key areas.

- First, Windows makes viewing the icon inside an .ICO file difficult. In fact, you can't see what an icon looks like until you assign it to a program while you're in the Program Manager, as described earlier in this chapter.
- Second, you can't make your own Windows icons. Paintbrush can't handle it. And changing the name of BART.BMP to BART.ICO doesn't fool Windows either.

The solution? Pick up an icon management program. Some of them enable you to create your own icons; you can use others to see the icons inside your icon files. And you can use still others to create animated icons that throw spitballs at each other and make splat sounds.

A Font of Font Wisdom

Different fonts project different images.

People with large mahogany desks and antique clocks that play Winchester chimes like the traditional **Bookman Old Style** look.

The arty types who like to buy clothes at thrift shops have probably experimented with the Arial look.

People who like gothic novels can't resist *Script*.

The key here is the *font* — the shape and style of the letters. Windows comes with a mere handful of fonts. Hundreds of additional fonts fill the store shelves, however, and you can find even more fonts on CompuServe or other on-line services.

Windows uses a breed of fonts called *TrueType*. TrueType is a fancy name for fonts that look the same on-screen as they do when you print them. Before TrueType fonts, fonts didn't look as good. In fact, a headline that looked smooth on-screen had jagged edges when you printed it out.

What are font files?

Each font needs two files, one ending in .TTF and the other ending in .FOT. But who cares? Windows comes with an installation program that handles all those loose ends, so you don't need to know what the filenames are called.

Fonts versus typeface

Traditional printers wipe the black off their fingers with thick towels and mutter, "The shape of the letters is called their *typeface*, not their *font*."

Computer users retort, "So what? Language is changing, and desktop publishing is putting you guys out of business, anyway."

Technically speaking, and that's why this stuff is down here in the small print, a *font* refers to a collection of letters that are all of the same size and style.

A *typeface*, on the other hand, simply refers to the style of the letters.

Most computer users merely shrug and wipe their hands of the whole controversy.

Where to put fonts

Just put the floppy disk in the disk drive. Windows handles the rest.

How to install fonts

Windows controls the font installation process through its Control Panel. Just follow these steps to font nirvana:

1. **From within the Program Manager, double-click on the Control Panel icon.**

   The Control Panel hops to the screen.

Control Panel

2. **Double-click on the Control Panel's Fonts icon, which is shown in Figure 3-13.**

   The Fonts box appears, as shown in Figure 3-14, and shows Windows current selection of fonts. Click on a font's name to see what it looks like.

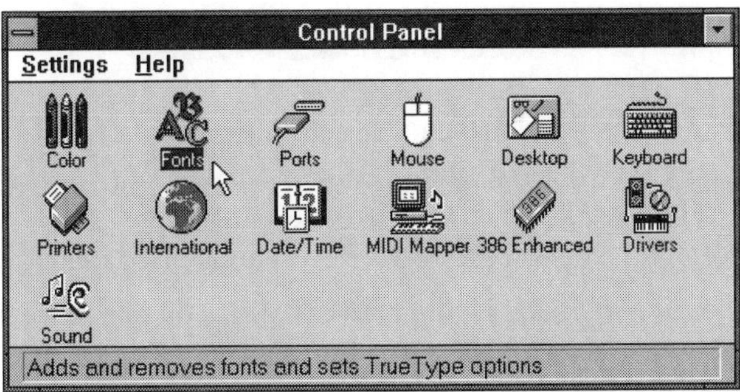

Figure 3-13: Double-click on the Fonts icon in the Control Panel.

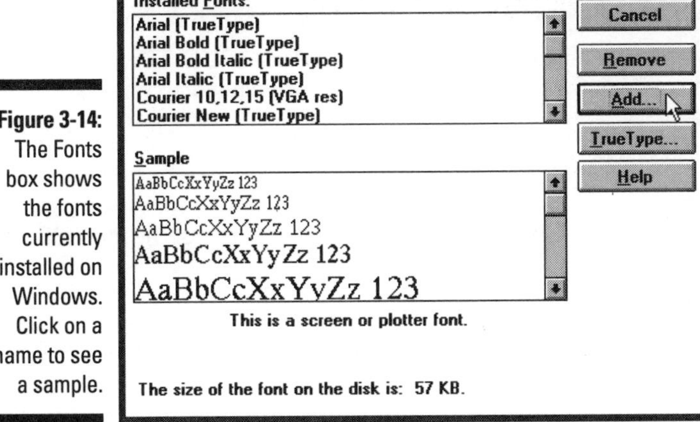

Figure 3-14: The Fonts box shows the fonts currently installed on Windows. Click on a name to see a sample.

3. **Click on the Add button.**

   The Add Fonts box shown in Figure 3-15 appears, eager to bring new fonts into the fold. But where are they? You need to tell Windows where those fonts are lurking, so move to Step 4.

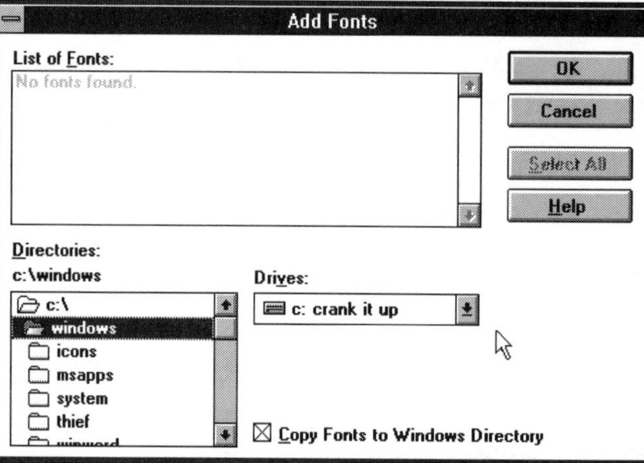

Figure 3-15: The Add Fonts box shows the fonts in the current directory, none, in this case.

4. **Click on the letter of the drive or directory that contains the fonts.**

   Are the fonts on a disk? Then click on the little arrow by the Drives box and choose the disk drive where you've placed the disk. (First make sure that you've put the disk in the correct drive and closed the little latch.)

   Or, if the fonts are already on the hard disk, click on the appropriate folder in the Directories box.

   After you click on the folder or drive where the new fonts live, their names appear in the List of Fonts box.

   If a little X isn't in the Copy Fonts to Windows Directory box, click in the box. You *want* Windows to copy the new fonts to its own directory.

   Windows copies incoming new fonts to the \WINDOWS\SYSTEM directory, but discussing that setup makes for exceptionally dry conversation in hotel lobbies.

5. **Select the fonts you want.**

   You probably want to install all the fonts, so just click on the Select All button. Or, if you're in a picky mood, click on the names of the individual fonts you're after.

6. **Click on the OK button.**

   A moment after you click on the OK button, Windows adds the new fonts to the list, one by one.

7. **Click on the Close button.**

   That's it! The next time you open the word processor, the new fonts will be on the list, waiting to be used.

How to get rid of fonts

Getting rid of fonts is even easier than installing them:

1. **From within the Program Manager, double-click on the Control Panel icon.**

   The Control Panel hops to the screen.

2. **Double-click on the Control Panel's Fonts icon (refer to Figure 3-13).**

   The Fonts box pops to the screen, showing the current selection of fonts.

3. **Click on the name of the font you're sick of.**

   After you click on a font's name, Windows reminds you what the little letters look like, as shown in Figure 3-16. If you click on more than one font, however, Windows stops showing you what *any* fonts look like.

   Information at the bottom of the Fonts box also tells how much space the font takes up on the hard disk and whether the font is a TrueType font.

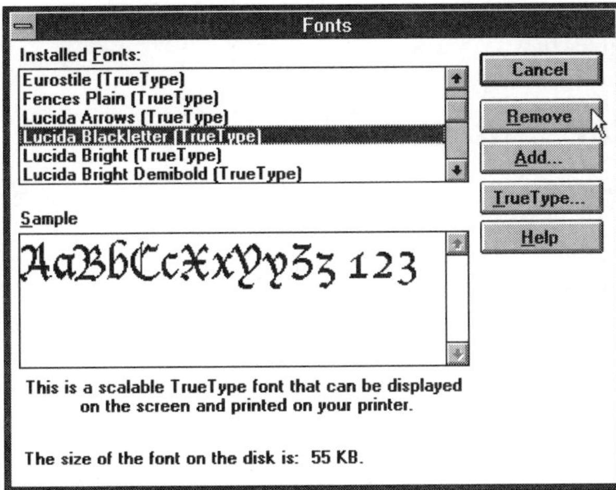

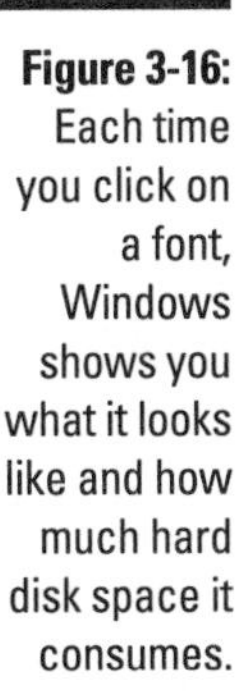
Figure 3-16: Each time you click on a font, Windows shows you what it looks like and how much hard disk space it consumes.

The fonts that came with Windows should stay with Windows. Only delete fonts that you know you have added. Many programs need Windows fonts to survive.

4. **Click on the Remove button**

   Windows asks whether you're sure you want to delete the font, as shown in Figure 3-17. If you're really sure, click on the Yes button. But first read the following tip.

Figure 3-17: Click on the Yes button, and check the Delete Font File From Disk.

Make sure that the Delete Font File From Disk box has a check mark in it. Otherwise, Windows doesn't delete the font's files from the hard drive — it simply removes the font from the menus and leaves the font files to clutter up the hard disk.

If you want to remove more fonts, back up to Step 3. Otherwise, move to Step 5.

5. **Click on the Close button.**

   That's it. You're back at the Control Panel, and the font has been erased from the hard drive.

What's the hard part?

The hardest part of fonts comes from the language. Table 3-1 explains some of the weirdness.

- If you're not already using Adobe Type Manager, then choose TrueType fonts whenever they're offered in Windows. They print more quickly and look better than the other fonts.
- TrueType fonts are great — except for use in professional-level desktop publishing, where PostScript fonts are more popular.

Table 3-1 Types of Fonts

These fonts . . .	*. . . do this*
Screen fonts	These fonts appear on-screen. (Many of them say VGA Res.)
Printer fonts Times	The printer uses these fonts to create letters and stick them on the printed page. (Some say Plotter.) Any printer fonts in a menu have a little picture of a printer next to them.
TrueType fonts Times New Roman	These fonts were introduced with Windows 3.1. Screen fonts and printer fonts are combined in one package to make fonts look the same on-screen as they do on the printed page. A little pair of Ts appears next to any TrueType fonts that are listed in a menu.
PostScript	An older type of font that is popular with professional-level desktop publishers. To use PostScript fonts in Windows, you need to have Adobe Type Manager (ATM).

Adding or Changing Sounds

For years, the howls of anguished Windows users provided the only sounds at the computer desktop. Today, however, Windows 3.1 can wail, as well.

But there's one big problem. Windows 3.1 can't make any sounds until you attach a sound card and some speakers. Sound cards usually cost about $50 – $200 for the medium-range ones.

Sometimes you *can* hear sounds without a sound card. If you install a speaker driver, Windows can play the sounds through the computer's little speaker. See "Adding or Changing Drivers," later in this chapter, to learn how to install a speaker driver; Chapter 7 tells where to find that particular driver. (It didn't come with Windows. . . .)

What are sound files?

Windows can play two popular types of sound files. The first type of files, known as .WAV files, contain real sounds — a duck quacking or the sound of a tree falling in a forest (if somebody was there to record it). Windows comes with several of these recorded sounds: CHORD.WAV, TADA.WAV, and a few others.

MIDI files are the second type of sound files. They aren't actual recordings. Rather, they're instructions for a synthesizer to play certain musical tones. MIDI files usually sound more like music than .WAV files do. In fact, Windows comes with one MIDI file — CANYON.MID. It's a pleasant, dentist's office jingle.

Because .WAV files contain actual recorded sounds, they can be huge. A ten-second sound can fill a floppy disk. MIDI files, in contrast, contain synthesizer instructions, not the sounds, so their size is smaller.

Finally, some MIDI programs save MIDI files in different formats that end with different extensions than .MID. Windows, however, prefers the MIDI format that ends in .MID.

You can find plenty more help with sound files in the multimedia chapter, Chapter 8.

Some sound cards come with sounds that are stored in an .SND format. Windows can't play those files, but the sound card may come with its own sound-playing program that can play them.

Where to put sound files

MIDI files can live anywhere on the hard drive. Chances are, the software included with your sound card contains a few MIDI files. Feel free to toss a few more .MID files in the same directories.

.WAV files can live anywhere on the hard drive, too. If you want to assign any sounds to events — hear a duck quack whenever you start Windows, for example — then copy those particular sounds to the \WINDOWS directory (the same place where you've been keeping wallpaper).

Chapter 2 explains how to create a directory on a hard drive and copy files to it from a floppy disk.

The Mod Squad

Okay, Windows can play a third type of sound file — a MOD file. A mixture of .WAV and MIDI, .MOD files contain actual sounds, plus instructions to play them in sequence. They sound sort of like MIDI files, but with real instruments.

The problem? To keep space to a minimum, most of the sounds are repeats — the same drumbeat, the same guitar riff, the same hand clap, ad nauseam. Most "MOD" files sound rather robotic. But, hey, add a few strobe lights and pretend you're in the, 70s again.

Windows doesn't come with a 'MOD player, but wherever you find 'MOD files, a 'MOD player shouldn't be far behind.

How to listen to sounds

After the sound card is hooked up and the driver is installed (described in the section, "Adding or Changing Drivers," later in this chapter), listening to sounds is a snap.

- From the File Manager, double-click on the file's name.
- If you double-click on a .MID file, the Windows Media Player leaps to the screen and begins playing it. Simple.
- If you double-click on a .WAV file, the Windows Sound Recorder leaps to the screen and just sits there, stunned. Gently remind it of its mission by clicking on its play button — the button in the middle with the triangle on it.

- Here's a quick way to listen to sounds: Load the Windows Media Player and minimize it — turn it into an icon at the bottom of the screen. Open the File Manager above it. To hear a sound, drag a .WAV or .MID file from the File Manager and drop it onto the Media Player icon. The sound plays immediately. Keep dragging and dropping sounds until you've heard them all. (Never dragged and dropped? Chapter 1 has a refresher course.)

How to assign sounds to events

Windows can let loose with different sounds at different times. Better yet, Windows lets *you* decide what sound it should play and when.

To assign different sounds to different events, follow these steps:

1. **From within the Program Manager, double-click on the Control Panel icon.**

The Control Panel, shown in Figure 3-18, hops to the screen.

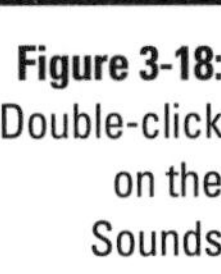

Figure 3-18: Double-click on the Sounds icon.

2. **Double-click on the Control Panel's Sounds icon.**

   The Sound box, shown in Figure 3-19, appears on-screen. It lists the sounds that are currently assigned to Windows events.

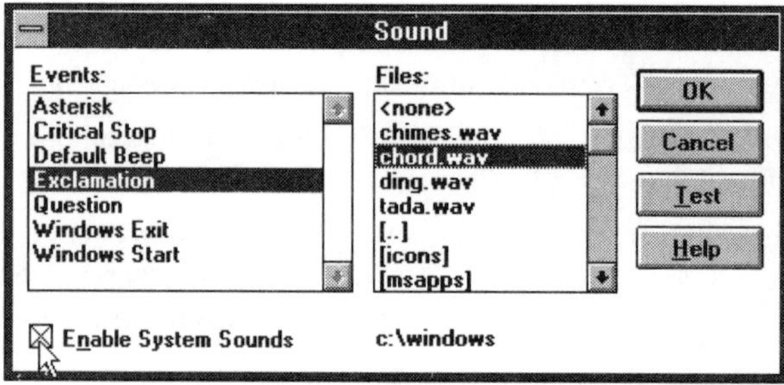

Figure 3-19: These sounds can be assigned to these Windows events.

If you haven't set up and installed a sound card, you can't play with the settings. The sounds look grayed out — dimmer than the rest of the text — and you can't click on them.

3. **Click on an event and then click on the sound that you want Windows to play when that event occurs.**

   Windows is rather vague about what words in the Events box are supposed to mean. An event is usually a box that pops up on-screen. For example, the message in Figure 3-20 occasionally pops up in the File Manager. See the exclamation point in the left side of the box? Windows considers that box an Exclamation event.

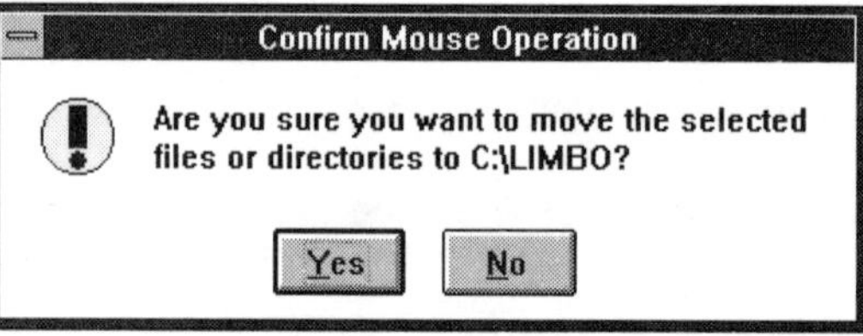

Figure 3-20: Windows considers the box to be an Exclamation event.

Now look at the sound files listed in the Files box that is shown in Figure 3-19. When you click on Exclamation, the CHORD.WAV sound is highlighted to indicate that Windows plays the CHORD.WAV sound whenever the box with the Exclamation point pops up.

Table 3-2 explains the events that you can assign sounds to.

Table 3-2 Windows Sound Events and Their Causes

This event and picture . . .	*. . . plays a sound because of this*
Asterisk/Information	A box has appeared on-screen, offering more information about your current situation.
Critical Stop	An urgent box warns of dire consequences if you proceed — but lets you click on the OK button to keep going, anyway.
Default Beep	The most common event, this means you've clicked outside of a dialog box, or done something equally harmless.
Exclamation	This box urges caution, to a slightly less degree than the Critical Stop Sign warning.
Question	A box is asking you to choose between a variety of choices.
Windows Exit	Plays when you shut down Windows.
Windows Start	Plays when you load Windows.

The Sound box lists all the sounds in the \WINDOWS directory. To see sounds in other directories, click on the names of those directories in the Files box.

Click on the [..] area to see even more directories.

Be sure that the Enable System Sounds box is checked; otherwise, Windows plays sounds only when it first starts and when it leaves the screen.

4. **Click on the Test button.**

   Windows dutifully trumpets the sound you selected. If you like it, click on the OK button, and you're done. If you don't like it, however, head back to Step 3 and click on a different sound.

Don't like any of the sounds? Then record your own! Head to Chapter 8 for the details.

How to get rid of sounds

MIDI files don't take up too much room in the hard disk closet, but .WAV files are clunkier than a cast-iron Hoover vacuum cleaner.

To get rid of sound files, head for the File Manager.

1. **Double-click on the File Manager icon from the Program Manager.**

2. **Call up the directory that contains the particularly dorky sound file.**

   Unlike wallpaper and screen savers, sound files don't have to live in any particular directory, so they can be scattered around the hard drive.

   Locating sound files is easier if you tell the File Manager to stick them all together. Make sure that the Sort by Type option is checked in the File Manager's View menu. The File Manager will dutifully list all the .WAV files together and all the .MID files together in each directory you examine.

   To find all the .WAV files on the hard drive, try this approach: Choose Search from the File Manager's File menu. When the Search box appears, type ***.WAV** in the Search for box, and type **C:** in the Start From box. Make sure that the Search All Subdirectories box is checked and click the OK button. The File Manager brings a new window to the screen, listing every .WAV file that lives on drive C:.

3. **Click on the name of the dorky sound file and press Del.**

   The File Manager dutifully deletes the file. Depending on how the File Manager is configured, it may even politely ask permission.

   Not sure whether you're deleting the correct sound file? Then double-click on its filename. The Sound Recorder comes to the scene, ready to play the file. Click on the Sound Recorder's middle button to hear the file. Still hate it? Then go back to the File Manager, make sure that the file is still highlighted, and press Del. Zap!

What's the hard part?

The hard part of using sound in Windows comes from the computer's sound card. If the sound card is installed correctly, with the right drivers, everything should work pretty smoothly. But until that sound card is set up right, things can be pretty ugly.

Adding or Changing Drivers

Even after you wrestle with the tiny screws on the back of the computer's case, slide in the new sound card, extract the tiny screws from the shag carpet, and reattach the computer's case, you're not through.

After you install a new gadget in the computer, you need to tell Windows how to use it. Those instructions come in the form of a *driver* — a piece of software that teaches Windows how to make that new gadget work.

Most gadgets — things like sound cards, video cards, and CD ROM players — come with a driver on a floppy disk. Some of the older gadgets can use the drivers that came with Windows.

If your gadget is not working right under Windows, chances are, it needs a new driver.

What are driver files?

Driver files end in .DRV, but you can promptly forget that bit of information. The Control Panel handles all the driver installation chores, sparing you the trouble of searching for individual files, moving them around, or trying to delete them.

When Windows tries to install a driver, it looks for another file. The file, called OEMSETUP.INF, contains even more driver instructions — where to copy the drivers and how to set them up. If Windows can't find this file, it screams for it. If Windows finds the file, however, everything moves smoothly. You don't even know that the OEMSETUP.INF file exists.

Where to put drivers

Drivers come on floppy disks. The Control Panel handles the installation chores, so merely put the disk in the disk drive and close the latch.

How to install drivers

To complicate matters, you can install drivers in Windows in two ways. The next section, "Adding a driver for a mouse, keyboard, monitor, or video card," tells you how to install those drivers. If you want to install a driver for a sound card, compact disc player, or movie player, check out the instructions in "How to install multimedia drivers," later in this chapter.

Adding a driver for a mouse, keyboard, monitor, or video card

Don't try to add a driver until you've installed the new mouse, keyboard, or video card. When you're sure that it's up and running, add the driver by following these steps:

1. **Double-click on the Windows Setup icon in the Program Manager's Main window.**

   The Windows Setup box appears on-screen.

2. Click on Change System Settings from the Options menu.

When you click on Options, a menu drops down, as shown in Figure 3-21.

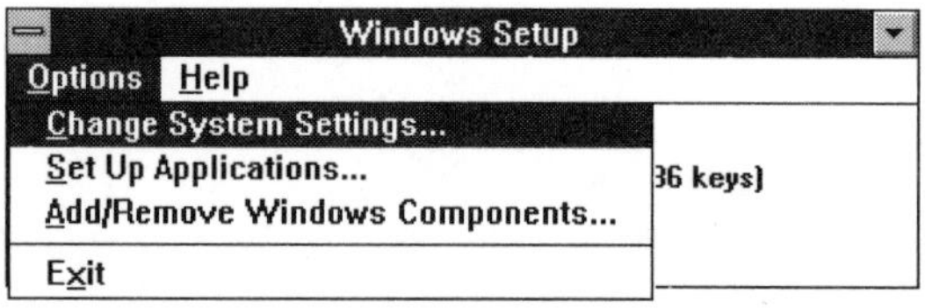

Figure 3-21: The Windows Setup Options menu.

Click on Change System Settings, and the Change System Settings box appears, as shown in Figure 3-22.

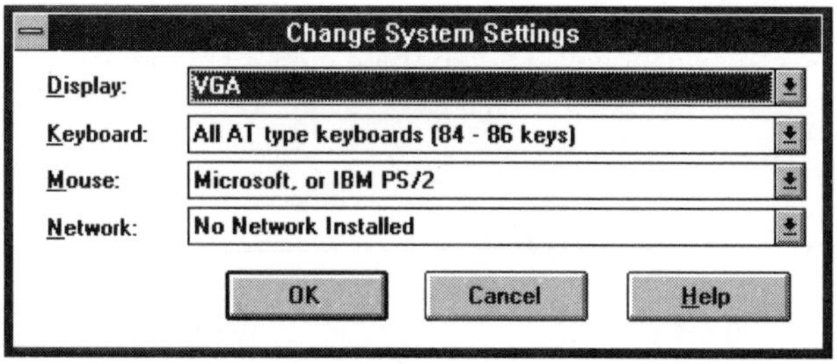

Figure 3-22: This box changes the Display, Keyboard, Mouse, or Network.

3. Click on the box next to the gizmo that you want to change.

A list of brands pops up. If you're lucky, Windows lists your brand by name. Click on its name, click on the OK button, and follow the instructions that appear.

Windows asks you to insert a disk. Do so, and follow the instructions that you see on-screen. (Different gizmos come with different instructions, each written by the manufacturer.)

- If your gizmo isn't listed, jump to the "But mine's not listed!" section, later in this chapter.
- Windows calls the monitor and video card combination a *display* because the two devices work together. The video card sends out the picture, and the monitor puts it on the screen. Video cards can send out the picture in different modes. Choose several video modes until you find the one you like best.

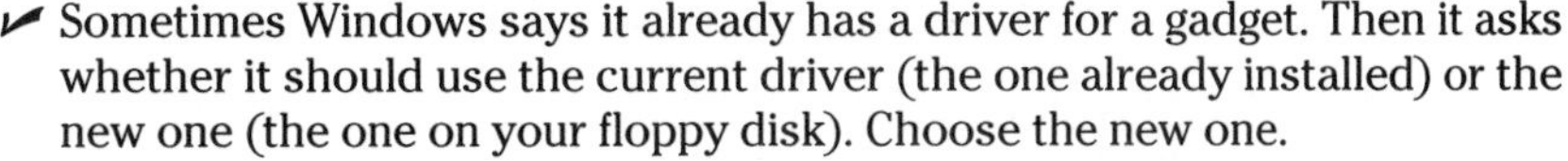

- Sometimes Windows says it already has a driver for a gadget. Then it asks whether it should use the current driver (the one already installed) or the new one (the one on your floppy disk). Choose the new one.

- If you choose a new video driver — or any other driver, for that matter — and Windows simply refuses to load, here's a solution. Type the following two lines at the DOS prompt, one after the other, and press Enter after each line:

  ```
  C:\> CD \WINDOWS
  C:\WINDOWS> SETUP
  ```

  The DOS version of Windows Setup will pop up. Use that program to change the driver back to the old one — the one that worked. That change should bring Windows back to normal.

How to install multimedia drivers (sound, movies, compact disc players)

First, install the sound card or compact disc player. If it comes with a test program, give it a shot. After you're sure the new gadget works, load Windows. If the new toy doesn't work with any DOS programs, it probably doesn't work under Windows, either.

Finally, check to see whether the gadget came with a Windows installation program. If it did, use the installation program — you don't need to bother with this chapter. If it didn't come with an installation program, however, keep reading.

If you're installing an updated version of a driver that you've already installed, remove the old driver first. (Removing a driver is covered in "How to get rid of drivers," later in this chapter.) You need to get the old driver outta there so Windows won't be confused when the new driver arrives.

To install a new driver:

1. **Double-click on the Control Panel icon from the Program Manager.**

   The Control Panel hops to the screen, as shown in Figure 3-23.

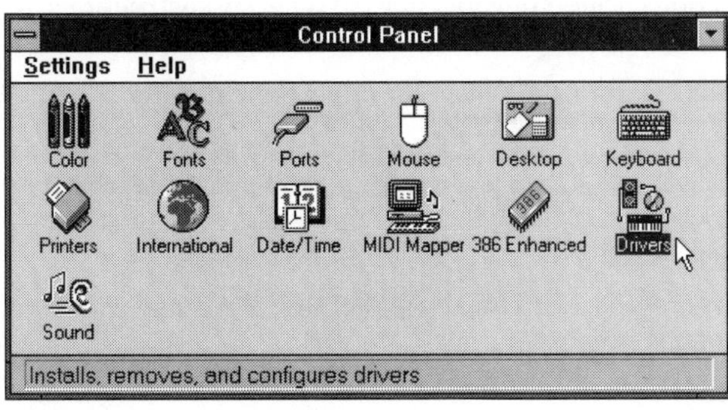

Figure 3-23: Double-click on the Drivers icon to add multimedia drivers.

2. Double-click on the Drivers icon.

The Drivers box shown in Figure 3-24 appears, showing a list of the currently installed drivers.

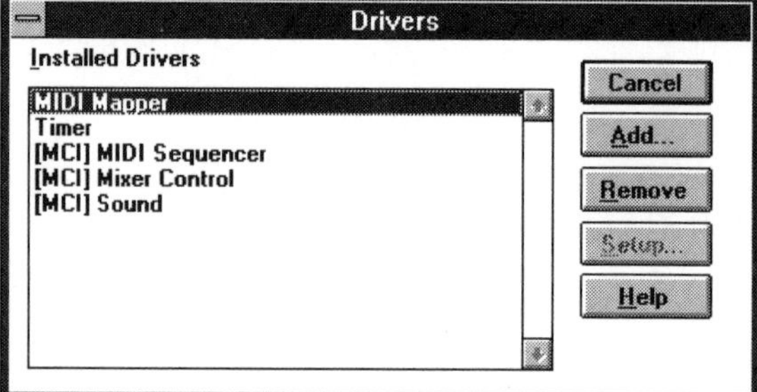

Figure 3-24: The Drivers box shows the drivers currently installed in Windows.

3. Click on the Add button.

A list of brand names pops up, as shown in Figure 3-25. This box lists the drivers that came packaged with Windows.

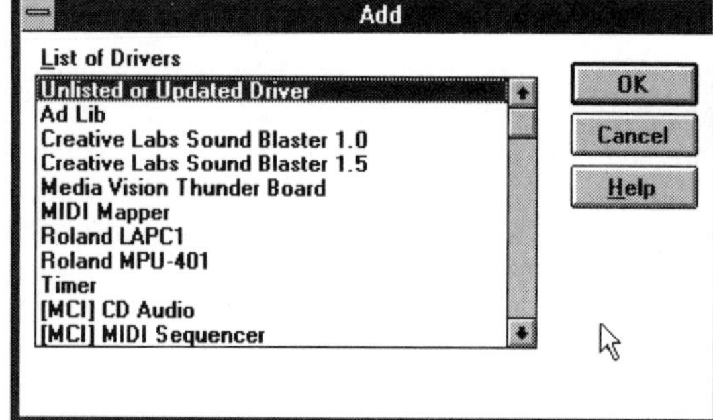

Figure 3-25: Windows comes with drivers for these gadgets.

4. If your new gadget is listed, double-click on its name.

Windows asks you to insert one of the disks that came in the original Windows box. Stick the disk in there, click on the OK button, and follow the instructions. Different gadgets have different instructions, unfortunately.

- If your gadget is not listed, head for the very next section, "But mine's not listed!"
- Windows always assumes that you're sticking your disk in drive A:. If you're sticking it in drive B: instead, change A:\ to B:\ in the box and then click on the OK button.
- For some more tips, head for the end of the "But mine's not listed!" section, coming up next.

But mine's not listed!

If your gadget isn't listed in the Windows menu, don't give up. Instead, follow the preceding Steps 1-4 and carry on with the steps listed below.

1. **Double-click on the Unlisted or Updated Driver option.**

   The Install Driver box pops up, as shown in Figure 3-26, asking you to insert the Windows Drivers disk that came with the gadget.

Figure 3-26: Insert the disk that came with the gadget in drive A.

Install Driver

Insert the disk with the unlisted, updated, or vendor-provided driver in:

A:\

OK

Cancel

Browse...

Help

   Rummage in the box until you find the disk and insert it in drive A:.

   Or, if the disk fits better in drive B:, change the `A:\` in the Install Driver box to `B:\`.

   Or, if the driver lives somewhere on the hard drive (perhaps you downloaded it from a BBS), click on the Browse button to find and select the file's current drive and directory.

   Finally, if the gadget didn't come with a Windows Drivers disk, head for this chapter's first section, "Where Can You Get These Things?," and track down a driver. Windows probably won't work right without it.

   Is the disk in the drive? Then head for the next step.

2. **Click on the OK button in the Install Driver box.**

   A box appears, listing the drivers on that disk or in the directory. If it can't find any, it will ask again. Try again with a different directory.

3. **Click on the name of the driver that you want and click on the OK button.**

   Windows copies the driver to the hard drive.

   Some drivers make you fill out a little form first. Fill it out to the best of your knowledge and try to avoid the technical gibberish.

   You're done. Windows copies the driver from the disk to the hard drive, and everything should work fine.

Ugly IRQs

Sometimes new computer gadgets — sound cards, for example — upset other parts of the computer. They argue over things such as *interrupts,* which are also known as *IRQs.* When you set up the card so it works right in DOS, remember its settings. For example, if the sound card says that it uses *IRQ 7* and *Port 220,* write that information down — no matter how technodork it sounds. Chances are, Windows will ask you for the same numbers.

If the gadget doesn't even work right in DOS, check out the book, *Upgrading and Fixing PCs For Dummies.* It may be able to give you a hand.

- Sometimes Windows, wants to exit and restart itself before the driver will work. You have to exit any of the currently running DOS programs first, however, or Windows will just sit there.
- Some gadgets make you install more than one driver, so keep repeating the preceding Step 3 until you install all of them.
- Didn't get the driver set up right when you first installed it? To get a second chance, double-click on the Drivers icon on the Control Panel, click on the driver that you want to change, and then click on the Setup button.
- Windows dishes out a few helpful spurts of information if you press F1 during any of the installation steps.

How to get rid of drivers

You only need to get rid of drivers under two circumstances:

- You're installing a new driver and you want to get rid of the old driver first.
- You've sold your gadget, or you've stopped using it for some other reason, and you don't want the driver installed anymore.

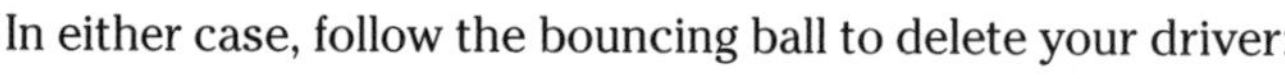

In either case, follow the bouncing ball to delete your driver:

1. **Double-click on the Control Panel icon from the Program Manager.**

   The Control Panel hops to the screen (refer to Figure 3-23).

2. **Double-click on the Drivers icon.**

   The Drivers box appears and lists the currently installed drivers (refer to Figure 3-24).

3. **Click on the name of the driver that you don't like and click on the Remove button.**

   Windows asks whether you're sure you want to get rid of that driver. If you are sure, click on the Yes button, and Windows sweeps it from the hard drive.

   You're through!

- Actually, Windows doesn't *really* sweep the removed driver from the hard drive. It just removes it from the menus. The actual driver file remains on the hard drive. And, short of pulling some bizarre technical strings, you can't reinstall it. If you want it back, reinstall it from the disk the same way you installed it the first time.
- Make sure that you really don't need a driver before you remove it, however; its gadget can't work without it.

What's the hard part?

The hardest part of working with drivers is getting the gadget set up right in the first place. Take the time to make sure that it's set up in DOS. If the gadget comes with any DOS programs, make sure that they work. Then, after it's past that step, try making it work under Windows.

The next problem is getting MIDI files to play. Unfortunately, different programs save them in slightly different formats, so you can have slightly different problems with each file.

Check out Chapter 8 for help when muddling with malfunctioning MIDI files.

The 5th Wave By Rich Tennant

"WELL, HECK—I CAN'T STEP AWAY FROM THE COMPUTER FOR A SECOND WITHOUT YOU BIRDS GETTIN' ALL RUFFLED ABOUT IT."

Chapter 4

Uh, Which Version of Windows Does What?

In This Chapter

- Finding out which version of Windows you have
- Windows Versions 1.0 and 2.0
- Windows Version 3.0
- Windows Version 3.1
- The Microsoft Windows Resource Kit
- The Windows Productivity Pack
- Windows for Workgroups
- Windows NT
- Windows 4.0 (Chicago)
- Windows NT Lite (Cairo)
- Windows for Pens

For the past several years, PC users lined up into two distinct rows. One group loved Windows. Everybody else stuck with plain ol' DOS. And unless the two groups tried to compute while they were in the same room, nobody hurled food at anybody else.

It's not simple anymore, though. That single row of Windows users now has more than six split ends.

Which version of Windows does what? Which one is best? Which version do you have? And are you using the right one?

This chapter rounds up all the different types of Windows — antique, modern, and the upcoming versions that are peeking right around the corner.

Which Version of Windows Do You Have?

Don't know which version of Windows you're using? Check the front of the Windows box; that's the easiest clue. No box? Then check the labels on the Windows floppy disks.

If all that stuff fell off the pick-up truck during the last move, then call up the Windows Program Manager. Click on Help from the menu bar and then click on About Program Manager when the little menu drops down.

A box like the one in Figure 4-1 lists the version number.

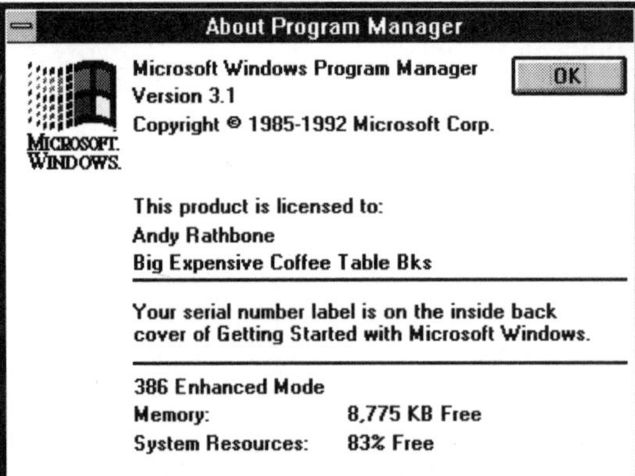

Figure 4-1: Click on About Program Manager from the Program Manager's Help menu to find your version of Windows.

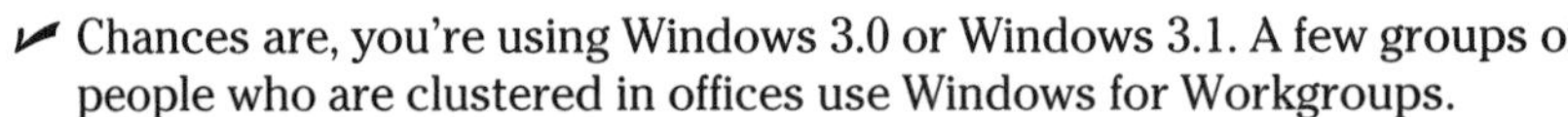

- Chances are, you're using Windows 3.0 or Windows 3.1. A few groups of people who are clustered in offices use Windows for Workgroups.

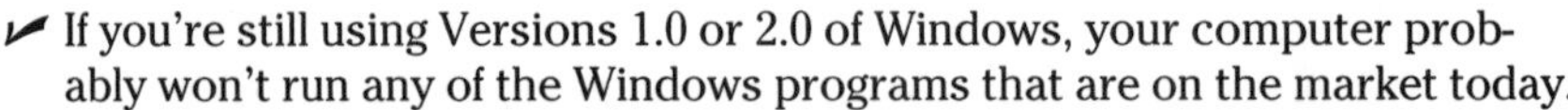

- If you're still using Versions 1.0 or 2.0 of Windows, your computer probably won't run any of the Windows programs that are on the market today.

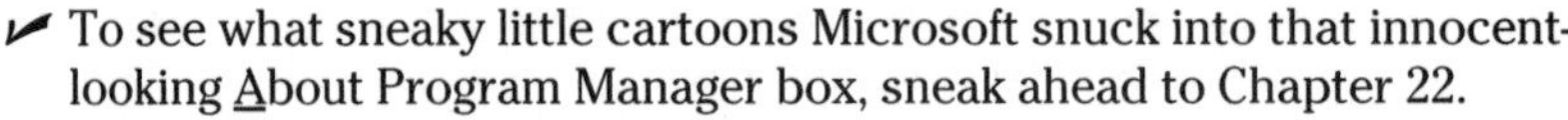

- To see what sneaky little cartoons Microsoft snuck into that innocent-looking About Program Manager box, sneak ahead to Chapter 22.

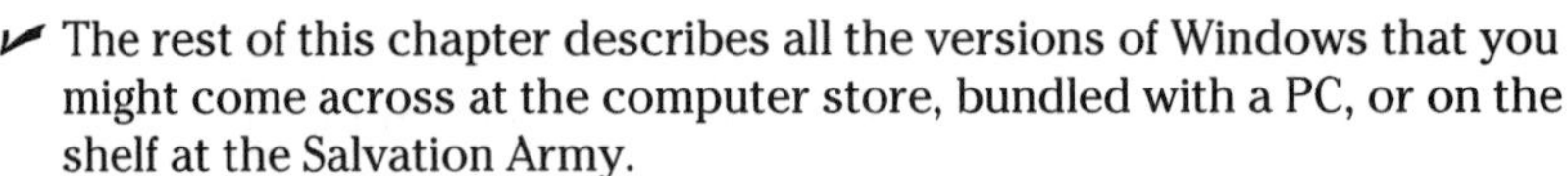

- The rest of this chapter describes all the versions of Windows that you might come across at the computer store, bundled with a PC, or on the shelf at the Salvation Army.

Windows Versions 1.0 and 2.0

Era: Announced in 1983, Windows 1.0 finally hit the shelves in November 1985. Windows 2.0 followed in December 1987.

Required hardware: Windows 1.0 required 256K of memory and two floppy drives. Anybody who wanted to do more than watch the mouse pointer turn into a perpetual hourglass needed a hard drive and a least 1MB of RAM.

Reason for living: Microsoft was trying to get rid of the computer's *typewriter look.* With DOS, people typed letters and numbers into the computer. The computer listened and then typed letters and numbers back at them.

It worked well — after people struggled through all the manuals. But it was, well, boring. A lot more boring than that fun Macintosh. Programmers designed DOS for other programmers, who thrived on elusive strings of techno-gibberish.

So, to camouflage DOS's shortcomings, Microsoft released Windows 1.0. Windows enabled people to boss around their computers much more pleasantly. They'd slide a mouse around on the desk, pointing at buttons on the screen and clicking a button on the mouse.

Major features: Everybody hated Windows 1.0. The colors were awful. They looked as if they'd been chosen by a snooty interior decorator who was trying to make a *statement.* Windows wanted every window to be the same awkward size, and they couldn't overlap. To fine-tune the concept and attract new users, Windows 2.01 added *Dynamic Data Exchange (DDE),* a dramatic marketing term for a simple concept — letting programs share information.

For example, the golf scores in the spreadsheet could be *hot-wired* to the club newsletter in the word processor. When somebody typed the latest golf scores into the spreadsheet, the spreadsheet automatically updated the golf scores in the newsletter.

For the first time, club members actually volunteered to serve as the newsletter editor.

Verdict: Like the first microwave oven, Windows offered something dramatically new — and dramatically frightening. Most people simply ignored it. The final straw? Windows required an expensive, powerhouse computer, and back then, tiny little XT computers ruled the desktops.

Interest in Windows 2.0 picked up a little, mainly because of IBM's new AT computer. The AT's rocking 286 chip could open and shut windows much faster than the XT.

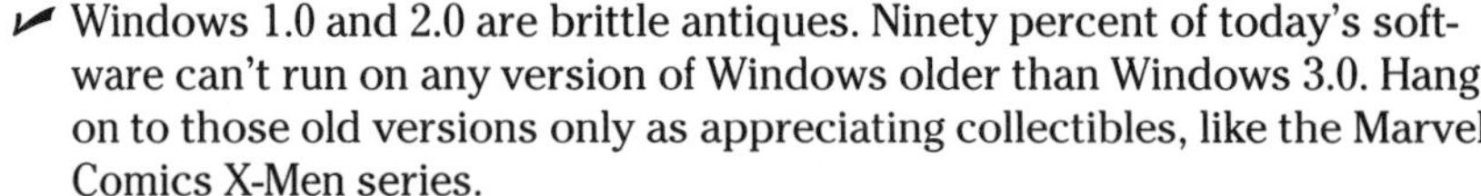

- Windows 1.0 and 2.0 are brittle antiques. Ninety percent of today's software can't run on any version of Windows older than Windows 3.0. Hang on to those old versions only as appreciating collectibles, like the Marvel Comics X-Men series.

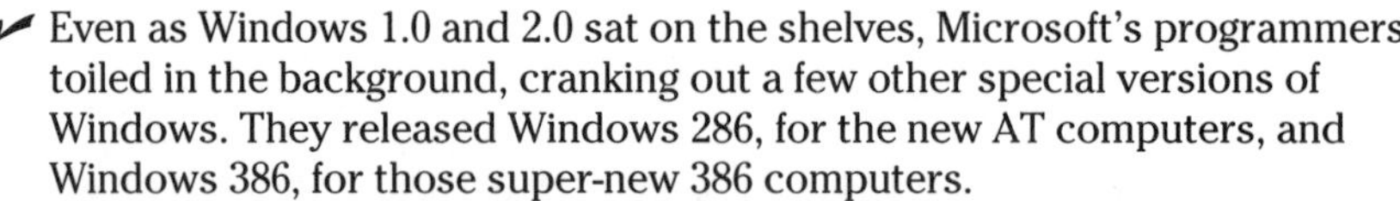

- Even as Windows 1.0 and 2.0 sat on the shelves, Microsoft's programmers toiled in the background, cranking out a few other special versions of Windows. They released Windows 286, for the new AT computers, and Windows 386, for those super-new 386 computers.
- Windows 386 could finally run a DOS program in a little on-screen window, instead of forcing it to hog the whole screen. These in-between versions were practice efforts for the upcoming Windows 3.0 version; neither can run most of the Windows software that is sold today.

Windows 3.0

Era: Born in May 1990.

Required hardware: Although the box said that Windows 3.0 worked on XTs, ATs, and 386s, it crawled on anything but a 386.

Reason for living: Windows finally grew up with this release. The powerful computers of the day could finally handle it, and Microsoft had sanded off the rough edges that plagued earlier versions.

Major features: Compared to the earlier Windows versions, Windows 3.0 took off like a cat stepping on a hot waffle iron. Cosmetically, Windows 3.0 *looked* better than earlier versions; plus, users could maneuver on-screen windows much more easily. Finally, it did a much better job of insulating users from ugly DOS mechanics; people could *point and click* their way through boring file-management tasks.

Windows 3.0 could handle networks for the first time (see "Windows for Workgroups," later in this chapter), and it did everything a lot faster.

Verdict: Most Windows software still runs under Windows 3.0. In fact, many people still use Windows 3.0, — although they're always muttering under their breath about upgrading "real soon now."

What mode are you?

Windows 3.0 brought three new Windows *modes* along with it.

Real: By loading Windows 3.0 in Real mode, users could still run some of the older Windows software that was written for Windows 2.0. Unfortunately, Real mode meant that Windows worked *Real slow.* But it was the only mode that XT computers could handle.

Standard: In Standard mode, Windows programs could run at their quickest, but DOS programs suffered. DOS programs couldn't run in little on-screen windows; they had to fill the whole screen. And although several DOS programs could run at the same time, only the currently running DOS program could show up on-screen. The rest had to lurk in the background, frozen as icons.

386-Enhanced: Designed specifically for the 386 chip (as well as any 286 chips), this mode let several DOS programs run simultaneously in their own on-screen windows. It also let Windows grab a chunk of the hard disk and pretend that it was memory, swapping information back and forth when *real* memory was too full to handle any more. (More swap file facts live in Chapter 5.)

Windows 3.1 dumped Real mode, but it still runs in the other two modes.

Windows 3.1

Era: Born in April 1992.

Required hardware: A 386SX or faster computer, at least 2MB of RAM, and at least 10MB of space on the hard drive. For best results, however, look for at least 4MB of RAM and at least an 80MB hard drive.

Reason for living: Ninety percent of Windows 3.1 is the same as Windows 3.0. That new ten percent, however, makes quite a difference. Windows 3.1 got rid of those ugly jagged fonts and added sound support so people can play with multimedia programs. It carries on the evolution toward making computers easier to use, as well as more fun.

Major features: Windows 3.1 continues the success of Windows 3.0. It adds a revamped, more efficient File Manager, easy-to-use TrueType fonts, more drag-and-drop features, and sound.

Verdict: People will be using Windows 3.1 for many years to come. Look for the next version sometime in 1994 or 1995.

- Chances are, you're using Windows 3.1. Microsoft has been selling about a million copies of it every month, and it comes preinstalled on many new computers.

- A Windows Software Development Kit (dubbed SDK by highly paid marketing workers) helps programmers make little windows and menus pop onto the screen at the touch of a button.

  A Windows 3.1 SDK, therefore, contains be a bunch of weird code words to help programmers write Windows 3.1 programs. Normal people find the SDK pretty useless.

  You're not missing much, though; SDKs can cost about five times as much as Windows.

The Microsoft Resource Kit for Windows 3.1

Era: 1992.

Required hardware: Same as for Windows 3.1.

Reason for living: Every large office keeps a haggard-looking computer guru to help computer-stunned people who wring their hands in anguish. Those haggard gurus spend their working hours paging through the Resource Kit for Windows.

Major features: Designed for folks who get *paid* to master Windows 3.1, the Resource Kit is a college textbook of Windows details. A disk contains a few programs that enable gurus to see what Windows is doing beneath the covers.

Verdict: The Resource Kit isn't a version of Windows. It's a bunch of programs and information to help technoids figure out why the File Manager stopped listing any files immediately after Robin finished sprucing up the color scheme in the Control Panel.

The Resource Kit fits well under the arms of computer gurus. Normal computer users don't bother with it.

The Microsoft Productivity Pack for Windows

Era: 1992.

Required hardware: Same as for Windows 3.1.

Reason for living: When some people buy groceries, they push the cart up and down every aisle — even if they don't need anything in the breakfast cereal aisle. If those cart pushers used Windows, they'd want the Productivity Pack.

Major features: The Productivity Pack isn't a version of Windows. It's a program that takes you up and down every Windows aisle. It's a huge tutorial that covers almost everything.

Verdict: If you want to spend your spare time rolling around in Windows, check out the Productivity Pack. If you'd just as soon get away from Windows whenever possible, ignore it. (In fact, if you've already been using Windows for a while, the Productivity Pack will seem pretty ho-hum.)

Windows for Workgroups

Era: 1992 – present.

Hardware requirements: Same as Windows 3.1, but toss in an extra megabyte or two of RAM.

Reason for living: For years, Steve printed out the spreadsheet and handed it to Jackie. Today, though, Jackie wants to read Steve's spreadsheet from her own computer. She needs a *network* — a way to link all the computers in the office so that everybody can share the same information.

Windows for Workgroups looks pretty much like plain old Windows. But Windows for Workgroups has all the networking stuff built into it. It comes with an enhanced version of Windows software, long cables, and special cards that plug into a computer's guts. Stringing cables from computer to computer enables everybody to share spreadsheets and Solitaire scores—and to send their party fliers to the same printer as well.

Major features: In addition to linking all the computers, this version of Windows has a special mail and scheduling system. Without leaving their desks, workers can decide where to meet for lunch *twice* as quickly as people without a network.

Verdict: Although Windows for Workgroups is compatible with many other network systems, the program hasn't been the overwhelming success that Microsoft expected. Some people even call it Windows for Warehouses. Many offices already had their computers set up on a network. Yet another version of Windows? Yawn.

Windows NT

Era: Born in August 1993.

Required hardware: A fast (at least 25 MHz) 386 computer or a 486. It needs at least 12MB of RAM and consumes about 75MB of hard drive space.

Reason for living: Windows doesn't replace DOS; it rides on top of it, like a shiny new camper shell on a rusty old pickup truck. And DOS, designed for computers that were created more than ten years ago, simply can't take advantage of today's more powerful computers. So Microsoft stuck its programmers in the closet for two years and came up with Windows NT.

Major features: Windows NT looks like plain old Windows, but it's designed specifically for today's speedy computers. It enables them to run bunches of programs at the same time without falling down and dropping everything.

Verdict: Windows NT may be the next big thing. However, it's expensive, requires an expensive machine, and doesn't really run Windows or DOS programs as quickly as Windows 3.1 can run them. Windows NT seems to work best when it's at the heart of a big network and is pumping files up and down cables into other computers. It's a little too fat for a normal desktop PC.

Operating system bores

Everybody agrees that DOS is on its last legs, but nobody agrees on which operating system should replace it. Some people say that Windows NT will take over because everybody is already using Windows 3.1.

Other folks say that IBM's OS/2 may shatter Windows' stronghold. OS/2 is cheaper, runs on cheaper computers, and even runs DOS and Windows programs *faster* than Windows NT can run them.

The real avant-garde folks mumble about UNIX, Solaris, NeXTStep, or something completely unintelligible.

Windows NT has Microsoft behind it, and all that Windows momentum. Which operating system will win? The power users are arm wrestling right now; look for a winner in about two years or so.

Windows 4.0 (Code-named Chicago)

WINDOWS 95

Era: Will probably be born in late 1994 or early 1995.

Required hardware: At least a 386, probably with 4MB to 8MB of memory.

Major features: Windows 4.0 will be an operating system. You won't need to run DOS in the background. It will probably combine some of the features that are found in Windows for Workgroups and Windows NT yet still run current DOS and Windows programs. Oh, and you'll be able to use filenames that are more than eight characters long — and you only had to wait 15 years!

Reason for living: Microsoft's Windows NT is too chunky for most people's desktops. So Microsoft has decided to spruce up Windows again. Code-named *Chicago,* Windows 4.0 will battle IBM's OS/2 to control the desktop PC market.

Verdict: Considering that Microsoft spends about two years building each new version of Windows, look for Windows 4.0 somewhere in 1994 or 1995.

Windows NT Lite (Code-named Cairo)

Era: Probably 1995.

Required hardware: Probably a 486 with at least 8MB

Reason for living: This *scaled-down* version of Windows NT will be yet another Microsoft bullet that's aimed at pushing IBM's OS/2 off the shelf.

Major features: Microsoft is mum.

Verdict: Your neighborhood grocer knows as much as anybody else.

Microsoft Windows for Pens

Era: 1992.

Required hardware: A pen-driven computer, like the ones advertised in fancy computer magazines. A pen-driven computer looks like an expensive Etch-A-Sketch without the little white knobs. (A product called PenDirect for Windows, from another company, lets you wipe a pen across a plain old desktop monitor and doesn't require a mouse or fancy Etch-A-Sketch.)

Reason for living: After years of technical research, programmers discovered that laps disappear when a person stands up. A few nerds experimented by wearing their laptops on trays like those worn by cigarette sales girls in casinos, but others turned to pen-driven computers. Mobile users can now poke Windows' on-screen buttons with a plastic pen rather than a mouse. Because using a pen-driven computer is like writing on a notepad, inventory crews can count cases of canned asparagus without sitting down and struggling with a laptop.

Major features: Windows for Pens is really Windows 3.1 with a special pen-like device that you use to *write* directly onto the computer's screen. Windows looks at the scribbles and translates them into words, letter by letter. (Yes, it's that slow.) Windows for Pens comes preinstalled on several pen-driven computers; you can't buy it separately.

Verdict: Those little pen tablets are somewhat pricey for everybody but supermarket chains that are trying to inventory their vegetables. In a few years, however, pen computers may be built into cars so that drivers can find out how far ahead their next Slurpee lies.

So, Which Windows Is for What?

In a nutshell, Microsoft is pushing three types of Windows, aimed at three types of users.

The person who wants to run Windows on a plain old desktop computer will probably stick with plain old Windows 3.1. Windows 3.1 runs on the average computer of the day.

For people who want to connect two or more computers, usually in a business setting, Microsoft is pushing Windows for Workgroups. Like Windows 3.1, it runs on the average computer of the day, yet it contains a special computer gizmo and some cable to string a bunch of computers together. Then everybody can shoot information back and forth.

And, for the big computing environments with big computers, Microsoft is serving up Windows NT. Windows NT requires a top-of-the line computer, and it's built for offices that need a serious computing platform for serious number crunching.

- All the other versions of Windows are just tiny fish in the huge Windows 3.1 sea. They haven't captured much of a market, although sales are increasing.
- One good point to all of these versions is that because they all have the same basic Windows look, they all work pretty much the same way. You click a word along the top of the screen, and a menu plops down.
- Solitaire is a *lot* easier to play with a pen than with a mouse, says Windows for Pens user Brian Bates. "What could be easier than picking up the Jack of Hearts and setting it on top of the Queen of Spades in one fluid pen movement?" Bates reports. "There's no hunt for the mouse pointer. Just put the pen on the Jack of Hearts, and it's ready to move."

Part II

Making Windows Do More

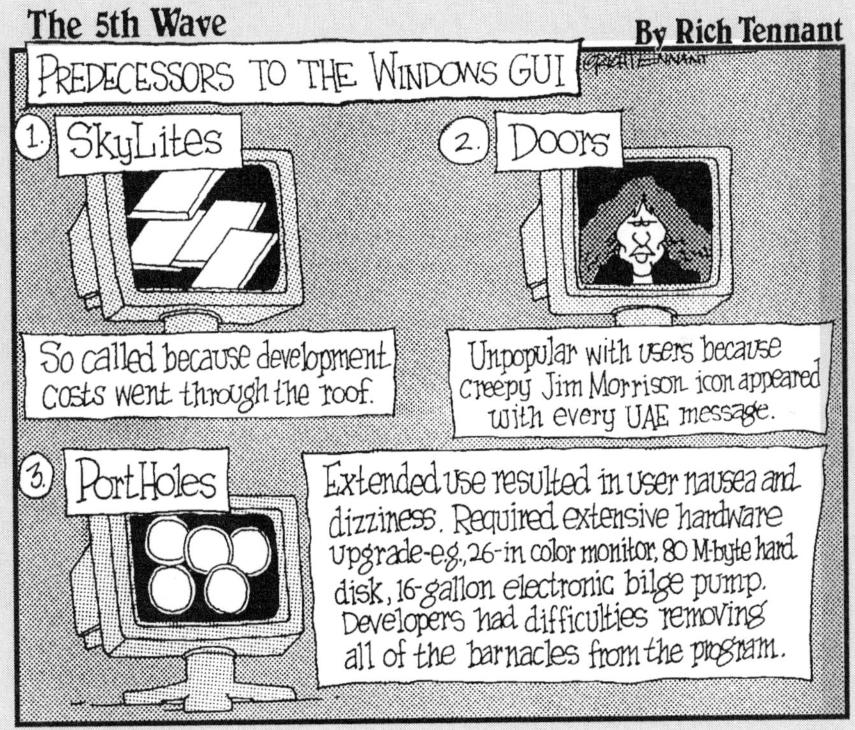

In This Part . . .

By now, you probably have figured out the Windows basics: Click here to make something appear; double-click there to make it disappear. Ho hum.

To keep things moving, this part of the book shows you how to handle that *new* stuff Windows always seems to throw in your face.

You learn how to dust off the Windows Terminal program, dial up Microsoft's Driver library, and pull the latest drivers off the shelf.

Another chapter in this part shows you how to cram all those Windows programs onto that new laptop. Plus, you find out the best way to keep that miniature mouse pointer visible as it scurries across that tiny laptop screen.

Yet another chapter shows which of those new DOS 6 Windows programs are worth bothering with — as well as what to do if Windows doesn't even run after DOS 6 has come aboard.

Finally, you find out how to put all that flashy Windows multimedia stuff to work. Groovy!

Chapter 5

Stuffing Windows onto a Laptop

In This Chapter

- Installing Windows on a laptop
- Making Windows easier to see
- Working with a mouse or trackball
- Making Windows run better on a laptop

For years, nobody bothered trying to run Windows on a laptop. Windows was simply too big and too clumsy, and the laptops of the day were too small to digest it.

Today, Windows is bigger than ever. But today's laptops are much more powerful than before: Most of 'em can digest Windows without even chewing. This chapter shows the *right* way to feed Windows to a laptop, as well as some things to try if the laptop tries to burp Windows back up.

Installing Windows on a Laptop

A laptop is a completely different organism than a desktop computer, so stuffing Windows onto a laptop takes a few extra tricks. To make sure that Windows knows it is heading for a laptop's hard drive, you have to push a few different buttons while installing Windows.

In fact, if you *already* have installed Windows on your laptop, head for the section "But I've already installed Windows!" and make sure that everything is set up correctly; you might need to tweak a few settings here and there.

If you're getting ready to install Windows on your laptop right now, however, keep a wary eye on the next few sections.

Before you install Windows on your laptop, *defragment* its hard drive. That leaves a big clean area on your hard drive for the Windows *swap file*, described later in this chapter. DOS 6 and 6.2 comes with a defragmentation program called Defrag, which is described in Chapter 6. Similar packages are available from Norton Utilities and PC Tools.

Reinstall Windows — don't "LapLink" it over

A program by Traveling Software called LapLink can be a lifesaver. By installing LapLink on both your laptop and your desktop computer — and then stringing a cable between the serial or parallel ports of the two computers — you can quickly copy or move files back and forth between the two computers.

- However, *don't* use LapLink to merely copy Windows from your desktop computer to your laptop.
- And don't use DOS 6 *Interlink*, a LapLink clone, to copy Windows to your laptop either.

- Sure, that would be the quickest way to install Windows. But Windows would still think it was living on your desktop. It wouldn't be able to find its favorite files, and it might not even show up on the laptop's screen: Windows wouldn't be set up to use your laptop's temperamental liquid crystal screen.
- Although it takes more time, install Windows on your laptop the old-fashioned way: by inserting the disks into the floppy drive, one at a time. Install your Windows programs on your laptop the same way — one disk at a time.

- When installing Windows on a laptop, choose Custom Setup, not the faster Express Setup. Windows sometimes doesn't know it's heading for a laptop; by choosing the Custom Setup, you can keep it on the right path.
- When Windows asks for your Display type, choose whatever option Windows tosses out. Chances are, it will be plain ol' VGA, which probably will work just fine. To fine-tune Windows' appearance after you have installed it, head for the "Making Windows Easier to See" section later in this chapter.
- If your laptop has a Suspend button — a gizmo that lets you shut the laptop's lid, eat breakfast, and open the lid to continue working where you left off — then check out the very next section. The Suspend button means your laptop has *Advanced Power Management*, and you need to let Windows know about it.

- Legally, you can install the same copy of Windows on both your desktop *and* laptop computers: You don't have to buy a second copy of Windows for your new laptop. However, your Windows package can only be used on *one* computer at a time. If somebody is using Windows on your desktop computer at the same time you're using Windows on your laptop, you're violating Microsoft's licensing agreement.

- When laptopping on a hot-air balloon, don't bother wearing a heavy jacket. All that hot air overhead keeps you surprisingly warm in that little dangling basket.

Installing Windows with Advanced Power Management

Batteries on a laptop never last long enough. To keep the Energizer Bunny kicking across your screen just a little bit longer, some laptops come with a bit of engineering called *Advanced Power Management* or *APM.*

APM is a fancy term that means your computer saves batteries by shutting down the parts you're not using. For example, if your software hasn't grabbed anything off the hard drive for a while, the laptop might save power by making the hard drive stop spinning. (Don't worry, the hard drive starts spinning again when either you or Windows needs it.)

On some laptops, APM adds a *Suspend* feature. You can shut down the laptop by merely closing its lid — even while Windows is on-screen. The next time you open the laptop's lid, Windows, looking just like you last left it, is there waiting for you.

Unless Windows *knows* it has been suspended, however, it freaks. It might not wake up the mouse, for example, or reset the computer's clock.

So, when you install Windows on a laptop with APM, watch the beginning screens carefully. Windows starts off by listing the type of computer it thinks you're using, as shown in Figure 5-1. If the list says `MS-DOS System`, press the up-arrow key until `MS-DOS System` is highlighted and then press Enter. A list of computers appears, and the two APM options are hiding near the bottom, as shown in Figure 5-2.

```
Windows Setup

    If your computer or network appears on the Hardware Compatibility List
    with an asterisk next to it, press F1 before continuing.

    System Information
       Computer:             MS-DOS System
       Display:              VGA
       Mouse:                Microsoft, or IBM PS/2
       Keyboard:             All AT type keyboards (84 - 86 keys)
       Keyboard Layout:      US
       Language:             English (American)
       Codepage:             English (437)
       Network:              No Network Installed

       Complete Changes:     Accept the configuration shown above.

    To change a system setting, press the UP or DOWN ARROW key to
    move the highlight to the setting you want to change. Then press
    ENTER to see alternatives for that item. When you have finished
    changing your settings, select the "Complete Changes" option
    to quit Setup.

 ENTER=Continue  F1=Help  F3=Exit
```

Figure 5-1: In this case, Windows is set up for a computer running MS-DOS, which won't take advantage of a laptop's power-saving options.

```
Windows Setup

  You have asked to change the type of computer to be installed. The
  following list also includes computers that require special handling.
  (They appear on the Hardware Compatibility List with an asterisk,
  because they are not 100% compatible with Windows version 3.1.). If
  your computer is not listed, accept Setup's original selection.

   • To select the computer you want from the following list
      1) Press UP or DOWN ARROW key to move the highlight to the item.
      2) Press ENTER.
   • To return to the System Information screen without
      changing your computer type, press ESC.

   Toshiba 5200
   Zenith: all 80386 based machines
   AT&T NSX 20 : Safari notebook
   MS-DOS System with APM
   Intel 386SL Based System with APM

  (To see more of the list, press the (↓) arrow key)
ENTER=Continue  F1=Help  F3=Exit  ESC=Cancel
```

Figure 5-2: The two APM options appear near the bottom of the computer list.

- If your laptop has a 386SL chip, choose the `Intel 386SL Based System with APM` option. This option lets Windows take advantage of all the energy-saving stuff built into the 386SL chip.
- If your laptop has Advanced Power Management stuff but *doesn't* have a 386SL chip, choose `MS-DOS System with APM`.
- If you see your laptop's brand name on the computer list, like the ones listed in Figure 5-2, choose it. Some laptops baffle Windows, so Microsoft lists those troublemakers by name. When Windows knows which brand of laptop it's shacking up with, everything works fine.
- Some laptops come with extra utilities designed to make Windows work more easily. Rummage through the box your laptop came in for any stray disks marked *Windows*. They probably contain special *drivers* (covered in Chapter 3) that make your laptop work better.
- Don't remember whether you set up the APM option when you installed Windows? Then turn to the "But I've already installed Windows!" section a few pages ahead.

- Toshiba's T2200SX, T3300SL, T4400SX, and T6400 laptops should be configured in Windows Setup as `MS-DOS System`, not as `MS-DOS System with APM` or `Intel 386SL Based System with APM`. Their power-saving features aren't APM compatible, and the APM setting can cause file glitches and clock problems.

- When Windows is installed with the Advanced Power Management option, a little battery icon sets up camp in your Control Panel. Double-click on the little battery, and you can fiddle with your laptop's APM options. Best bet: Set Power Management to Advanced and CPU speed to Auto (under Options). For more excruciating details, read the boring technical stuff that follows.

Going "APE" over APM

Windows lets you fine-tune the energy-saving features built into your laptop with Advanced Power Management. Double-click on the little battery icon living in the Control Panel, and Windows lets you start tweaking. Although different laptops may have slightly different settings, here's a short guide to what each knob does.

Power Management

This area controls how Windows should interact with your laptop's built-in power-saving functions.

Advanced: The best choice, this option reminds Windows to turn on your mouse when the laptop wakes up from Suspend mode and to reset the current time. However, if the opposite happens — your laptop's power-saving features suddenly stop working — then choose the Standard option described next.

Standard: This option takes advantage only of the energy-saving stuff built into the laptop — Windows won't try to help out at all. Choose this setting if the Advanced setting causes problems.

Off: Choosing this option disables all of the laptop's energy-saving features. Only use this option when your laptop is plugged into the wall with its AC adapter.

Battery Level

If your laptop comes with a built-in battery-life gauge, Windows displays it in the Battery Level box. This box also says whether your computer is currently plugged into the wall or sucking life out of your batteries.

SL™ Options

This box displays even more additional energy-saving features of this SL chip, which are described in the following list.

CPU Speed. Your computer's main chip can work more slowly to save power. You can leave the CPU racing along at 100-percent efficiency or slow it down to 10-percent efficiency. The slower speed saves battery power but makes your laptop run about as slowly as a cat-nibbled cockroach with five legs pulled off. Best bet: Leave CPU Speed set on Auto. With the Advanced option set, the CPU automatically turns itself on or off, depending on its workload.

Manual Suspend. This feature controls how Windows deals with a laptop's Suspend feature, which usually is activated by opening and shutting the laptop's lid.

Immediately: Windows immediately suspends all the currently running programs when the laptop's lid is closed. This usually is the best bet.

Delayed until idle: This option lets any Windows program finish its current work — sorting a database, for example — before Windows goes into Suspend mode.

Auto Suspend. This option controls how Windows deals with a laptop that shuts itself off if it hasn't been touched for a while.

After: Want Windows to save its batteries by resting if you haven't touched the mouse or keyboard in a while? Click this box; then enter the number of minutes you want Windows to wait for your touch before sleeping.

Delayed until idle: As with Manual Suspend, this option tells Windows to wait until any currently running program finishes its work, such as downloading a file, before shutting down — even if the Auto Suspend deadline has passed.

Resume. This box controls how and why Windows should wake up from Suspend mode if something exciting happens.

On Modem Ring: Windows stays in Suspend mode and saves battery power until your laptop's modem receives an incoming call. Then it wakes up and crankily answers the phone.

On Date/Time: Enter the date and time when you want Windows to wake up, and be sure to use military time. For example, to make Windows wake up at 1 p.m., type the number **13**, not 1.

Installing Windows on a Smaller Hard Drive

Although Windows normally gobbles about 10MB of a laptop's precious hard drive space, that amount can be snipped down to less than 3MB of space. (Hop ahead to Chapter 16 for tips on what parts to prune.)

The key to paring down the amount of space consumed by Windows is to decide what parts of Windows you can leave behind. For example, do you really need Paintbrush, except to impress kids on the airplane? Don't install Paintbrush or its Help file, and you have saved 224K of hard disk space.

To leave portions of Windows off the hard drive when you install it, choose the Custom Setup option. Then, look for the screen shown in Figure 5-3; it appears relatively early in the installation process. Make sure that a check mark appears in the box next to Set Up Only Windows Components You Select.

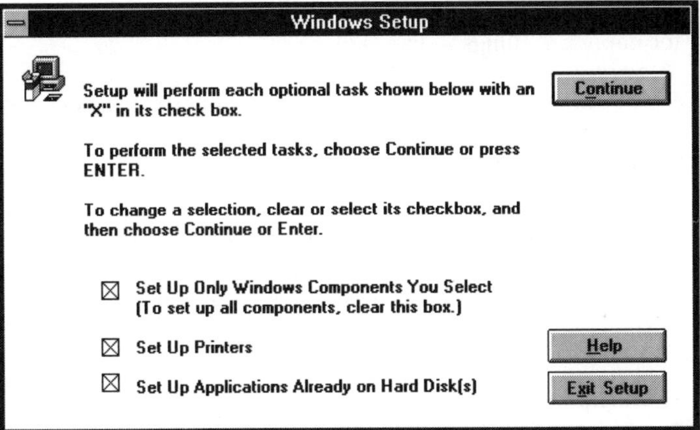

Figure 5-3: The Set Up Only Windows Components You Select box lets you decide which Windows features to install.

Click on Continue, and the screen shown in Figure 5-4 pops up.

Click the Windows component you want to leave out. For example, to prevent Windows from installing any screen savers, make sure that there is no check mark next to the Screen Savers option.

Or, if you want to pick and choose which screen savers to remove, click on the Files button. Another box appears that lets you specify which screen savers to install and which to leave out. (See Chapter 13.)

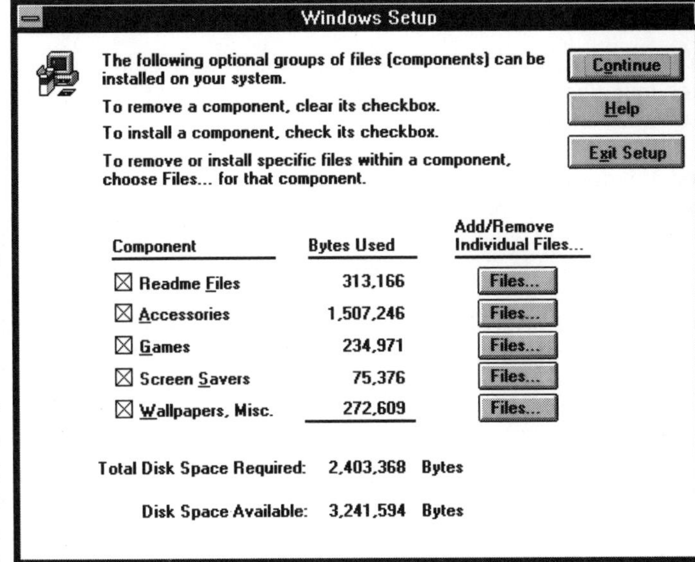

Figure 5-4: Click on the Files button next to each part of Windows you don't want to install.

By whittling down the unnecessary goods, you will have more room on the hard drive for important things — like games.

- You probably don't need Media Player or Sound Recorder; most laptops don't have sound or video. You can find plenty of other disposable files listed in Chapter 16.

- Feel free to keep Paintbrush off your laptop's hard drive to save space, but consider copying Paintbrush — and any other programs you have left out — to a floppy disk. The disk won't take up much weight in your laptop bag, the files won't clutter up your hard drive, and you'll still have them if you need them.
- When installing programs on your laptop, look for "light" versions. Word for Windows, for example, can be installed without the programs containing graphs and pictures that are bundled with it. Leave out the thesaurus, tutorial, and other stuff you won't need on the road.

Installing those sneaky swap files

When Windows hops onto a computer for the first time and starts fluffing up the pillows, it immediately asks for more room.

The extra room Windows is requesting is called a *swap file;* it's simply a large file that Windows creates on your hard drive. When Windows runs out of room to store things in your computer's memory, it starts storing stuff in the hard drive's swap file.

Swap files create two big problems on laptops. First, Windows sometimes grabs way too much hard drive space for its permanent swap file. Laptops often don't have much room to spare.

Second, Windows gets nauseous when a laptop's battery runs down. That means you shouldn't choose a swap file option called 32-Bit Disk Access. The swap file runs faster when this option is selected, but when the laptop's batteries begin to fade, Windows can lose data.

The solution? Buy as much RAM for your laptop as possible. More RAM results in a smaller swap file, more space on your hard drive, and longer battery life. (Swap files eat more power than RAM.)

- When you are running a laptop, don't choose the Use 32-Bit Disk Access option, which is listed under the Virtual Memory area of the Control Panel's 386-enhanced icon. You can lose data when the laptop's batteries run down.

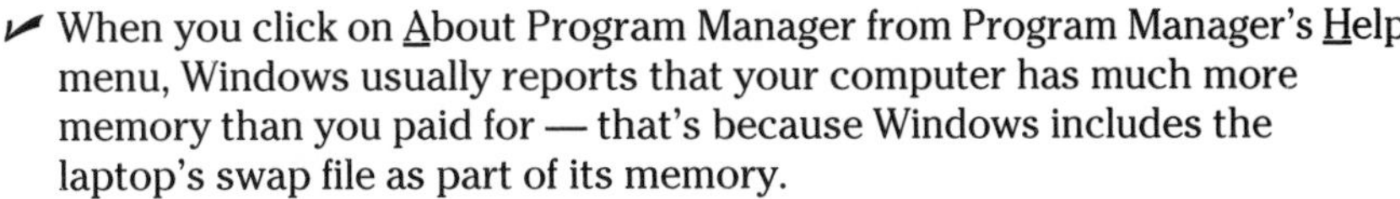

- When you click on About Program Manager from Program Manager's Help menu, Windows usually reports that your computer has much more memory than you paid for — that's because Windows includes the laptop's swap file as part of its memory.

- If you ever spot files named 386SPART.PAR or SPART.PAR sitting on your hard drive, don't delete them: Those are Windows *permanent* swap files. Don't delete a file called WIN386.SWP, either; that's Windows *temporary* swap file.
- To see how much room Windows has snatched for its swap file (and to check on the 32-Bit Disk Access area), head for the section "But I've already installed Windows!" coming up soon in this chapter.
- Windows asks permission for creating a swap file. If your laptop has 4MB of RAM or more, don't let Windows grab more than 4MB for its permanent swap file. If your laptop has less than 2MB of memory, don't let Windows grab more than 6MB. And certainly don't let it grab anything ridiculous — like 23MB. (Don't laugh — Windows has certainly tried.)
- Windows only needs a swap file when it's running in 386-Enhanced mode. It doesn't use one while it's in Standard mode.

But I've already installed Windows!

Have you already installed Windows? Then here's how to make sure it's installed on your laptop the *right* way.

Checking up on Windows swap files and 32-Bit Disk Access

To see how Windows is handling your swap files (and to make sure the 32-Bit Disk Access option is turned off), follow these steps. Oh, Windows calls its swap file *Virtual Memory*, so don't be surprised to see that term trying to crash the party.

If you plan on making any changes to the Windows swap file, be sure to save your work first. Chances are, everything will work fine. But you can never have too many backup copies of your work.

Follow these steps to check up on your swap file:

1. Double-click on the Control Panel icon from within the Program Manager.

2. Double-click on the Control Panel's 386 Enhanced icon

A box appears that lists information too complex to bother with here.

3. Click on the Virtual Memory button.

A box appears similar to the one shown in Figure 5-5. The box lists the size and type of the swap file Windows currently is using.

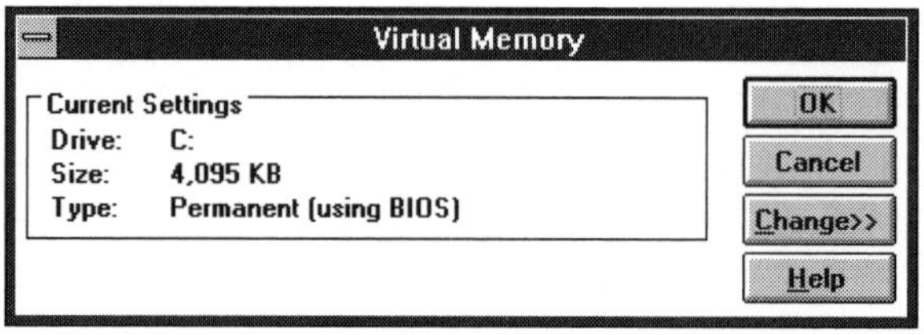

Virtual Memory
Current Settings
Drive: C:
Size: 4,095 KB
Type: Permanent (using BIOS)
OK
Cancel
Change>>
Help

Figure 5-5: Windows is using a Permanent swap file of 4,095K or about 4MB.

4. Click on the Change button, and make the desired changes.

The box expands to display more information, as shown in Figure 5-6.

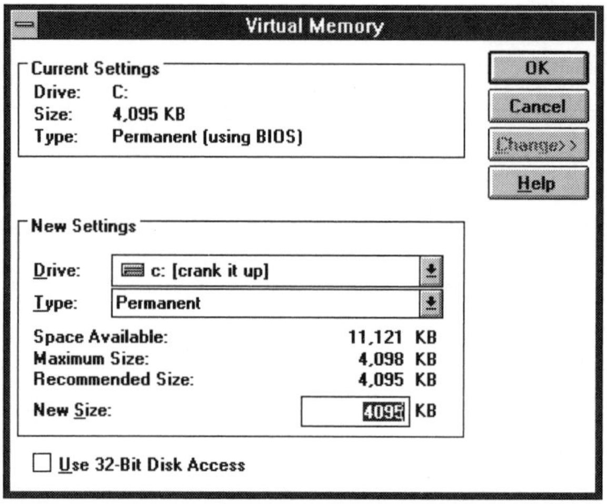

Virtual Memory
Current Settings
Drive: C:
Size: 4,095 KB
Type: Permanent (using BIOS)
OK
Cancel
Change>>
Help
New Settings
Drive: c: [crank it up]
Type: Permanent
Space Available: 11,121 KB
Maximum Size: 4,098 KB
Recommended Size: 4,095 KB
New Size: 4095 KB
Use 32-Bit Disk Access

Figure 5-6: In this box, you can change your Windows swap file from Temporary to Permanent.

If the swap file looks too big, type a new number under New Size. Or to change the swap file to Permanent, Temporary, or None at all, click on the Type: box.

If the number you enter is too small, Windows complains about not being able to create it; but it won't tell you why.

5. Make sure that the Use 32-Bit Disk Access option is not checked.

If you are using a battery-powered laptop and the 32-Bit Disk Access box has a check mark in it, click in the box until the check mark disappears. Using 32-Bit Disk Access on a laptop can damage your files.

6. **Click the OK button, followed by the Yes button**

   Are you done making changes? Then click the OK button. Windows asks whether if you are sure you want to make changes (even if you haven't changed anything). Go ahead and click the Yes button.

   If you changed anything, Windows tosses another screen in your face, as shown in Figure 5-7. Click on the Restart Windows button. Windows clears the screen and returns with its new settings.

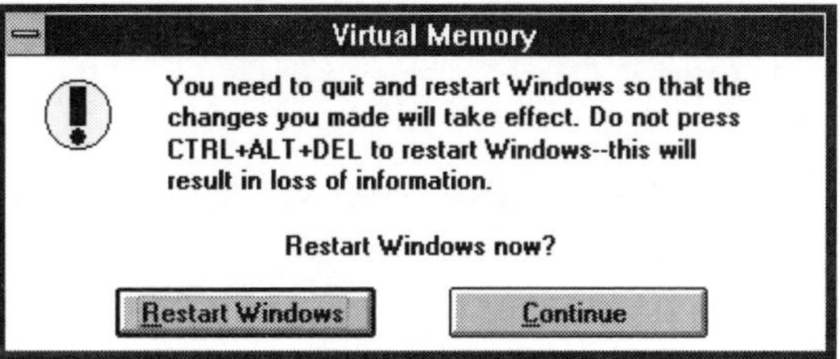

Figure 5-7: The Restart Windows button makes your changes take effect.

Setting up Windows for APM

Does your mouse pointer disappear when Windows comes back after the laptop "suspends" itself? Does your laptop lose track of time while it's suspended? If either of these things happens, then Windows probably doesn't know how to handle your laptop's power-saving options.

Here's how to make sure Windows is set up correctly if your laptop has power-saving features or a 386SL chip:

1. **Exit Windows.**

   Don't shell to DOS. Instead, exit Windows: shut down the Program Manager by double-clicking in its top, left-hand corner. Or, if the mouse isn't working right, open Program Manager and press Alt+F4.

2. **Move to your Windows directory.**

   This part is important. You *must* be in your Windows directory before you can make any changes. The following two DOS commands should move you to the proper directory:

```
C:\> C:
```

   Type the letter of your hard drive where Windows lives, a colon, and then press Enter. If Windows lives on drive D, for example, you would type `D:` and press Enter.

```
C:\> CD \WINDOWS
```

Type the letters CD, a space, a backslash, and the word WINDOWS; then press Enter.

3. **Type SETUP and press Enter.**

   The Windows Setup program appears, as shown in Figure 5-8.

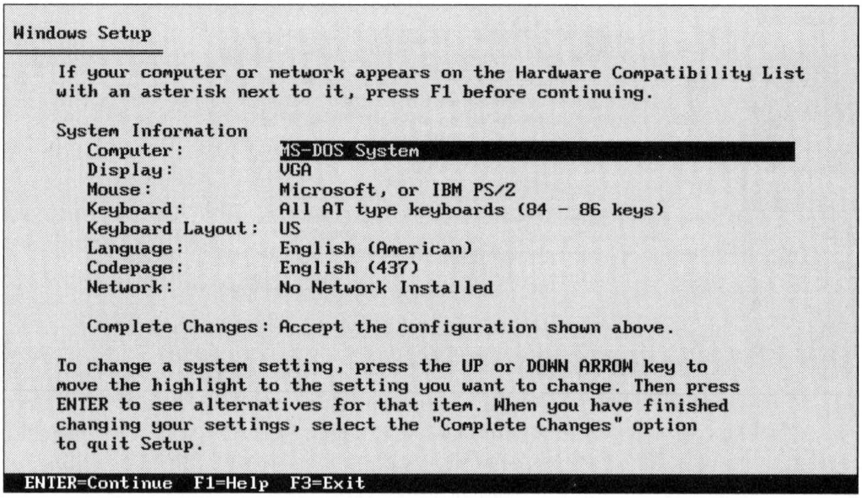

```
Windows Setup

    If your computer or network appears on the Hardware Compatibility List
    with an asterisk next to it, press F1 before continuing.

    System Information
       Computer:          MS-DOS System
       Display:           VGA
       Mouse:             Microsoft, or IBM PS/2
       Keyboard:          All AT type keyboards (84 - 86 keys)
       Keyboard Layout:   US
       Language:          English (American)
       Codepage:          English (437)
       Network:           No Network Installed

       Complete Changes: Accept the configuration shown above.

    To change a system setting, press the UP or DOWN ARROW key to
    move the highlight to the setting you want to change. Then press
    ENTER to see alternatives for that item. When you have finished
    changing your settings, select the "Complete Changes" option
    to quit Setup.

 ENTER=Continue  F1=Help  F3=Exit
```

Figure 5-8: Windows lists the equipment it thinks it currently is running on.

4. **Look at the Computer: listing.**

   The top line under System Information lists the type of computer Windows thinks it is running on. If it says MS-DOS System, you need to change it, so go to Step 5.

   If the box lists something with APM in the title, you're OK. No need to proceed further. You also are OK if the box lists your computer by name, such as the AT&T NSX 20 Safari notebook or the Toshiba 1600.

5. **Press the up-arrow key to highlight the Computer: line and press Enter.**

   A box appears, as shown in Figure 5-9.

6. **Choose a different computer type and press Enter.**

   To change the Computer: setting, press the down-arrow key until you spot the two APM options near the bottom of the list. When the right one's (a 386SL chip or anything else) is highlighted, press Enter.

   Windows might ask you to insert some of your original Windows disks. Rummage around until you find the one with the number that Windows is requesting, stick it in the appropriate disk drive, and press Enter.

```
Windows Setup

    You have asked to change the type of computer to be installed. The
    following list also includes computers that require special handling.
    (They appear on the Hardware Compatibility List with an asterisk,
    because they are not 100% compatible with Windows version 3.1.). If
    your computer is not listed, accept Setup's original selection.

      • To select the computer you want from the following list
          1) Press UP or DOWN ARROW key to move the highlight to the item.
          2) Press ENTER.
      • To return to the System Information screen without
          changing your computer type, press ESC.

      MS-DOS System
      AST Premium 386/25 and 386/33 (CUPID)
      AT&T PC
      Everex Step 386/25 (or Compatible)
      Hewlett-Packard: all machines

    (To see more of the list, press the (↓) arrow key)
  ENTER=Continue  F1=Help  F3=Exit  ESC=Cancel
```

Figure 5-9: Windows lists the different types of computers on which it can run.

Eventually, Windows tells you it is finished and leaves you at the DOS prompt. The next time you start Windows, it runs the *right* way.

It's easy to get in the habit of using the laptop's Suspend feature. Just be sure that you save your work before shutting the lid. When you return to your laptop, you might not remember it is suspended. If you inadvertently flip the power switch, thinking you're turning the laptop on, you actually will be turning it off.

Making Windows Easier to See

The biggest problem with running Windows on a laptop becomes apparent when you look at the screen: It's hard to see what's going on. Some of the boxes have funny lines running up and down the screen; the mouse pointer often disappears at the worst possible moment; and your finger can get a workout adjusting the laptop's contrast or brightness knobs.

Unfortunately, there's no sure-fire cure. Unlike desktop computers, laptops find themselves under various lighting conditions. Working beneath a tree in an Amtrak station calls for a slightly different screen setup than working under the little swiveling overhead light on an airplane.

Here are some lighting weapons to keep in your armament bag; keep trying them until you find the one that works for your particular situation.

Wallpaper may look cool on a desktop computer, but don't bother with it on a laptop. Most wallpaper just gives the mouse pointer another place to hide.

Adjusting the contrast knobs

Your first line of defense comes from the little contrast knob found on nearly every laptop, either along one edge or near the screen.

Whenever the laptop's screen looks a little washed out, try giving the knob a quick turn to bring the light source under control.

Changing your display

Windows comes with several settings that are custom designed to stand out on a laptop's display. When you first install Windows on your laptop, try out each setting until you find the one that makes Windows show up most clearly.

Or if you have already installed Windows, follow the steps below to change the colors to something a little more appealing.

Some manufacturers toss in a floppy disk containing video drivers designed especially for their laptop's screen. Refer to Chapter 3 if you're not sure how to get those drivers off the disk and onto your hard drive.

Feel free to test each color scheme in Windows until you find the one that looks best for your particular laptop:

Control Panel

1. **Double-click on the Control Panel icon in the Program Manager.**

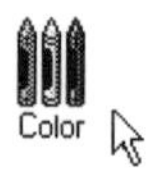

2. **Double-click on the Color icon (those three crayons).**

   The Windows Color box appears, as shown in Figure 5-10, and lets you change Windows' colors. Unless you are using an expensive, color-screen laptop, everything on-screen is a mottled-gray color. Your mission: To choose the *clearest* shade of mottled gray.

3. **Click on the Color Schemes box, and then click on a new scheme.**

   Click on the Color Schemes box and a menu drops down, as shown in Figure 5-11. Each time you click on a different scheme from the menu, Windows offers a "preview" in the lower box of what the color scheme looks like.

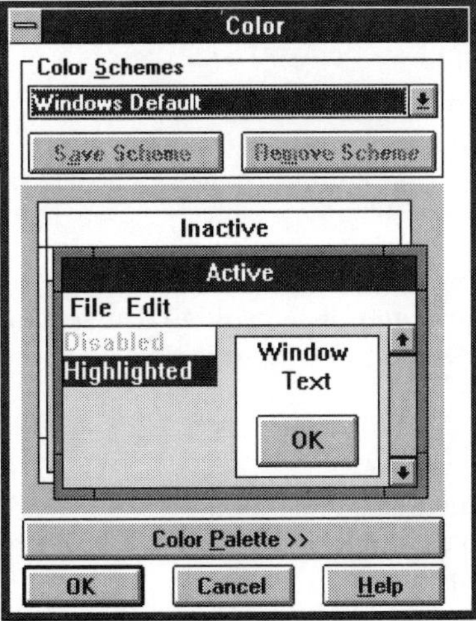

Figure 5-10: The Windows Color option lets you change the colors Windows uses on your laptop.

Laptoppers should try out these color schemes:

Windows Default: Chances are, Windows is already set up like this on your computer, which is why some parts look sort of faint.

Black Leather Jacket: Give this one a try when you're feeling kinky. It looks better than you might think.

LCD Default Screen Settings: Designed specifically for a laptop's display, this setting works well in some dimly lit coffee shops.

LCD Reversed - Dark: This puts white letters on a black background.

LCD Reversed - Light: You guessed it: Black letters on a white background.

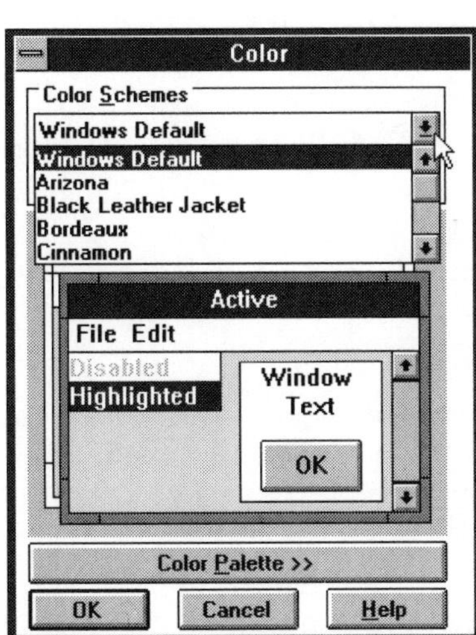

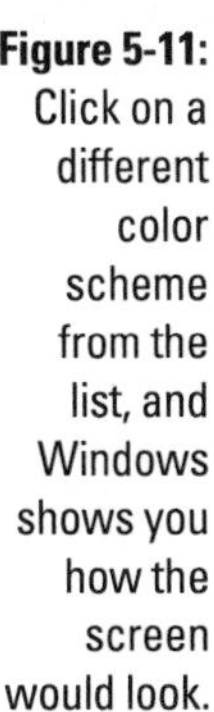

Figure 5-11: Click on a different color scheme from the list, and Windows shows you how the screen would look.

Plasma Power Saver: This one's for those older laptops with glaring orange screens. (You can tell right away if you have one of those monsters.)

Monochrome: This setting works best on my laptop — a Dell 320SLi without a backlit screen. Most color schemes use 16 shades of gray; the Monochrome color scheme cuts that down to a clearly visible four: black, white, light gray, and dark gray.

Don't confuse the Control Panel's Monochrome color scheme with the Setup screen's VGA with Monochrome Display video driver. They are two different beasts. The Setup screen's video driver is designed for a specific type of video card.

4. **Click on the OK button.**

   Your newly chosen color scheme takes effect. If the screen is still hard to read, head back to Step 2 and try a different color scheme. Sooner or later, you will find one that looks right.

The Color option lets you assign your own choice of colors to different parts of Windows. Be very careful, however, when you change your Text colors. If you suddenly can't see any text on your menus, you probably changed your Text color to white — and white doesn't show up very well on a white background. Review Chapter 21 for tips on how to make things go back to normal.

Changing to a better mouse pointer

Even when the laptop's screen is easy to read, your troubles aren't over. The mouse pointer on a laptop usually disappears whenever it's moved. And, unfortunately, the mouse pointer is moving about 90 percent of the time.

Here's one way to make the pointer easier to spot:

1. **From the Program Manager, double-click on the Control Panel icon.**

Mouse

2. **Double-click on the Mouse icon.**
   The Mouse control box appears, as shown in Figure 5-12.

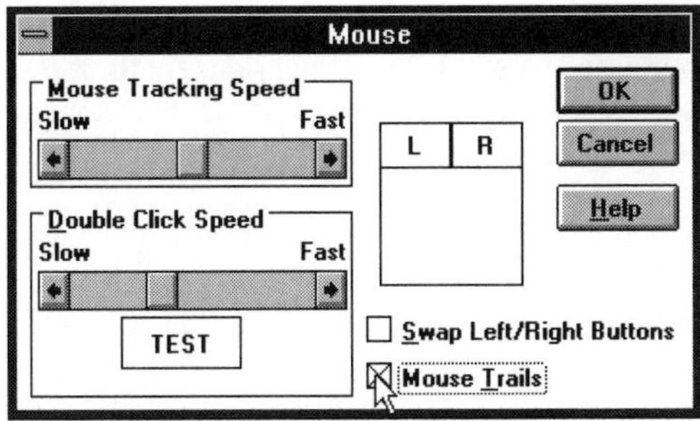

Figure 5-12: The Mouse control box lets you change how your mouse acts.

3. **Click in the box next to Mouse Trails.**

   As soon as a check mark appears in the Mouse Trails box, your mouse begins leaving mouse droppings all over your screen (see Figure 5-13).

- Some mice or trackballs come with software that makes their pointers easier to spot. For example, Microsoft's clip-on trackball comes with a special Control Panel that makes the mouse pointer as big and black as a Happy Hour meatball.
- Several shareware and public domain programs also can make mouse pointers easier to spot. Turn to Chapter 7 for tips on downloading those programs.

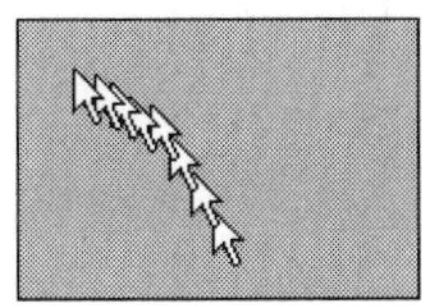

Figure 5-13: The Mouse Trails option makes the mouse pointer much easier to spot on a laptop.

The letters are all too small!

A laptop's screen is nearly always smaller than a desktop monitor. Text often looks smaller than the ingredients list on a package of Hostess Chocodiles. Luckily, fonts are easy to enlarge in both DOS and Windows programs.

Windows programs: When using Windows word processors, spreadsheets, or other windows programs with text, tell the program to use larger fonts. Usually the program's *Format* menu contains a *Font* or *Size* option.

If you're using Word for Windows or another word processor that uses *style sheets*, change your Normal style to something big and easy to read, such as 14-point Arial. This adjustment causes the word processor to display your text in a larger, more visible font.

DOS programs: Windows can enlarge the fonts used by DOS programs, but only while the program runs in an on-screen window and doesn't use any fancy graphics. To enlarge the fonts, click on the little box in the DOS window's upper-left corner (or press Alt+spacebar) and choose Fonts from the menu that drops down. Click on the 10 x 18 option to make the window larger and easier to see.

The DOS window's new, larger size probably will keep it from fitting completely on-screen, but Windows automatically shifts your point of view, keeping the cursor within view.

If the DOS program looks too small when run in an on-screen window, press Alt+Enter. The DOS program fills the screen, making it much easier to see. Press Alt+Enter again to return it to its own window.

Making the Windows Help screen easier to read

The Windows built-in Help program can be an eye-strainer as well as a lifesaver. Those little green *jump* words — the words you click on to make Windows flip to a new helpful page — can be almost invisible on a laptop's gray screen.

The ever-pleasant Windows can change those dim green letters to any color you want. The trick? Add a few lines to a file called WIN.INI that resides in your WINDOWS directory.

Look for the section in WIN.INI marked [Windows Help] and insert these lines:

```
IfJumpColor=0 0 0
IfPopUpColor=0 0 0
JumpColor=0 0 0
PopUpColor=0 0 0
```

Those secret code numbers change the Help system's dim green words to a basic black. The jump words are still underlined, however, which makes them relatively easy to spot.

If you have never edited WIN.INI — or any other .INI file, for that matter — then hop ahead to Chapter 15 for the complete .INI-editing steps, explained most carefully.

Who wants purple jump words?

You can change Windows' Help colors to anything you like by changing those three code numbers in the [Windows Help] section of the WIN.INI file. The numbers work somewhat like finger paints: The first number tells Windows how much red color to mix in; the next number represents green; and the last number adds blue. The number zero means to mix in the *most* of a color, so the numbers 0 0 0 turn everything black.

To find out which code numbers create your favorite color, double-click on the Control Panel's Color icon. Click on the Color Palette button and choose Define Custom Colors. See the numbers currently listed in the Red, Green, and Blue boxes? Those numbers stand for the color currently appearing in the Color|Solid box.

Click on a favorite color or shade in the big square; then, fine-tune the color's brightness by clicking on the tall bar sitting right next to the square. Find a color you like? Write down the numbers that are showing in the Red, Green, and Blue boxes.

To get out of the Custom Color Selector, click on Close and choose Cancel from the next menu. (So you won't mess up your currently selected desktop color scheme.)

Finally, replace the 0 0 0 numbers in the WIN.INI file with the three numbers you wrote down. The next time you load Windows, your newly selected colors will show up in the Help screen's jump words.

Yes, it's a whole lotta effort for a lotta different shades of gray. But bothersome details like this are what these Technical boxes are designed for.

Playing with a Mouse on the Airline Tray

A mouse makes Windows easier to use on a desktop computer, but it often gets in the way on a laptop. Luckily, there are a few alternatives.

Trackballs: These little guys look like tiny upside-down mice that clip to the side of your laptop. Some laptops come with a trackball built in near the screen. Just give the ball a deft spin with your thumb, and the mouse pointer stumbles across the screen. Definitely give yourself a few days to get used to it.

Trackballs work on desktop computers as well as laptops. To get used to the trackball's different feel, clip it to your desktop computer's keyboard. After giving it a whirl for a few days, you will feel more confident thumbing a trackball when you are on the road.

Keyboard: Some laptops let you move the mouse pointer by pressing a special "function" key and tapping the arrow keys. It's as awkward as it sounds, but arrow keys are better than the last alternative, described next.

Memorizing keystrokes: Windows can be controlled exclusively through the keyboard. See those underlined letters on the menus of just about any Windows program? Press and release Alt, and then press one of those underlined letters, which activates the command. For example, press Alt,F while you are in Program Manager, and the File menu drops down.

- Ever tried to change a window's size by using a trackball? Grabbing a window's border is like trying to pick up a toothpick with salad tongs. The border is just too skinny to get a grip on. To enlarge the border, double-click on the Control Panel's Desktop icon. Then, in the bottom, left-hand corner, change the Border Width to 5 and click on OK. If the border is still hard to grab, increase the number to 6 and try again.

- Don't have much space to move your mouse on the airplane's fold-down tray? Head for the Control Panel's Mouse icon and change the Mouse Tracking Speed to fast. A subtle push then sends the mouse flying across the screen. Keep fine-tuning until you have the speed adjusted the way you like it.

Portable Problems

Windows still doesn't work right on your laptop? Then check out this section. Some ways to break up the most common Windows/laptop fights, plus a few tips to keep their arguments from escalating into something serious are listed here.

My mouse doesn't come back when my laptop does!

Some laptops have a Suspend feature to save batteries: Just close the lid and everything turns off. Open the lid, and everything turns back on — with Windows looking just like it did when you closed the lid.

Except, sometimes the mouse pointer doesn't come back, or it's frozen in place. The solution? Head for the Advanced Power Management section earlier in this chapter. You need to tell Windows to wake up the mouse when it wakes itself up.

Windows won't go into Suspend mode!

This one's yet another Advanced Power Management problem. First, make sure Windows is set up to use your laptop's power management features, as described earlier in this chapter.

Next, click on the Power icon (the little battery) in the Windows Control Panel. Under Options, make sure Immediately is selected in the Manual Suspend box.

That should fix it.

My laptop's clock is always off

Unless Windows knows it's on a laptop with a Suspend feature, it shuts down everything — including the laptop's internal clock — when it heads for Suspend mode.

To make sure Windows resets your laptop's internal clock when it wakes up from Suspend, review the APM section in the beginning of this chapter. Windows has to know it's living on a laptop with power-saving features.

If you're using DOS programs (gasp), make sure the program POWER.EXE is living in your AUTOEXEC.BAT file. That program helps DOS handle your laptop's Advanced Power Management functions. (Chapter 11 covers AUTOEXEC.BAT insertions.) POWER.EXE should be on one of the disks that came with your laptop.

Plain Old Windows/Laptop Tips

- When traveling, don't forget to change your laptop's internal clock to match the time zone in your current location. Double-click on the Date/Time icon in the Control Panel and type the new time in the little box.

- Do you frequently change your laptop's time? Then create a Program Manager icon to simplify the process. While you hold down the Alt key, double-click on a blank spot in a Program Group. When the Program Item Properties box appears, type **Control Date/Time** in the Command Line box. Click the OK button and a new Control Panel icon appears called Control Date/Time. A double-click on that icon immediately brings the Date/Time box to the screen, ready for a quick time change.

- When using Solitaire, click on Game, choose Options from the menu, and click on the Outline dragging option. That makes the cards a *lot* easier.
- Using a trackball while on an airplane? Then make sure all the confirmations are turned on under the File Manager's Options menu. It's all too easy to drag and drop a file into the wrong place when choking on the airline's pasta dish dinner. By setting the confirmation settings, File Manager will ask if you're *sure* you want to do what the trackball just did.

Testing before Traveling

Did you just buy a new laptop for that upcoming business trip? Then copy all your programs onto it and use it exclusively for two or three days before you leave. By trying out your laptop beforehand, you can determine which programs you forgot to copy — before it's too late to take them with you. Plus, you can decide which pages of the Help manual you should Xerox and stick in your laptop bag!

Chapter 6

DOS 6 and Windows

In This Chapter

- Installing DOS 6.0 or DOS 6.2 over Windows
- Installing Windows over DOS 6
- Killing viruses with Windows Anti-Virus
- Undeleting files with Windows Undelete
- Backing up a hard disk with Windows Backup
- Optimizing memory with DOS MemMaker
- Optimizing a hard disk with Defrag
- Expanding storage space with DoubleSpace
- DOS 6 commands not to use under Windows

Adding DOS 6 to a computer is pretty easy, thank goodness. The screwdriver can stay tucked away in the kitchen's knick-knack drawer.

Chances are, you'll stick the DOS 6 disks into the computer, and punch a few buttons. Then, when the computer wakes up after the operation, you'll wonder why everything on-screen still looks the same.

Keen-eyed users, however, will find a few new icons lurking in the Windows Program Manager: Anti-Virus, Backup, and Undelete.

What do these strange new DOS 6 programs do? Are they worth a click or two? This chapter provides the exposé.

(Oh, yeah — check out the Windows Character Map to put little squiggles in words like exposé; the Character Map is that little key cap icon in the Program Manager's Accessories window.)

Installing DOS 6.0 and DOS 6.2

For the most part, DOS 6 doesn't influence Windows much one way or the other. Like older versions of DOS, DOS 6 sits buried in the background, occasionally waving its antennae to befuddle users.

Luckily, it's pretty easy to install. Just exit Windows, slide the installation disk in drive A:, and type **A:\SETUP** at your DOS prompt. Then, DOS 6 installs itself. It sniffs around on the hard drive, searching for Windows. If DOS 6 finds Windows, it assumes that you want the special Windows versions of its special DOS 6 programs: a program called Undelete that revives deleted files, a program called Backup that simplifies backing up a hard disk, and a program called Anti-Virus that stamps out those evil, infectious virus programs that you hear about on the evening news and at cocktail parties.

Before installing these three new Windows goodies, DOS 6 asks your permission. Feel free to click the OK button. Those new programs are about the only things DOS 6 has to offer.

And DOS 6.2? It just fixes some of the rough edges left by DOS 6.0. If DOS 6.0 gave you problems, try DOS 6.2; they install the same way. But if DOS 6.0 works fine, don't bother switching.

In fact, this book considers DOS 6.0 and DOS 6.2 to be the very same beast. A DOS 6.2 icon in the margin of this book indicates material for DOS 6.2 users *only*. But when you see DOS 6 in the text, it means DOS 6.0 and DOS 6.2. After all, who wants yet another version of a DOS icon clogging the book's margins?

- Be sure to back up the hard drive before you install DOS 6 or any other new operating system upgrade.
- At the very least, copy WIN.INI, SYSTEM.INI, PROGMAN.INI and any file ending in the letters .GRP (all of these files live in the Windows directory) to a floppy disk for safekeeping. If something goes awry while you're installing DOS 6 — the Windows Program Manager looks completely blank, for example — copy those files back to the Windows directory.
- If your hard drive is big enough, tell DOS 6 to install both the DOS and the Windows versions of Backup, Undelete, and Anti-Virus. That way, if Windows breaks, a neighboring DOS computer guru can still fiddle with the DOS versions.
- Hard drive too small for both the DOS and Windows versions? Then just install the Windows versions. Many computer gurus come equipped with a utility-filled disk in a shirt pocket, anyway.

- Already installed DOS 6 and want to install Windows now? Then check out the section, "Installing Windows after DOS 6," that lurks a little later in this chapter. It's devoted specifically to that topic.
- One more confusion lifter: DOS 6.0 and DOS 6.2 are practically indistinguishable from each other. If you'd like a magnifying glass, read the boring comparison of the two DOS versions below.

The Free Windows Toys in DOS 6

Microsoft tossed in a handful of Windows programs with DOS 6. If DOS 6 installed itself right, they'll be waiting for you in the Program Manager the next time you load Windows.

Look for a Program Group called Microsoft Tools, as shown in Figure 6-1.

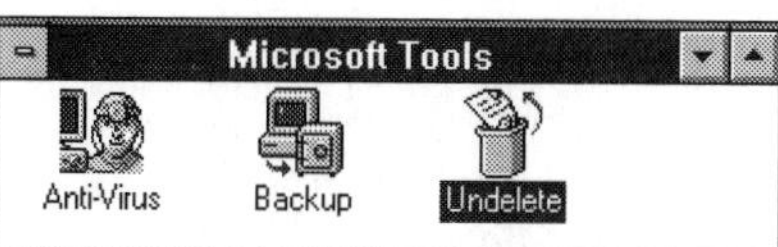

Figure 6-1: The DOS 6 Windows programs.

What's the difference between DOS 6.0 and DOS 6.2?

Just like a car that's been recalled to have an engine part replaced, DOS 6.2 simply repairs a few rough edges on DOS 6.0. On the outside, everything in DOS 6.2 looks and feels pretty much the same as DOS 6.0.

Basically, DOS 6.2 fixes these parts of DOS 6.0:

DoubleSpace makes sure your hard drive is working right *before* it starts compressing it. Plus, DoubleSpace is a little more careful when storing files on your hard drive. Finally, it works better under Windows when dealing with floppy disks.

SmartDrive now works more conservatively. When you want to copy information to a disk, SmartDrive does it *immediately*. Under DOS 6, SmartDrive waits for the most convenient, time-saving moment before writing the information: That means you could accidentally turn off your computer before SmartDrive has written down the important stuff. Finally, the DOS 6.2 SmartDrive speeds up CD-ROM drives, too.

DOS users will find a few benefits in DOS 6.2, as well: DOS now punctuates numbers with commas. For the past ten years, DOS would display things like `1000000 bytes free`. With DOS 6.2, it now displays, `1,000,000 bytes free.` Miracles!

Because both versions really look the same, this book says DOS 6 when it means DOS 6.2, as well. A DOS 6.2 icon in the margin of this book indicates material for DOS 6.2 users *only*.

The next few sections explain what these strange new programs are, whether they're worth bothering with, and, if so, how to bother with them.

Anti-Virus

What Anti-Virus does: As if computers didn't screw up enough on their own, some brooding programmers write programs that are *designed* to botch things up.

Called *viruses*, these evil programs disguise themselves as helpful, everyday computer programs. The worst of these viruses can sneak onto the hard drive from a floppy disk and start destroying files and programs. Other, weirder viruses display funky *bumper-sticker-like* slogans or exotic graphics on the screen. Either way, viruses are nuisances to be avoided.

The DOS 6 anti-virus program, *Anti-Virus*, works like a computerized version of Detective Columbo. It searches for viruses that live in the computer's memory or camp on its hard drive. If Anti-Virus finds something evil going on, it tells you about it, as shown in Figure 6-2. Then it tries to kill the culprit.

How to install Anti-Virus: DOS 6 automatically puts an Anti-Virus icon in the Program Manager. Don't see its icon in the Microsoft Tools box? Trot a little farther ahead in this chapter. The section, "Putting Anti-Virus, Backup, and Undelete in Windows," explains how to put icons for those new DOS 6 programs into the Windows Program Manager.

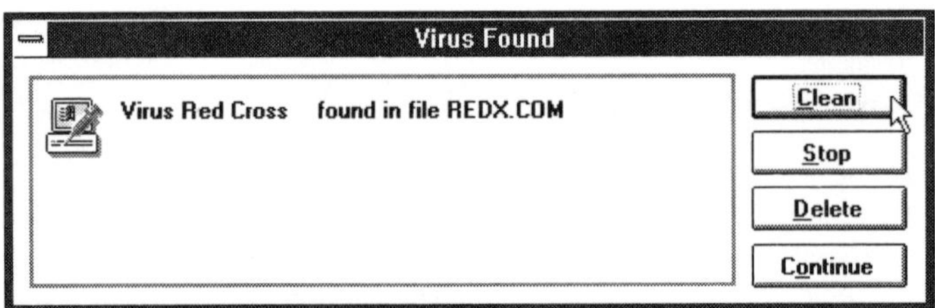

Figure 6-2: Anti-Virus finds the evil Red Cross virus. (*Nothing* to do with the Red Cross.)

How to search for viruses: Follow these steps to make Anti-Virus seek and destroy enemy viruses that live on the computer or on any suspicious-looking floppy disks.

1. Double-click on the Anti-Virus icon from the Microsoft Tools box in the Program Manager.

Or, if you're closer to the File Manager, load Anti-Virus by clicking on the File Manager's new Tools menu. (DOS 6 added that new menu when you weren't looking.)

Whether you load Anti-Virus from the Program Manager or the File Manager, it works the same way. It shoots a little advertisement onto the screen and then pops onto the screen itself, as shown in Figure 6-3.

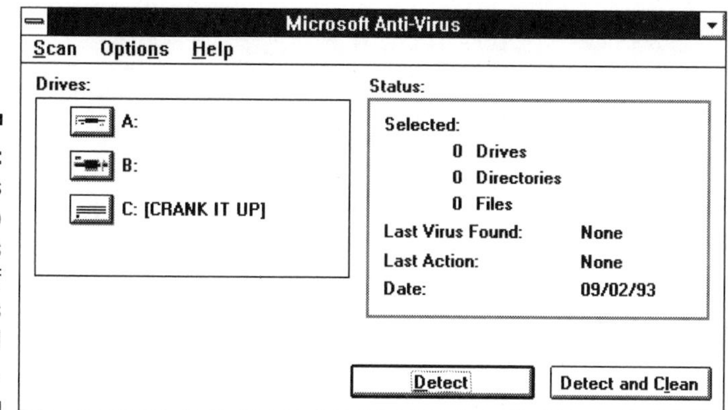

Figure 6-3: Anti-Virus is ready to sweep disks clean of infectious viral organisms.

2. Click on the disk that you want to scan.

If you want to scan a floppy disk — which is a good idea whenever a suspicious-looking person hands you a floppy — stick that disk in the floppy drive and click on the drive's icon. (You can see icons for each drive in Figure 6-3.)

Or, to scan the entire hard drive, click on the hard drive's icon.

After the click, Anti-Virus prepares for anti-viral warfare. It counts all the directories on the chosen drive and then waits for further instructions.

Want Anti-Virus to scan another drive at the same time? Then click on the other drive's icon as well. Anti-Virus will add that drive to the warfare list by counting all of its directories too. Done? Move to Step 3.

3. Click on the Detect and Clean button.

At the press of the Detect and Clean button, Anti-Virus begins to rummage through the disks you chose in Step 2, looking for tell-tale signs of a potentially damaging virus. If it recognizes a virus, it deactivates it.

In fact, if Anti-Virus spots a program that has changed in size — often an indicator that something naughty has been stuffed inside it — Anti-Virus lists that file's name in the Verify Error dialog box, as shown in Figure 6-4. Then it tosses you a real head-scratcher: What should it do now?

The four buttons on the right side of the dialog box show your choices: Update the file's size in Anti-Virus's master list and keep going, Delete the file and keep going, Stop looking for more viruses, or simply Continue to plow through the rest of the files on the drive and check for any other threatening evidence.

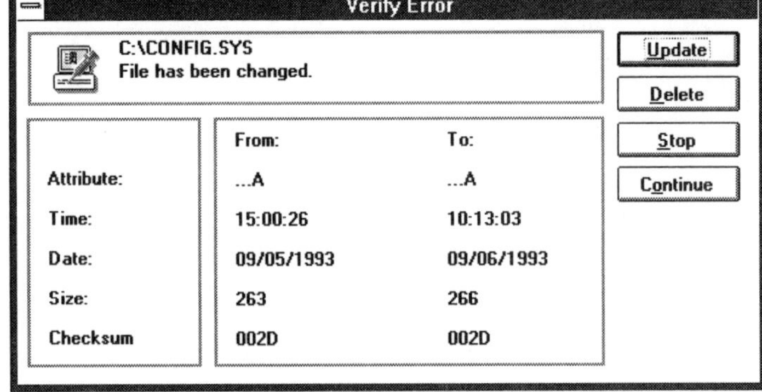

Figure 6-4: Don't choose the Delete option unless you're sure that a virus has infected the file.

The problem is that there's no sure-fire answer. Some programs and files are *supposed* to change their size. In fact, some files change size all the time. So don't choose the Delete option unless you're sure that a virus has taken over. Your best bet is to call over a computer guru for advice. This virus-detection stuff is full of false alarms.

Why do you need help? Because the size change is only evidence that something *may* have gone wrong. If Anti-Virus finds a real, smoking-gun virus, it tells you, as shown in Figure 6-2. If you see a screen like the one in Figure 6-2, click the Clean button and breathe a sigh of relief.

When Anti-Virus finishes picking through the hairs of the hard drive, it lists the number of viruses that it has found and destroyed.

The verdict: Anti-Virus can seek and destroy hundreds of viruses that it recognizes. The key word is *recognizes*. New viruses pop up every month. The more popular the anti-virus program, the more likely that viruses are being written specifically to defeat it. In fact, some evil virus programmers have already discovered how to outwit Anti-Virus.

Don't let Anti-Virus give you a false sense of security; Microsoft offers updates, as shown in Figure 6-5, but virus programmers can evade them.

Anti-Virus is better than nothing; don't be afraid to use it. Better still, however, observe the *safe computing* rules in this section. They can be just as effective as Anti-Virus in keeping a computer virus-free and healthy.

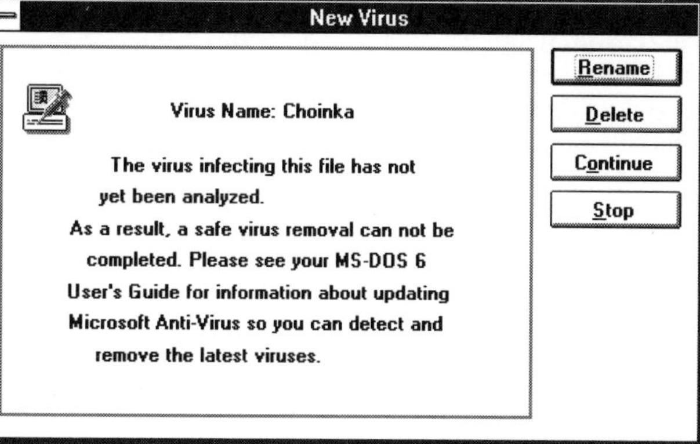

Figure 6-5: Anti-Virus must be constantly updated so that it can destroy newly written viruses.

- Chances are, you'll never come across a virus, especially if you follow the safe-computing rules. But if you *do* find a virus on the hard drive, scan all your frequently used floppy disks as well. The virus may have spread to those disks.
- Whenever you upgrade to a newer version of a program, Anti-Virus will probably report that something is wrong. The newer files will probably have a different size and date that confuse Anti-Virus. Check with a computer guru if you're not sure what's going on.
- Most virus checkers can't catch a virus if it's living in a zipped file. If you've downloaded a zipped file — described in Chapter 7 — head to Chapter 12 to figure out how to unzip it. After you unzip the file, check it with Anti-Virus or any other virus-checking program.

- Be careful when you are scanning more than one floppy disk. Whenever you stick a new floppy disk into the disk drive, *click on that floppy drive's icon* in Anti-Virus. If you don't, Anti-Virus won't realize that you've swapped disks, and it may leave some viruses undetected.
- Anti-Virus places a small file called CHKLIST.MS in every directory on the hard drive. Those little files keep the computer more secure, but they take up space on the hard drive. To make Anti-Virus stop creating them, choose Set Options from the Anti-Virus Options menu. When the box appears, click on the Create New Checksums option until the little check mark disappears.

- To make Anti-Virus erase all the CHKLIST.MS files that are already hanging around on the hard drive, choose Delete CHKLIST files from the Anti-Virus Scan menu. Anti-Virus will delete them from every drive you choose.
- To see a list of the viruses that Anti-Virus can purge, choose Virus List from the Scan menu. The famous Michelangelo and Stoned viruses are on the list, as well as the lesser-known Burger and Jebberwocky (yep—they misspelled it) viruses. No mug shots of the programmers, however.

- For some reason, Windows doesn't like to play a musical MIDI file while it's checking for viruses. In fact, if you try to play one, Windows may toss an error message in your face and shut down a program or two. To avoid this problem, don't play MIDI files while you're checking for viruses; instead, hum an old Patsy Cline standard.

Safe computing guidelines

Don't swap programs with friends or coworkers. Buy your software in sealed boxes from reputable software dealers.

Don't leave any floppy disks sitting in drive A. When you're through copying information to or from a floppy disk, *take the disk out of the drive.* Many viruses spread when the computer accidentally tries to boot off a virus-laden floppy disk that has been left in drive A.

Don't download files from a computer Bulletin Board System (BBS) unless you're *sure* the board is run by a reputable owner.

If you do a great deal of disk swapping or file downloading from computer bulletin boards, don't rely exclusively on Anti-Virus. Buy another virus checker from a second company. You can order one good program, VIRUSCAN, by McAfee Associates, by calling 800-383-0257. You also can download VIRUSCAN from CompuServe and most other online services. (Chapter 7 covers that *downloading* stuff.)

Finally, get *update disks* for your virus-checking programs as soon as they're released. Having the latest update is the best way to make sure that your virus checker can recognize the newest virus on the block. The Anti-Virus update order form sits in the back of the MS-DOS 6 booklet. McAfee Associates also issues updates on a regular basis.

Pretty boring vital statistics about CHKLIST.MS

Anti-Virus puts a file named CHKLIST.MS in every directory on the hard drive. That file contains the vital statistics for each program that lives in the directory.

Why? Because program files, unlike data files, usually stay the same size. So, whenever Anti-Virus runs, it compares each program's size with the sizes that are listed in the CHKLIST.MS file. If the sizes differ, Anti-Virus knows that something suspicious may be going on.

To keep a close watch, CHKLIST.MS stores the size, time, date, and attributes of all the files that have the following extensions: .386, .APP, .BIN, .CMD, .COM, .DLL, .DRV, .EXE, .FON, .OV*, .PGM, .PRG, and .SYS. Those types of files are the most vulnerable to viral organisms.

Also, CHKLIST.MS contains the checksum for those files. The *checksum* is an error-detection scheme that adds up little snippets of a file's data and then checks later to see whether the sum has changed. If the checksum has changed, then Anti-Virus knows that something is fishy.

Plenty of 12-year-old virus programmers can bypass that CHKLIST.MS stuff, unfortunately, so don't think that those files make your hard drive invulnerable.

Undelete

What Undelete does: Just about everybody has accidentally deleted a file and ended up chewing their palm in frustration. Undelete brings the deleted file back from the dead and extracts that chewed-up palm from your mouth.

How to install Undelete: When you first installed DOS 6, it thoughtfully put an icon for Undelete in the Windows Program Manager. Don't see it in the Microsoft Tools group? Then tiptoe ahead in this chapter till you find the section, "Putting Anti-Virus, Backup, and Undelete in Windows." It tells you how to put Undelete back in there.

How to make Undelete work: The key to using Undelete successfully is to work quickly. Don't leave skid marks on the mouse pad — just run Undelete as soon as possible after you discover that you've deleted the wrong file. The more files you've saved since deleting a precious file, the worse your chances of retrieving it.

Follow these steps to undelete a deleted file from a hard disk or floppy disk:

Undelete

1. **Double-click on the Undelete icon from the Program Manager's Microsoft Tools window.**

Microsoft Undelete rises to the rescue, as shown in Figure 6-6. Undelete lists the names of files recently deleted from the Windows directory.

Or, to launch Undelete from the File Manager, click on File and then click on Undelete from the little menu that drops down. Either way, Undelete looks like the screen shown in Figure 6-6.

Microsoft Undelete
File Options Help
Undelete Drive/Dir Find Sort by Print Info
File Condition Size Date Time
C:\WINDOWS
?LBGCPGD Destroyed 0 bytes 09/06/93 11:22AM
?LVIS.LVS Excellent 3863 bytes 06/12/92 04:34PM
Deleted Date: N/A Deleted Time: N/A Protected by: N/A
Path:

Figure 6-6: Microsoft Undelete lists the names of files recently deleted from the Windows directory.

2. **If Undelete lists the deleted file, click on its name. If the deleted file is not listed, move to the directory containing the deleted file.**

   Does Undelete list the deleted file you're after? Great; click on its name. Undelete highlights the file, as shown in Figure 6-7. Then you can move to Step 3.

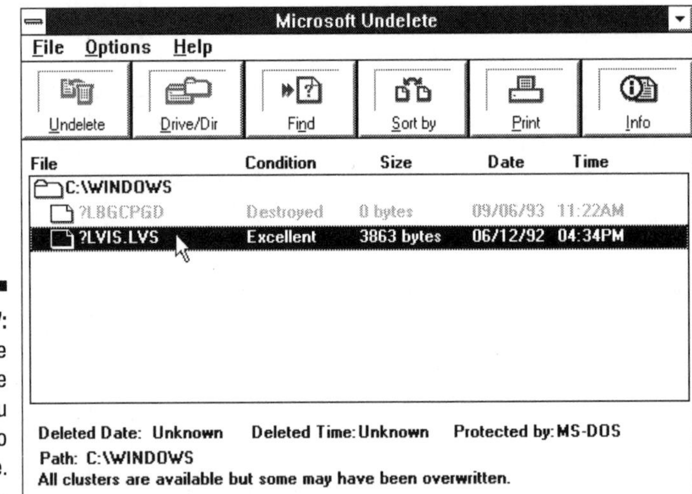

Figure 6-7: Click on the name of the file that you want to undelete.

Did you delete the file from a different disk or directory? Then click on the big Drive/Dir button along the top of Undelete's window. Undelete tosses up a box that lists the hard drive's directories and drives; click on the ones that you want to peek into, and Undelete will show you their deleted files.

Again, click on as many deleted files as you want to revive and then move to Step 3.

Can't find your deleted file anywhere? Then click on the big Find button, and a new window will appear. If you remember the file's name, type it in the first box and click on the OK button. Don't remember it? Then leave the *.* stuff in the File specification box and click the OK button anyway. After a few seconds of searching, Undelete will list the names of every recoverable deleted file in every directory.

3. **Click on the Undelete button.**

   After highlighting the name of the deleted file that you want to retrieve, click on the Undelete button — the picture of the reddish-orange trash can.

4. **Type the first letter of the deleted file and click OK.**

   Whenever a computer deletes a file, it maliciously shaves off the first letter of that file's name. So, to undelete the file, type the first letter of the file's name, as shown in Figure 6-8.

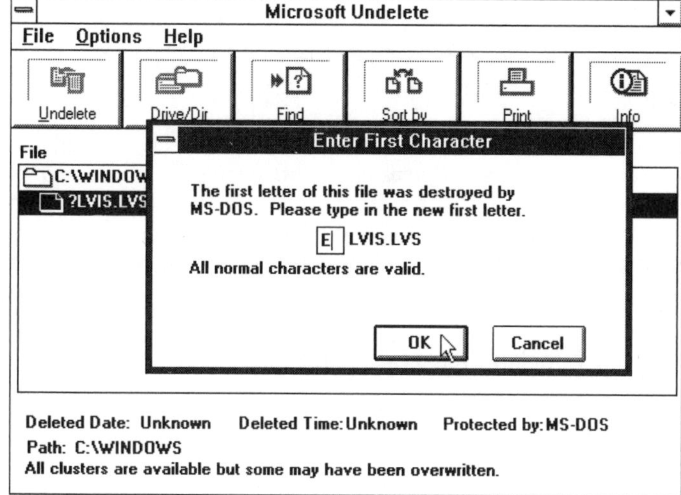

Figure 6-8: Type in a letter, and Undelete will try to bring the deleted file back from the dead.

If you don't remember the first letter of the deleted file, type any letter. Undelete isn't picky; it will happily use any letter you type.

Unfortunately, Undelete can't retrieve every deleted file that it lists. Look at the Condition column, as shown in Figure 6-9. If the file's condition is listed as Excellent or Good, the file's name is black, and you can probably resurrect it. If the condition is listed as Poor or Destroyed, the file's name is light gray, and the file is a goner. If the file's name doesn't show up at all, give up: The deleted file can never be retrieved from the computer's catacombs.

File	Condition	Size	Date	Time
?ARROT1.ICO	Excellent	766 bytes	12/20/92	06:57PM
?ART.ICO	Destroyed	766 bytes	12/20/92	06:55PM
?ARTY.ICO	Excellent	766 bytes	12/20/92	06:57PM
?ARTY1.ICO	Good	766 bytes	12/20/92	06:57PM
?ARX.ICO	Destroyed	766 bytes	12/20/92	06:56PM
?AT.ICO	Destroyed	766 bytes	12/20/92	06:55PM
?AT1.ICO	Destroyed	766 bytes	12/20/92	06:55PM
?AT2.ICO	Destroyed	766 bytes	12/20/92	06:55PM
?AT3.ICO	Destroyed	766 bytes	12/20/92	06:55PM

Figure 6-9: Undelete can bring back deleted files only if they're in Excellent or Good condition.

Verdict: Undelete can work very well, provided that you use it as quickly as possible after you notice that you've snuffed out the wrong file. The longer you wait, the farther your deleted file floats irretrievably toward the ninth concentric circle, where not even Dante could bring it back.

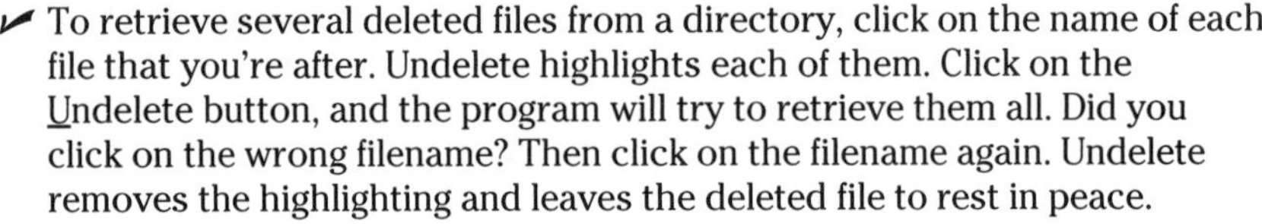

- To retrieve several deleted files from a directory, click on the name of each file that you're after. Undelete highlights each of them. Click on the Undelete button, and the program will try to retrieve them all. Did you click on the wrong filename? Then click on the filename again. Undelete removes the highlighting and leaves the deleted file to rest in peace.
- Want Undelete to list all your deleted files, sorted by the time and date you deleted them? Click on the Sort by button and choose Deleted Date and Time to put the most recently deleted files at the top of Undelete's list.
- Undelete offers several options to make undeleting files easier and more reliable. These options slow down Windows, however, as described in this section's boring technical box.
- If you choose Delete Sentry or Delete Tracker and decide later to turn them off, click on Configure Delete Protection from Undelete's Options box. Then click on Standard. Windows updates the AUTOEXEC.BAT file to remove the former level of protection.

- If you choose Undelete's Delete Sentry or Delete Tracker options, Windows tosses a box in your face, telling you to reboot the computer. *Don't do it!* Instead, exit Windows the normal way, by closing down the Program Manager. *Then* reboot the computer. Rebooting the computer while Windows is still running is a definite no-no that can kill more files than Undelete can retrieve.

Backup

What it does: Everybody has lost data on a computer — pushed the wrong button during a sneeze or noticed that a file has simply vanished for no apparent reason. Computers can destroy work just as easily as they can help create it.

For that reason, having a second copy of all the files on the hard drive is important. Then, when your most important files wander off, you can use the second copy to put things right back on track.

Unfortunately, backing up a computer's hard drive to floppy disks is tiring work. Who can remember which files need to be copied? Plus, copying the entire hard drive onto floppy disks each day can take an hour.

The Windows Backup program simplifies matters by enabling you to choose which files to back up. For example, you can save both time and floppy disks by telling Backup to copy only the files that you've changed since the last backup.

How to install Backup: When you installed DOS 6, it stuck an icon for Undelete in the Microsoft Tools group of the Program Manager. Don't see the icon? Then flip ahead to the "Putting Anti-Virus, Backup, and Undelete in Windows" section a little later in this chapter. It tells you how to stick Backup's icon into the Program Manager.

How to make Backup work

Backup works well at copying important files from the hard drive to floppy disks for safekeeping. However, Backup needs a little preparation.

First, Backup needs to *configure* itself to the computer. Backup makes a quick, two-disk test to see whether the floppy drives are up to snuff.

When the test ends, you need to decide on a backup schedule that's easy enough to follow and then tell Backup about your decision.

Both chores are described in the next two sections.

Delete Sentry, Delete Tracker, and Boredom Alert

To make files easier to undelete, click on Configure Delete Protection from Undelete's Options box. Then scratch your head and agonize over the three options:

Standard: If you don't bother changing anything, Undelete stays at the Standard level of protection.

> **Pros:** The Standard level doesn't slow Windows down, and it doesn't eat up hard drive space.
>
> **Cons:** Undelete can retrieve plenty of deleted files, but only if you haven't saved a lot of other files since the accident.

Delete Tracker: One step of safety above Standard protection, Delete Tracker stores some key information when Windows deletes a file, so it makes Undelete a little more reliable.

> **Pros:** Delete Tracker doesn't consume as much extra hard drive space as Delete Sentry does, and it makes files a little easier to undelete.
>
> **Cons:** Windows works a little more slowly than with Standard protection — especially when you're deleting files.

Delete Sentry: The most reliable option, Delete Sentry, pulls a fast one: Windows doesn't *really* delete files when you push the delete button. Instead, Windows simply makes them invisible and stores them in an invisible directory, called SENTRY, on the hard drive. Because the files weren't really deleted, you can pull them back in perfect condition.

Delete Sentry enables you to choose how much hard drive space to devote to your deleted-file SENTRY graveyard; you also can choose how many days Windows should wait before *really* deleting the files. Finally, you can choose which types of files Delete Sentry should hang onto. For example, you can tell Delete Sentry to save DOC files — Word for Windows files — and let all the other deleted files slide over the waterfall.

Also, Delete Sentry doesn't save temporary files that Windows or Windows programs often create and delete for their own nerdy uses.

> **Pros:** Delete Sentry is the best option for people who constantly delete the wrong files. Its beauty lies in its configurability. For example, you can tell Delete Sentry to save only deleted spreadsheet files for three days before deleting them for good.
>
> **Cons:** Because the *deleted* files aren't *really* deleted, they eat up space on the hard drive very quickly. Plus, Windows lags when you delete files because it has to copy them to the SENTRY directory every time you push the delete button.

If you choose Delete Sentry or Delete Tracker, Windows asks which drives to protect. Putting a floppy drive on the list makes Windows very slow at deleting files. Protect only the hard drives for best results.

One last thing: Windows doesn't really use its own version of Undelete. It just grabs the version that comes with DOS and puts it to work. When you choose Delete Tracker or Delete Sentry, Windows sneakily copies the DOS version of Undelete into the AUTOEXEC.BAT file. Then Windows asks you to reboot the computer. Rebooting your computer makes the computer reread its AUTOEXEC.BAT file, and that makes Undelete start working in the background.

Configuring Backup for the first time

Scrounge around for two floppy disks with nothing important on them. You need two disks to set up Backup for the first time, and this process will wipe out anything that is stored on them.

1. **Double-click on the Backup icon from the Program Manager's Microsoft Tools window.**

If you happen to be working in the File Manager, look for the File Manager's new Tools menu; DOS 6 added it when your back was turned. Click on Tools and choose Backup from the little pull-down menu.

Whether you load Backup from the Program Manager or the File Manager, it hops to the screen, as shown in Figure 6-10.

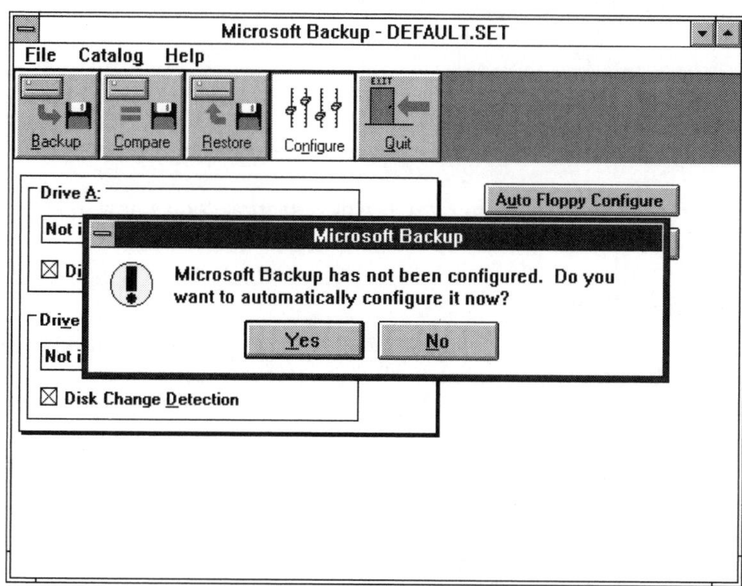

Figure 6-10: When you start Backup for the first time, it asks whether you want to configure it; click the Yes button.

2. **Click the Yes button.**

Before Backup will trust your computer's disk drives with this important backup mission, it needs to test them. So when Backup first pops onto the screen, click the Yes button and follow the instructions on-screen.

Backup fiddles around with the floppy drives, making you insert disks as it copies some of the files. When it's done, it tells you that it's finished and displays the Backup DEFAULT.SET window, as shown in Figure 6-11.

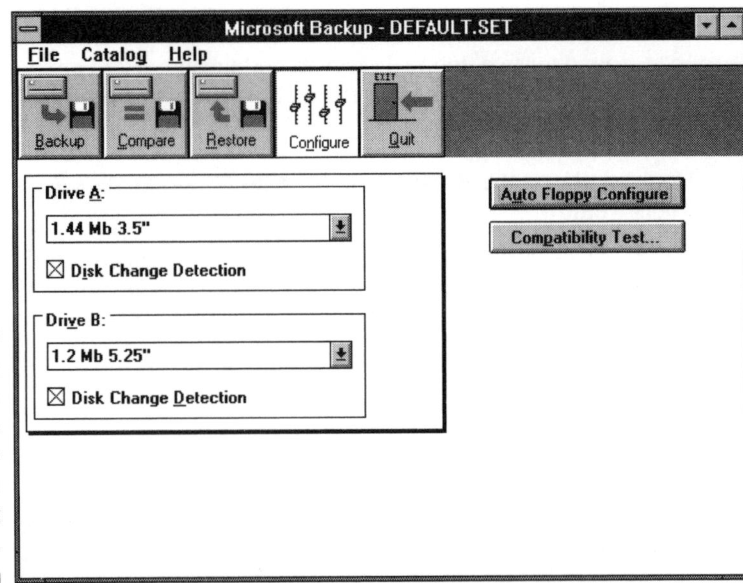

Figure 6-11: Backup presents this window when you configure it properly.

Now that Backup is set up right, the next section shows how to make your first backup.

Making a Backup

Here's how to make a backup copy of the hard drive. Copying all your information onto floppy disks will keep all those important letters and high scores safe even if the hard drive suddenly gasps and withers away.

1. **Click on the Backup icon and bring the Backup window to the screen.**

   Or, if you happen to be fiddling with the File Manager, choose Backup from the File Manager's new Tools menu. Whether the Program Manager, the File Manager, or the Auto Shop Manager starts Backup, it hops to the screen, as seen in Figure 6-12.

   Your screen looks a little different than Figure 6-12? Then click the big Backup button to make sure that the window in Figure 6-12 is currently showing.

2. **Choose a Setup file from the Setup File menu.**

   If you are using Backup for the first time, you won't have a Setup file yet. Don't worry; just move on to Step 3 and keep going. You'll have some Setup files by the end of all this stuff, and they'll speed things up for later.

   If you've already made your Setup files, then click on the Setup file that you want to use and jump ahead to Step 7, you lucky dog.

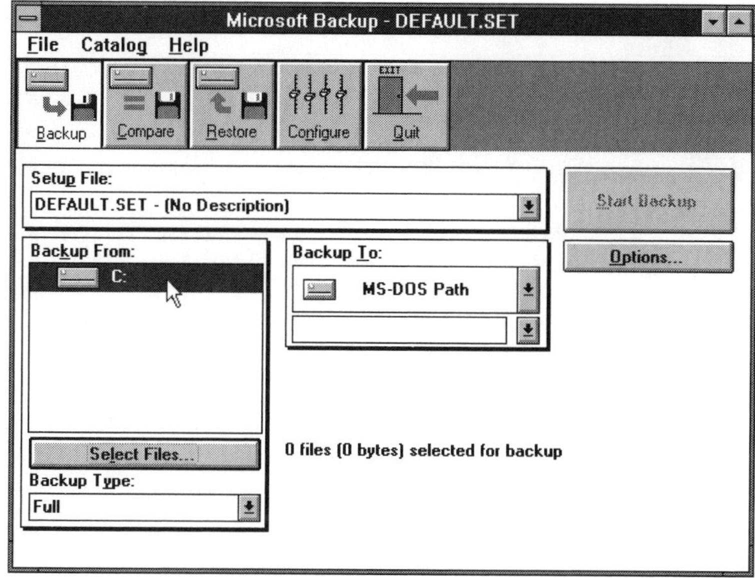

Figure 6-12: Backup is ready for you to tell it which files to copy.

3. **Choose the drives or files that you want to back up and choose OK.**

   To back up the entire hard drive, double-click on the hard drive's icon, as seen in Figure 6-12.

   Or, to pick and choose which directories and files you want to back up, click on the Select Files button near the window's lower-left corner. The file and directory window shown in Figure 6-13 appears.

   Double-click on the names of the files and directories that you want to back up. Mess up? Then double-click again on the wrong names to take them off the list.

   A big black square appears next to each filename or directory that you choose for backup.

   Backup's file and directory window works just like the one in the File Manager. Double-click on a directory's little folder to see all the subdirectories below it; double-click on the directory's little folder again to hide all the subdirectories.

   Finished choosing? Click on the OK button near the window's lower-right corner to return to the preceding screen.

4. **Click in the Backup Type box and choose a backup type.**

   Click on the tiny Backup Type box in the lower-left corner of the screen. Then, it's decision time, because Backup offers you three different ways to back up files.

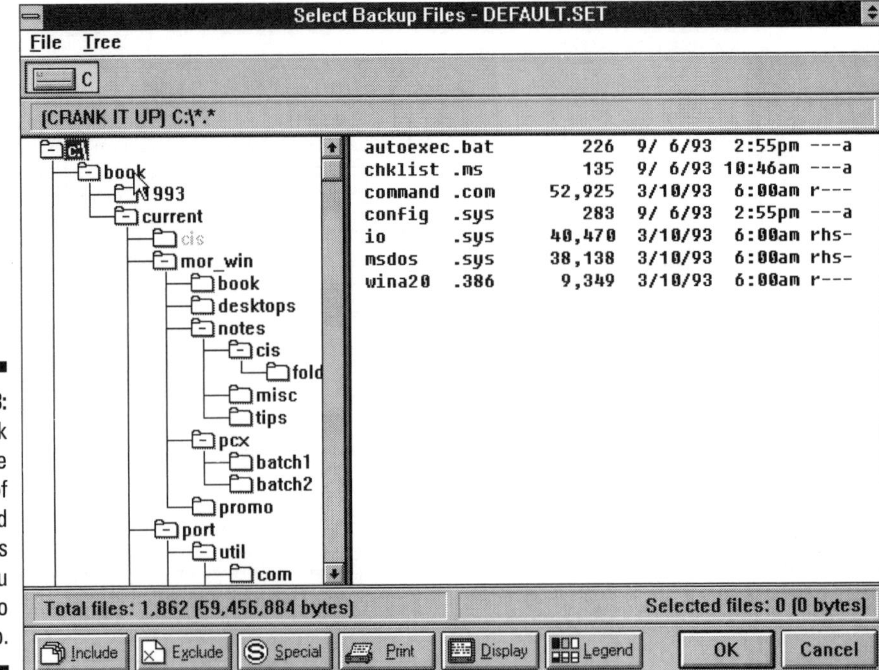

Figure 6-13: Double-click on the names of the files and directories that you want to back up.

Here's the scoop:

Full backup: This option makes Backup copy the entire hard drive to floppy disks. It takes a *lot* of time and floppy disks. Backing up a 60MB hard drive, for example, can take more than a half hour and more than 30 disks. However, a Full backup is the best way to insure a computer against disaster.

For best results, perform a Full backup once each month.

Differential backup: This option tells Backup to copy only the files that have changed since the last Full backup. A Differential backup tends to eat up a lot of floppies, however; and you can easily lose important disks.

Incremental backup: This option tells Backup to copy only the files that have changed since the last Incremental backup.

For best results, perform an Incremental backup at the end of each day.

5. **Click on the Backup To box and choose the floppy drive that you want to use.**

   For example, if you want to copy everything to floppy disks in drive A, choose drive A.

Choose the floppy drive that uses the highest-capacity disks. Backups move a little faster that way.

6. **Save the settings in a Setup file to use next time.**

   The next time you back up the hard drive, will you want to use the same settings? For example, will you always be copying the same files from drive C to drive A? Then save the current settings to a handy Setup file. Choose Save Setup As from the File menu, type a new filename, and click OK.

   Set up Backup to create a Full backup of the hard drive and save those settings in a Setup file named MONTHLY.SET.

   Next, tell Backup to make an Incremental backup of the hard drive and save those settings in a Setup file named DAILY.SET.

   Having those Setup files saves time when you are backing up the hard drive. Call up the MONTHLY.SET Setup file once a month and use the DAILY.SET Setup file every day that you're not making a full, monthly backup.

7. **Look to see how many disks Backup will need and make sure that you have enough disks handy.**

   After you choose the files to back up — or open a Setup file that already contains that information — Backup lists the number of disks that you need, as shown in Figure 6-14. The information is in the fine print near the lower-right corner of the screen.

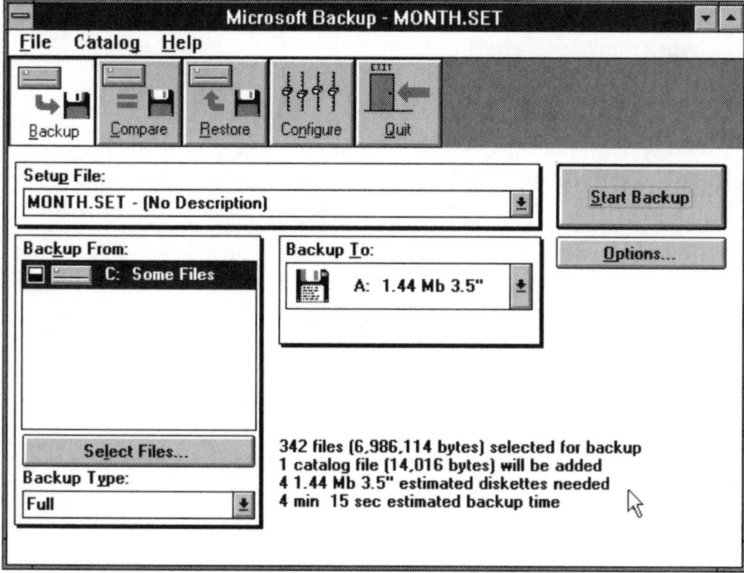

Figure 6-14: Backup lists the number of disks and the amount of time required to perform the backup.

Make sure that the backup disks have labels, or this whole backup concept will wither on the vine. In the next step, you write numbers on those labels.

Don't reuse old backup disks for new backups until you perform another Full backup. Then, when you have a current backup of the entire hard disk, go ahead and reuse the old incremental disks. Better buy those floppy disks in bulk. . . .

8. **Click the Start Backup button.**

   Backup begins copying the selected files to floppy disks, telling you when to remove one disk and insert the next.

   As soon as you know the disk's label number, write it on the disk. Doing so is the only way to keep track of which disk is which.

- If the Start Backup button is a faded-gray color, you haven't selected any files to back up. Head back to Step 3 to make sure that you've set everything up right.

- To shorten the time required to do a backup, don't make backups of the *programs* on the hard drive; you can always install them again from their installation disks.
- For quick backups, keep all current data in a directory called \CURRENT. Then just back up the \CURRENT directory at the end of the day. This practice can save a lot of time and floppies. Chapter 11 contains a few more hard drive tips.
- Yes, backing up the hard drive is still a lot of boring, thumb-twiddling work. Following the steps in this section just makes the thumb-twiddling work more organized.
- If you tire of feeding floppies to your computer, think about buying a *tape backup unit*. It's a miniature tape recorder that's the size of a floppy drive. The unit fits in the front of the computer, and you slide tapes in and out. At the end of a day, slide in a single tape, push a button, and relax. The tape backup unit automatically copies all your data to the tape for safekeeping.
- Also, the price of hard drives keeps dropping. Some people install a second hard drive inside their computer. At the end of the day, they simply copy everything from one drive to the other. Wham — quick backup copy. Of course, if lightning or a power surge ever fries your computer, the second hard drive won't be of much help.

How to restore a backup

If you're lucky, all your dutifully performed backup work will be a complete waste of time. If nothing goes wrong, you never have to salvage information from the floppy disks.

But if something *does* go wrong with the hard disk, here's how to bring the backup files on those floppies back to life.

1. **Click on the Backup icon from the Program Manager and bring the Backup window to the screen.**

   Fiddling with the File Manager? Then choose Backup from the File Manager's new Tools menu. Either way, Backup hops to the screen, as shown in Figure 6-12.

2. **Click the Restore button and, in the Backup Set Catalog, choose the session that you want to restore.**

   You probably want to choose the most recently completed backup; chances are, it's at the top of the list.

3. **Make sure the Restore From and Restore To boxes show the correct drives.**

   For example, you're probably copying information from the floppy in drive A to the hard drive — drive C. Or, if you've copied from other drives, click on the names for those drives instead.

   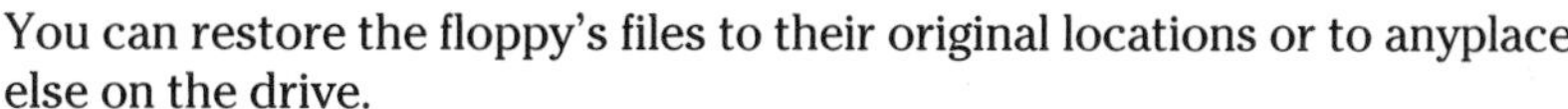

   You can restore the floppy's files to their original locations or to anyplace else on the drive.

4. **To pick and choose among the files you'd like to restore, click the Select Files button. Otherwise, to restore *all* the files, simply double-click on the drive A icon.**

5. **Click the Start Restore button.**

   Backup obediently begins its task of restoring the files to normal. Congratulations! All your backup work has finally paid off.

Less Obvious DOS 6 Goodies

Not all DOS 6 programs put their icons in the Windows Program Manager or dangle from menus in the File Manager. Here's a look at some of the other DOS 6 programs that can affect Windows.

MemMaker

What MemMaker does: Computer memory is a maddening mess. When memory is being discussed, even the babble of computer nerds reaches a fever pitch. In fact, many people turn their backs on DOS and head for Windows because Windows keeps all that memory stuff in the background so they don't have to deal with it.

The DOS 6 program MemMaker is a computerized computer guru of sorts. It looks at how the computer is currently using memory and then tries to tweak things so that the computer uses its memory in the most efficient way.

Specifically, it fiddles with the computer's memory so that DOS programs will run better — whether they're running on their own or running with Windows in the background.

MemMaker won't work on an XT or 286 computer; it's built for 386 and 486 computers.

How to install MemMaker: MemMaker is a DOS 6 program, not a Windows program. It's already living in the DOS directory, ready to roll.

How to make MemMaker work: To make MemMaker work, exit Windows. Then type MEMMAKER at the DOS prompt to make MemMaker whir into action.

Verdict: If you've completely weaned yourself from DOS — for example, you're running Windows programs exclusively — then don't run MemMaker. In fact, running MemMaker can make Windows run worse.

If all your programs are running fine right now — both DOS and Windows programs — then don't run MemMaker. It may just louse things up.

But if you're having trouble running DOS programs from within Windows, MemMaker may be worth a try.

MemMaker can freak out and stop your computer from working. Before running MemMaker, make sure you have a bootable floppy disk that contains a copy of your AUTOEXEC.BAT and CONFIG.SYS files. If MemMaker freezes up your computer, boot your computer off the floppy, and copy your original files back to drive C.

Defrag

What Defrag does: Defrag organizes the hard drive so that the computer can grab files faster. In buzzword language, the process is called *defragmenting*, but because that word sounds too dopey, many people simply call it *optimizing* the drive.

Either way, If Windows seems to be running a little slower than usual, Defrag may be able to speed things up.

Defrag's mundane micro mechanics

Putting files onto a hard drive is like dropping ice into a glass: Sometimes you need to break apart the larger ice chunks before they'll fit into the glass.

Normally, the computer simply drops a file's information onto the hard drive in one big chunk. But when hard drive space runs scarce, the computer breaks the file into smaller pieces, stuffing bits and pieces wherever it can find room on the hard drive.

The computer keeps track of where all the bits and pieces lie, so figuring out their location is not a problem. The problem comes when the hard drive needs to retrieve the file. Things slow down when it has to jump around to different spots to collect all the pieces.

Defrag solves this problem by pulling all the files off the hard drive and then copying them back on again. It puts all the pieces of a file next to each other, where the hard drive can grab all of them in one quick pass.

Don't know whether you're at a *real* DOS prompt or just in a *shell* with Windows still lurking in the background? Type **EXIT** at the DOS prompt before you enter any other command. If Windows pops back up, you were in a shell. If the command prompt just looks bewildered, you're sitting safely at the DOS prompt.

How to install Defrag: When you installed DOS 6, it put Defrag in the computer's DOS directory.

How to make Defrag work: To run Defrag, exit Windows by exiting the Program Manager as you normally do. Then, when you're *sure* Windows isn't running in the background, move to Step 1 in the instructions that follow.

1. **Type the following at the DOS prompt and press Enter:**

```
C:\> DEFRAG
```

   Defrag hops to the screen, ready to roll.

2. **Choose the disk that you want Defrag to optimize and press Enter.**

   Defrag starts by asking which drive you want to optimize. You simply press Enter to make Defrag go to work on drive C.

   After you choose a disk drive, Defrag analyzes where all the files are stored. Then it offers its recommendation on how the drive should be optimized.

3. Accept Defrag's recommendation by pressing Enter.

Defrag goes to work. Sometimes it merely moves all the pieces of each file next to each other; at other times it reorganizes the entire hard drive.

Defrag tells you when it has finished moving things around. Expect to wait anywhere from three minutes to — yawn — half an hour. You don't need to do anything while it's working, though, so feel free to head for the refrigerator.

4. When Defrag has finished, choose Exit DEFRAG — unless you want Defrag to optimize another disk.

- To keep the hard drive running smoothly, run Defrag once a month. If you use the computer a lot, run Defrag once a week. The more often you run Defrag, the less time it will take each time.

- Run Defrag *before* you install or reinstall Windows over DOS 6. When the hard drive is optimized, Windows can create a much healthier *swap file.* (Look for information about swap files in Chapter 11; swap files for laptops get their due in Chapter 5.)
- Don't turn off or reboot the computer while Defrag is running. Defrag is constantly picking up and moving pieces of files, so it may drop crucial file pieces and lose them forever if you interrupt it.
- Defragmenting a floppy disk can take a long time; it's rarely worth the effort unless you constantly copy files back and forth from the hard drive to the same floppy.

DoubleSpace

What DoubleSpace does: DoubleSpace compresses all the information on the hard drive into one big file. Then it installs a little program that makes that big, compressed file mimic a regular ol' hard drive.

By squishing everything, DoubleSpace opens up more room to store stuff on the previously packed hard drive.

How to install DoubleSpace: DoubleSpace came with DOS, so it's already waiting in the DOS directory.

How to make DoubleSpace work: Don't try to run DoubleSpace from within Windows. Instead, exit Windows and install DoubleSpace from a DOS prompt.

If you haven't installed Windows yet, don't install DoubleSpace. Instead, run Defrag, as described in the preceding section. Then install Windows. *Then* install DoubleSpace. The order is *very important.*

To install DoubleSpace, type **DBLSPACE** at the DOS prompt and press Enter:

```
C:\> DBLSPACE
```

Follow the instructions on the screen, and depending on how full the hard drive is, be prepared to wait for an hour or two while DoubleSpace gives all your information a long, slow squeeze.

- After you install DoubleSpace, you can't remove it without wiping out all your files. So be *sure* that you want to use DoubleSpace before you install it.
- Using DoubleSpace can bring more empty space to the hard drive, but like putting a patch on a tire, it can cause problems down the road.
- For example, DoubleSpace can take up more memory, making it harder to run some DOS programs.
- Depending on the programs you're using, DoubleSpace can make the computer run a little slower, as well.
- For best results, don't bother with DoubleSpace at all. Bite the bullet and buy a larger hard drive.

Installing Windows after DOS 6

Windows and DOS 6 work fine together, as long as they're installed in the right order.

First, before installing Windows, run the DOS 6 Defrag program, as described previously.

Then, if you're using the DOS 6 virus checker, disable it. That DOS 6 virus checker, VSAFE, thinks that parts of the Windows installation program are doing some naughty virus stuff.

DOS loads VSAFE from the computer's AUTOEXEC.BAT file, so you need to edit the AUTOEXEC.BAT file.

Don't follow these steps to edit the AUTOEXEC.BAT file if you've already installed Windows and it's running in the background. Follow these steps *before* you install Windows.

1. **Load your AUTOEXEC.BAT file into the DOS Edit program.**

   To call AUTOEXEC.BAT into the Edit program, type this at the DOS prompt:

   ```
   C:\> EDIT C:\AUTOEXEC.BAT
   ```

A little DOS 6 program called Edit leaps to the screen, bringing the AUTOEXEC.BAT file along with it.

2. **Type REM before VSAFE.**

   Look at the lines on the screen until you find one that says *VSAFE.* Then type REM right before VSAFE so the VSAFE line looks like this:

   ```
   REM VSAFE.EXE
   ```

3. **Press Alt,F,X,Y to save the changes.**

   A little menu pops down when you press the F, but you can ignore it. Just press those keys, in that order, to save the changes.

4. **Reboot the computer by pressing Ctrl+Alt+Delete.**

   You need to reboot the computer before it will notice your handiwork. So hold down Ctrl and Alt, and press Delete at the same time. The computer reboots, disabling VSAFE in the process.

- Never edited an AUTOEXEC.BAT file before? Head for Chapter 15 before you begin. To edit an AUTOEXEC.BAT or CONFIG.SYS file, you need to use the same precautions that you use when you edit an INI file, as described Chapter 15.
- That REM business tells DOS not to load VSAFE, so that you can safely install Windows. Then, when Windows is on the hard drive, use the Windows Anti-Virus program to bring VSAFE back to life.

- Check the AUTOEXEC.BAT and CONFIG.SYS files after you install Windows in DOS 6. Those files should refer to the SMARTDRV.SYS and HIMEM.SYS files in the DOS directory, not in the Windows directory.
- DOS 6 and DOS 5 come with an MS-DOS Shell that looks kind of like a wimpy Windows File Manager. The shell enables DOS users to *point and click* their way through many tedious DOS commands. But don't start Windows from the MS-DOS Shell, or Windows won't work at its best.
- Feel free to start the MS-DOS Shell when you are *within* Windows, however. Rev it up from the File Manager, start it from an MS-DOS window, or make the shell an icon in one of the Program Groups.

Putting Anti-Virus, Backup, and Undelete in Windows

Install Windows *after* you installed DOS 6? Then all those DOS 6 goodies won't be waiting for you when Windows finally comes to the screen.

The following steps make DOS 6 put those icons in the Program Manager, as well as update the File Manager's menus.

If you installed DOS 6 by typing SETUP at the command prompt, then follow these three steps:

1. **Put Setup Disk 1 in drive A and close the latch.**
2. **Type these two lines at the command prompt, pressing Enter after each line:**

   ```
   C:\> A:
   ```

   You press A, followed by a colon, and then press Enter. The computer's attention turns to drive A, ready for you to type the next line:

   ```
   A:\> SETUP /E
   ```

3. **Follow the instructions on-screen.**

   DOS 6 will find Windows and generously offer to install the freebie Windows utilities.

Or, if you installed DOS 6 by inserting Setup Disk 1 in drive A and restarting the computer, follow these three steps:

1. **Put Setup Disk 1 in drive A and close the latch.**
2. **Type these two lines at the command prompt, pressing Enter after each line:**

   ```
   C:\> A:
   ```

   You press A, followed by a colon, and then press Enter. The computer's attention turns to drive A.

   ```
   A:\> BUSETUP /E
   ```

3. **Follow the instructions on-screen.**

   When the computer wakes up from its DOS installation slumber, load Windows. The new Windows programs will be waiting for you.

- Don't remember how you installed DOS 6? Then try the first option — the SETUP method.
- Contrary to the DOS 6 manual, the BUSETUP command works only on a disk in drive A. It doesn't work in drive B.
- For some reason, the SETUP /E command sometimes deletes the Undelete icon. To put the icon back, exit Windows. From *any* DOS prompt, run SETUP /E again and choose Windows Only for Undelete, and None for Backup and Anti-Virus.

DOS 6 Commands to Avoid While You Are Running Windows

The DOS 6 commands listed in this section work fine — except when Windows is running in the background. So don't click on the names of these programs while you're in the File Manager and don't type these commands at the DOS prompt while Windows is waiting in the background.

Don't know whether you're at a *real* DOS prompt or just in a *shell* with Windows still lurking in the background? Type **EXIT** at the DOS prompt before you enter any other command. If Windows pops back up, you were in a shell. If the command prompt just looks bewildered, you're sitting safely at the DOS prompt.

DBLSPACE

What it does: DoubleSpace compresses all the files on the hard drive, giving you more space to store even more files.

Why you shouldn't use it: If you run DoubleSpace before you install Windows, Windows may not be able to create a *permanent swap file*, a bit of computer mechanics that's batted around in Chapter 11. And don't try to run DoubleSpace while Windows is running in the background, either. Windows tries to detect DoubleSpace, and it usually steps in with a warning if it detects that the program is rearing its head.

DEFRAG

What it does: Defrag organizes the files on the hard drive so the computer can locate them easier and faster.

Why you shouldn't use it: Defrag may drop some bits and pieces of files if it runs when Windows is in the background. In fact, if Defrag detects that Windows is lurking in the background, it's supposed to refuse to run.

EMM386

What it does: EMM386 cooks up and dishes out different types of memory to different types of programs.

Why you shouldn't use it: EMM386 is a complicated little beast; running it from within Windows confuses the computer.

MEMMAKER

What it does: MemMaker organizes the memory of 386 or 486 computers so all the programs can get the right slice.

Why you shouldn't use it: Windows has already grabbed a bunch of memory, so MemMaker won't run until you exit Windows.

MSCDEX

What it does: MSCDEX tells the computer to look for a certain disk drive.

Why you shouldn't use it: When Windows is loaded, it counts all the disk drives; it doesn't like to see that new ones are trying to jump in.

NLSFUNC

What it does: NLSFUNC helps set up a keyboard for foreign language characters.

Why you shouldn't use it: If you switch from English to Greek while Windows lurks in the background, Windows may not understand anything you type when it returns to the screen. In fact, it will all look like Greek to Windows.

SMARTDRV

What it does: SmartDrive sets a chunk of the computer's memory aside as a little cardboard box. Whenever you grab something from the hard drive, SmartDrive puts a copy of it in the box. Then, if you need that information again, SmartDrive whips it back out of the box. That method is often much faster than pulling the information off the hard drive again.

Why you shouldn't use it: SmartDrive should already be running *before* you start Windows. In fact, both DOS and Windows put it in your computer's AUTOEXEC.BAT file so it will load automatically when you turn on your computer.

VSAFE

What it does: VSAFE is the DOS version of the Windows Anti-Virus program.

Why you shouldn't use it: To keep track of things, Windows prefers that you use the Windows version of the Anti-Virus program. Running VSAFE from within Windows just confuses the computer.

Other DOS commands to avoid

Don't use any of the following commands unless you've completely exited Windows: CHKDSK /F, FDISK, RECOVER, SELECT, FORMAT C:, APPEND, ASSIGN, JOIN, SUBST, SHARE, and FASTOPEN.

I Installed DOS 6, and Now Windows Doesn't Work!

Installing DOS 6 and finding out that Windows doesn't work is like buying a fancy new sport utility vehicle with ski racks and hearing the ski racks get scraped off as you drive the car into a *little bit too short* garage.

DOS 6 can add plenty of life to Windows — as long as it doesn't kill it in the process. The next few sections point out how to loosen those ski racks when things aren't working well.

Windows says Corrupt Swap File Warning *with DoubleSpace*

Because Windows 3.1 hails from an earlier era, it doesn't recognize some of the tricks that DOS 6 tosses out. Perhaps the trickiest trick is DoubleSpace.

With DoubleSpace, DOS 6 grabs a bunch of files from the computer's hard drive and compresses them all, leaving a bunch of empty space on the hard drive. The whole process works so transparently that the hard drive seems to double in size.

Unfortunately, it works so transparently that Windows grabs part of the newly compressed hard drive and tries to use it as a *swap file* — a place to stash information quickly. And a compressed file just doesn't work as a swap file, no matter how much huffing and puffing Windows does.

The solution isn't pretty, as shown by all the techno-boogerish stuff in the following instructions:

1. **Add a line to the Windows SYSTEM.INI file.**

   You need to find the `[386Enh]` section of the SYSTEM.INI file. Then you need to add the following line to that section:

   ```
   PAGING=OFF
   ```

   Chapter 15 thoroughly covers editing the SYSTEM.INI file. This task is a great deal easier that it sounds.

   Oh, that `PAGING=OFF` business tells Windows not to bother loading a swap file the next time you load it.

2. **Restart Windows in 386-Enhanced mode.**

   To make sure that you're starting Windows in Enhanced mode, start it by typing the following line at any DOS prompt:

   ```
   C:\> WIN /3
   ```

   To find out whether Windows is running in Enhanced mode, choose About Program Manager from the Program Manager's Help menu. A box appears, and the current Windows mode shows up on the third line from the bottom, as shown in Figure 6-15.

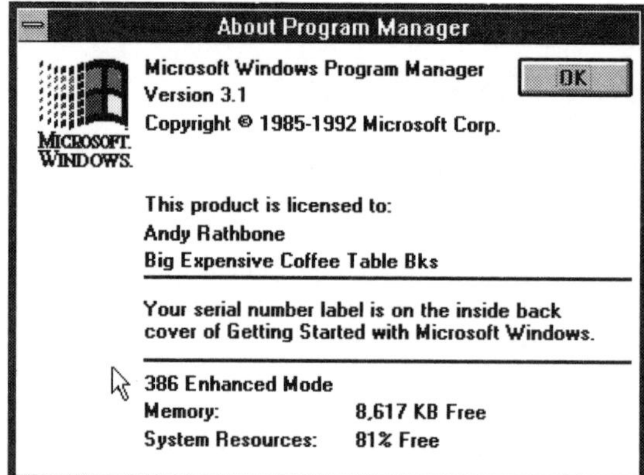

Figure 6-15: The third line from the bottom of this window reveals the mode that Windows is using.

3. **Set up a permanent Windows swap file on a noncompressed drive.**

   Microsoft's answer is to create a new permanent swap file on a drive that DoubleSpace hasn't compressed.

   Unfortunately, most people who have installed DoubleSpace don't have much room left on their noncompressed drive (which is also called a *host* drive).

   The solution? You should probably change over to a Temporary swap file. That chore is covered for laptops in Chapter 5 and for desktops in Chapter 11.

- After DoubleSpace compresses a hard disk, you can't de-compress the disk without losing your data unless you follow a lengthy, twelve-step procedure that's too complicated to describe here. If you're desperate, however, upgrade to DOS 6.2: That new, improved version of DOS *can* uncompress a DoubleSpace disk.
- Or you can stick with DOS 6.0 and agonize your own way through decompressing a drive: Copy all the files from the DoubleSpaced hard disk to floppy disks. Then delete the DoubleSpaced hard disk and copy all the files back from the floppy disks.

My compact disc player doesn't work any more!

DOS 6 comes with some new software to make compact disc players — CD-ROM drives — work even better than before.

Unfortunately, that new software also can make some compact disc players stop working at all.

The problem? DOS 6 put a new version of something called MSCDEX.EXE in the AUTOEXEC.BAT file. And that new version isn't getting along well with the CD-ROM drive's own drivers.

The solution? Hand this book to a computer guru and tell the guru to take care of the problem. The instructions are carefully laid out in the rest of this section.

Greetings, Computer Guru. Your mission is to remove the reference to the new version of MSCDEX.EXE from the computer's AUTOEXEC.BAT file.

After it's gone, you should add a reference for the old MSCDEX.EXE file — the one that used to work. Chances are, it's still living somewhere on the hard drive or on the installation disks that came with the compact disc drive.

Found it? Then you're ready to edit the AUTOEXEC.BAT file to get rid of the old version and put in the new one. Then make sure that this line appears in the CONFIG.SYS file:

```
DEVICE=C:\DOS\SETVER.EXE
```

Finally, after saving both files, make sure that Windows isn't running in the background and reboot the computer. When Windows starts back up, the compact disc player should work right.

Collect your usual fee of Hostess snack cakes, barter for some extra Doritos, and move on.

The Program Manager is blank!

If you choose to *uninstall* DOS 6, you may encounter a curious phenomenon: the Program Manager doesn't have any little group windows in it anymore.

The cure? Grab the backup disk that you made before you installed DOS 6. (You did make one, didn't you?)

Then copy three files — PROGMAN.INI, WIN.INI, and SYSTEM.INI — to the Windows directory.

When you've exited Windows and are at the DOS prompt, reboot the computer. These measures should cure the problem.

If taking those steps doesn't work, try this:

1. **From the Program Manager's File menu, choose Run.**

   A little box appears.

2. **In the Command line box, type SETUP /P and press Enter.**

   That is, type SETUP, a space, and a forward slash and then press P and Enter.

Windows puts the original five groups back into the Program Manager, complete with the icons they contained when you first installed Windows.

It doesn't show any customized icons you've done, but, hey, you're better off than if you had no windows or icons at all.

Chapter 7

Dialing Up Other Computers with Terminal

In This Chapter

- Getting new drivers from Microsoft
- Logging onto CompuServe
- Downloading shareware
- Calling another computer
- Capturing information from the computer screen
- Downloading a file
- Receiving a call
- Changing Terminal's default settings
- Making Terminal work better
- Unzipping a file

Every once in a while, the newspapers expose some sneaky kids who have used a modem to hook up their computers to the phone lines.

With the modem, they can order a pizza, charge it to somebody else's bank account, and have the pepperoni-and-mushroom, crispy crust delivered during their social studies class.

Those kids probably didn't do all that sneaky stuff with Terminal, Windows' built-in telecommunications program. No, Terminal is definitely a bare-bones operation, lacking most of the fancy features cherished by devious computer nerds.

Even though Terminal is a relatively simple program, it's not particularly easy to use. Unfortunately, it is one of the most unfriendly programs packaged with Windows.

This chapter shows how you can pry something useful from that grim Terminal screen. (You won't find any tips on prying a pizza out of it, however.)

Why Bother with Terminal?

Some people are afraid to fly. To get from point A to point B without wearing out a few pairs of tennis shoes, however, an airplane is the best tool for the job.

The same holds true for Terminal and a *modem* — the gizmo that hooks your computer up to the phone line. With a modem connected to your computer, Terminal can handle all the tasks described in the following sections.

Terminal might not be the best program for bossing modems around, but hey, it's free. Besides, *all* modem programs are unfriendly, and Terminal's no exception.

Calling Microsoft's BBS to grab the latest drivers

Sooner or later, Windows starts asking for new *drivers* — special pieces of software that let Windows talk to different parts of your computer. But where do you get those drivers? A few nice companies mail them to you on a floppy disk — if you mail them a check.

But the quickest way to find a driver is to grab it directly off Microsoft's own computer. Yep, using Terminal you can tell your computer's modem to call up Microsoft's computer. When Microsoft's computer answers the phone, you tell Terminal to grab the driver. Got the driver? Then you're done. Hang up and put that new driver to use.

Best of all, you're only paying for a few minutes of long-distance charges.

Sure, all this Terminal stuff sounds kind of nerdy. It *is* nerdy. But it's also the fastest and cheapest way to shut up Windows when it starts asking for new drivers, like the one it's demanding in Figure 7-1.

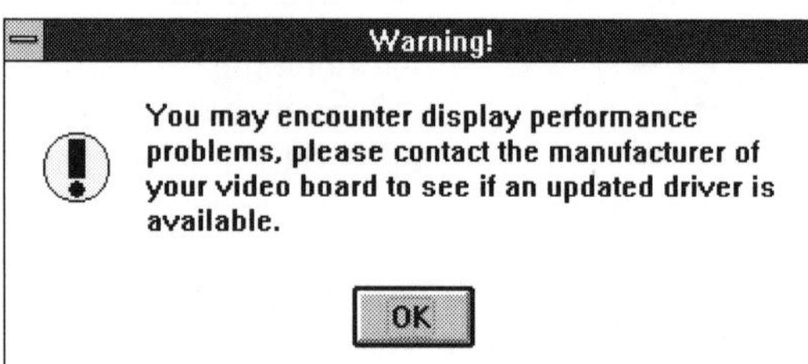

Figure 7-1: Windows wants a new driver.

- After you have grabbed the new drivers, review Chapter 3 for the dance steps required to install them.
- Just buy a new video card? Chances are, the video drivers on Microsoft's BBS are more up-to-date than the video drivers that came with your new card.
- Microsoft's computer — called a *Bulletin Board System*, or *BBS* — offers drivers and helpful information about Windows, DOS, Word, Excel, Works, and a few other Microsoft products. You may even find some goodies for your friend's Macintosh.

- Can't afford a sound card? Call Microsoft's BBS and grab — or *download* — Microsoft's *speaker driver.* The speaker driver lets Windows play sounds through your computer's built-in speaker, the one that beeps when you turn it on. (Oh, baby!)

Call CompuServe for Microsoft's help forums

Is Windows giving you some grief? And you don't want to wait on hold for Microsoft's Tech Support folks to help fix the problem? Then use Terminal to join CompuServe. Unlike Microsoft's BBS, CompuServe runs on H&R Block's gargantuan income-tax computers, and thousands of people can call in at the same time.

Using Terminal, you can call CompuServe and type a question for Microsoft's Technical Support staff. Windows Technical Support people then read your question and type an answer.

If you're leery of typing messages into a strange computer, browse through the messages other confused people have already typed into CompuServe. Chances are, somebody before you has had the same question, and the answer may be waiting for you to read and hastily scribble onto a sticky note.

- The bad news? CompuServe costs money, charged by the hour. Most of the on-line services, including Prodigy, GEnie, and America Online, charge a fee of some sort.
- For more information about CompuServe (including the current hourly rates), call 1-800-848-8990. After you have signed up for the service, type **GO MSWIN** to reach the forum where Microsoft's helpful technical folks hang out.

- You can find support for many Windows programs on CompuServe. Type **FIND WINDOWS** at the CompuServe prompt for an up-to-date list of helpful Windows topics.

- CompuServe isn't just about Windows, however. CompuServe attracts more than one million callers who meet in various forums to discuss everything from politics to which vintages of Cabernet Sauvignon turn your teeth red.

Finding wacky shareware programs

Where do your friends get all those cool new icons? All that fun wallpaper? Those wild screen savers that make winged zucchini flap across your screen?

Chances are, they found all that stuff on CompuServe, American Online, or on any of the thousands of other computers set up for callers around the world. Some computers, like CompuServe, are set up by big corporations who charge big hourly rates. Others computers are plain ol' PCs — just like yours – set up by nerds in their living room.

And best of all, most of those programs you can grab from these computers are either free or cost just a few dollars.

- Don't know what a shareware program is? Trot back to Chapter 2 for a quick refresher.
- Oh, and if your new shareware programs start asking for some weird VBRUN thing, you can find an explanation of that in Chapter 2 as well.
- Can't see your mouse pointer very well? Explore CompuServe's Windows Shareware Forum for some shareware mouse pointer enlargers.
- To see what some of these shareware programs look like, sneak a peek at Chapter 9.

Making Terminal Call Another Computer

No doubt about it, computers are downright hostile to their users. Computers are even *more* hostile when they're dealing with other computers. Consequently, the whole world of *telecommunications* — making computers talk to each other over the phone lines — can be pretty stressful. Too many things can go wrong.

First, your modem may be having a bad data day. Or the cable connecting it to the phone jack might have a few fibers out of place. Or Terminal might not be set up correctly to talk to your particular modem.

The problem might even be out of your reach: The phone lines could be crackling, or the *other* computer's modem may be turned off. The problem might even be that the other computer is out of commission or its software isn't properly set up.

The next few sections cover all the hoops you can jump through in your quest to get Terminal up and running. If you have called up other computers before, but just want a quick refresher on a particular area, jump ahead to the section that's got you stumped. Otherwise, read each section in order for the whole scoop on how to have your computer make that first phone call.

Plugging a modem into your computer

Terminal's main purpose is to talk to a modem — that gadget that attaches to your computer and hooks up to the phone line. Modems come in two basic models:

Internal modems come on a *card* that lives inside your computer, hidden from sight.

External modems come in a little box that sits next to your computer. A cable runs between the modem and a little plug on the back of your computer called a *serial,* or *COM,* port.

The biggest problem? Your computer can talk to the modem through one of *four* different COM ports. Unless Windows knows which COM port your modem is connected to, nothing exciting happens.

- Internal modems grab a COM port from their bunk inside the computer. No need for connector cables, on\off switches, or power cables.
- External modems grab a COM port through a cable that plugs into the back of your computer. External modems also need power, which usually is supplied by an AC adapter that plugs into the wall.
- Most internal and external modems come with two phone jacks. Look for a little picture of a telephone by one jack; that's where the cord from your normal telephone plugs in. Plug a phone cord into the second jack, with the other end plugging into the phone jack in your wall.

- COM ports are little pathways that your computer uses to send and receive information. Although your computer can talk through four COM ports, it can only use two of those ports at the same time. So if your mouse plugs into one COM port, your modem has to grab the other COM port. If they both try to grab the same port, they'll bicker like rude neighbors on a party line, and neither will work.
- If you have an external modem, look to see where its cable plugs into the back of your computer. Does it fit into a plug that is about ½-inch long? That's probably COM1. If it fits into a plug that's a little longer than 1-inch, it's probably COM2.

- Most internal modems are set up initially to use COM2, but you can flip little switches to change that. You might have to dig through the modem's manual for those bits of switch-setting trivia.
- After you have figured out what COM port your modem is using, write it down. You have to tell Terminal about it, which is described in an upcoming section.
- Having trouble installing your modem? Check out *Modems For Dummies*. It offers a guiding hand to help tame a squiggling octopus of problems.
- Windows hates *skipped* COM ports. If you want to use COM2, make sure you're first using COM1, as well.

Loading Terminal

Loading Terminal is the easiest part of the entire process. See the icon named Terminal with the telephone sitting in front of a computer? Double-click on that icon, and Terminal hops to the screen.

- Terminal's icon looks a great deal like two other icons, shown in Figure 7-2. (Terminal's icon is circled.)
- The first time you double-click on Terminal, a box pops up and asks you to choose a COM port. If you know which COM port your modem uses, click on that option in the list that appears next.
- If you don't know which COM port your modem uses, simply click on COM2 and keep your fingers crossed. Choosing the wrong COM port isn't like pulling the pin from a grenade; nothing explodes, and down the road you can safely switch to a different port if necessary.
- If Windows doesn't like your choice of COM ports — and a box will pop up saying it can't find it — then head to the next section for the COM port dirt.

Figure 7-2: Terminal's icon has a little telephone next to it.

Introducing Terminal to your COM port

Unfortunately, Terminal can't tell which brand of modem you could afford. It's not smart enough to know where that modem is plugged in, either. Nobody's wearing name tags, so you have to introduce Terminal to your modem and hope that they get along.

First, check to see whether Terminal has found your computer's COM port. To check, click somewhere inside Terminal's window. Next, type **AT** and press Enter.

If you have chosen the correct COM port, the modem responds quickly with `OK`, as shown in Figure 7-3.

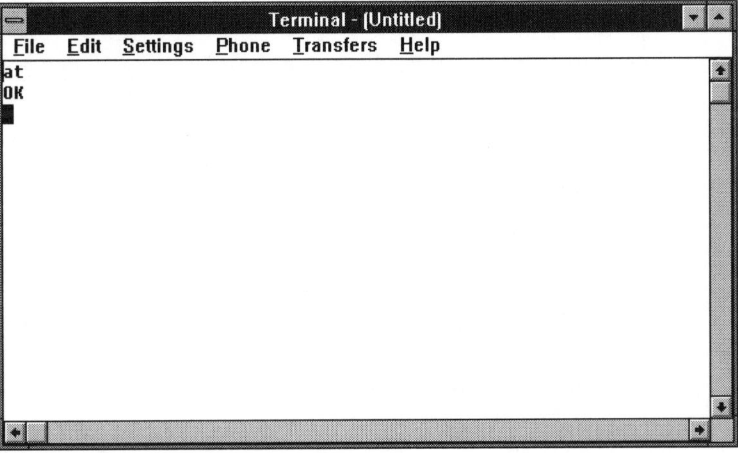

Figure 7-3: When you type **AT** into Terminal's window; a properly-connected modem should respond with the word `OK`.

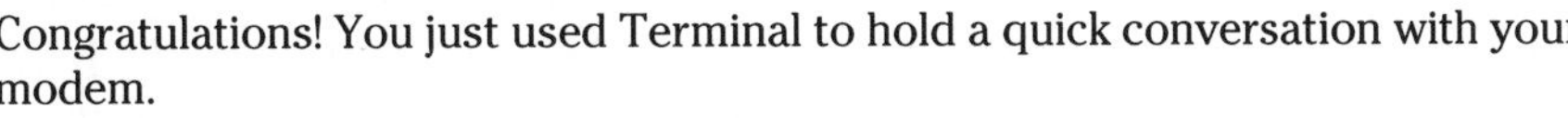
Congratulations! You just used Terminal to hold a quick conversation with your modem.

If the modem *didn't* say anything, don't give up. Try a different COM port, a point-and-click process described below.

1. **From Terminal's Settings menu, choose Communications.**

   A dialog box appears, like the one shown in Figure 7-4.

2. **Click on a different COM port in the Connector drop-down list.**

   See the COM ports listed in the Connector box? Click on a COM port other than the one that's highlighted. For example, if COM2: is selected, try COM1:, or vice versa. Then, click on the OK button, try typing **AT** again, and press Enter.

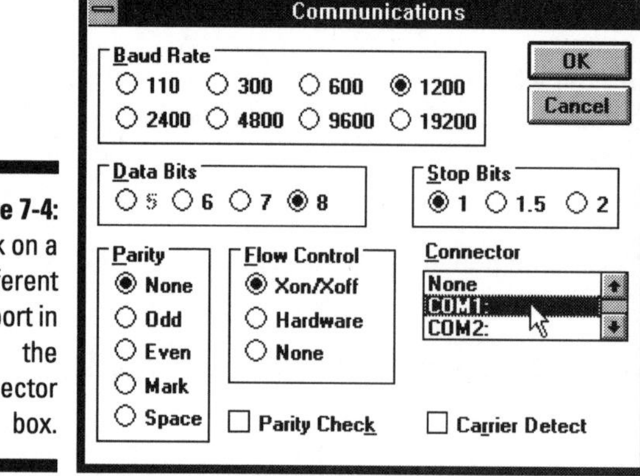

Figure 7-4: Click on a different COM port in the Connector box.

- Most modems use either the COM1: or COM2: setting. Very few modems use COM3:, and Windows gets especially ornery if you try to use COM4:.
- If you can't get Terminal to recognize your computer's COM port, then something inside your computer is amiss. Perhaps another computer toy, such as a scanner, is grabbing a COM port and won't let go. It's time to find a computer guru for some help. If you're bound and determined to do it yourself, tighten your belt a notch and check out *Modems For Dummies*.
- After you tell Terminal what COM port your modem is using, Terminal writes it down. That means you only have to mess with this setting once. If Terminal is remembering the *wrong* COM port, however, you can edit the entry in your WIN.INI file (a process meticulously described in Chapter 15).

- Some video adapters grab the same *interrupt* — also known as IRQ — that your computer uses for COM4:. To cure the conflict, call up the Ports icon in Windows' Control Panel, click on Settings, choose the Advanced button for COM4:, and try changing the Interrupt Request Line (IRQ) to 3 or 4. The manual for your internal modem may tell you which IRQ to use, as well as offering an *address* to enter in the box above the IRQ box.

Getting Terminal ready to call another computer

After you have introduced Terminal to your modem — and to your computer's ever-important COM port — you must tell Terminal a few facts about the computer you are trying to call.

First, you must know the other computer's *phone number*. For example, the phone number for Microsoft's BBS is 1-206-637-9009.

Second, you need a bizarre bit of babble known as the computer's *parameters*. Parameters boil down to two numbers and a letter. For example, the parameters for Microsoft's BBS are 8-N-1.

Third, you have to tell Terminal how fast your modem can talk to the other computer's modem. Terminal measures modem speed as *baud rate*.

Here's how to pass that information along to Terminal (as well as how to fudge it if you haven't the foggiest idea of what's going on).

Entering the phone number

This one is pretty easy. Just type the other computer's phone number into Terminal's Phone Number box, as described below.

1. **From Terminal's menu bar, click on Settings.**

   A box drops down, listing nearly a dozen confusing settings.

2. **Click on Phone Number.**

   A little box (shown in Figure 7-5) hops onto the screen.

Figure 7-5: Enter the phone number you want to dial.

3. **Type the phone number in the Dial box and click on OK.**

   Type the other computer's telephone number. Be sure to add a 1 and the area code if you're dialing long distance.

   Feel free to add the little hyphens between numbers if you think it looks better. Put the area code in parentheses, too, if you prefer. Or leave them out — Terminal doesn't care either way.

   For example, to call Microsoft's BBS, you type **1-206-637-9009**, just as it appears in Figure 7-5.

   Do you have to dial 9 for an outside line? Then type **9,** — that's the number 9 followed by a comma — before the actual phone number. For example, to call the Microsoft BBS you would type **9,1-206-637-9009.**

   Done? Click the OK button to put the Phone Number box away.

Entering the settings and baud rate

This one is much simpler than it looks. Terminal has to know the settings, or parameters, for just about every place you call, including Microsoft's BBS.

The most common settings are known as 8-N-1, which stands for 8 *data bits*, a *parity* of None, and 1 *stop bit*.

1. **From Terminal's menu bar, click on Settings and choose Communications from the drop-down menu.**

   A familiar-looking box pops up; it's the same box you saw in Figure 7-4 when you entered your modem's COM port.

2. **Click on `8` under Data Bits, `1` under Stop Bits, and `None` under Parity.**

   Terminal usually comes already set up like this, so you probably won't have to click on anything at all.

3. **Enter the Baud Rate and click the OK button.**

   Modems can chatter to each other at different speeds, measured as their *baud rate*. The trick is to make sure that they're both talking at the *same* speed. If you know the other modem's baud rate, click on it in the Baud Rate box. Make sure that you don't enter a speed faster than your own modem can speak, however.

   Don't know what speed to choose? Then click on `2400`. It's possible that the two modems could talk at a faster speed; however, nearly all modems can talk at a speed of 2400, so that setting is a pretty safe bet.

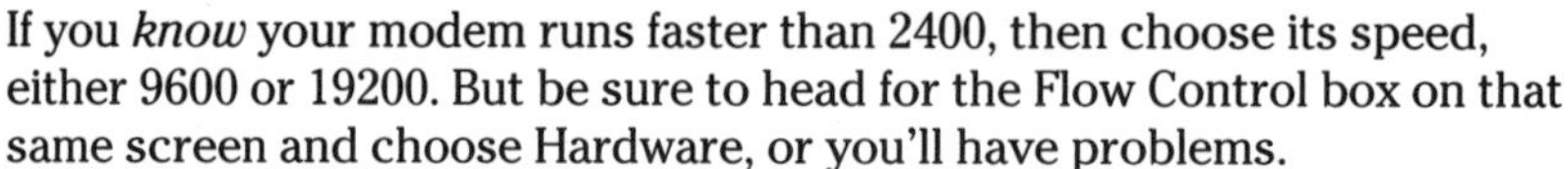

   If you *know* your modem runs faster than 2400, then choose its speed, either 9600 or 19200. But be sure to head for the Flow Control box on that same screen and choose Hardware, or you'll have problems.

   Done? Click on OK.

4. **From the File menu, choose Save, and type a name in the File Name box.**

   Terminal can remember your newly entered settings if you save them to a file. So, when the File Name box pops up, shown in Figure 7-6, type a filename that's easy to remember.

   For example, if you have been entering the settings from the Microsoft BBS, type **MICROSFT** and press Enter. Don't bother entering a file extension; Terminal adds one automatically. (Terminal automatically uses .TRM for an extension, even if you *try* to type something else.)

- Just like any other filename, the name used to save Terminal's settings cannot contain more than eight characters. It also cannot include characters such as |, *, ?, or the other weird characters mentioned in Chapter 2.

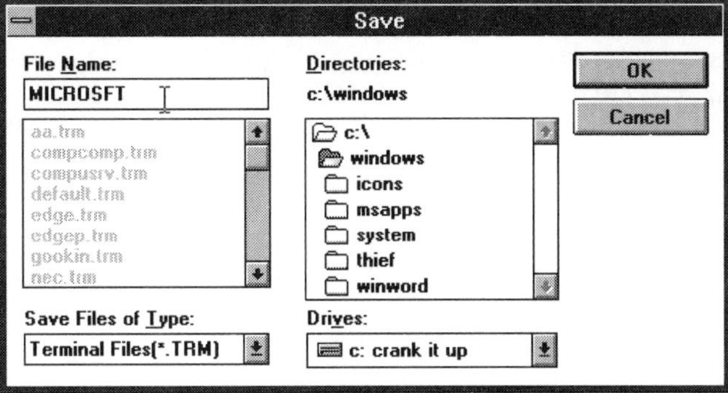

Figure 7-6: Enter a filename in which you can save Terminal's settings.

- The term *baud* is named for the French engineer, J.M.E. Baudot. Several computer literates, however, insist that French poet Charles Baudelaire was involved, as well.

Telling Terminal to call another computer

After you have told Terminal the vital statistics on the computer it is preparing to call, it's time to tell Terminal to begin dialing.

Have you already saved the settings for the other computer, as described in the preceding section? Then here's how to call them up and put them to use:

1. **From Terminal's menu, choose the File menu, choose Open, and then load the other computer's settings.**

   For example, if you saved the settings for Microsoft's BBS as MICROSFT, the file MICROSFT.TRM will be listed in the File Name box (see Figure 7-7). Double-click on the filename, and Terminal loads the settings.

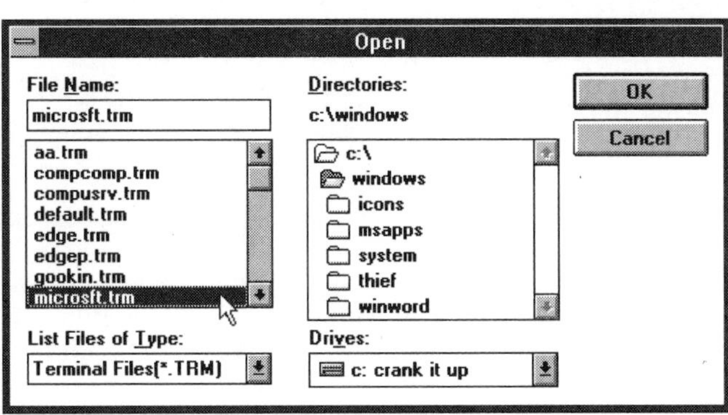

Figure 7-7: Double-click on MICROSFT.TRM to load the settings for the Microsoft BBS.

2. **From Terminal's Phone menu, choose Dial.**

   Click on Dial from the drop-down menu, and, depending on your brand of modem, you should hear the sound of a phone number being dialed. (Some modems won't make any noise at all, unfortunately, adding to the legion of confusion.)

   After a moment or two, you should hear the other modem answer the phone. The two modems make spitting sounds at each other for a moment, embrace, and then a `CONNECT` message should appear on-screen.

Congratulations! You have connected to another computer!

If Terminal didn't connect, a few things may have happened. The phone line might be busy: somebody else's modem may have beat you to it. Wait a few minutes and try again.

If things still seem awry, head for the end of this chapter for some troubleshooting tips. Unfortunately, it may be time to call in a computer guru.

- After you dial the Microsoft BBS, as with most other computers you dial, you have to type your name, your city, and your state. That invasion of privacy is called *logging on*.
- When other computers begin sending information over the phone lines, Terminal's screen looks like a strange new program, complete with menus.
- If you are calling a new computer for the first time, you might want to capture everything that flows by to a text file (described in an upcoming section). Then, when the stress level isn't so high, you can review exactly what transpired while you were on-line.

Capturing Something from the Screen

After you are connected to another computer, the fun begins. Terminal's window fills up with information sent by the computer on the other end of the phone line.

See anything interesting? Tell Terminal to grab it right off the screen. For example, to grab a few interesting paragraphs off the screen, follow these steps:

1. **Find the paragraphs you want to grab.**

   If the interesting paragraph has already scrolled off the top of Terminal's screen, it's not gone for good. Bring it back from the dead by clicking on Terminal's scroll bar — the long skinny thing along the right edge (see Figure 7-8). Keep clicking near the top of the scroll bar until the information slides back onto the screen.

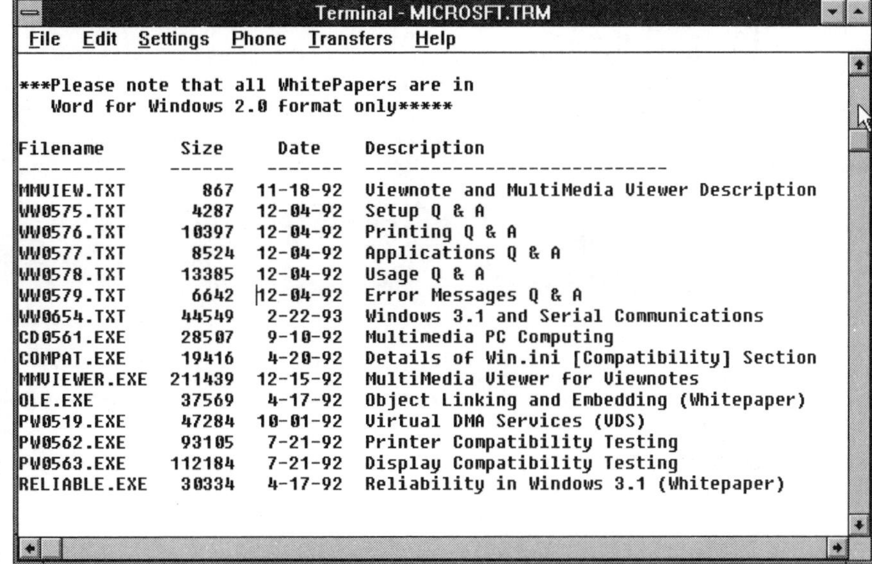

Figure 7-8: Click on the scroll bar to bring back information that has already shot beyond the screen.

2. **Hold down the mouse button and slide the pointer over the information.**

   Point to the beginning of the first word you want to grab. Then, while holding down the mouse button, slide the mouse until it points to the last word you want to grab. The stuff you want to grab changes color, or becomes *highlighted.*

3. **From Terminal's Edit menu, click on Copy or press Ctrl+C.**

   When you choose Copy or press Ctrl+C (see Figure 7-9), the highlighted information you grabbed is sent to the Windows clipboard.

4. **Paste the information into Notepad or some other program.**

   To save the information quickly, call up Notepad from the Program Manager, and choose Paste from Notepad's Edit menu. The clipboard dumps your newly grabbed information into Notepad, and then you can save it to a file.

   Actually, you can paste the information into any program; Notepad just makes a nice place to store it for a while.

   - If Terminal doesn't have a scroll bar, bolt one back on: Choose Terminal Preferences from the Settings menu. Then, make sure that the Show Scroll Bars button is checked. (It's hiding near the bottom of the box.)

   - Sometimes the information goes by too fast to grab. To keep that from happening, make Terminal hold on to a bigger chunk of information. Choose Terminal Preferences from the Settings menu. Then, type **300** in the Buffer Lines box near the bottom of the dialog box. Now you can scroll back to read the preceding 300 lines. Normally, Terminal retains only the last 100 lines: about four pages of information.

```
Terminal - MICROSFT.TRM
File  Edit  Settings  Phone  Transfers  Help
      Copy        Ctrl+C
      Paste       Ctrl+V
      Send        Ctrl+Shift+Ins
      Select All
      Clear Buffer

***Pl                          ePapers are in
   Wo                          at only*****

Filen                          Description
-----                       -- ----------------------------
MMVIE                       92 Viewnote and MultiMedia Viewer Description
WW0575.TXT     4287  12-04-92  Setup Q & A
WW0576.TXT    10397  12-04-92  Printing Q & A
WW0577.TXT     8524  12-04-92  Applications Q & A
WW0578.TXT    13385  12-04-92  Usage Q & A
WW0579.TXT     6642  12-04-92  Error Messages Q & A
WW0654.TXT    44549   2-22-93  Windows 3.1 and Serial Communications
CD0561.EXE    28507   9-10-92  Multimedia PC Computing
COMPAT.EXE    19416   4-20-92  Details of Win.ini [Compatibility] Section
MMVIEWER.EXE 211439  12-15-92  MultiMedia Viewer for Viewnotes
OLE.EXE       37569   4-17-92  Object Linking and Embedding (Whitepaper)
PW0519.EXE    47284  10-01-92  Virtual DMA Services (VDS)
PW0562.EXE    93105   7-21-92  Printer Compatibility Testing
PW0563.EXE   112184   7-21-92  Display Compatibility Testing
RELIABLE.EXE  30334   4-17-92  Reliability in Windows 3.1 (Whitepaper)
```

Figure 7-9: By highlighting information and choosing Copy, the information is sent to the Windows clipboard.

- If Ctrl+C makes the other computer act weird — and Terminal refuses to grab the information — here's the fix: Choose Terminal Preferences from the Settings menu. Then, make sure that there's a check mark in the Use Function,Arrow,and Ctrl Keys for Windows box (it's at the very bottom of the dialog box).

- If you grabbed a horrendously huge chunk of information, Notepad won't be able to handle it. Notepad is not a big enough program to handle files of more than about 50K. Dump the information into Write, instead.

Capturing Everything from the Other Computer

Want to make sure that you're not missing anything sent by the other computer? Then capture *everything* that flows across Terminal's screen.

With this technique, if something has flown past too quickly to see, you still have the information stored in a file. After you *log off* — hang up and disconnect from the other computer — you can read the file at your leisure.

Here's how to make Terminal stuff everything that flows by into a file of your choosing.

1. **From Terminal's Transfers menu, choose Receive Text File.**

   I know "Receive Text File" is an awfully weird way to say "capture all the information that flows across the screen." But that's the hoop Terminal wants you to jump through.

2. **Enter the name of the file in which you want to store the information and click OK.**

   When typing the name of a file in the File Name box, make sure that it's not more than eight characters long and doesn't have any forbidden characters. (Those scary forbidden characters are described in Chapter 2.) Done? Click OK.

From that point on, Terminal stores everything that goes by in the file you specified.

- Tell Terminal to begin "receiving its text file" *before* you call the other computer. This technique gives you a copy of everything that flows by, even during that scary moment of first typing in your name and location.
- Terminal is extraordinarily picky about the name you choose for your incoming text file. You *must* put an extension on it. For example, Terminal lets you use TRASH.TXT as a filename. But if you just type TRASH, Terminal sends you the disturbing message shown in Figure 7-10. To be on the safest side, only receive text to a hard drive, unless you have to dump it onto a floppy.

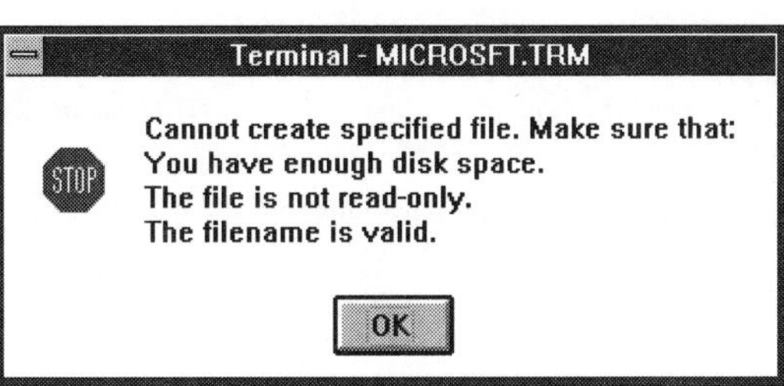

Figure 7-10: This box appears if you tell Terminal to create a file, and you don't add an extension.

- Want to use a single file as a storage pot for everything? Then don't keep entering a new filename. Instead, click on the Append File button. Then click on the name of an existing file to which you want to add additional information. Terminal keeps tossing new information into that same old file but won't overwrite the older stuff.

- When you call a particular computer for the first time, it's a good idea to capture everything. That way you can always print out that computer's help menu for later reference.

Downloading a File

Now it's time to start grabbing some files from the other computer. Believe it or not, you're not stealing. Those other computers are set up so that people can grab files from them.

Here are the official file-grabbing procedures:

1. **Find the file you want to grab.**

   Before you get to the name of the file you want to grab, you may want to spend a few minutes navigating the menus on the other computer. Check the menus for the words *file library*, or *download area.*

   For example, pressing F on Microsoft's BBS brings the File Index to the screen, as shown in Figure 7-11. That's where all the files are stored.

```
Terminal - MICROSFT.TRM
File  Edit  Settings  Phone  Transfers  Help
IBM.EXE        114753   6-29-92  Audio-IBM M-Audio Adapter
MARBLE.EXE      24476  10-27-92  Marble Wallpaper
MMHELP.EXE     181095  10-27-92  Microsoft Mail Help
MONO.EXE        16043   7-10-92  Create More UMB Space with Mono Video
MSEXE.EXE       41175   8-12-92  Windows MS-DOS Executive
-More-
NOVELL.EXE     251802   7-10-92  Novell Netware Upgrade & IPX Upgrade Utility
REVERS.EXE      28462   7-10-92  Contains the Game Reversi
SPEAK.EXE       22312   6-19-92  Audio-PC Speaker Driver
SPHELP.EXE     204019  10-27-92  Microsoft Schedule Plus Help
SSMYST.EXE      25834  10-27-92  Mystify Screen Saver
TADA.EXE        37014  10-27-92  TADA Sound File
TARTAN.EXE      19806  10-27-92  Tartan Wallpaper
THUNDR.EXE      26339   6-19-92  Audio-Thunderboard Drivers
UPDATE.EXE      40802   7-02-93  List of WDL changes (txt file)
VPD386.EXE      17114   7-10-92  VPD.386 for LPT Contention Management
WFWADD.EXE     112342   5-20-93  WFWG Accessory Files
WRI.EXE         74981   7-10-92  SYSINI.WRI and WININI.WRI Write Help Files

<D>ownload, <P>rotocol, <E>xamine, <N>ew, <L>ist, or <H>elp
Selection or <CR> to exit:
```

Figure 7-11: Microsoft's Speaker driver is called SPEAK.EXE and is listed alphabetically among the list of drivers and other files.

2. **Tell the other computer what file you want and how it should send that particular file.**

   Did you find the file you were after? Then look on the other computer's menu for a *download* option. Choose the download option from the menu and type in the name of the file you want to grab.

   Next, tell the other computer what *protocol* to use when it sends the file. Choosing the protocol is easier than you might think: Always choose XMODEM when using Terminal. The other computer will immediately say it's starting to send the file.

   In Figure 7-11, pressing D told the Microsoft BBS you wanted to download a file. Then, as you can see in Figure 7-12, pressing X tells the Microsoft BBS to send the file using XMODEM.

   Now that the other computer has started sending the file, you have to tell Terminal to start receiving it.

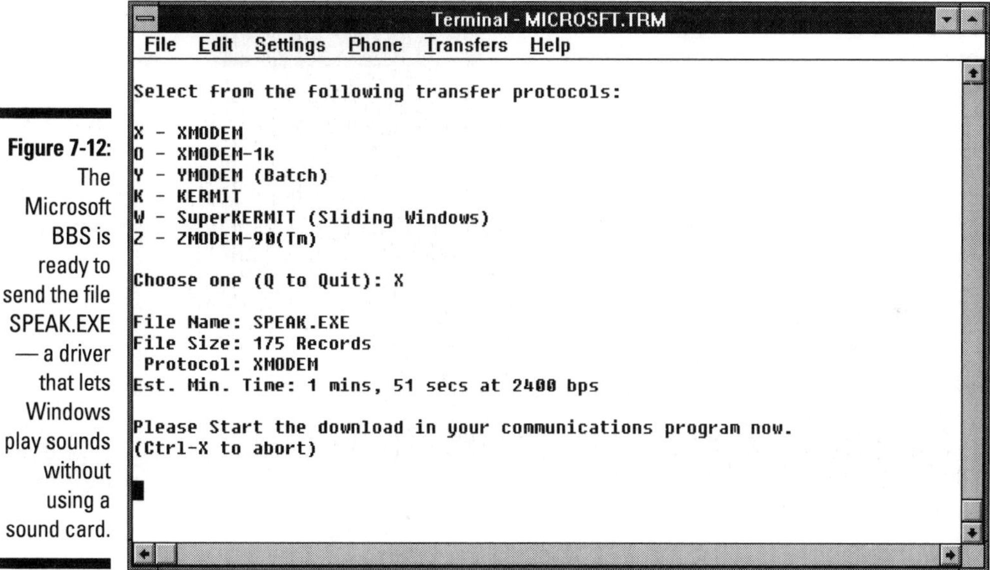

Figure 7-12: The Microsoft BBS is ready to send the file SPEAK.EXE — a driver that lets Windows play sounds without using a sound card.

3. **From Terminal's Transfers menu, choose Receive Binary File.**

   After you have told the other computer to send a file using XMODEM, it's time to tell Terminal to receive that incoming file.

   Click on Transfers and choose Receive Binary File, as shown in Figure 7-13.

   Terminal then asks where you want to store the incoming file.

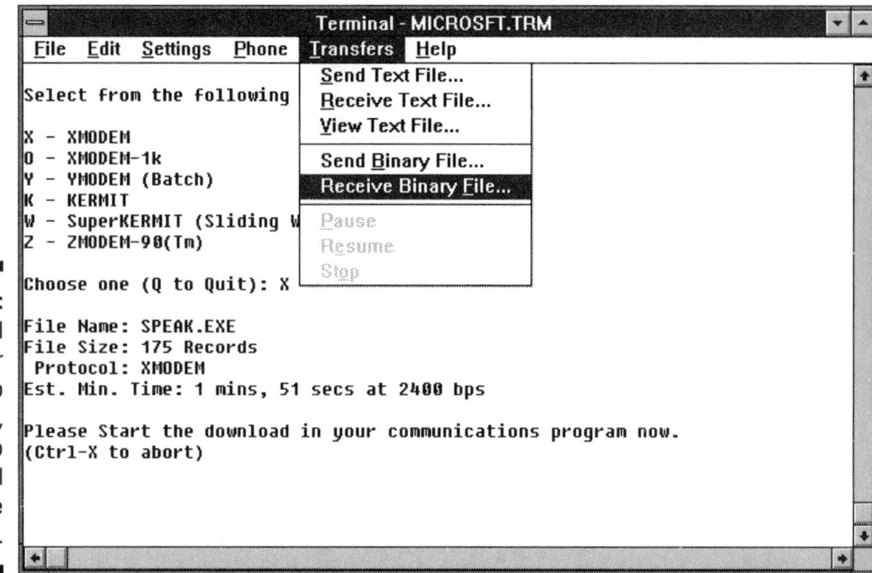

Figure 7-13: After you tell the other computer to send a file, you have to tell Terminal to receive the file.

4. **Tell Terminal where to put the incoming file, what to call it, and then click OK.**

   When you tell Terminal to receive an incoming file, Windows needs to know where to put it. Terminal places a familiar-looking box on-screen so that you can specify where the file should go (see Figure 7-14).

   Click on the directory — the little folder — in which you want Terminal to store the incoming file.

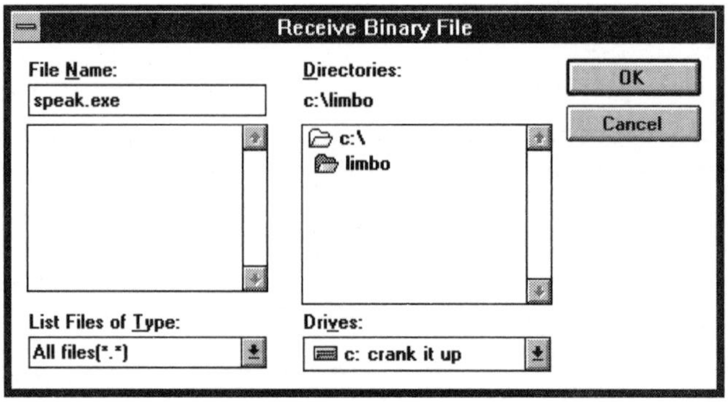

Receive Binary File
File Name: speak.exe
Directories: c:\limbo
c:\
limbo
OK
Cancel
List Files of Type: All files(*.*)
Drives: c: crank it up

Figure 7-14: Click on the directory where you want to store the incoming file; then type the name of the incoming file in the File Name box.

If you're going to be downloading a number of files, create a directory called \JUNK or \LIMBO, and always download your files into that directory. They will be easier to find when you're ready to take a look at them.

Next, type the file's name in the File Name box. Terminal is pretty dumb — it makes *you* type the name of the file the other computer is sending.

When you click OK, Terminal begins receiving the incoming file. You can watch the progress of the download along the bottom of the screen, as shown in Figure 7-15.

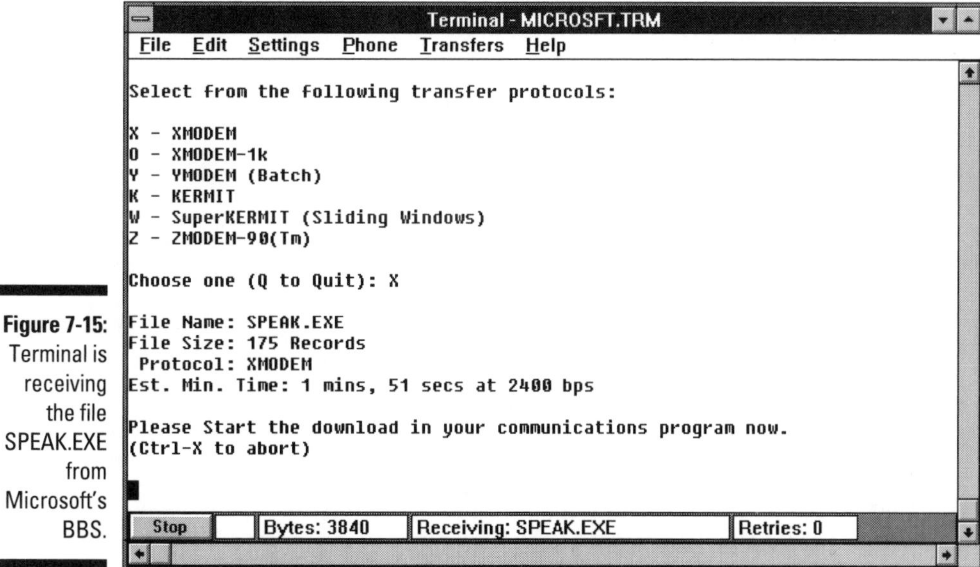

Figure 7-15: Terminal is receiving the file SPEAK.EXE from Microsoft's BBS.

5. **Press Enter when the transfer is complete.**

   When your computer is finished sucking a copy of the file onto its hard drive, the little messages along the bottom of Terminal's screen disappear.

   When the messages disappear, Terminal has finished grabbing the file. Press Enter, and the other computer wakes up and starts sending menus again.

6. **Choose Exit from the other computer's menu.**

   When you are done using the other computer, don't just tell Terminal to hang up. Always let the other computer hang up first. Look for the words Exit, Off, or Log Off from the other computer's menu. For example, pressing E on the Microsoft BBS causes it to hang up, as shown in Figure 7-16.

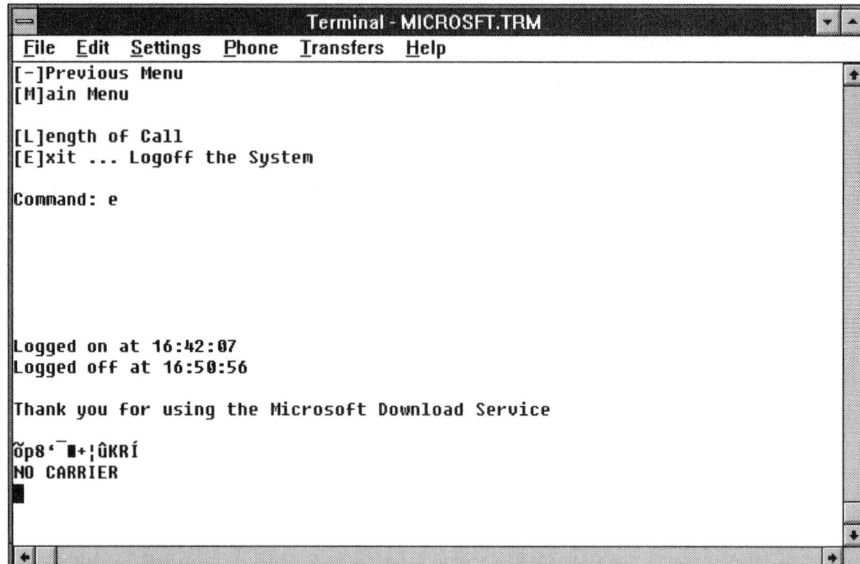

Figure 7-16: Pressing E tells Microsoft's BBS that you are done grabbing files and you want to hang up.

- So what do you do with the file now? If the file ends with the extension .ZIP or .ARC, head for Chapter 12. You must *unzip* or *de-archive* the file before you can do anything with it. Your work's not over, unfortunately.
- If you downloaded SPEAK.EXE, Microsoft's speaker driver, double-click on it from within the File Manager. Then, turn to Chapter 3 for tips on installing a sound driver. *Hint:* When Windows asks you to insert a disk containing the driver, click on the Browse button; then click on the directory where you downloaded SPEAK.EXE.

- To find the Microsoft Speaker driver, follow the Microsoft BBS menus and choose the File Index option. From there, move to the Windows and MS-DOS area and then the Windows 3.1 Driver Library. Finally, choose the Audio Drivers & Misc. Files area. At that point, download the SPEAK.EXE file.

- Terminal lists two ways to download or *transfer* information. To capture information as it flows across the screen, choose the Receive Text File. To download a particular file, choose Receive Binary File and tell the other computer to send using XMODEM.
- Want to send a file? Follow the same steps: Make sure that the other computer is ready to receive your file and then send it. Click on the Send option instead of the Receive option just described.

Receiving a Call

Sometimes calling another computer isn't enough. Some folks want another computer to call *their* computer.

Terminal is up for the challenge. Here's how to tell Terminal to wake up and answer the phone:

1. **Load Terminal.**

   Double-click on the Program Manager's Terminal icon to bring it to the screen.

2. **Click in the Terminal window, type `ATS0=1`, and press Enter.**

   That's a *zero* after the ATS part, not a capital *O*. The S0=1 command tells your modem to answer the phone on the first ring; change it to S0=2 to answer on the second ring, or S0=3 to answer on the third ring.

   That's it; just sit there and wait. When the phone rings, Terminal tells your modem to answer. When you want to make Terminal *stop* answering the phone, fer cryin' out loud, move to the next step.

3. **Click in the Terminal window, type `ATS0=0`, and press Enter.**

   This makes Terminal stop picking up the phone. And you *gotta* type that ATS0=0 stuff in, by the way. If you exit Terminal *without* typing it, your modem will keep answering the phone again and again and again....

- When Terminal answers the phone, you should see a `CONNECT` message on-screen. Then, as someone begins typing on the other computer, you should see whatever is being typed (including misspellings) in Terminal's window.
- When you type back, remember the other person can also see *your* misspellings.

Uh, It Doesn't Work Right

Sometimes only part of Terminal works. Here are a few places you can prod when Terminal doesn't walk the straight and narrow.

It almost connects, but then the timer runs out!

Sometimes you can hear the other computer's phone ring, and then the modems start spitting at each other. Before the modems make their actual connection, however, the little timer runs out and Terminal gives up. Bottom line: the computers never connect.

Terminal normally waits 30 seconds for the other computer to connect. To give Terminal a little more patience, change that 30 seconds to 45.

From Terminal's Settings menu, click on Phone Number. A box like the one in Figure 7-17 appears.

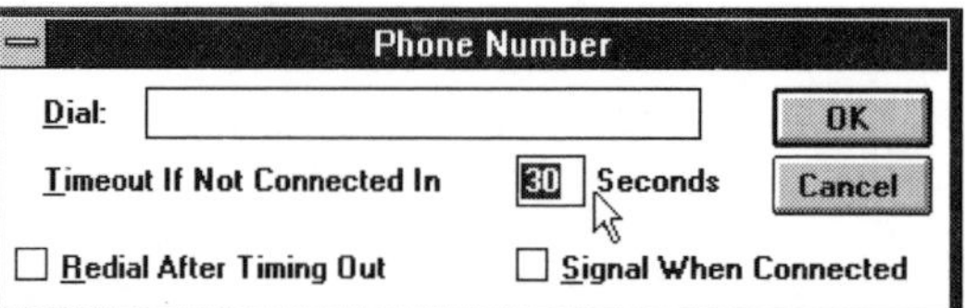

Figure 7-17: Change the number of seconds from 30 to 45.

Delete the number 30 from the box labeled Timeout If Not Connected In, and type **45**. Terminal will then wait 45 seconds for a connection, which should be plenty of time.

Terminal thinks it's still connected, even when I hang up

Terminal is pretty dopey. In fact, it can't even tell when your modem has hung up the phone. If you try to exit Terminal after calling another computer, Terminal often sends the message displayed in Figure 7-18.

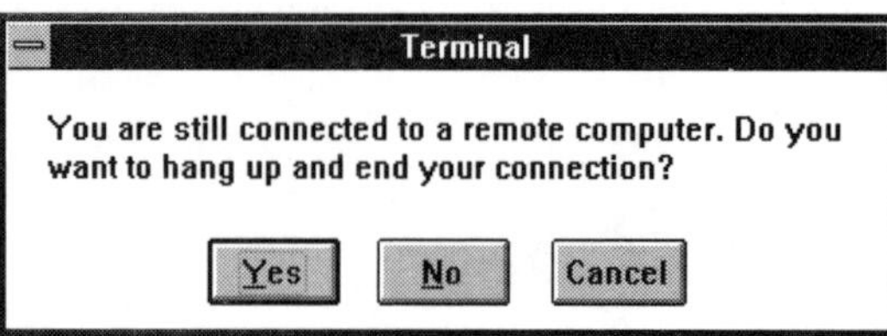

Figure 7-18: Terminal can't tell whether the modem is still connected.

There might be a solution, however. From the Settings menu, choose the Communications box; click the Carrier Detect box until a check mark appears (see Figure 7-19). Selecting this option sometimes convinces Terminal to check with the modem to see whether it is still talking to another computer.

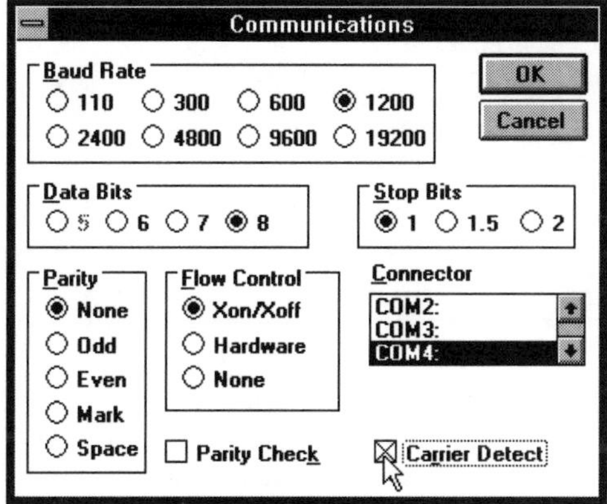

Figure 7-19: The Carrier Detect box option sometimes makes Terminal more aware of whether your modem is on the phone.

- Unfortunately, selecting the Carrier Detect box is not a sure-fire solution. Modems can be set up in too many ways for Terminal to cope. If changing the Carrier Detect box makes things worse, or even more confusing, click in the box again and make the check mark disappear.
- If choosing Carrier Detect *does* work, be sure to save those settings by choosing the Save command from the File menu.
- If you can't fix the problem, don't worry; it's not serious. The modem has already hung up, so it doesn't really matter whether you click the Yes or the No button in Figure 7-18. So save a little time by clicking No.

Terminal won't show any colors or graphics

Some bulletin boards greet their callers with lavish colors and fancy graphics. Unfortunately, Terminal can't handle any of those colors. Terminal is strictly from the black-and-white era — not even Ted Turner can help.

In fact, if the other computer tries to send fancy graphics, Terminal will look something like Figure 7-20.

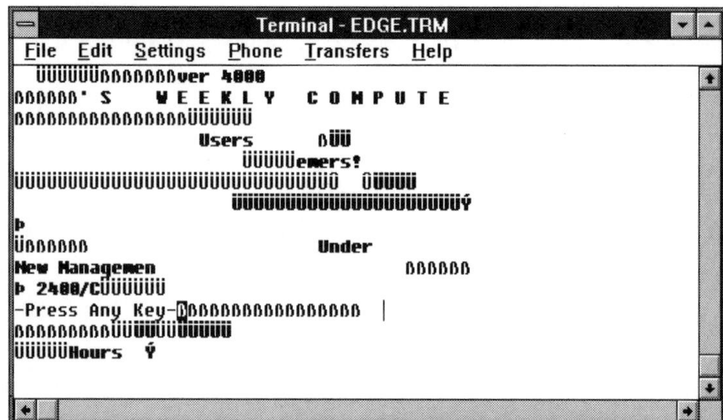

Figure 7-20: Fancy ANSI graphics won't show up correctly in Terminal and may even look this weird.

- The best you can do is click on Terminal Emulation from the Settings menu. Then choose DEC VT-100 (ANSI). Chances are, however, that's already been chosen and the screen looks the best it can.
- Look for a menu option on the other computer to turn off ANSI Graphics and IBM Graphics. Your screen will look a lot more appealing when Terminal can stick to black-and-white letters.
- If you really miss those colors, you probably should buy another kind of telecommunications program.

I can't send Ctrl characters like Ctrl+C

Windows eavesdrops on everything you type on the other computer through Terminal. Windows is listening for keys that tell it what to do. For example, if you press Ctrl+C to activate a command in CompuServe, Windows won't let that command pass through.

Instead, Windows grabs that Ctrl+C for itself, races to see if you set up any Ctrl+C macros in that complicated Macro Recorder, and then just throws the Ctrl+C away. That Ctrl+C never makes it through the phone lines to CompuServe.

To make your Ctrl characters pass through to the other computer, choose Terminal Preferences from the Settings menu. At the very bottom of the box, click on the Use Function,Arrow,and Ctrl Keys for Windows option until the X disappears from the box.

This option keeps Windows from intercepting your keystrokes: Everything you type — including your arrow keys, function keys, and Ctrl keys — is passed directly to the other computer.

I have a pulse phone, not touch tone!

Terminal assumes everybody has a *touch tone* phone — the kind that sounds a different tone for each button you press.

If you still have a pulse phone — the kind with the little round dial that makes clicks — Terminal won't work without some adjustment.

To fix it, choose Modem Commands from the Settings menu. See the `ATDT` listed in the Dial Prefix box? Change that to `ATDP`, click on OK, and your troubles will be over.

You must change the `ATDT` setting every time you enter settings for another computer you want to call. To simplify things, hop to the Changing Terminals Defaults tip, coming up in the next section.

How can I change Terminal's defaults?

Whenever you click on New from the File menu, Terminal is ready and waiting for you to enter the settings for another computer you want to call.

However, Terminal always starts out with the same basic settings — and those aren't always the settings you want. There is a solution, however.

Click on New from the File menu and change Terminal's settings so that they match the settings of your phone and modem. Then save those settings under the filename DEFAULT.TRM. Now, whenever you want to add another computer to your list of places to call, just call up the DEFAULT.TRM file. Type the new phone number, save the new settings with Terminal's Save As command, and then assign a new name to that file. This technique can save you time, as well as make sure that your settings are consistent.

My modem keeps answering my phone!

This problem has several answers. Try each of the following solutions until you find the one that works for your particular bunch of gizmos:

1. **Check the Modem Commands box from Terminal's Settings menu.** Make sure that the characters in the Originate box start with the letters `AT` and include `S0=0` in there somewhere. For example, the characters `ATQ0V1E1S0=0` are fine.

2. **Check your modem manual; a tiny switch on the modem's bottom tells it whether or not to answer the phone.** Flip the switch to the Stop Answering position. Then turn the modem off and on again, and the modem should stop confusing people who call your house.
3. **Keep the modem turned off when you are not using it.**
4. **Buy a second phone line specifically for your modem.**

One of the preceding steps should cure the problem.

Call Waiting keeps bumping me off-line

Many people choose the Call Waiting option from the phone company. Then, when they're talking to one person on the phone and another person calls, they hear a little beep.

Unfortunately, that little beep makes your polite modem hang up instantly if it happens to be talking to another computer.

Modems solve everything with a string of numbers, and Call Waiting is no exception.

To make your modem turn off Call Waiting before it dials, call up the Modem Commands box from the Terminal's Settings menu. Then, in the Dial Prefix box, change `ATDT` to `ATDT*70,` and click on OK.

- This technique should turn off Call Waiting when your modem makes a call.
- When your modem is done making the call, Call Waiting turns itself back on automatically.

That XMODEM Stuff Doesn't Work!

To keep modem newcomers helplessly confused, a bunch of technoids keep developing new ways for modems to talk to each other when sending files back and forth.

Terminal keeps things simple by only supporting two methods: XMODEM and a rarely used method called Kermit. (Yep, it's named after the frog.)

- Nearly every computer you will ever call offers XMODEM as a choice.
- So why bother with any of those other ways? Because they're faster, which translates to cheaper when any per-minute expenses are involved.

- If you are going to be downloading a number of big files, look for a modem program that can handle something called ZMODEM. It's one of the fastest.

- Download methods are called *File Transfer Protocols*. XMODEM, developed by a pioneer computer hacker named Ward Christensen, was one of the first protocols. Back then, it was also the fastest. Today, protocols include YMODEM, ZMODEM, CompuServe B, CompuServe B+, and more. Most of them are faster than XMODEM, but Microsoft is in no hurry to add them to Terminal.

How Do I Unzip or De-Arc a File?

By turning to Chapter 12 and digging in. Files ending in the extensions .ZIP and .ARC won't run right off the bat. They come in a special software *bag*. You have to take them out of the bag before you can use them.

Am I Gonna Get a Virus?

Probably not. If you have DOS 6, however, head for Chapter 6. There you can find out how to put Microsoft's virus checker to work. Otherwise, look for programs called VIRUSCAN by McAfee Associates. Most computers that offer files for downloading also offer VIRUSCAN.

The 5th Wave **By Rich Tennant**

"NO, SIR, THIS ISN'T A DATING SERVICE. THEY INTRODUCE PEOPLE THROUGH A COMPUTER SO THEY CAN TALK TO EACH OTHER IN PERSON. WE INTRODUCE PEOPLE IN PERSON SO THEY CAN TALK TO EACH OTHER THROUGH A COMPUTER."

Chapter 8

Sound! Movies! Multimedia Stuff!

In This Chapter

- Figuring out Media Player
- Figuring out Sound Recorder
- Playing music (those .MID files)
- Playing sounds (those .WAV files)
- Playing musical CDs (those shiny round things)
- Watching movies (those .AVI files)
- Recording sounds
- Fixing sound and video problems

All the really *fun* computers — from that somber-voiced "working" computer on "Star Trek: The Next Generation" to that flailing-armed "Danger! Danger!" robot on "Lost In Space" — have one important thing in common: They can make *noises*, for cryin' out loud.

For years, *real* computers could only cut loose with a rude beep, which they issued whenever a confused user pressed the wrong key. Windows 3.1, however, bursts onto the screen with a triumphant *ta-da* sound; and it plays melodious chimes when it leaves the screen. Add a microphone and a sound card, and you can even record your own (or your neighbor's) belches and burps.

Of course, computer game players know that computerized sound is nothing new; they've been listening to screeching tires and giggling maidens for years. But Windows brings a glorious new name to this conglomeration of sound and video: *multimedia*.

This chapter shows how to push the on-screen buttons on your computer's new multimedia VCR — one that will never flash a blinking *12:00*.

Media Player

The best noisemaker that comes with Windows 3.1 is Media Player. Depending on how much money you paid for your computer — or how much money your computer has absorbed since you first plopped it on your desk — you can use the Windows Media Player to listen to prerecorded sounds, play back music, and even watch movies.

To see what Media Player can do on *your* particular computer, double-click on the Media Player icon from its hideout in the Program Manager's Accessories window. If you're lucky, you won't see the message in Figure 8-1.

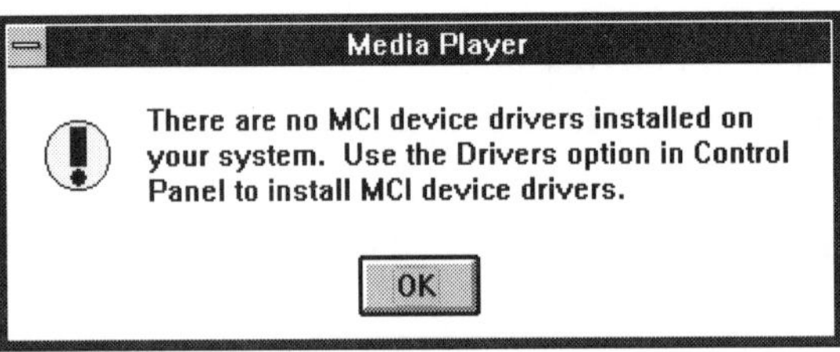

Figure 8-1: Media Player can't find any drivers for your particular computer's sound or video cards.

That ugly message means that Media Player won't come out of its box: It can't find any Windows drivers for the sound or video goodies that are stuffed inside your computer. For example, if you installed a sound card, you need to install Windows drivers for that sound card. Without them, Media Player doesn't know how to make the sound card squawk.

Windows drivers are a necessary evil, so Chapter 3 shows how to install them. Head for Chapter 7 if you're still searching for drivers — especially new drivers to replace old ones that are driving in the wrong direction.

Drivers installed? Good; then a double-click on Media Player's icon will bring Media Player to the screen, as shown in Figure 8-2.

- Actually, Media Player is nothing more than a big, fancy button. Before that big button can do anything, you need to connect it to something — a sound card, for example, as well as the right software.
- You also need a *sound* to play. Like corporate reports and Bart Simpson icons, sounds are stored in files. Your version of Windows came packaged with a few sound files; and most sound cards include a disk that is packed with sound files.

- To see what Media Player can play on your particular computer, choose Device from its menu. A menu like the one in Figure 8-3 drops down; the menu lists the kinds of things that your version of Media Player is currently set up to play.
- Media Player has changed in appearance over the years; in fact, your version may look a little different from the one that came in the Windows 3.1 box. To learn about the newer, souped-up version, check out "The fancy new version of Media Player," later in this chapter.

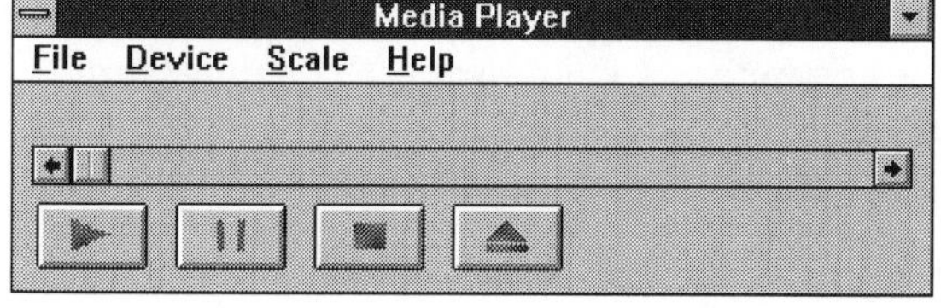

Figure 8-2: Media Player can play sounds and music; an updated version can play movies, as well.

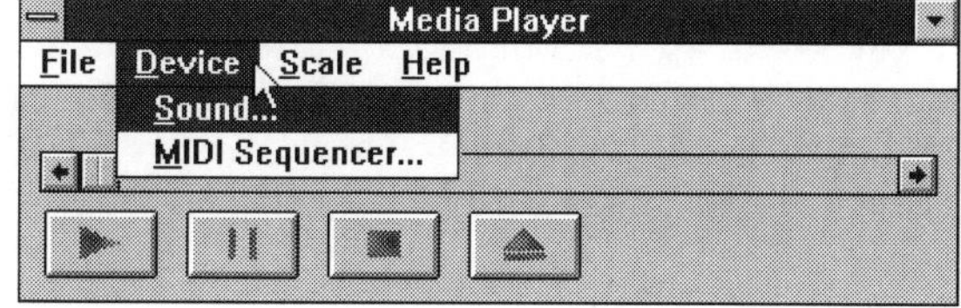

Figure 8-3: Media Player is set up to play sounds and synthesized music, known as *MIDI.*

Differences between .WAV and .MID files

Savvy New Age musicians know that Media Player can play two different types of sound files: digitized and synthesized. Table 8-1 describes the two types of files, which sound completely different from each other.

Table 8-1	Sound Files	
This type of Windows file . . .	*ends in these letters . . .*	*and contains this stuff*
Digital recording	.WAV	A recording of a sound that actually occurred.
Synthesized sound, also called MIDI	.MID	A list of musical sounds for the computer to synthesize and play.

A .WAV sound *actually* happened when somebody was nearby with a microphone to record it. The microphone grabbed the sound waves from the air and pushed them into the computer's sound card. The computer turned the incoming sound waves into numbers, stuck them into a file, and slapped the letters *.WAV* on the end of the filename.

To play back the .WAV file, Media Player grabs the numbers from the file and converts them back into sound waves; then the sound card pushes the sound waves out of the speaker. The end result? You hear the recording, just as if you played it from a cassette tape or compact disc.

A .MID or MIDI sound, on the other hand, never really happened. A computer with a sound card listened as some long-haired hippie type played an electronic instrument, usually a keyboard. As the computer heard each note being played, it wrote down the name of the instrument, the name of each note, its duration, and its timing. Then it packed all that information into file and added .MID to the end of the filename.

When Media Player plays a .MID file, it looks at the embedded instructions. Then it tells whatever synthesizer is hooked up to the computer to re-create those sounds. Most sound cards come with a built-in synthesizer that creates the sounds.

.MID files stand for *MIDI* files — a fancy new way for musicians to store their music.

- .WAV files contain actual *sounds*: chirping birds, yodeling Swiss cheese makers, or honks from New York cabbies.

  .MID files contains synthesized *music:* songs that re-create the sounds of instruments ranging from saxophones to maracas.

- In real life, MIDI is a pretty complicated concept that only *looks* easy when the guy on the stage hammers out a few notes and flicks cigarette ashes off the keyboard. In fact, most MIDI musicians are also closet computer nerds. (Or they pay other nerds to handle all the complicated MIDI stuff for them.)

- A .WAV file sounds pretty much the same when you play it back on anybody's computer, using anybody's sound card.

Snoring .WAV sounds

What's really inside a .WAV file? Basically, it contains a bunch of numbers — measurements of how that particular file's sound waves should look. But the .WAV file also contains a *header.* The header gives Windows some information about the file's sounds: their *sampling* rate, whether they're mono or stereo, and whether they're recorded in *8-bit* or *16-bit resolution.*

Without that header, Media Player will gag on the sound, throwing an error message in your face.

For example, sound files that end in .VOC have a different header than sound files that end in .WAV. Because the header is different, Media Player chokes on .VOC files, the format that many SoundBlaster cards use. (You can find some .VOC to .WAV converters on CompuServe; see Chapter 7 for more information.)

If you're bored, check out the end of this chapter for definitions of italicized words such as *sampling* and *8-bit resolution.*

- A .MID file, in contrast, sounds different when you play it back on different computers. The sound depends entirely on the type of synthesizer — or sound card — that Windows uses to play it back. Some synthesizers sound great; the cheapest ones sound kinda soggy.
- Compared to .MID files, .WAV files consume huge chunks of hard drive space. For example, Windows comes with a two-minute-long MIDI song called CANYON.MID that takes up 33K. The Windows TADA.WAV file lasts less than two seconds; yet it grabs 27K.

Listening to a .MID file

A MIDI file is sort of like the pages of sheet music that sit on a conductor's podium. The file tells the computer which instruments to play, when and how loud to play them, and how often to empty the mouthpiece of spittle. Media Player handles the first three categories; keep an eye on your own drool bucket.

Follow these steps to make Media Player play back a MIDI file:

1. **Double-click on Media Player's icon from the Program Manager.**

   Media Player hops to the screen, looking like Figure 8-2.

2. **Click on Device and choose MIDI Sequencer from the menu that drops down.**

   Don't see MIDI Sequencer on the list? Then you need to install a driver for the sound card in Windows. To find out how to install this piece of software that the sound card uses, head to Chapter 3.

   Otherwise, MIDI Sequencer should appear on the menu, as in Figure 8-4.

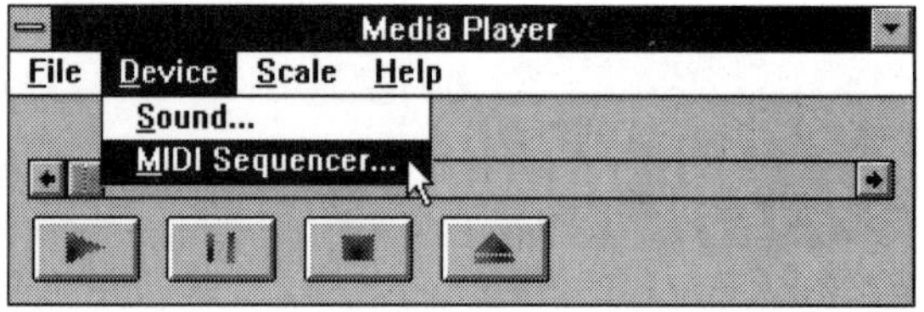

Figure 8-4: Choose MIDI Sequencer to play a .MID file through the Media Player.

3. **Double-click on the name of the file that you want to play.**

   When you choose MIDI Sequencer, Media Player shows a familiar-looking box — the same box that you've been using to open a file in any Windows program. As Figure 8-5 shows, the box filters out everything but the MIDI files that live in the current directory.

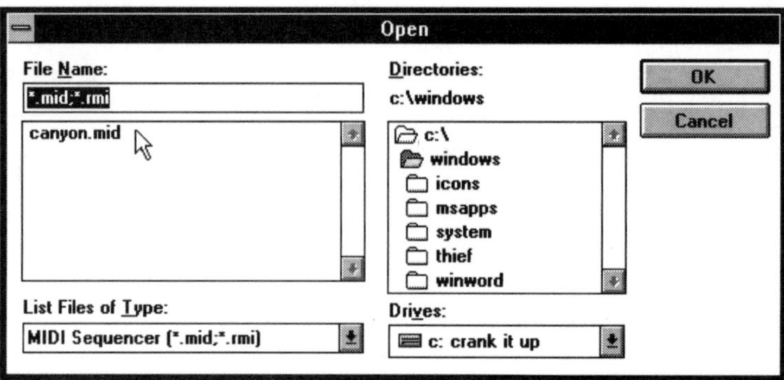

Figure 8-5: Click on the name of the .MID file that you want to hear and then click on the OK button.

   If you see the .MID file that you're itching to hear, double-click on it.

   Don't see the .MID file you want? Then click on the icons for other directories or drives; Media Player will show you any MIDI files that are lurking in those areas, too. Double-click on the .MID file that you want to hear.

   When you double-click on a .MID filename, Media Player loads the file and gets ready to play it back.

4. **Click on the play button.**

   Click on Media Player's play button — the black triangle — and the file should begin playing. Figure 8-6 shows what all the little Media Player buttons do.

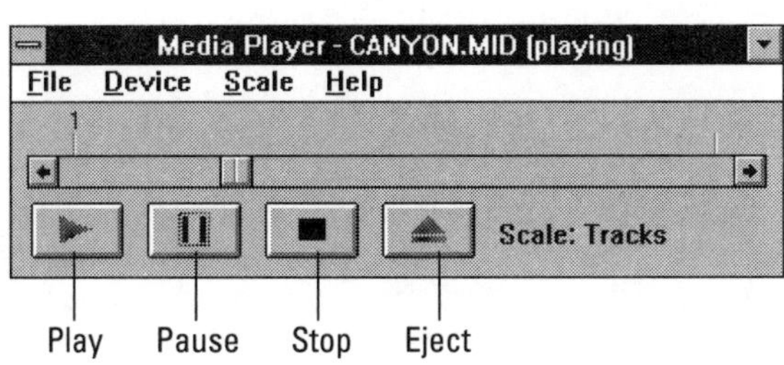

Figure 8-6: The first three buttons tell Media Player how to play, a file; eject tells a compact disc player to eject a disc.

- Chances are, you'll have good luck playing CANYON.MID, the file in the Windows directory. Microsoft designed the song specifically for Media Player. If something goes wrong, however, and you're not hearing pretty tunes, head for the troubleshooting section, "Media Player Doesn't Work!" It's near the end of this chapter.
- Most of the .MID files you'll come across weren't designed with Media Player in mind, unfortunately. They use a slightly different MIDI standard, so you have to mess with the tricky MIDI Mapper. The "MIDI Mapper Madness" section, a little later in this chapter, tackles this ugly beast.

- MIDI stands for *Musical Instrument Digital Interface*, but most people try to forget that right away.
- Microsoft's Internal Speaker driver — the one that plays sounds through the computer's own tiny speaker — doesn't have enough guts to satisfy Media Player. The Speaker driver simply can't play MIDI files.
- The Media Player may look a little bit different from the one that's pictured in this section. If so, it has probably been upgraded to play videos, as described in "Watching movies (those .AVI files)," later in this chapter.
- Instead of opening .MID files by clicking on the Device menu, you can choose Open from the File menu. But then Media Player will promptly show all the files in the current directory — not just the .MID files — and finding the .MID files is harder when they are among all the other files.

- The fastest way to play a .MID file is to find it listed in the File Manager. Double-click on its filename, and Media Player will leap to life and begin playing that file immediately.

Scale, Time, Tracks, and Tedium

Media Player always displays a bar with an arrow on each end and a box inside it, as shown in Figure 8-6. That bar stands for the *media clip* that you're playing. (Suave and debonair multimedia folks use the term *media clip* when they're talking about sound, music, or movies.)

As Media Player plays a file, the little box moves along the bar with the arrows on it. When the box reaches the end of the bar, the clip is over.

Two options, Time and Tracks, lurk in Media Player's Scale menu. Neither one affects the quality of whatever is being played. They just change the little numbers that Media Player displays above the bar while it's playing a media clip.

Choosing Time makes Media Player display how much time that media clip takes to play. For example, Figure 8-14 shows Media Player when it's displaying the Time. The number at the far right shows how many minutes and seconds the current sound or movie will last.

Choosing Tracks, however, tells Media Player to display which song it's currently playing out of a series of songs. When you are playing music from a compact disc, for example, the Tracks setting may display song number 5 out of a total of 12 songs. Figure 8-13 shows Media Player when it's displaying Tracks.

People who bother to change the setting usually set Scale to Time. Setting it to Tracks almost always makes Media Player display a *1* — after all, unless you're listening to a compact disc, you're probably playing a single sound from a queue of 1.

Finally, if you install a movie-playing driver, Scale offers a new option: Frames. A movie is composed of dozens of individual pictures, or *frames*, that are flipped in rapid succession. If you choose Frames, Media Player displays how many frames are in the movie that is currently loaded.

Playing .WAV files

Media Player can play recorded sounds — .WAV files — as well as .MID files. Here's how to let one loose:

1. **Double-click on Media Player's icon from the Program Manager.**

   Media Player rises to the occasion.

2. **Click on Device and choose Sound from the menu that drops down.**

   The Device menu drops down, as shown in Figure 8-7. Choose Sound to hear a .WAV file.

   A familiar-looking box appears, listing all the .WAV files in the current directory. Just as in Figure 8-5, you click on the little folders in the Directories box to see the sound files that are stored in different directories. Click on Drives to look for sounds on different drives.

If Sound doesn't show up on the Device menu, you have a loud problem: You don't have a Windows driver installed for the sound card. Chapter 3 describes how to install the sound card's driver so that Windows can play with it.

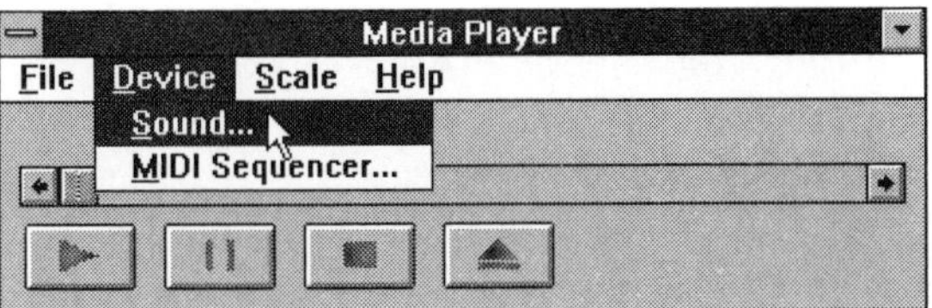

Figure 8-7: Choose Sound from the Device menu to play a .WAV file, or sound.

3. **Double-click on the sound that you want to hear.**

   After you double-click on the .WAV file that you want to hear, Media Player loads it.

4. **Press the play button to hear the sound.**

   The play button has a single black triangle on it. (Figure 8-6 shows what all the buttons do.)

   When the sound starts to play, the words change in the title bar at the top of Media Player. For example, instead of saying *Media Player CHIMES.WAV (stopped),* they say *Media Player CHIMES.WAV (playing),* as shown in Figure 8-8. A little box moves along the other bar to indicate how much of the clip has been played.

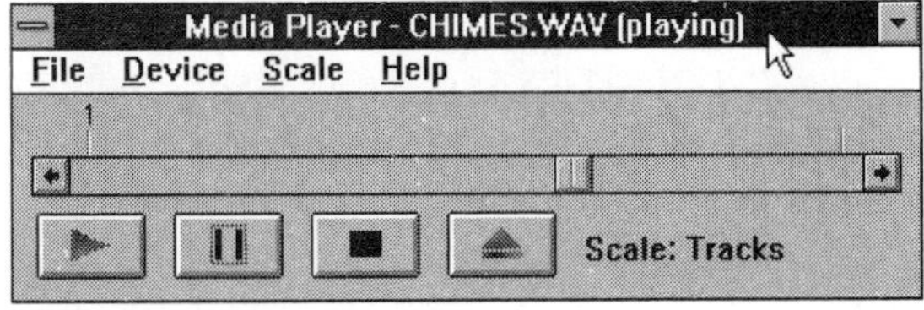

Figure 8-8: When Media Player is playing a media clip, `(playing)` appears in the title bar.

- If Media Player's title bar changes from *(stopped)* to *(playing)* and you don't hear anything, your suspicions are right: Something is wrong. To figure out why you aren't hearing anything, head for the troubleshooting section at the end of this chapter, "My .WAV Files Won't Play Right."
- The version of Media Player that comes packaged with Windows can't play .WAV files by using the little Microsoft speaker driver that is described in Chapters 3 and 7. (The updated version of Media Player, however, can push .WAV files through the Speaker driver. For a description of the updated version, see the section, "The fancy new version of Media Player," later in this chapter.)
- You can run two or more copies of Media Player at the same time. But don't get too fancy. If you try to play two MIDI or two .WAV files at the same time, an error message chastises you for being so bold.

Playing musical CDs on a computer's compact disc player

Adding a new compact disc player to a home stereo is a big hassle. You may not have enough wall outlets to go around, and figuring out which wires plug into which gizmo is a pain.

Windows makes using a compact disc player even more of a headache, unfortunately.

First, you need to set up the CD-ROM drive so it works under DOS.

Then, when the compact disc player finally works with DOS, head to Chapter 3 and install any Windows drivers for the CD-ROM drive. If you're lucky, a floppy disk came in the box.

Finally, before you can hear any music, you need to make sure that the Windows [MCI] CD Audio driver is installed. The following section describes this bothersome burden. (You only need to bother with this step *once*, thank goodness.)

MCI stands for *Music Control Interface*. It's a set of rules that programmers have to follow to make Windows play their sounds and music.

Adding the CD Audio driver to Windows

You need to hit Windows over the head before it will play music from a compact disc player. After you install the drivers that came with the CD player, as described in Chapter 3, follow these steps to make sure that the Windows [MCI] CD Audio driver is installed and ready to go:

1. **Double-click on the Control Panel icon in the Program Manager.**

   The Control Panel hops to the screen.

2. **Double-click on the Drivers icon.**

   The Drivers icon is the one with the little compact disc and cassette tape. A double-click on the icon brings the Drivers box to the screen, as shown in Figure 8-9.

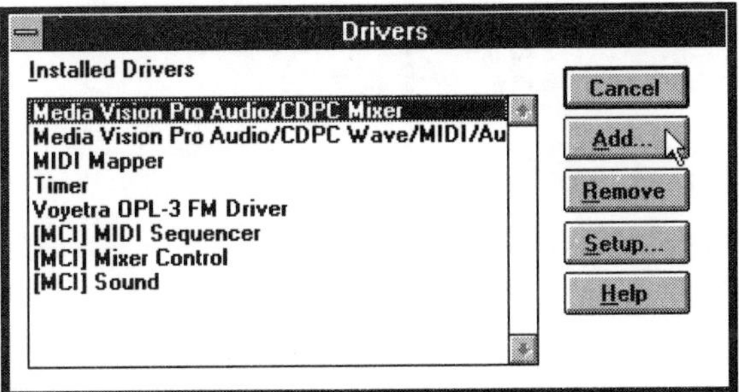

Figure 8-9: The Drivers box shows the drivers that are currently installed in Windows.

   If you see `[MCI] CD Audio` on the list, you don't need to go any further. Windows is set up to play compact discs, and you can move to the next section.

   If you don't see that driver listed, however, hop along to Step 3.

3. **Click on the Add button.**

   A list of brand names pops up, as shown in Figure 8-10. Windows comes packaged with drivers for all those brand names.

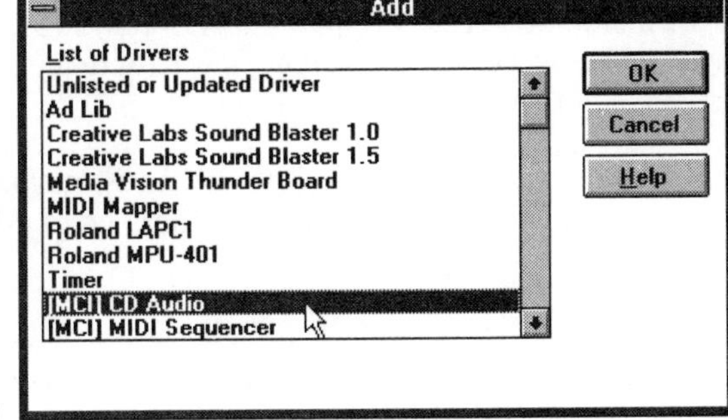

Figure 8-10: Windows comes with drivers for these gadgets.

   See the driver that's listed near the bottom of Figure 8-10? That driver is the one you want, so move to Step 4.

4. **Double-click on the [MCI] CD Audio driver.**

   If the [MCI] CD Audio driver has already been installed — but it's lost somewhere — a double-click will make Windows dredge the driver up.

Windows then asks whether you want to install the New or Current driver, as shown in Figure 8-11. Choose Current. (If that trick doesn't work, come back to this step and tell Windows to install the New one. Feel free to put an *X* in this book's margin so you can find your way back here.)

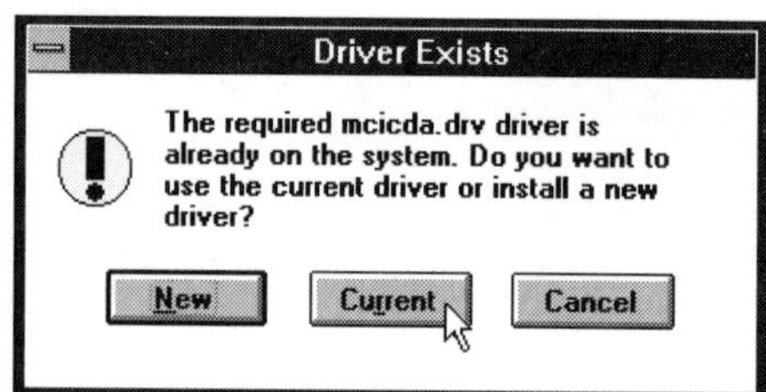

Figure 8-11: If Windows finds a CD Audio driver already installed, it asks whether you want to reuse it.

If Windows doesn't show you the box in Figure 8-11 (or if you clicked on New from that box in Figure 8-11), then pull the Windows disks out of the software box. Windows will ask you to insert one of them, probably disk #4.

When Windows asks, stick the disk in drive A, click on OK, and follow the instructions.

Windows installs the driver and asks you to reboot the computer. Close Windows the normal way — by exiting the Program Manager — and press Ctrl+Alt+Delete at the C:\> prompt.

After Windows loads up, it should be ready to play that hot new Pearl Jam CD in the compact disc player. The next section describes how to actually hear some tunes.

While you are installing Windows drivers for the CD-ROM drive, leave a compact disc sitting in the drive. Sometimes having the disc there helps Windows know what's going on.

Discs, DOS, and boring CD Data

A compact disc player is new technology. MS-DOS is old technology. So setting up a compact disc player to work under Windows can be a laborious process. Sometimes the CD-ROM drive's Setup program handles everything. At other times, the drive makes you do all the grunt work.

Either way, the CD-ROM drive probably wants two files to live in two separate places.

First, most CD-ROM drives want you to add a program called MSCDEX.EXE to the AUTOEXEC.BAT file.

Second, they usually want a driver — often a file ending in SYS — in the CONFIG.SYS file.

Those two files enable DOS to recognize a compact disc player, and getting DOS to recognize it is half the battle toward getting Windows to recognize it.

Finally, after you change the AUTOEXEC.BAT or CONFIG.SYS files, save them and reboot the computer. Doing so is the only way to make the computer notice the changes you've made.

Listening to music CDs

After you install the CD-ROM drive correctly in the computer, and its DOS drivers are in place, and its Windows drivers are in place — Whew! — the time finally arrives to listen to some tunes. Here's how:

1. **Double-click on the Media Player icon in the Program Manager.**

   Media Player rises to the surface.

2. **Put the compact disc in the compact disc player.**

   Don't forget to put the compact disc in that small, outrageously expensive plastic caddie before you slide it into the CD player. (The edge of the caddie with that little silver thing needs to slide in first. Also, a few outrageously expensive CD players don't use caddies at all.)

3. **Click on Device and choose CD Audio from the drop-down menu.**

   The Device menu drops down, as shown in Figure 8-12. Choose CD Audio to hear the compact disc.

   If CD Audio isn't listed on the Device menu, stop right now. Make sure that you've added that [MCI] CD Audio thing, a chore described in the previous section, and subsequently rebooted the computer. If you have performed these tasks and CD Audio still isn't listed under Device, throw your hands up in despair and head for the troubleshooting section near this chapter's end, "Media Player Doesn't Work!"

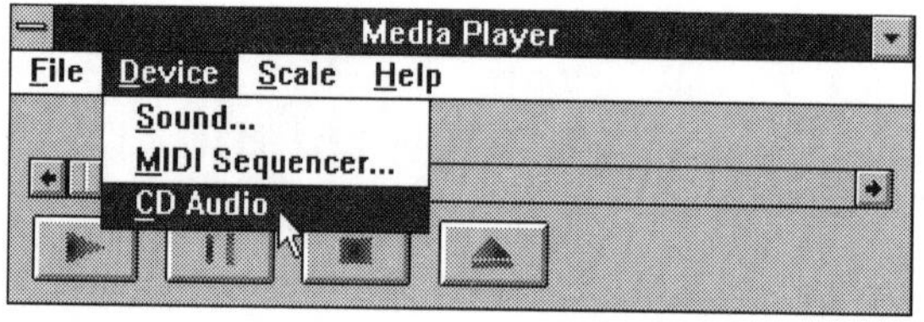

Figure 8-12: Choose CD Audio from the Device menu to play a file or sound.

4. **Press the play button to hear the sound.**

   The play button is the one on the left, with the black triangle on it, as shown in Figure 8-13. Give it a click and give your compact disc a listen.

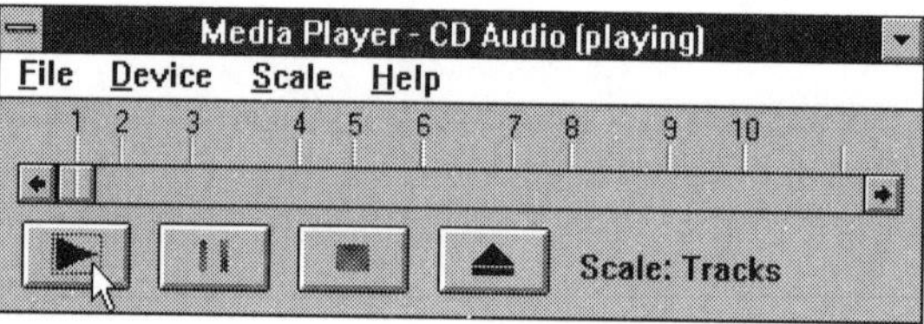

Figure 8-13: Click on the black triangle to start playing the musical compact disc.

   To pause, hit the button next to the triangle. To stop everything, click on the button with the black squarish rectangle. Finally, the upward-pointing triangle will eject the disc — if the disc player has that nifty feature. If you forget this stuff, flip back to Figure 8-6 for a refresher on what all the buttons do.

- When the sound starts to play, the words in Media Player's title bar change. For example, instead of saying *Media Player CD Audio (stopped),* it says *Media Player CD Audio (playing).* So, if you see *(playing)* but don't hear anything, head toward the end of this chapter and read the trouble-shooting section, "Media Player Doesn't Work!"
- See the ten numbers above that long horizontal bar in Figure 8-13? Those numbers stand for the number of songs — the *tracks* — on the current compact disc. For example, Figure 8-13 shows the ten tracks on Stevie Ray Vaughan's *Texas Flood* CD.
- To skip one song and play the next, drag the little box forward and drop it on the next number. (Chapter 1 covers drag-and-drop mouse manipulations.) Or, if you have the newer, fancier version of Media Player, push the fast-forward buttons, as described in Figure 8-24.

- With some CD players, Media Player's buttons don't work until you start playing the CD. You can't drag the little box forward or backward until you first punch the play button.
- If you're using the new, improved version of Media Player, pictured in Figure 8-15, head to this chapter's "The fancy new version of Media Player" section. The newer version of Media Player enables you to do even more fun stuff with compact discs.
- Don't know whether you have enough time to hear an entire CD on your lunch hour? Click on Scale and choose Time from the menu that appears. Instead of displaying the number of songs on the CD, Media Player shows the CD's length in minutes, as shown in Figure 8-14.

Figure 8-14: Media Player shows that Stevie Ray Vaughan's *Texas Flood* CD is a short but tough 38 minutes and 53 seconds long.

Watching movies (those .AVI files)

The version of Media Player that came with Windows simply can't handle movies. So Microsoft wrote a piece of software, called Video for Windows, to overhaul Media Player. Video for Windows adds new buttons, new options, and fresher gum between the seats.

The new, sleeker version of Media Player appears in Figure 8-15.

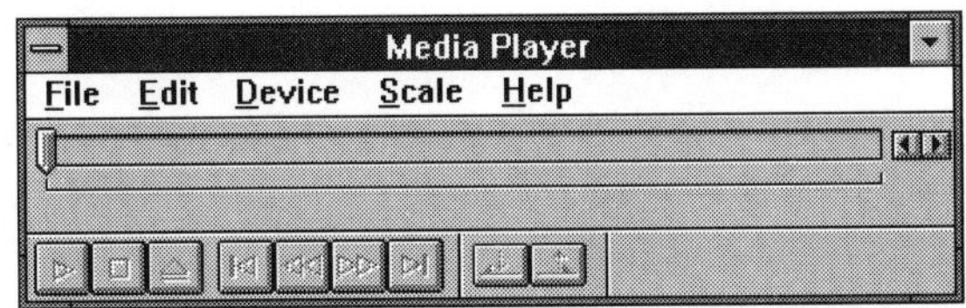

Figure 8-15: Microsoft Video for Windows updates Media Player so that it can play movies.

You don't have to buy Video for Windows in a store. Microsoft wrote a special version of Video for Windows that's up for grabs — free — on the Microsoft BBS. It's called a *run-time* version. (Chapter 7 covers that BBS stuff.)

The run-time version gives Media Player a face lift that extends to other areas. You can make CDs replay automatically, for example, or play a few songs rather than a whole CD.

To play a video, follow the bouncing ball along these steps:

1. **Install the run-time version of Microsoft Video for Windows.**

   You have to perform this step only once, thank goodness. After you install Media Player, it is ready to roll some flicks, and you can move to Step 2.

   The run-time version of Video for Windows comes packaged in a file called VFWRUN.EXE. If you have a modem, you can use Terminal to grab it off Microsoft's BBS or CompuServe. (See Chapter 7 for that merry procedure.)

   After you download VFWRUN.EXE, use the File Manager to create a directory called TRASH on the hard drive. Move VFWRUN.EXE into the TRASH directory and double-click on its filename.

   VFWRUN runs, breaking itself into bunches of smaller files. (Press F5 from within the File Manager to see those files; the File Manager is too lame to update the screen automatically.)

   Finally, double-click on the SETUP.EXE program in the TRASH directory. The program installs itself, as shown in Figure 8-16.

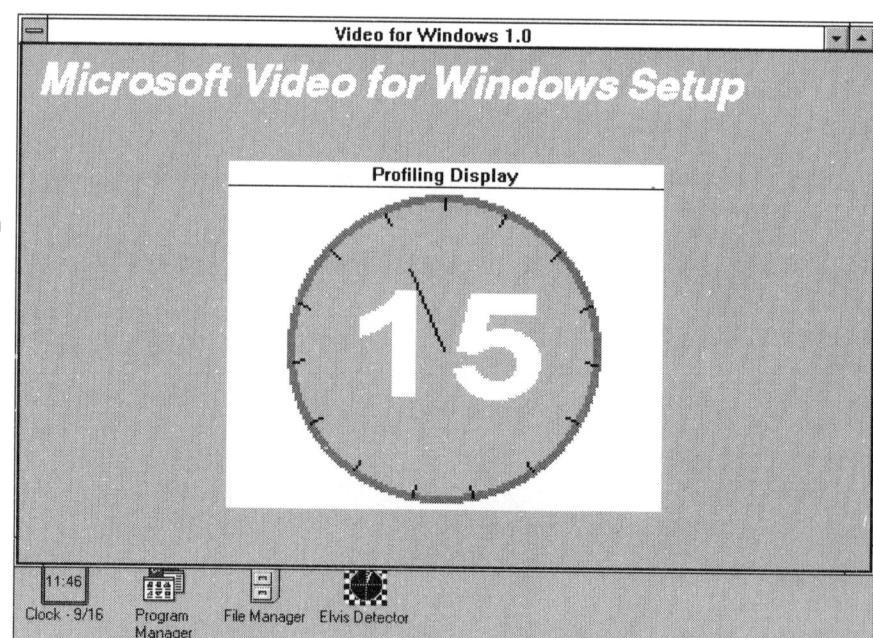

Figure 8-16: Microsoft Video for Windows tests the monitor and video card to see whether they can keep up with fast-paced movies.

Video for Windows usually sends out a box that tells you to look for a newer video driver. Head for Chapter 3 to find out about that hassle.

Finally, when the Video for Windows program finishes installing itself, delete the \TRASH directory and everything in it. (The video player has already copied all of its important files to the right place — the Windows \SYSTEM directory.)

Can't find VFWRUN.EXE anywhere and don't have a modem? Then look for Microsoft Video for Windows in your favorite software store. Sure, it'll cost you some cash, but it comes with some movies.

Checklist time: Is the run-time version of Video for Windows installed? Have you closed the program's SETUP window? Then head for Step 2.

2. **Double-click on the Media Player icon in the Program Manager.**

   The new, improved Media Player leaps to life, as shown in Figure 8-17.

Figure 8-17: The Microsoft Video for Windows version of Media Player offers more features.

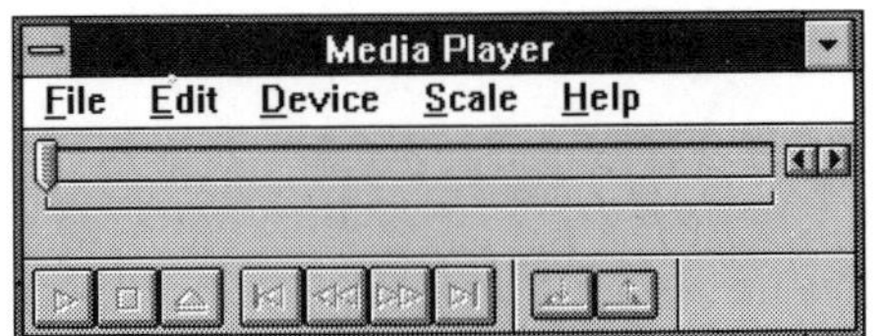

3. **Click on Device and choose Video for Windows.**

   A click on Device brings down a menu, as shown in Figure 8-18. Click on Video for Windows.

   Movies come in files that end with .AVI, so Media Player lists any .AVI files that live in the current directory. Don't see any? Then click in the Directories or Drives boxes to scout around in different parts of the hard drive.

   Windows doesn't come with any .AVI files; you have to get them from friends or download them, as described in Chapter 7. You might find some .AVI files hanging out in the same place you found the VFRUN.EXE file. Also, you'll find some .AVI files for sale at software stores.

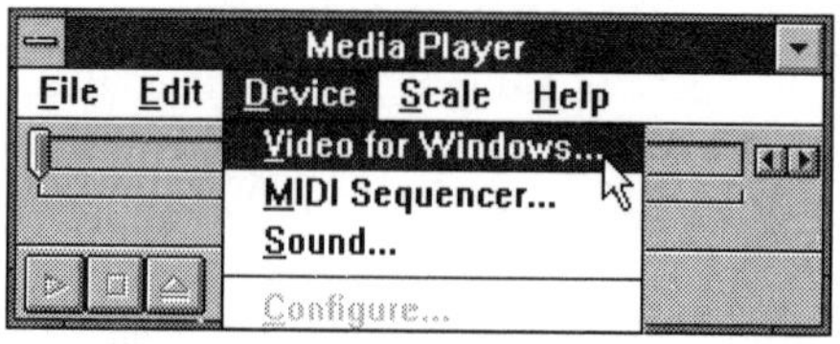

Figure 8-18: Click on Video for Windows to see a list of available movies.

4. **Double-click on the filename of the movie that you want to watch.**

   The movie rises to the screen in its own little window.

5. **Click on the play button.**

   To start the reel rolling, click on the play button — that button with the little black triangle on the left side of Media Player. The movie starts to play, as shown in Figure 8-19.

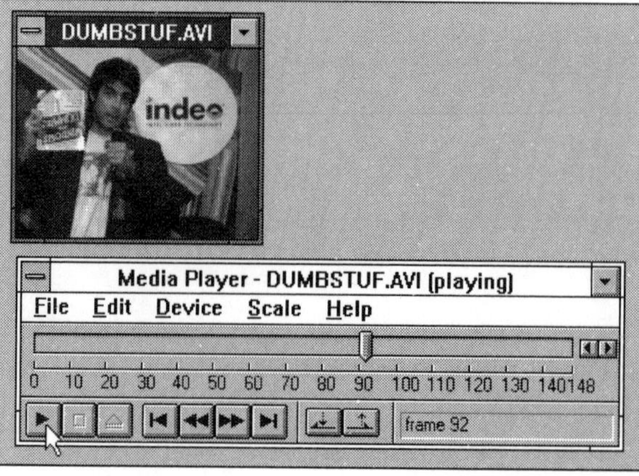

Figure 8-19: Click on the button with the little black triangle to play the movie.

Media Player starts playing the movie in a postage-stamp-size window. Because of the small size, the computer doesn't have to work as hard as it does when the picture is larger, so the movie looks better. You can enlarge the picture up to three times, as shown in Figures 8-20 through 8-23, to see how well the computer handles high-powered, thrill-packed video action.

- To make movies always start up in a certain size, check out the Configure option from Media Player's Device menu. Click on Full Screen, for example, to make movies take up the whole screen. Zoom by 2 makes the movies play twice as large as normal; pressing Ctrl+2, Ctrl+3, or Ctrl+4 will make the picture even *larger*. Just play with the buttons for a while, and you'll get the hang of it.

- Microsoft's run-time version of Video for Windows — that VFWRUN.EXE file — doesn't come with any movies, because movies are huge. A ten-second movie clip can take up 1MB of hard disk space.

Figure 8-20: Press Ctrl+2 to see movies in this size.

- Most movies contain 256 colors — usually known as *SVGA* mode. If you're using Windows in plain ol' VGA mode, movies will look grainier than Spoon-Size Shredded Wheat. If the video card can handle 256 colors, make sure that you've installed a 256-color Windows driver along with it. (Chapter 3 describes how to install drivers; Chapter 7 shows how to find drivers.)
- You need a sound card to hear any sound with movie clips; Microsoft's Speaker driver just doesn't cut it.

Figure 8-21: Press Ctrl+3 to see movies in this size.

- Movies come stored in files that end in .AVI. *AVI* stands for *Audio Video Interleaved*, a boring term that means the file contains both sound and video.

Figure 8-22: Press Ctrl+4 to see movies in this size.

Figure 8-23: Press Ctrl+1 to see the pictures in this, normal size

- For some real fun, start playing a movie and then minimize its window. The movie will still play, but from a tiny, icon-sized window at the bottom of the screen. Ho!

The fancy new version of Media Player

When you update Media Player to run videos, you also update Media Player's ability to play sounds. Adding a compact disc player adds a few more buttons and options. They're all described in the next two sections.

The new Media Player buttons

Don't know what all those fancy new little buttons do? Check out Figure 8-24 for all the answers.

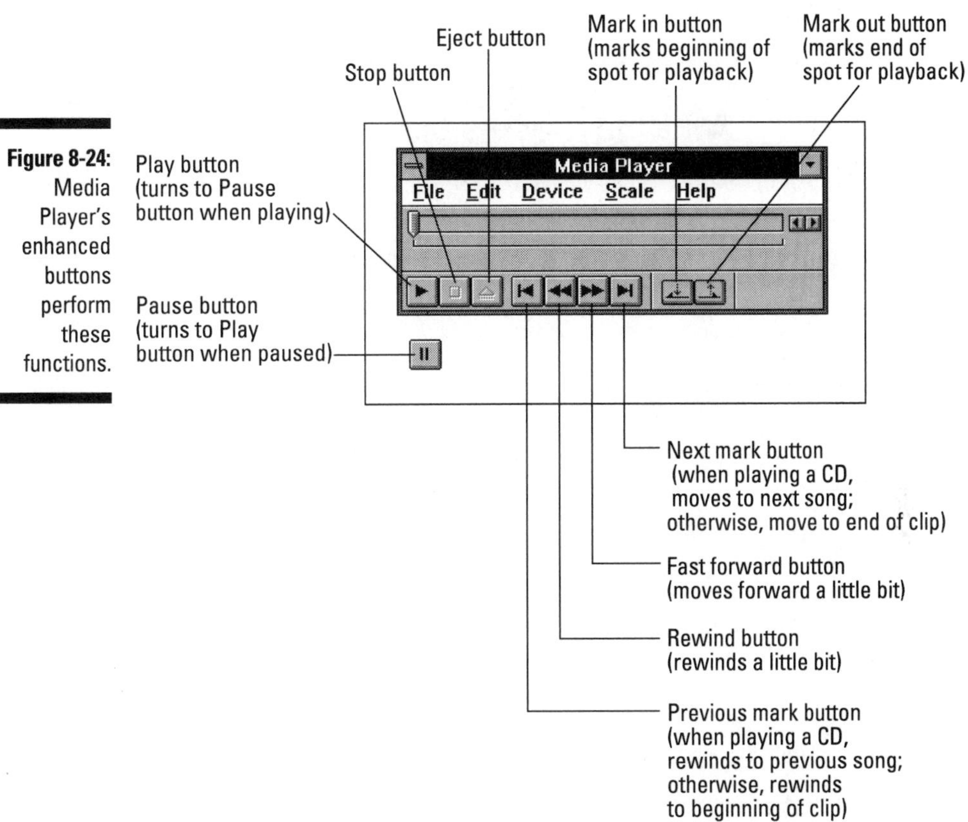

Figure 8-24: Media Player's enhanced buttons perform these functions.

- The improved, cholesterol-free version of Media Player has a lot of new buttons. But if they don't all show up, grab the side of Media Player's window and drag it out a few inches. Media Player swallows some of its buttons when it doesn't have enough room to display them.
- What's the difference between the stop and pause buttons? Not much — they both make Media Player stop what it's currently doing. If you select Media Player's Auto Rewind button (under Options, found on the Edit menu), pressing the stop button will stop the clip and rewind it. Otherwise, pause and stop are about the same.
- A click on the fast-forward or rewind buttons moves the clip about 10 percent of its length. So, if you start at one end, five clicks moves the clip to the half-way point. (At least, that's what Microsoft says Media Player is supposed to do. That maneuver doesn't work on my CD-ROM player.)

- With some CD players, you have to push the play button before any of the other buttons will have an effect. After the CD is playing, you can use the buttons to move from track to track or rewind.

Making movies play better

Movies don't always play back smoothly. If the video card isn't fast enough and expensive enough to keep up the fast pace, the movie looks jerky. The problem is that Media Player skips part of the movie in order to keep up with the sound track. Here are a few tips for smoother sailing when you're watching movies:

- Be sure to use the latest drivers for the video card, as described in Chapter 3. If that doesn't work, buy an accelerated video card. If that doesn't work, buy a faster computer.
- Computers take longer to grab files from a compact disc than from a hard drive. Try copying movies from the compact disc to the hard drive. Or buy a faster, double-speed compact disc player.
- The Defrag program that comes with DOS 6 can organize the hard drive so that Media Player can grab the movies a little more quickly. Head for Chapter 6 to learn how to Defrag.
- Movies sometimes play a little faster if you turn off the Don't buffer offscreen option. (That option hides on the Configure menu that hides on Media Player's Device menu.)
- Movies play back at their fastest when they are either full-screen (not contained in a window at all) or in the smallest possible window.
- If the sound turns on and off while the movie plays, perhaps the video card isn't fast enough to display the picture. Media Player plays some sound, turns it off until the video catches up, and turns it on again. To keep the sound from going off, head for the Configure option on the Device menu. Then click on Skip video frames if behind until a check mark appears next to it.

The new Media Player options

The biggest change in the new, upgraded version of Media Player is in the addition of the Edit command to the menu bar at the top of Media Player. Here's what to expect from the Edit menu's commands:

Copy object: Click here to copy whatever you're playing into the Windows clipboard. You can paste a movie, sound, or song into Write, for example, and play it back between paragraphs. Fun!

Options: The two important options are Auto Rewind — which makes Media Player automatically jump back to the beginning of a clip — and Auto Repeat — which not only rewinds, but starts playing the clip again and again and again (press Esc to shut it up). The OLE Object stuff, listed near the bottom, is described in the boring technical box.

Selection: Got a favorite song on the CD? Type that song's track number in the From box and type the next song's track number in the To box. Move to the beginning of the CD, hold down Alt, and press the play button. The CD will jump to the song and begin playing it.

Plus, if you select the Auto Repeat button, described earlier, Media Player plays the same song, over and over. Unfortunately, you can select only *consecutive* portions of a compact disc or video clip. You can't make it play songs 5 and 7 and skip over that dreary ballad on track 6.

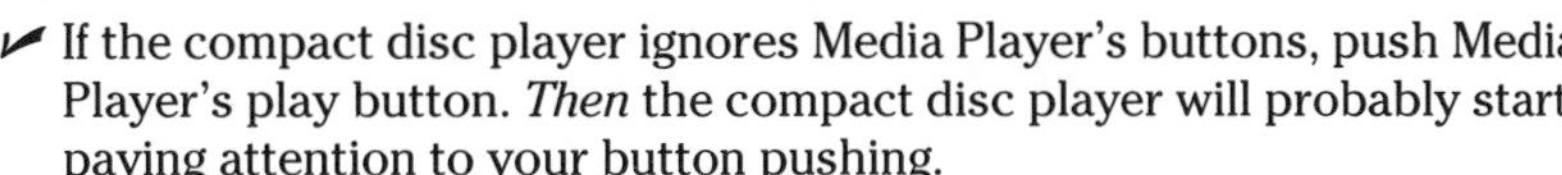

- If the compact disc player ignores Media Player's buttons, push Media Player's play button. *Then* the compact disc player will probably start paying attention to your button pushing.

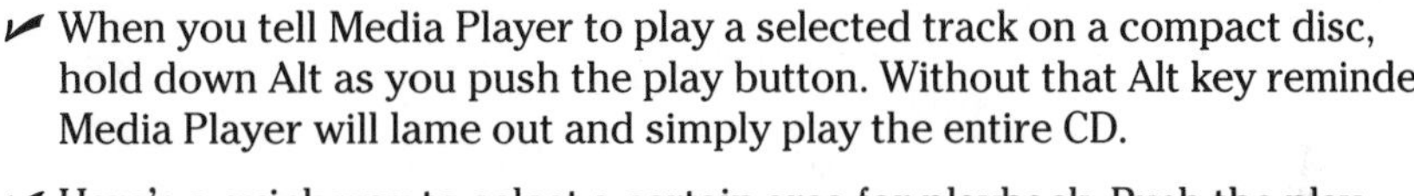

- When you tell Media Player to play a selected track on a compact disc, hold down Alt as you push the play button. Without that Alt key reminder, Media Player will lame out and simply play the entire CD.

- Here's a quick way to select a certain area for playback. Push the play button and drag the little box on the bar to the part of the clip that you want to play. Then hold down Shift and drag the little box to where you want Media Player to stop. Those actions quickly mark the area for playback.

- Finally, here's one technical tip: If something goes afoul when you're playing an embedded movie, double-click on the movie's title bar. If you're lucky, Media Player will pop to the surface, complete with all its buttons, for immediate fine tuning.

Sound Recorder

Windows comes with some decent sounds, but only four of them. After a while, those same old dings and chimes can grow as tiresome as a friend's answering machine message that never changes.

When you're tired of listening to the same old sounds, grab a microphone, grab the Windows Sound Recorder, and start recording your own sounds. In fact, Sound Recorder can add special effects to sounds that you've already recorded, such as adding a little *echo* to make your burp sound as if you made it in a huge, empty warehouse.

Also, Sound Recorder isn't limited to voices. You can grab tidbits from a CD player, as well.

Despite its name, Sound Recorder can play sounds as well as record them. In fact, if you're using Microsoft's Speaker driver, using Sound Recorder is the only way to hear sounds. Media Player doesn't work with Microsoft's Speaker driver.

Say OLE, sit back down, and fall asleep

Despite its terrible name, Object Linking and Embedding (OLE) is a novel little toy that's revitalizing a ho-hum computer task.

For years, people have copied words from one document and pasted them into another. Known as *cut-and-paste*, it's also called *boring*.

OLE, however, finally adds some new dazzle. Instead of just moving words around, people can paste sounds, movies, and songs into documents.

For example, load your favorite media clip into Media Player and then choose Copy Object from its Edit menu. That option sends the media clip to the Clipboard. (Call up the Clipboard Viewer and peek inside, if you're skeptical.)

Next, call up Windows Cardfile, Write, or any other fancy Windows program and choose Paste. The Media Player clip will appear in the program. If you copied a movie, you see its first frame; if you copied a sound, you see the Sound Recorder icon. (Nobody could say what a sound looks like.)

Now, while in Cardfile, Write, or wherever you pasted the clip, double-click on the pasted movie or the Media Player icon and watch as the clip starts playing. Fun!

Media Player enables you to control how that clip looks when you play it. Click on Options from Media Player's Edit menu to choose from these OLE Object choices:

Caption: Want to create a title that sits beneath the little clip when it's embedded somewhere? Click on Captions and type the new title in the Captions box. Oh, here's some terrific news: The title can be as long as you want, and you can put spaces between the letters. None of that 8-character filename stuff here. (If you don't type anything, however, Media Player uses the file's name for a title.)

Border around object: If you want a thin black line for a picture frame around the clip, click here. Don't like frames? Leave this box blank.

Play in client document: When you double-click on a media clip that you've embedded somewhere, Media Player usually rises to the screen and begins playing it. If you check this box, however, Media Player doesn't pop up. The movie or sound simply comes to life and starts playing, right inside the program where you pasted it.

Control Bar on playback: If you click in this box, the clip pops up in a little window when you play it back. What's new? The new window doesn't look like Media Player. It simply shows the bar with the little box that you can use to skip around in the clip. You have control while the clip is playing, without having to see the complete Media Player.

Dither to VGA colors: Most little movies are filled with 256 dazzling colors in a format known as SVGA. Click in this Phyllis Dither box to make an embedded movie use only 16 colors when it sits embedded in a document. When you play the movie, it returns to its normal 256 colors.

Recording .WAV sounds

Before you can set up your computerized recording studio, you need a sound card; there's no getting around it. To record voices or sound effects, you need a microphone as well. (You can skip the mike if you just want to record from CDs on a CD-ROM drive.)

Sound card installed? Microphone plugged in? Then here's how to make Sound Recorder capture your magic Karaoke moments:

1. **Double-click on Sound Recorder's icon in the Program Manager.**

   The Sound Recorder icon looks like a little microphone. A double-click brings Sound Recorder to the screen, as shown in Figure 8-25.

Figure 8-25: The Sound Recorder can record sounds and add special effects as well.

2. **Prepare to record the sound.**

   If you're recording something with a microphone, make sure that the microphone is plugged into the sound card's microphone jack.

   Or, if you're recording something from a compact disc, make sure that the CD is loaded and ready to play.

   Some sound cards, such as those in MediaVision's ProAudio Spectrum series, come with *mixer* programs. You can use the mixer programs to record from the microphone, CD player, stereo, or synthesizer, or from several of them at the same time. Rummage through the disks that came with the sound card; a mixer comes in handy when you want to route different sounds to Sound Recorder.

3. **Click on the Sound Recorder button that has a picture of a microphone on it.**

   Sound Recorder starts to record any incoming sounds, and it stores them temporarily in the computer's memory.

4. Start making the sound that you want to record.

Start making noise. Talk into the microphone or play the music CD. If everything is hooked up right, the little green line inside Sound Recorder begins to quiver, reflecting the incoming sound (see Figure 8-26). The bigger the quiver, the louder the sound.

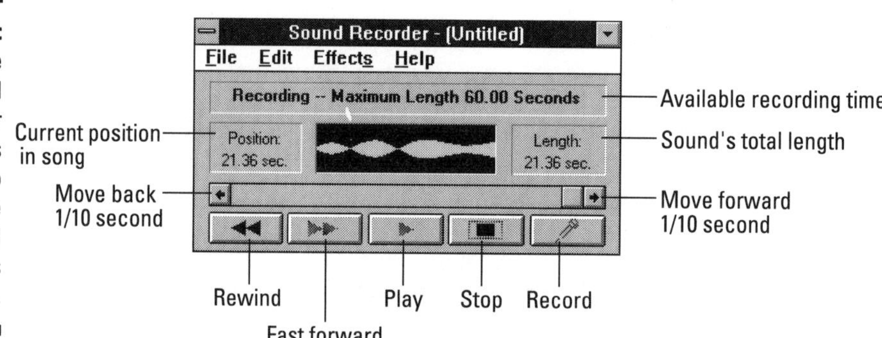

Figure 8-26: The little line in Sound Recorder changes shape to show the sound waves it's recording.

In Figure 8-26, see where Sound Recorder says `Maximum Length 60.00 Seconds`? That message tells you how many seconds of sound that Sound Recorder can capture. The more memory that the computer has, the more seconds of recording time that Sound Recorder gives you.

Don't record any sounds for too long, though — they consume an incredibly large amount of disk space. In fact, when you're through recording the sound, jump to Step 5 as soon as possible.

If the little wavy green line gets too wavy and starts bumping into the top or bottom edges of its little window, the sound is too loud. To avoid distortion, turn down the volume.

5. Click on the button with the black square on it to stop recording.

A click on the button with the black square on it, shown in Figure 8-26, makes Sound Recorder stop recording new sounds.

6. Click the rewind button to rewind.

The rewind button has two black triangles that face left.

7. Click the button with the single black triangle to hear the recording.

Does it sound OK? Congratulations. But if the recording doesn't sound perfect, erase it. Just choose New from Sound Recorder's File menu to wipe the slate clean for a new recording. Jump back to Step 2 to make any necessary adjustments and try again.

When the recording sounds perfect — or just needs a little editing — move on to Step 8.

8. **Choose Save from the File menu and save the sound to a file.**

   Type a name for the file, just as if you were saving a file in a word processor. Sound files add up quickly, though; without a lot of room on the hard disk, you won't have enough space to save a particularly long, drawn-out wail.

   Sound Recorder lames out when you save files. You need to type in the .WAV extension yourself. Unlike most other Windows programs, Sound Recorder doesn't add an extension automatically.

   You're done — unless you have some empty spots that you want to edit out of the recording. If so, head for the Technical Sound Engineer's box.

Technical Sound Engineer's stuff

It's hard to click Sound Recorder's start and stop buttons at exactly the right time. You usually have some blank moments before the sound begins and after it ends.

To edit them out, first save the file. Then start editing out the blank spots, as follows:

1. **Locate where the sound begins.**

   Listen to the sound again and watch the quivering line. The sound starts when the green line first starts to quiver. When you locate the spot right before where the sound begins, write down the number that's listed under Position.

   Then rewind the sound. Next, click the right-pointing arrow, one click at a time, until you position yourself immediately before the spot where the sound starts. Listen to the sound a few times until you're sure that you're at the right place.

2. **Click on Delete Before Current Position from Sound Recorder's Edit menu.**

   Sound Recorder asks whether you're sure that you want to delete that part of the sound. If you're sure, click on OK, and Sound Recorder will snip out that blank spot before the place where the sound starts.

3. **Locate where the sound ends.**

   Just as before, position Sound Recorder's little bar at the spot where your sound has ended and nothing but empty sound remains.

4. **Click on Delete After Current Position from Sound Recorder's Edit menu.**

   Again, click on the OK button if you're sure that you're at the right place.

5. **Rewind and listen to the edited sound.**

   Is it perfect? Then save it. If it's not perfect, ditch it by choosing Revert from the File menu. Or call up the sound file that you started with and head back to Step 1. Sound editing usually takes a few tries before everything sounds perfect.

Editing out blank spots always shrinks the file's disk size. Even recorded silence takes up a lot of disk space, for some reason.

- Sound Recorder can add special effects to recorded sounds. Make sure that you've saved the file and then experiment with the goodies in the Effects menu. You can change the sound's volume and speed, add echo, or play the sound backward.

- Record strategic snippets of Beatles albums, make Sound Recorder play them backward, and decide for yourself whether Paul is Dead.
- To copy a sound to the Clipboard, choose Copy from Sound Recorder's Edit menu. Then paste your belch into a corporate memo that you created in Write (or almost any other word processor). When the chairman of the board of directors clicks on the Sound Recorder icon near your signature, the whole board will hear your signature sound.
- Sound Recorder's Edit menu enables you to insert other sounds and mix them with the current sound. The Insert File command can add one sound after another. You can insert a splash sound after a boom sound to simulate the sound that a pirate ship makes when it's firing at the natives. The Mix File command mixes the two sounds together. You can make the boom and the splash happen at the same time, as if the pirate ship blew up.

- Add an effect that sounds just awful? Click on Revert from Sound Recorder's File menu to get rid of it and bring the sound back to the way it was.
- Before you edit a newly recorded sound, make sure that you save it to a file. Taking that precaution is the safest way to make sure that you can retrieve the original sound if the editing commands mess it up beyond recognition.
- The little Sound Recorder window shows $\frac{1}{10}$ second of the current sound. Click the right-pointing arrow, shown in Figure 8-27, to view the next $\frac{1}{10}$ second; click the left-pointing arrow to view the previous $\frac{1}{10}$ second.

- .WAV files can eat up ten times as much disk space as .MID files. So recording a .MID file as a .WAV file usually isn't very practical. To save hard disk space, keep .MID files stored as .MID files, not as .WAV files.

Playing .WAV sounds

Both Sound Recorder and Media Player can play recorded sounds — those .WAV file things. If you've installed Microsoft's Speaker driver, as described in Chapter 3, Sound Recorder can play sounds even if you don't have a sound card. Media Player, on the other hand, requires a sound card before it can play any sounds.

Playing sounds in Sound Recorder is pretty simple:

1. **Double-click on the WAV file's name in the File Manager.**

   Sound Recorder hops to the screen.

2. **Click on Sound Recorder's play button.**

   The play button is the little button with the triangle on it. Give it a click, and the sound will start playing.

   Or, after opening Sound Recorder, choose Open from Sound Recorder's File menu and double-click on the .WAV file. Click the Play button and listen to an earful.

- Chapter 3 is full of tips on what to do with sound files after you've recorded them. It also explains how to get rid of the ones you're sick of. (After all, how many times can you listen to a Beavis and Butthead chortle every time you exit the Program Manager?)

- One quick way to hear .WAV files is to minimize Sound Recorder to an icon at the bottom of the screen. Then drag .WAV files from the File Manager and drop them onto the Sound Recorder. You'll hear them instantly. (Chapter 1 covers this drag and drop stuff.)

MIDI Mapper Madness

Rich people argue over how long a fine red wine should be decanted — if at all. Just as the rich folks chew their cigars and ponder, technoid computer musicians argue over how the computer world should store its music files.

Most electrified musicians use *MIDI* — the Musical Instrument Digital Interface, but a problem rears its ugly head when they have to decide which parts of the MIDI standard to use. Different MIDI gadgets pick and choose different bits of the MIDI standard.

The Windows MIDI Mapper solves this problem. Just as a printer driver tells Windows how to deal with a particular printer, MIDI Mapper tells Windows how to treat a particular MIDI gadget.

If a MIDI song's trombones sound like cymbals, or vice versa, the time has come to give MIDI Mapper a few tweaks. The sound card's installation program may not have kicked MIDI Mapper in the right spots.

To call up MIDI Mapper, follow these steps:

1. **From the Program Manager, double-click on the Control Panel icon.**

Control Panel

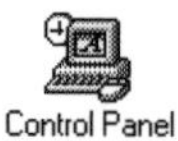

The Control Panel pops up, as shown in Figure 8-27, complete with the MIDI Mapper icon.

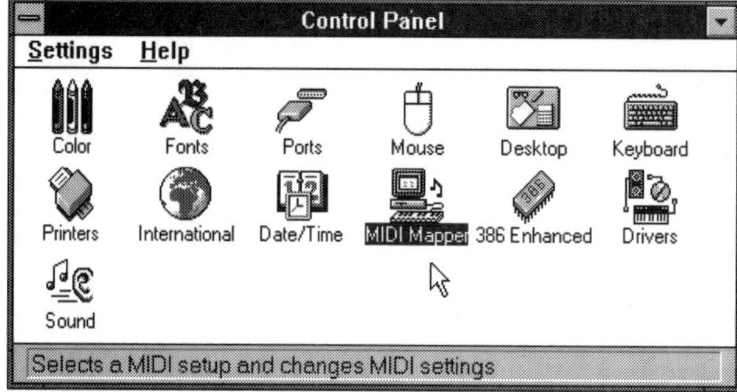

Figure 8-27: When Windows MIDI drivers are installed correctly, MIDI Mapper appears in the Control Panel.

2. **Double-click on the MIDI Mapper icon.**

MIDI Mapper

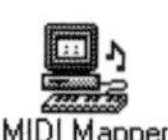

The MIDI Mapper rises to the occasion, as shown in Figure 8-28.

Look in the Name box. Is your sound card or synthesizer listed? Great; you're done. If it's not listed, grab the manual to see which sound card or synthesizer it emulates.

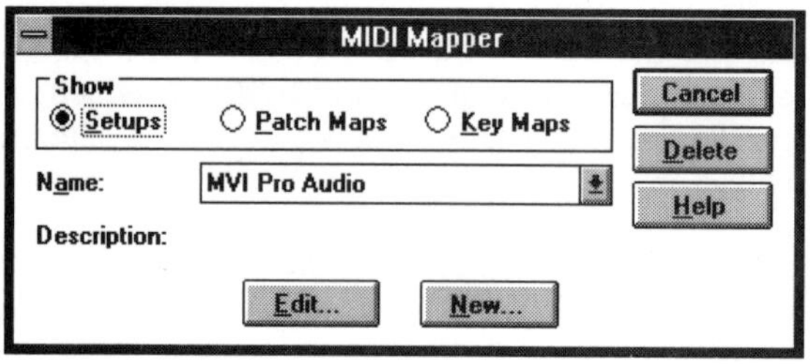

Figure 8-28: MIDI Mapper enables you to synchronize Windows with your particular sound card.

3. **Choose your type of MIDI gadget in the Name box.**

   After you click on the MIDI Mapper's Name box, a list like the one in Figure 8-29 drops down. See the name of your gadget or the one it emulates? Then click on it. MIDI Mapper will use that gadget's rules when you play MIDI files.

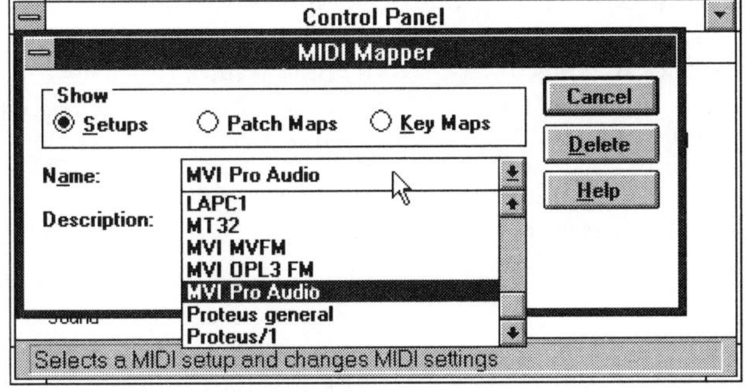

Figure 8-29: Click on the name of your MIDI gadget or the gadget it emulates.

4. **Click the Close button.**

   MIDI Mapper heads back to its closet, but it remembers which gadget your computer is using.

Unfortunately, different MIDI songs use different parts of the MIDI format. Even when a sound card or synthesizer is hooked up perfectly, certain MIDI songs may still sound weird when you play them under Windows.

Welcome to cutting-edge computer music technology.

- If the MIDI Mapper icon doesn't even show up in the Control Panel, the sound card's drivers probably aren't installed correctly. Better head for Chapter 3.
- When you first install many of the newer sound cards, they automatically tweak MIDI Mapper to add their own special settings, thank goodness. That feature can save you a lot of grief.
- The installation program of some sound cards adds three choices to MIDI Mapper: Basic, Extended, and All. Try choosing the Basic option, first. If CANYON.MID plays OK, you're done. If not, try the other options.
- Even after you understand how MIDI Mapper works, MIDI Mapper doesn't always work with every song. It requires a lot of time and fiddling, kind of like painting a seascape with Magic Markers.
- In fact, you may find yourself constantly switching between different MIDI Mapper settings in order to hear different MIDI songs. An especially boring technical box that's nearby tackles the reason for these horrendously complicated shenanigans.

- When you connect a keyboard or synthesizer to a sound card, the MIDI OUT or MIDI THRU cables of one MIDI gadget always connect to the MIDI IN port of the other MIDI gadget. (You can ignore the MIDI THRU stuff altogether unless you're connecting two or more MIDI gadgets to a sound card.)

- If a MIDI file sounds *almost* right on an Ad Lib-compatible sound card, try something called *disabling Channel 10*: Open MIDI Mapper from the Control Panel, click on Setups, and click on the Edit button. Then, in the row for channel 10, click in the Active column until the *X* disappears. Click on OK to save the changes, and click on Close to get rid of the window. That Band-Aid sometimes fixes the problem.
- When certain songs still don't sound right, try switching to some of the other Name settings that are listed under MIDI Mapper. Table 8-2 offers some clues on what to choose.

Media Player Doesn't Work!

Because MIDI is such a complicated mess of a concept, and because Windows is so picky about its formats, you'll probably happen across the box in Figure 8-30.

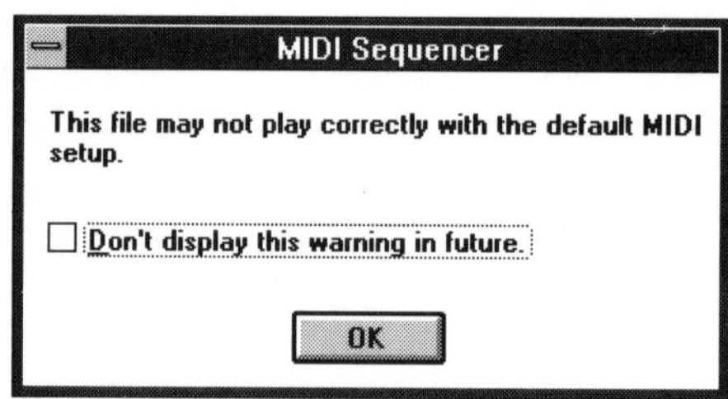

Figure 8-30: This message merely means that you're playing a file that may not meet the strict Windows MIDI guidelines.

The message doesn't necessarily mean that the song won't play. It just means that the file doesn't have a little message inside it that says that the file is up to Microsoft's standards. The file may still sound fine — or it may sound terrible. The only way to know for sure is to play it.

If you don't like that message, click in the Don't display this warning in future box. Or just ignore the the message completely. It's one of the least critical decisions you have to make in Windows.

Table 8-2 MIDI Options for Different Sound Cards

This MIDI Mapper option . . .	*usually works for these gizmos*
Ad Lib	Choose this option for the original AdLib sound card (not the newer AdLib Gold sound card). This setting sends MIDI channels 13 – 16 to the AdLib sound card.
Ad Lib general	If the plain AdLib sounds weird, try this setting. Here, all 16 MIDI channels head for the AdLib card; however, channels 10 and 16 are swapped because AdLib was built to use channel 16 for percussion, but other folks put percussion on channel 10.
Extended MIDI	This option usually works for a synthesizer that is hooked up to an early Sound Blaster, MediaVision's Thunderboard, or many other inexpensive sound cards. This setting routes MIDI channels 1 – 10 to the sound card.
General MIDI	Choose this setting if Extended MIDI sounds weird. This option routes all 16 of the MIDI channels to the sound card.
LAPC1	Roland's LAPC-1, one of the more expensive-sounding cards, uses this setting. Here, channels 1 – 8 and channel 10 head for the LAPC-1 card.
MT32	Choose this setting if you have a Roland MT-32 hooked up to the MIDI OUT port of the sound card. Channels 1 – 8 and Channel 10 head for the sound card, where they're piped out its MIDI-OUT port (if you bought that extra MIDI box, that is).
Proteus/1	Choose this option if the sound card's MIDI OUT port heads for the E-mu Systems Proteus/1 sound module. This setting sends channels 1 – 10 through a sound card's OUT port for the Proteus/1. It doesn't work for the Proteus/2 or Proteus/3 modules, however.
Proteus General	Give this setting a shot if Proteus/1 doesn't work right. It's the same as Proteus/1, except that all 16 channels head out the SoundBlaster-compatible card's MIDI OUT port.

MIDI Channel Surfing

MIDI works kind of like a cheap TV set that was built before the cable era. One of MIDI's many problems is that it can handle only 16 channels.

Basically, MIDI assigns a number to each of its instrument sounds—known primarily as *patches.* For example, an electric guitar sound could be one patch; a French Horn or Glockenspiel patch would get their own number, as well. Each of the 16 channels plays a different patch. For example, a MIDI file could say to play Instrument #89 on Channel 3.

Unfortunately, different synthesizer/sound-card manufacturers assigned different patch numbers to their instruments. So, if a friend wrote a piano solo, stored it as a MIDI file, and gave it to you, your brand of sound card may play it back as a bagpipe.

After hearing one bagpipe solo too many, the industry wised up and finally gave each instrument its own number. This new General MIDI standard worked fine for the long hairs with expensive synthesizers. But 16 channels of musical information was still a little over the heads of the computer industry's cheap sound cards.

So, to try to please both the musicians and the computer crowd, Microsoft broke General MIDI's 16-channel standard into two pieces — Basic and Extended.

Basic: Designed for most inexpensive computer sound cards, Basic sends its MIDI information on channels 13 through 16 — with channel 16 containing all the percussion. The Basic cards should ignore channels 1-12. AdLib, Sound Blaster, Sound Blaster Pro, and Pro Audio Spectrum are all Basic sound cards; so are most of their clones.

Extended: This setting tells the sound card to listen to anything that comes through on channels 1 through 9, with channel 10 used for percussion. The Roland MT-32/LAPC, Roland Sound Canvas series (including the SCC-1), Turtle Beach's MultiSound card, and a Sound Blaster 16 ASP with the Wave Blaster add-on are all considered Extended gadgets.

Here's the point to all this rambling: Microsoft wants composers to write MIDI files that can play on Basic and Extended MIDI gizmos. So musicians are supposed to put two versions of a song in one MIDI file. One version — the Basic one — should live on channels 13 through 16, and the Extended version should live on channels 1 through 10.

Most MIDI files, however, aren't written Microsoft's way. In fact, some MIDI files don't even use the same instrument numbers that Windows expects. So many MIDI files sound weird unless you fiddle with MIDI Mapper.

Very few people who read this book care about bagpipe solos, but those of you who do can find much more of this ugly MIDI detritus living in the book *Multimedia For Dummies.* It's coming right around the bend.

If Media Player is messing up in some other way, check out this list of cheap fixes:

- Check the volume. Some sound cards have a little rotary knob on the back, and you need to wiggle your fingers through the octopus of cables in the back of the computer in order to reach the knob. Other cards make you push certain keyboard combinations to control the volume. You may have to pull out the manual for this one.

- Does the sound card work while you're in DOS? Run any Setup or configuration programs that came with the sound card. Sometimes CD-ROM drives, scanners, fax cards, and other goodies argue with the sound card for the computer's attention. If the computer freezes when you try to play a sound, another part of the computer is probably arguing with the sound card.
- Are the Windows drivers installed correctly? Check out the driver's sections in this chapter and in Chapter 3.
- Did you list new drivers in the computer's AUTOEXEC.BAT or CONFIG.SYS files and then rush back to Windows to see whether Media Player works? It won't work until you reboot the computer. Shut down the Program Manager, reboot the computer, and then load Windows and Media Player.
- Did you plug speakers into the sound card? That sound has to come from somewhere. . . . (And is the speaker cord plugged firmly into its jack on the sound card?)
- Is the MIDI Mapper set up correctly for the particular sound card or device? Better go back to the "MIDI Mapper Madness" section. It's just before this one.
- For some reason, Norton Desktop for Windows 1.0 and MIDI files don't get along. Give Peter Norton a tap on his pink-shirted shoulder by asking Symantec for an update to his program.

My .WAV Files Won't Play Right!

When .WAV files aren't working, look at this checklist for things to fix:

- If the sound card isn't playing at all, check the volume, cables, speaker, and installation. If the card doesn't work under DOS, it won't work under Windows.
- Windows uses .WAV files; some DOS sound cards use a .VOC file — or something with an even weirder name. Sound Recorder and Media Player can't handle anything but .WAV files. And no, you can't just rename that BEAVIS.VOC file to BEAVIS.WAV and play it. It doesn't work.
- Sound Recorder can play stereo sounds, but it can't record them in stereo. Most stereo sound cards come with their own recording programs so that you can record that rocket as it whoooshes from left to right.
- Sound Recorder won't record any sounds until you have a sound card. Microsoft's PC Speaker driver doesn't cut it.

Bitter MIDIMAP.CFG file juggling

Windows stores all its settings for the computer's MIDI gadgets in a file called MIDIMAP.CFG. If that file is lost, Windows will be lost the next time you tell it to play a MIDI file.

So, if you know that a MIDI device is installed correctly, yet Windows shoots you a message like the one in the following figure, stop. If you have a backup copy of the MIDIMAP.CFG file, copy it to the Windows SYSTEM directory pronto.

No backup copy? Then follow these steps to retrieve a fresh copy of the MIDIMAP.CFG file from the Windows floppy disks.

1. **If you're using the 1.44MB disks, place Windows Disk #4 in the floppy drive. Using the larger, 1.2MB disks? Then place Windows Disk #6 in the floppy drive.**

   Be sure to close the latch to keep the disk inside.

2. **Type one of the following lines at the DOS prompt:**

   If the floppy disk is in drive A, type this line:

   ```
   C:\> expand a:\midimap.cf_
   c:\windows\system\midimap.cfg
   ```

   Or, if the floppy disk is in drive B, type this line:

   ```
   C:\> expand b:\midimap.cf_
   c:\windows\system\midimap.cfg
   ```

Windows copies a fresh version of MIDIMAP.CFG to the Windows SYSTEM directory, making things work better. You may still need to make a few tweaks.

You may need to rerun any installation programs that came with the sound card or synthesizer, as well. Then, when everything is finally working right, put a backup copy of the MIDIMAP.CFG file onto a floppy disk for safekeeping.

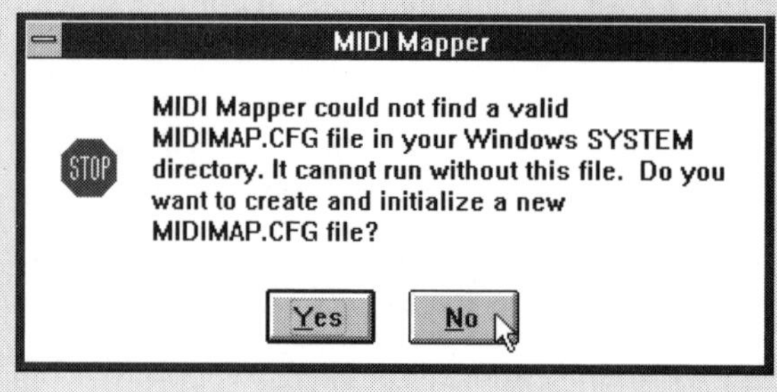

Bizarre Multimedia Words

Here's what some of those weird multimedia buzzwords are supposed to mean. Use caution when murmuring them in crowded elevators.

16-bit: The newer, 16-bit sound cards can measure a sound's variations to 65,536 different levels. That capability means that the card's sound is almost as good as a compact disc.

8-bit: The older, 8-bit sound cards divvy up a sound's waves to only 256 different variations — kind of like using a huge spoon to measure sugar for a cup of coffee. An 8-bit card sounds about as good as a voice over the telephone.

AdLib: One of the first popular sound cards, AdLib merely plays back synthesized music — it can't record or play back *real* sounds. Most sound cards are now *AdLib compatible*, which means that they can play music written for the AdLib card.

AVI: Short for *Audio Video Interleaved,* AVI is video-playing software for IBM-compatible PCs. (It competes with Macintosh's QuickTime movie player.)

Digital or **Waveform:** A sound that has been converted into numbers so that a computer can play it.

FM: Short for *Frequency Modulation,* FM is the technology that's used to create instrument sounds from most AdLib-compatible sound cards.

MCI: Short for *Media Control Interface,* MCI helps programmers write multimedia programs under Windows.

MIDI: It's short for *Musical Instrument Digital Interface*, but most people try to forget that right away.

OEMSETUP.INF: A certain file that's tossed onto a diskful of drivers. The OEMSETUP.INF file lists the names of the drivers on the disk, as well as what Windows should do with them. Usually, OEMSETUP.INF tells Windows how to change its WIN.INI file. (Chapter 15 tackles more INI file tedium.)

ProAudio Spectrum: The first ProAudio Spectrum mimicked the AdLib, but it wasn't SoundBlaster compatible. Later versions added compatibility and 16-bit quality.

Roland MPU 401: A popular sound card among musicians, it connects a computer to a MIDI keyboard, synthesizer, or sound module.

Run-time version: A version of a program that enables you to play other programs, but not create them. For example, you can use Microsoft's run-time version of Video for Windows to play movies, but not create them.

Sampling: How closely the computer pays attention to the sound. The higher the sampling rate, the more attention the computer's paying. A higher sampling rate translates to a better sound — and a much bigger file when saved to disk. Most cards sample at 11, 22, or 44 KHz.

Sound module: A box-like contraption that creates sounds but doesn't have a keyboard: A drum machine, for example.

SoundBlaster: Another popular sound card, Creative Lab's SoundBlaster was one of the first cards that could record and play back sounds.

Speaker Driver: Written by Microsoft, the Windows Speaker driver plays sounds through the PC's internal speaker. Unfortunately, the driver doesn't work for MIDI songs, it freezes up the computer while it's playing any sounds, and it doesn't even sound that good. But hey, it's free.

VOC: The format that SoundBlaster uses to store and play digitally recorded sounds in DOS.

WAV: The format that Windows uses to store and play digitally recorded sounds.

Weighted keys: If a synthesizer's keyboard feels like a keyboard on a real piano, it probably has weighted keys — and up to $2,000 more on its price tag.

The 5th Wave **By Rich Tennant**

"AND TO COMPLETE OUR MULTI MEDIA PRESENTATION,..."

Part III

Getting More Out of Windows

"GATHER AROUND, KIDS. YOUR MOTHER'S WINDOWING!"

In This Part . . .

A little lube in the tracks can make a window much easier to open and close. The same holds true for the Windows on your computer. But forget this metaphor stuff. Where are the tracks? Where's the lube?

This part of the book explains how to make Windows work a little bit faster, a little bit easier, and without crashing as much.

Chapter 9

Desktops on *Other* People's Computers

In This Chapter

- Windows desktops from other people so that you can see what other folks are doing

People don't sip coffee in sidewalk cafes because those white plastic chairs are so comfortable. No, they're sitting outside so that they can ogle the people walking by: that woman with the purple hair and brass nose ring, the cool kid with the Speed Racer T-shirt, and the guy who looks *just like* Dustin Hoffman.

That's where this chapter comes in. The headlines on the newsstand say that Windows lives on twenty million PCs. And each Windows desktop looks a little bit different than the all the rest. So this chapter is an open house invitation into the desktops of Windows users from across the nation. You'll see how each person has rearranged his Windows furniture to meet his computer needs. In fact, some of the desktops don't even look like Windows anymore. Shocking!

Robin Garr's Toshiba T4500C Color Notebook

What it is: Robin Garr, a journalist who shared a Pulitzer prize while at Kentucky's *Louisville Courier-Journal,* now hits the keys on his Toshiba T4500C color notebook. (He snaps on a trackball to play Solitaire.) The Toshiba's active-matrix color screen eats up the batteries a little faster than normal, but its brilliant color screen sure looks purdy — especially with Robin's Rocky Mountain wallpaper (see Figure 9-1).

Figure 9-1: Robin Garr's Rocky Mountain wallpaper never fails to draw gasps when he brings his laptop to meetings.

Running out of room for icons along the bottom? PC Tools for Windows stacks them along the side, as well.

Robin can click on any of these buttons to bring up different desktops, each set up for a different purpose.

What he uses it for: Robin uses the notebook as his desktop computer while working at World Hunger Year, a non-profit organization in New York City. When he needs to hit the road for business or to write travel stories for *The New York Times*, the notebook — and his Windows desktop — travel with him.

How he set it up: Frustrated with the Windows bare-bones Program Manager and File Manager, Robin installed PC Tools for Windows. That program replaces the Windows File Manager by adding a handy feature. PC Tools for Windows lets him see stuff inside a file without having to load the file into a program.

"A lot of my use for the computer involves considerable file handling," Garr says. "Being able to click on a filename and see the contents almost instantly, right on the same screen, is critical."

PC Tools also lets Robin switch back and forth between several of his custom-designed desktops. Do you see the four big desktop icons along the screen's right-hand side in Figure 9-1? Robin can click on the TeleComm desktop, for example, and PC Tools switches to a desktop that holds all his modem programs. His Writing Desk holds programs and files for his current project, a book describing his work traveling around the U. S. to find the most creative grassroots initiatives against hunger and poverty.

Although Robin has spent a great deal of time making his desktop "just so," it's the Toshiba's brilliant color screen that draws all the raves. "When I was demonstrating the CompuServe Wine/Beer Forum at a home brewers' national convention in Portland, Oregon," Robin said, "the wallpaper got a lot more attention than anything else."

Vital Stats:

- Robin's desktop runs in 640 x 480 mode, 256 colors.
- PC Tools for Windows can be ordered from Central Point Software, 15220 N.W. Greenbrier Parkway, Suite 200, Beaverton, OR 97006-5764, (503) 690-8090.

Bill Chau's Hong Kong Desktop

What it is: Bill Chau's idea of a perfect Windows desktop is "uncluttered, but with everything just a click away." To cut down on both clutter and clicks, Chau chose Norton Desktop for Windows.

What he uses it for: A power user, Bill likes to keep a wary eye on his PC. That little wavy line along the top of the screen in Figure 9-2 displays how much pressure Windows is putting on his computer. The taller the wave, the more his computer is sweating under the pressure. An icon in the screen's bottom left corner shows how much RAM Windows currently has to work with.

An Unattended Events Scheduler icon along the bottom of the screen can automatically back up Bill's hard drive, even if he's not around. Plus, the icon automatically grabs his e-mail so that Bill's letters are waiting when he sits down at his computer.

A program launcher from hDC along the right side of the screen puts all his most frequently used icons in one place without taking up the whole screen, as the Program Manager does.

How he did it: First, Bill's high resolution, 1024 x 768 video driver gives him plenty of screen room for Hong Kong's shining night lights. Norton's desktop plopped some new menu options along the screen's top and some new icons along the desktop's edges. If the cursor gets lost, Bill looks at the Bart Simpson icon along the bottom. Bart's eyes always face toward the mouse pointer.

Bill's desktop is like an oil painting: He's constantly adding a stroke here, removing a dab there. "My desktop's an ongoing thing, like anything good," Bill said. "However, I built the basic layout relatively quickly 'cause I had seen the Macintosh and the NeXT desktops and knew what I wanted. Along the way, I spruced it up with more appropriate icons and wallpapers. And bless my tape drive for saving me from screwups and change of minds."

Figure 9-2: Born in Hong Kong but working in the states, Bill Chau's Hong Kong wallpaper reminds him of home.

Vital Stats:

- Bill's desktop runs in high-resolution, 1280 x 768 mode, with 256 colors.
- Norton Desktop for Windows can be ordered from Symantec Software, 175 West Broadway, Eugene, OR 97401, (800) 441-7234.
- hDC's program launcher, part of hDC First Apps, can be ordered from hDC Computer Corporation, 6742 185th Avenue NE, Redmond, WA 98052, (206) 885-5550.
- Blackhole, a freebie program, can be downloaded from CompuServe's Windows Shareware Forum (GO WINSHARE) in Library 2. Simply drag unwanted files to the Blackhole and whoosh! They're gone.
- BartEyes, the mouse pointer tracker, can be downloaded from CompuServe's Windows Fun Forum (GO WINFUN), in Library 3.

Paul Mareks' Bunches of Buttons

What it is: As you can see, Paul Mareks *loves* buttons. More than 50 buttons flood the edges of his current desktop, a mixture of Norton Desktop for Windows, hDC's Windows utilities, and some pretty spectacular wallpaper, as you can see in Figure 9-3.

hDC's Power Toolbox can launch programs.

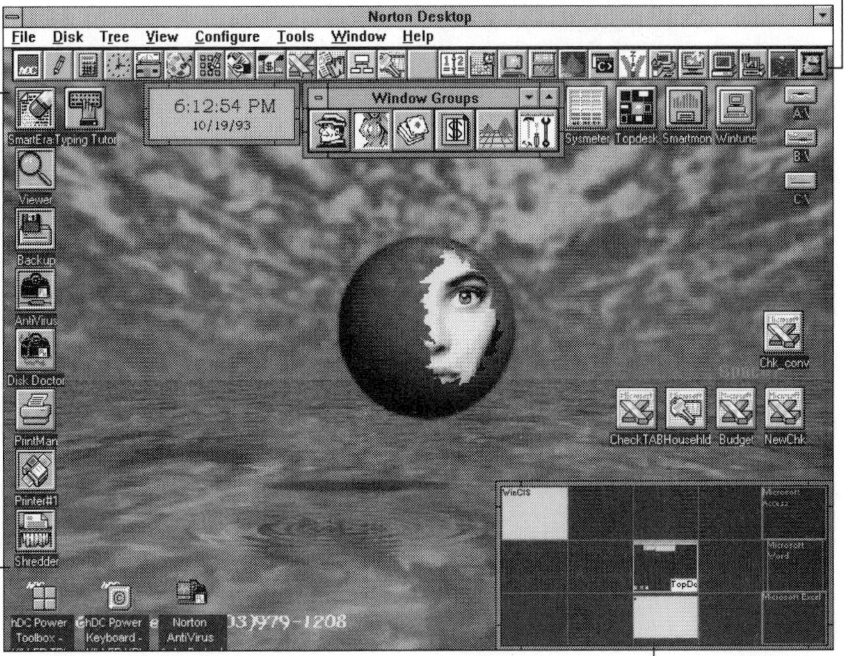

Figure 9-3: Paul Mareks keeps his rows of buttons around the perimeter so that they do not interfere with his cool wallpaper.

Norton Desktop for Windows lets Paul stick icons right on his desktop.

Microsoft Windows Resource Kit's Top desk lets Paul switch to different desktops.

What he uses it for: This desktop lives on Paul's home computer, where it organizes his household needs.

Do you see the little Window Groups toolbox at the top center of the screen? A click on each of those icons brings up a window with even *more* icons, each designed to handle a specific task. The Dick Tracy icon brings up a box of Paul's icons, for example; a click on his girlfriend's icon, sitting next to Dick Tracy, brings up icons for her favorite programs.

Icons for Microsoft's Excel spreadsheet live near the bottom-right corner, ready to tackle Paul's budget and checking account needs.

How he did it: Who needs the Program Manager? Instead of opening the Program Manager to click on a button, Paul prefers seeing his favorite icons directly on the desktop, ready to roll. Norton Desktop for Windows handles that task.

But because permanently attached buttons can take up a great deal of working space on the desktop, Mareks puts hDC's Power Toolbox, the long string of slightly smaller icons, along the top edge. "I leave these items around the perimeter of the screen because I prefer an uncluttered look," Paul says. "One of the reasons is because I like nice wallpaper; I find this scene to be especially soothing to the eyes."

Finally, Paul uses software included with Microsoft's Windows Resource Kit. The Resource Kit's desktop switcher (in the bottom-right corner) lets him switch between 12 desktops, each set up to fulfill a particular computing need.

Vital Stats:

- Paul's desktop runs in 256 colors at 800 x 600 resolution.
- Norton Desktop for Windows can be ordered from Symantec Software, 175 West Broadway, Eugene, OR 97401, (800) 441-7234.
- hDC's PowerToolbox comes with hDC's PowerLauncher package and can be ordered hDC Computer Corporation, 6742 185th Avenue NE, Redmond, WA 98052, (206) 885-5550.
- To order the Windows Resource Kit within the United States, dial (800) 642-7676. (Touch-Tone phone lovers will be disappointed. I reached a friendly *human being* on the first call.)

BillyBob Johnson's Desk Calendar

What it is: Who needs wallpaper? BillyBob Johnson uses his computer for just one thing — a computerized replacement for his old desk calendar and organizer, as you can see in Figure 9-4.

What he uses it for: A calendar in the desktop's top-left corner tracks the current month. BillyBob clicks on a specific day, and any scheduled appointments pop up in the adjoining window.

BillyBob can launch programs by clicking here.

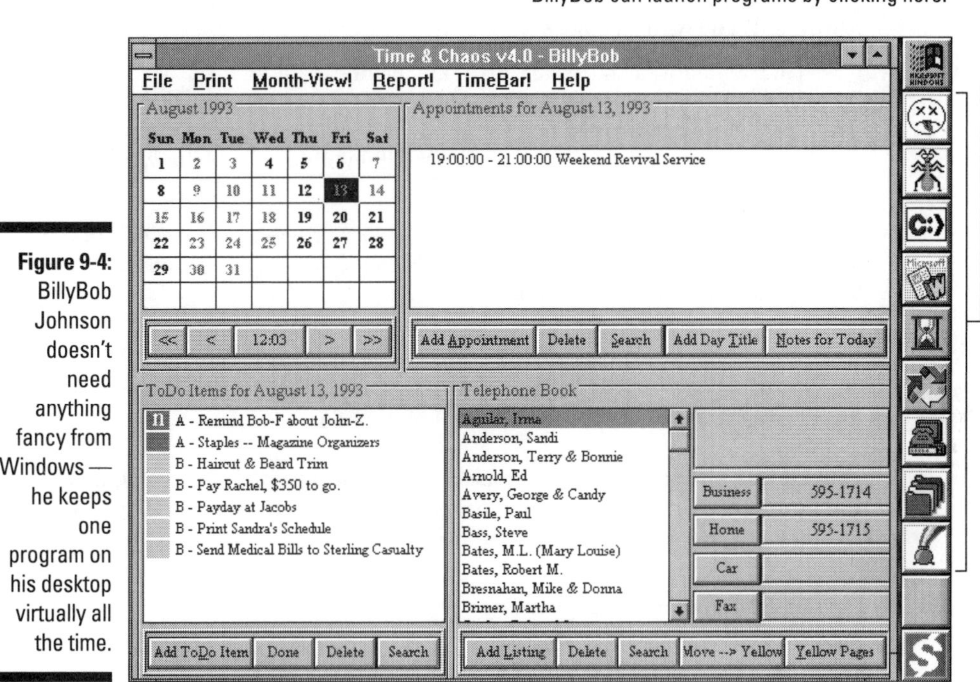

Figure 9-4: BillyBob Johnson doesn't need anything fancy from Windows — he keeps one program on his desktop virtually all the time.

BillyBob keeps this program on-screen most of the time.

Beneath the calendar lies the current "ToDo" list. If he needs help with a project, a telephone book sits nearby. BillyBob clicks on a name, and up pops that friend's number: business, home, fax, or car phone.

How he did it: BillyBob uses Time & Chaos, a shareware Personal Information Manager, that tracks his daily schedule. Because an icon for Time & Chaos lives in the Startup group of BillyBob's Program Manager, Time & Chaos jumps to the screen whenever BillyBob fires up Windows.

The Program Manager lurks behind the Time & Chaos window, should BillyBob ever need another program's services. But more often than not, he simply double-clicks on one of the icons lined up along the desktop's right side. There, a program called WinDock lets BillyBob launch any of his ten most-used programs with a simple double-click.

Vital Stats:

- BillyBob runs Windows in the default VGA mode, a snappy 640 x 480 resolution with 16 colors.
- Time & Chaos, a shareware program, can be ordered for $30 from iSBiSTER International, 1314 Cardigan Street, Garland, TX 75040, (214) 495-6724. Or if you have a modem and CompuServe account, you can find Time & Chaos saved as TCHAOS.ZIP in Library 12 of the Windows Shareware Forum (GO WINSHARE).
- You can find WinDock, the other shareware program, in Library 2 of the same CompuServe forum. WinDock is called WINDCK.ZIP, and the programmer is asking a $15 registration fee.

Ray Hendrickson's Dashboard

What it is: Unlike many Windows users, Ray Hendrickson hasn't given up on the Program Manager. In fact, he still keeps the Program Manager center stage, as shown in Figure 9-5. The supporting cast brings the act together, however.

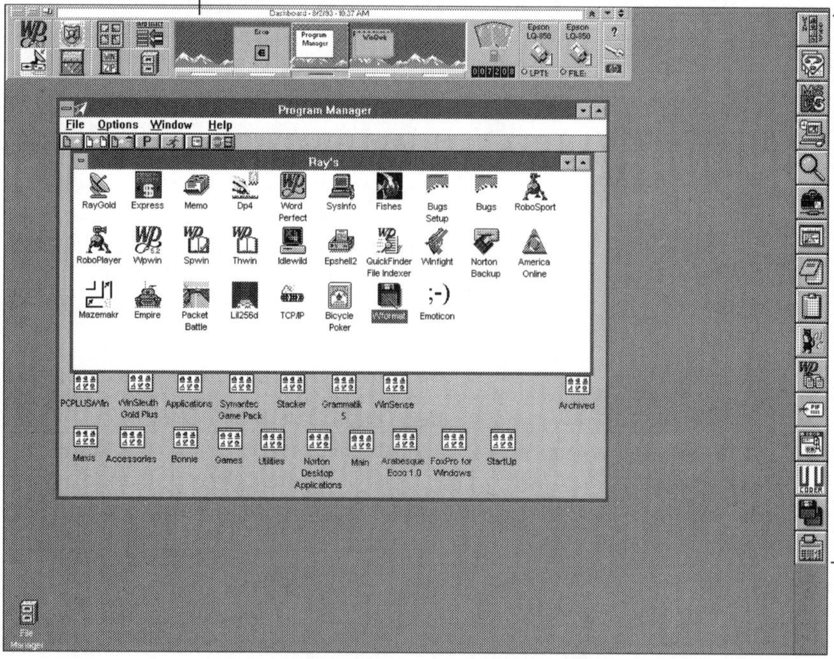

Ray's Dashboard lets him launch programs, print files, switch to other desktops, and more.

Ray can launch programs from here.

Figure 9-5: Although Ray Hendrickson is sticking with Program Manager, Hewlett-Packard's Dashboard lets him steer Windows a little easier.

What he uses it for: Ray shares his home computer with his wife, Bonnie. Her program group, Bonnie, has all the "cooking stuff," Ray says.

How he did it: Although Ray's still using the Program Manager, he is keeping it very organized. He has no overlapping program groups, and the icons for all the most frequently used programs sit in a large, open window.

Like Bill Johnson's desktop, described previously, Ray uses WinDock. A long barber's pole of frequently used icons sits along the screen's right edge, ready for a quick double-click.

Riding along the top of the desktop, Hewlett-Packard's Dashboard packs an amazing amount of gizmos into a Hundai-sized space. First, Dashboard lets Ray switch between five different desktops, each set up for a different task. Plus, he can embed a few of his favorite icons in the Dashboard's left side, ready for instant launching.

Do you see the Dashboard's fuel gauge? This icon is a quick and easy way to tell how much RAM Windows has left — and whether you'll have to shut down some smaller programs to make room for a bigger one.

Ray's video card pulls a fast one. Although he's running at 800 x 600 resolution, his Fahrenheit 1280 Plus video card lets him slide stuff around on the desktop as if it were a 1024 x 768 card.

Finally, those strange buttons embellishing the top of the Program Manager come from a SuperBar shareware program.

Vital Stats:

- Ray runs his desktop at 800 x 600 resolution, but his video card driver lets him move around Windows as if he had a 1280 x 760 desktop.
- Hewlett-Packard's Dashboard for Windows can be ordered from Hewlett-Packard Company, PC Software Division, 5301 Stevens Creek Blvd., Santa Clara, CA 95052-8059, (800) 554-1305.
- You can find WinDock in Library 2 of CompuServe's Windows Shareware Forum (GO WINSHARE). WinDock is called WINDCK.ZIP, and the programmer is asking a $15 registration fee.

Dave Christensen's Bare Bones Desktop

What it is: When you double-click on Windows wallpaper, a Task List pops up, showing all the currently running programs. The Task List is handy, but, for such a handy appliance, not very spectacular.

Dave liked to be able to switch to different desktops instantly, like Paul Marek, described previously. So, he replaced the Task List with a program called WinTools. "By double-clicking the background," Dave says, "I open up a map of the six screens I use. WinTools supports up to 64 screens, although I hope I never need that many." Dave's bare-bones desktop appears in Figure 9-6.

Figure 9-6: Dave Christensen prefers the Spartan look; a double-click on the background brings up a program that lets him switch to other, custom-designed desktops.

After the map of desktops pops up, Dave double-clicks on the screen he wants to visit. In this way, Dave keeps his desktop uncluttered, but he has dozens of other, more cluttered desktops just a double-click away.

What he uses it for: Dave uses this Windows desktop on his home computer, where he uses it for his work as a technical writer and for just plain messing around.

How he did it: Besides using WinTools, Dave also uses SmartFind, a quick file searcher from PC Tools for Windows.

In addition, do you see the icon called drag 'n vu at the bottom of the screen? Dave drags a filename from the File Manager and drops it on the drag 'n vu icon. Presto! A drag 'n vu window pops up, showing him what's inside the file. Currently, drag 'n vu can peek inside most major spreadsheets, databases, word processed files, and graphics.

The HALT button lets him bail out of Windows immediately — no waiting around for the "Are you sure that you want to exit Windows?" message.

Finally, Dave took the normal Windows start-up graphic and tweaked it a bit in Fractal Design's Painter 2.0.

Vital Stats:

- Dave's desktop runs in 1024 x 768, high-resolution mode, with 256 colors.
- WinTools can be ordered from Tool Technology, 3030 Bridgeway, Sausalito, CA 94965, (415) 289-7400.
- The handy drag 'n vu program (It's *really* called Drag and View — Dave merely changed the icon's title.) can be ordered for $25 from Canyon Software, 1537 Fourth St., Suite 131, San Rafael, CA 94901, (415) 453-9779.
- PC Tools for Windows can be ordered from Central Point Software, 15220 N.W. Greenbrier Parkway, Suite 200, Beaverton, OR 97006-5764. (503) 690-8090.
- HALT, a $5 shareware program, can be downloaded from CompuServe's Windows Shareware Forum (GO WINSHARE) in Library 6.

What Do All These Different Desktops Mean?

At a glance, it's not easy to tell that all these desktops come from Windows users. The next few sections describe some of the most common enhancements they're using. (After all, those Windows utility programs on the store shelves must do *something*.)

Each is customized to its user's tastes

Each of these desktops looks very different, and that's the attraction. Each desktop is designed to meet its user's individual needs (and, in some cases, the spouse's needs, as well). Some of the desktops are constantly evolving because their owners spend a great deal of time on-line, testing out new Windows shareware utilities. Other desktops, such as Bill Johnson's desk calendar, are finished. Why mess with something that works?

Either way, don't be afraid to change around your Windows desktop to meet your own needs. Keep shaving off the default frustration levels, bit by bit.

Most have more than one desktop

Your desk in the office probably looks different from your desk at home, which looks different from the woodworking area in the garage. Simply put, nobody keeps the same items on all the various desks. But Windows is limited to one desktop. Or is it? Many of the people described in this chapter use *multiple desktop* utilities. They can set up one desktop to use while word processing, for example, and then set up another one for spreadsheets.

A click on the desktop map changes views to a different desktop. Multiple desktops keep things from getting cluttered, yet Windows' ever-lurking Clipboard keeps it easy to cut and paste information.

Icons besides the ones in the Program Manager

The Program Manager works well to hold a collection of icons. But after a while, the program groups appear to blur together. Where did that Word for Windows icon go? And isn't it a bother to open the Program Manager and search for the Word for Windows icon, when you merely want to whip out a quick anticorporation letter?

To save start-up time, most of the Windows desktops I have described in this chapter use program launchers, which allow you to stick icons for your favorite programs directly onto your wallpaper. Program launchers are quick, easy to start, and use no Program Manager to get in the way. Other utilities put a small, moveable box containing your favorite icons on-screen.

Best yet, these program launchers come with their own installation program, so you can easily launch the launcher.

Handy file viewers

The File Manager doesn't offer many hints as to what's inside a certain file. Looking for a favorite .BMP file? You better get ready to fire up Paintbrush and spend some time loading files.

That viewing hassle led many of the users in this chapter to check out file viewers. Instead of loading a file to see what's inside, drag it to the drag 'n vu icon at the bottom of the screen. A window appears, letting you see exactly what's inside that file — just as if it were loaded into the program that created it.

Finding Windows desktop fixers

Many of the people in this chapter have joined on-line services, such as CompuServe. By using a modem, these people can meet other Windows users, swap desktop talk, and download Windows programs. (Read Chapter 7 for all the download stuff.) Other users check out the computer stores because most of the programs described in this chapter can be purchased there.

Chapter 10

My Mouse *Still* Doesn't Work!

In This Chapter

- Shutting down Windows without a mouse
- Retrieving a missing mouse pointer
- Calming down jumpy mouse pointers
- Making the mouse work with a DOS program
- Making the mouse work with a DOS program in a window
- Doing something with that *right* mouse button
- Using cordless mice

The side of the Windows box says that the program is "mouse optional." But the person who wrote this bit of wisdom probably never tried to draw a party flier in Paintbrush by using the arrow keys or play a game of Solitaire by using just the Tab and arrow keys.

You can use Windows without a mouse — just like you can drive a car with your toes gripping the steering wheel — but it takes a little longer, and it's embarrassing if anybody is watching.

So if your mouse has stopped working in Windows or the little arrow's suddenly taking wild leaps around the screen, this is the chapter you've been searching for. And as an extra, no-frequent-flier-miles-required bonus, this chapter also tackles DOS mouse-pointer problems. You'll be armed with the weaponry required to break up fights when DOS and Windows both argue madly over that single mouse pointer. After all, which program gets the clicks?

Emergency Keyboard Trick to Shut Down Windows

Is your mouse pointer frozen? Do double-clicks suddenly stop working? Did your mouse pointer simply walk off the screen without leaving an explanatory sticky note?

If your mouse takes a hike, use the following easy-to-find trick to shut down Windows by simply pecking at the keyboard — no mouse activity required:

1. **Press Ctrl+Esc.**

   The Windows handy little Task List surfaces, listing your currently running programs. The Task List should look something like Figure 10-1.

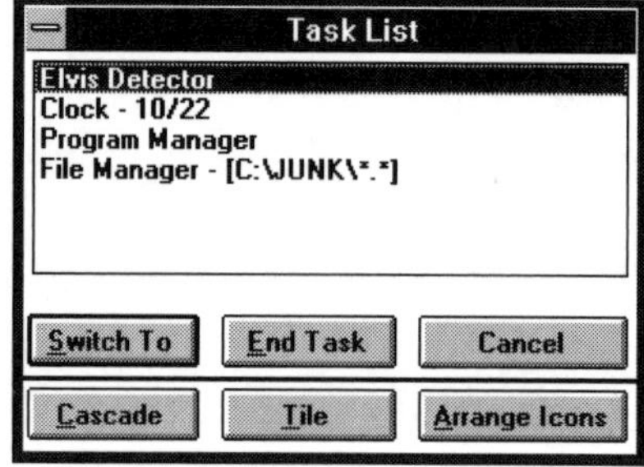

Figure 10-1: Pressing Ctrl+Esc opens the Windows Task List.

If Ctrl+Esc doesn't work for some frustrating reason, hold down Alt and press Tab. Keep pressing Tab until the little pop-up box says Program Manager and then jump to Step 3.

2. **Select Program Manager and press Enter.**

   Push your up- or down-arrow keys until you've highlighted the Program Manager. Press Enter and the Program Manager hops to the forefront.

3. **Press Alt+F4 and then press Enter.**

   Pressing Alt+F4 tells the Program Manager to shut down and take all the rest of Windows with it. Whew.

After you shut down Windows, try typing **WIN** at the DOS prompt to start up Windows again. My wife uses this technique if her mouse pointer isn't waiting for her when she loads Windows in the morning. After she loads Windows a second time, however, the pointer shows up on-screen, ready for action. If the mouse pointer still doesn't show up, however, all is not lost. You just have to read a little further along in this chapter.

If the mouse dies, but you want to keep working in Windows for a while before popping open the hood, use your keyboard. While in a program, press and release Alt and then press the down-arrow key. A menu appears out of nowhere. Now press your arrow keys to move around in the menus and press Enter when you've found your choice. (Pressing Esc gets you out of Menu Land if you haven't found your choice.)

My Mouse Pointer Doesn't Show Up When I Start Windows!

Like a car's steering wheel, Windows' little mouse pointer is pretty much taken for granted. But when the pointer isn't on-screen, don't panic. First, try chanting some of the following spells to purge the mouse-stealing gremlins that have taken refuge in your computer.

Is the mouse really plugged in?

Aw, go ahead and check, even if you're *sure* that the mouse is plugged in.

A mouse needs to be plugged in *before* you start playing with Windows because the instant Windows hops to the screen, it looks around for the mouse. If Windows can't find a mouse as it's first waking up, it probably won't notice a mouse you plug in as an afterthought a few minutes later.

The solution? If you've loaded Windows before plugging in your mouse, exit Windows by using the emergency keyboard trick described in the preceding section. Then plug in the mouse and reload Windows. This time, the pointer should be waiting for you. Keep the following points in mind when working with the mouse:

- Make sure that the mouse is tightly plugged in. Frantic mouse movements during computer games can dislodge its tail from your computer's rear.
- If your mouse comes unplugged while you're working in Windows, the little arrow probably freezes on-screen, even after you plug in the mouse's tail again. The solution? Exit Windows, plug in the mouse, and start up Windows again.
- Some computers are even pickier. If the mouse comes unplugged, you need to exit Windows, turn off the computer, plug in the mouse, turn on the computer, and load Windows again. This procedure is worth a try to restore mousehood.

Is the mouse plugged into the right hole?

Computer mice have looked like a bar of soap from the beginning. What's changed, however, is the type of plug on the ends of their tails. Each of the new types of plugs fits into different holes on the back of your computer. To complicate matters further, sometimes a mouse's plug can fit into two different holes. Which hole is which?

For example, the plug on a PS/2-style mouse looks just like the plug on the cable of a PS/2-style keyboard. How can you tell you're not accidentally plugging your mouse's tail into the keyboard's hole? Start by looking for any labels or pictures. Some computers put a little picture of a mouse next to the mouse's hole. If you're not lucky, however, flip a coin and plug the mouse in one of the holes. You have a fifty-fifty chance for success. If the mouse doesn't work, you still have solved the problem: you now know that the other hole is the correct one.

If you're using a *serial* mouse, plug it in to COM1 or COM2. Windows doesn't listen to a serial mouse set up to use COM3 or COM4.

Is the mouse set up correctly under Windows?

If the mouse is on vacation, or dancing wildly, use the following steps to see if you set up the little critter correctly in Windows:

1. **Exit Windows.**

   To get out of Windows without using a mouse, follow the emergency keyboard exit steps listed at the beginning of the chapter.

2. **Type the following at the DOS prompt and press Enter:**

   ```
   C:\> CD \WINDOWS
   ```

   This step should bring you to your Windows directory in DOS. (If you've installed Windows on drive D, switch to drive D before typing the command.)

3. **Type the following at the DOS prompt and press Enter:**

   ```
   C:\WINDOWS\> SETUP
   ```

   The Windows Setup screen pops to the forefront, as shown in Figure 10-2.

   Look at the Mouse information to see what sort of mouse Windows *thinks* you have. Did Windows guess right? If you're sure that it is your type of mouse, then stop right now. You must have some other mouse problem. But if the Setup screen lists the wrong type of mouse, head for the next step.

4. **Highlight the Mouse category by pressing the arrow keys and then press Enter.**

   The Windows Setup screen shows you the various types of mice it can relate to, as shown in Figure 10-3.

   If you see your type of mouse, press the arrow keys to highlight it. Then press Enter and follow the instructions. You'll probably need to insert one of your original Windows disks so that you can copy a new mouse driver to your hard drive.

If you don't see your type of mouse, choose the Other (Requires disk provided by a hardware manufacturer) option. Now, your mission is to find that particular disk because it contains a mouse driver that lets Windows know its language. (Chapter 3 covers drivers.) Hopefully, your mouse came with a floppy disk for your to insert.

```
Windows Setup

  If your computer or network appears on the Hardware Compatibility List
  with an asterisk next to it, press F1 before continuing.

  System Information
     Computer:          MS-DOS System
     Display:           VGA
     Mouse:             Microsoft, or IBM PS/2
     Keyboard:          All AT type keyboards (84 - 86 keys)
     Keyboard Layout:   US
     Language:          English (American)
     Codepage:          English (437)
     Network:           No Network Installed

     Complete Changes:  Accept the configuration shown above.

  To change a system setting, press the UP or DOWN ARROW key to
  move the highlight to the setting you want to change. Then press
  ENTER to see alternatives for that item. When you have finished
  changing your settings, select the "Complete Changes" option
  to quit Setup.

 ENTER=Continue  F1=Help  F3=Exit
```

Figure 10-2: The DOS version of Windows Setup lets you change Windows settings, just like the Windows version of Setup.

```
Windows Setup

  You have asked to change the type of Mouse to be installed.

   • To select a Mouse from the following list

      1) Press the UP or DOWN ARROW key to move the highlight to the
         item.
      2) Press ENTER.

   • To return to the System Information screen without changing your
     Mouse type, press ESC.

   Genius serial mouse on COM1
   Genius serial mouse on COM2
   HP Mouse (HP-HIL)
   Logitech
   Microsoft, or IBM PS/2
   Mouse Systems serial mouse on COM2

  (To see more of the list, press the (↓) arrow key)
 ENTER=Continue  F1=Help  F3=Exit  ESC=Cancel
```

Figure 10-3: The Windows Setup screen shows the types of mice it knows how to use.

If the mouse still doesn't work, even after you're sure that it's set up right under Windows, you have two choices. You either can install the newest mouse driver you can find for your particular brand of mouse or, if that doesn't work, you can consider buying a new mouse. If your mouse isn't working in your DOS programs either, it simply may have died.

Where do you find these new mouse drivers? If you have a modem, check out the beginning of Chapter 7. You probably can find a new driver within a half hour. If you don't have a modem, call or write the mouse manufacturer to see whether its people can mail you one. If you need the latest Microsoft mouse driver, call Microsoft at 1-800-426-9400. Unfortunately, Microsoft is charging $20 for Version 9.0, the latest one.

You have one more chance: your mouse may have a conflict with other parts of your computer. Check your AUTOEXEC.BAT or CONFIG.SYS files for any DOS mouse utilities, such as CLICK, LOGIMENU, or CPANEL. You also may have problems if your MS-DOS mouse driver is older than version 7.04 or if your Logitech mouse driver is older than Version 6.0. (See Chapter 11 for more information about AUTOEXEC.BAT and CONFIG.SYS files.)

The Mouse Pointer Is There, but Now It Doesn't Work!

After a mouse starts working in Windows, its little arrow rarely disappears. The arrow may freeze up solid, but it usually stays on-screen. If your mouse pointer suddenly bails out, however, give these suggestions a shot before giving up:

- Roll your mouse across your desktop in big circles. Sometimes, pointers hide in corners or get lost in the flashy wallpaper.
- Do you have an energy-saving "green" or laptop computer that shuts down if you haven't poked the keyboard for a while? If your mouse pointer doesn't reappear when your slumbering computer wakes up, head for Chapter 7: You need to set up Windows for Advanced Power Management, which reminds the computer to turn on the mouse after it wakes up from a snooze.
- If the pointer freezes up solid, your mouse may have come unplugged from the back of your computer. You should exit Windows, plug in the mouse, and start over again.
- If none of these tricks fixes the mouse problem, head for the preceding section to see whether your mouse is set up right under Windows. Sometimes, a disappearing mouse is a sign of a conflicting driver.

The Mouse Pointer Is Starting to Jerk Around!

If your little arrow dances around the screen like a drop of water on a hot griddle, your mouse is probably just dirty. To clean your mouse, grab a toothpick, and follow the steps in the next section.

Cleaning a mouse

Mouse balls must be cleaned by hand every so often to remove any stray hairs and grunge. To degrunge a spastic mouse, do the following:

1. **Turn the mouse upside down and find the little plastic plate that holds the ball in place.**

   An arrow usually points out which way to push the plate in order to let the ball fall out.

2. **Remove the plastic plate, turn the mouse right-side up, and let the mouse ball fall into your hand.**

   Two things will fall out: the plate holding the ball in place and the ball itself. (Surprisingly, mouse balls give off a very disappointing bounce.)

3. **Pick off any hairs and crud coating the mouse ball. Remove any other dirt and debris from the mouse's ball cavity.**

   A toothpick works well for scraping off the gunk living on the little rollers inside the mouse's ball cavity. (Rollers are those white or silver thingies that rub against the mouse ball.) If the toothpick isn't doing the trick, move up to a Q-tip moistened with some rubbing alcohol. The Q-tip usually removes the most stubborn crud.

   Roll the little rollers around with your finger to make sure that you can see no stubborn crud hiding on the sides. Also, make sure that the crud falls outside the mouse and not back into the mouse's guts. If you find some really gross stuff caked on to the mouse ball (dried-fruit remnants, for example), mild soap and warm water usually removes it. Make sure that the ball is dry before popping it back inside the ball cavity.

   Never use alcohol to clean a mouse ball because the alcohol can damage the rubber.

4. **Place the mouse ball back inside the mouse and reattach the plate.**

   Turn or push the plastic plate until the mouse ball is firmly locked back in place.

This cleaning chore cures many jerky mouse-arrow problems, and it's a good first step before moving on to the more bothersome jerky-mouse solutions. But keep these points in mind:

- A mouse ball stays only as clean as your desk. Especially-hirsute computer users should pluck stray hairs from their mouse ball every month or so.
- After you've cleaned the mouse, sponge off any grunge hanging on to your mouse pad, as well. Be sure to let the pad dry completely before using it again.
- If all this hair-picking has put you in that special mood, feel free to pick off the hairs and dust that are clogging the fan vent on the back of your computer. (Your hands are already dirty, anyway, and a clean vent helps keep your computer from overheating.)

The pointer still jerks!

Hmmm, your clean mouse is still jerking around? Try the following fixes before knocking the mouse against the file cabinet. (Hard knocks merely give the mouse a lived-in look, anyway.)

- Could the mouse have come unplugged? If the mouse is unplugged, even slightly, and plugged back in while Windows is on-screen, the little arrow probably starts squirming out of control. To make the arrow stop dancing, exit Windows by using the keyboard trick (shown at the beginning of this chapter) and then reload Windows.
- If you're using a mouse with a laptop, disable the laptop's special keyboard mouse or any attached trackballs. Laptops get confused if they think that they're hooked up to more than one mouse.
- If you're using a laptop that powers down when you haven't touched it, make sure that you've installed the Advanced Power Management described in Chapter 5. If your mouse still hovers near the left edge of the screen after the laptop wakes up, tap the laptop's manufacturer on the shoulder: You need a PS/2 mouse port BIOS upgrade.
- Sometimes the mouse jerks around if you're printing a big file in the background. This action is supposed to happen. The jerking stops after the printer stops.

- If the mouse goes wild right after you install some new gizmos — a scanner or modem, for example — your mouse may have an *interrupt* conflict. To fix this problem, pull out the new gizmo's manual and see how to change its IRQ. (That usually boils down to one thing: Flipping a switch somewhere on the new gizmo. Unfortunately, they all use different switches.)
- If none of these suggestions helps, look for a more up-to-date mouse driver. (Chapter 3 covers this topic.)

Fine-Tuning a Mouse's Performance

After the mouse pointer shows up on-screen and moves around at the same time the mouse does, most Windows users breathe a sigh of relief. Sigh.

For others, however, who are bothered when the mouse is still just a little bit off — when the mouse mistakes a relaxed double-click for two single-clicks or when the mouse arrow becomes hyper and whizzes across the screen at the slightest nudge — productivity comes to a standstill.

The Windows Control Panel offers a few ways to tweak a mouse's performance. After you double-click on the Mouse icon from the Windows Control Panel, the Mouse dialog box appears, as shown in Figure 10-4. You can adjust your mouse's work habits in this dialog box.

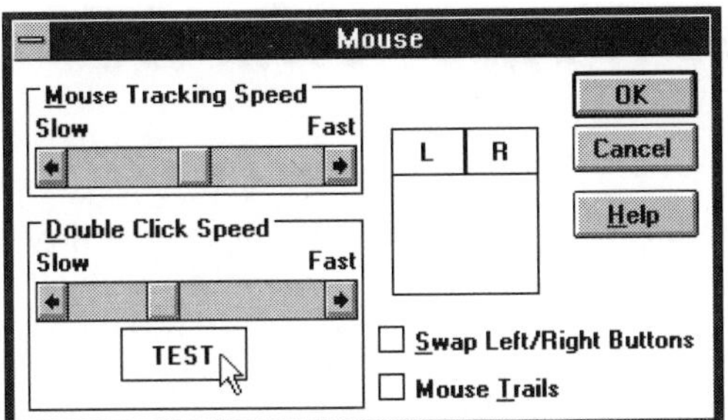

Figure 10-4: The Mouse dialog box lets you fine-tune your mouse's performance.

- **Mouse Tracking Speed:** Do you see the little box in the Mouse Tracking Speed groove in Figure 10-4? Move the little box back and forth to adjust how far your mouse should scoot when you nudge it. If you move the bar to the Slow side, the mouse barely moves. If you move the bar to the Fast side, however, even a slight vibration turns it in to Speed Racer.
- **Double Click Speed:** If you can't click quickly enough for Windows to recognize your handiwork as a double-click, scoot the little box in the Double Click Speed groove toward the Slow side. If Windows mistakes your double-clicks for single clicks, scoot the box toward the Fast side.

  To test your settings, double-click in the TEST box. The box changes color each time you make a successful double-click.
- **Swap Left/Right Buttons:** Left-handed users may want to click in this box because it switches the mouse's buttons so that left-handers can click with their index fingers, just like the rest of the world. The button swap takes place instantly. To undo the change, click in the box again, but be sure that you use the mouse button on the *right.*
- **Mouse Trails:** Described in Chapter 5, mouse trails are little ghosts that follow your mouse pointer and make the pointer easier to see on laptops and more fun to use on desktops. Mouse trails need to be supported by your video driver, however, and some video drivers — especially the high-resolution ones — simply can't handle mouse trails. If the trails aren't supported, the Mouse Trails option is grayed out.

After you've adjusted your mouse so that it's *just* so, close the box, and the mouse will remember your new settings from thence forth.

Windows comes with the preceding settings for a Microsoft mouse. If you're using a different brand of mouse, or if you're using the latest Microsoft mouse driver, your settings may look different. For example, Version 9 of Microsoft's mouse driver lets you magnify parts of the screen to take a closer look, and it has a Snap-to feature that automatically plops the little arrow on to some of the menu buttons.

Waiter, There's No Mouse in My DOS Programs

Although Windows certainly helped to popularize the mouse, dozens of DOS programs also let their users point and click their way through menus. But when a DOS program is running under Windows, which program gets the mouse clicks — DOS or Windows?

My DOS program has the whole screen but no mouse!

Windows can run DOS programs and Windows programs on the same screen. But Windows programs often snatch the mouse pointer for themselves — even when a DOS program is filling the whole screen. Before you throw out your DOS programs in frustration, consider the following possibilities as to why you don't have that mouse on-screen.

Does the DOS program really support a mouse?

Some programmers simply don't like mice and, therefore, didn't design their DOS programs to use a mouse. If your DOS program can't use a mouse when it's running by itself in DOS, it can't use a mouse when it's running under Windows, either. In fact, most DOS programs *don't* support a mouse. (That's why everybody is using Windows now.)

Is the mouse driver loaded in DOS?

Windows comes with its own built-in mouse driver, described earlier in this chapter. That Windows driver works for *Windows* programs. If you want to use a mouse with your *DOS* programs, you need to load a DOS mouse driver, and you need to load that DOS mouse program before you load Windows.

So before loading Windows, type the following at the DOS prompt and press Enter:

```
C:\> MOUSE
```

Then load Windows and try out your DOS program. If the mouse finally works, you've solved your problem: you simply need to load a DOS mouse driver before you start Windows. The easiest way to load the mouse driver is to put the word MOUSE in your AUTOEXEC.BAT file, a delicate process described in Chapter 11.

Using a mouse pointer in a windowed DOS program

Back in Windows 3.0, the mouse worked in DOS programs. But the mouse didn't work the way many people expected. The mouse couldn't point and click on the program's menus. Instead, the mouse merely copied text from the DOS program's screen and copied the text to the Windows clipboard, ready to be pasted in to other programs.

Windows 3.1 fixed that oversight. Finally, a mouse worked on a windowed-DOS program's menus, as seen in Figure 10-5, just as if the program spread over the whole screen. (The mouse also could copy text to the Clipboard, just as before.) This new feature brought a new slough of problems, unfortunately, which led to the slough of fixes that I discuss in the next sections.

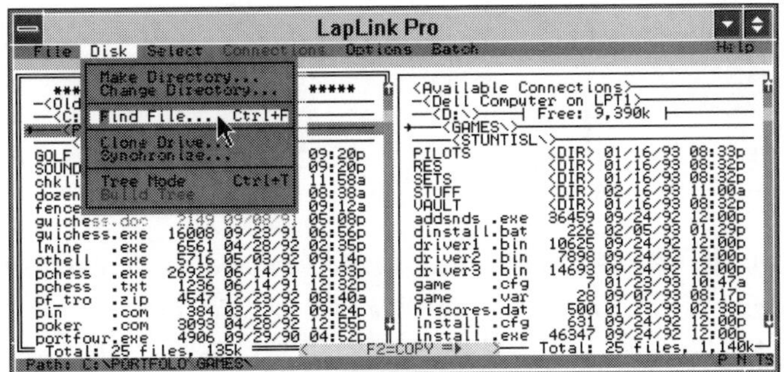

Figure 10-5: The mouse can work with DOS programs running in a window, as seen here with Laplink.

Does the mouse work when the program runs full-screen under Windows?

If the mouse ain't there when the DOS program's running full-screen, it won't be there when the program's running in a window. Before going any further, check out the section just before this one. Make sure that your DOS mouse driver is loaded — also described in that same section.

Is your DOS mouse driver new enough?

Being able to control a DOS program with a mouse while the program is on-screen in Windows is the height of computer fashion. Some of the older mouse drivers are simply behind the times, however, and they cannot function in DOS programs running in Windows.

To see whether your mouse software is up to snuff, watch the screen carefully after you turn on your computer (or when you load your mouse driver from the DOS prompt). You should see a version number head across the screen. Figure

10-6, for example, shows that the mouse is using Version 8.20 of Microsoft's mouse driver. If your DOS mouse driver is earlier than Version 8.20, you'll need a new driver. Drivers older than that version can't control a DOS program while it's in a window.

```
C:\>mouse
Microsoft (R) Mouse Driver Version 8.20
Copyright (C) Microsoft Corp. 1983-1992.  All rights reserved.
Existing Mouse driver enabled

C:\>
```

Figure 10-6: To see the version number of your mouse software, watch the screen as you turn on your computer or when you type **MOUSE** at your DOS prompt.

Does your Windows screen driver support mice in DOS windows?

Even if your mouse driver can control a DOS program in a window, you're still not off the hook. Your Windows video driver needs to allow the mouse action, as well. The video drivers that come with Windows let mice work in a windowed-DOS program. But some of the third-party video drivers written for the newer video cards, especially the high-resolution ones, wimp out: no mice allowed in DOS windows.

To see if your driver's one of the wimpy ones, switch to the plain ol' VGA video driver that came with Windows (described in Chapter 3). If a change of video drivers gets your mouse up and running in the DOS program, then your video driver is at fault. You better start bugging the video card manufacturer for a newer, wimp-free driver.

Is your DOS mouse driver installed?

Even though a DOS program may be running in Windows, it's still a DOS program.

So, just as with full-screen DOS programs, the windowed-DOS programs needs a DOS mouse driver. And that driver needs to be loaded before Windows hits the screen.

Head back a page or two to the section on full-screen DOS programs for the scoop.

A somber taste of INI

Before giving up on making your mouse work in your windowed-DOS program, open up your SYSTEM.INI file to make sure that the following line appears under the [NonWindowsApp] section:

```
MouseInDosBox=1
```

If you don't want the mouse to work when a DOS program's in a window, change the line to the following:

```
MouseInDosBox=0
```

If this SYSTEM.INI stuff has your ears twitching in confusion, see Chapter 15 for some anti-itch information.

- If Windows 3.0 doesn't let your mouse work in a DOS window, simply upgrade to Windows 3.1.
- Some Logitech mice have trouble with DOS programs running in Windows. If the DOS program starts from a PIF that launches it in a window, the Logitech mouse may not work. You should get an updated driver from Logitech. (At last check, Logitech's phone number is (510)795-8100.) Until then, start the program in a full screen and then press Alt+Enter, which allows the mouse to work. (That PIF stuff is covered in Chapter 14.)

What's That Right Mouse Button For?

Windows users can click up a storm with their left mouse button. But the right mouse button is about as useful as a hood ornament. It just sits there. In fact, I've only been able to find three ways to use the right mouse button:

- **Paintbrush:** When you click on the colors with your left mouse button, you can choose between colors or you can paint with that color. But when you click on a color with your right mouse button, you're choosing the background color.

  To experiment, choose a background color with your right mouse button and open a new file: Your new file will be awash with that new background color. Check out the Text's Outline and Shadow options for more fun.
- **Minesweeper:** In this Windows game, the left mouse button turns over a square to see whether a mine is lurking underneath. The right mouse button, however, marks suspicious squares with a little red flag that warns you not to click on that square again.

- **Grabbing DOS text:** Windows lets you copy text from a DOS program that is running in a window. Press Alt+spacebar, click on Edit, and choose Mark. Then hold down the left mouse button and move the mouse over the text you want to grab, which highlights the information. Press Enter, and Windows copies the text to the Clipboard.

  So? After you highlight the information, just press your right mouse button to copy the information to the Clipboard without taking your hands off the mouse to push Enter. Slick, eh?

Although Windows itself doesn't take much advantage of the right mouse button, many Windows programs do. Microsoft's Word for Windows, for example, lets you highlight a column of text by holding down the right mouse button and moving the mouse.

Windows manuals and help screens don't use the terms *left* or *right* when talking about mouse buttons. They use the more mousily correct terms of *primary* button (the left mouse button) and *secondary* button (the right mouse button. Very few Windows programs use a three-button mouse.

Miscellaneous Mouse Madness

As more and more brands of mice hit the shelves, more and more types of mouse problems bite their users. This section covers some of the other problems that may go wrong with your mouse in Windows.

My cordless mouse acts weird

Cordless mice don't have tails. They squeak their signals through the air to a *receiving unit.* The receiving unit has the tail, which then plugs in to the back of your computer.

Like a TV remote control, these mice need fresh batteries every few months, so change the batteries if they're acting up. Sometimes the mouse's receiving unit needs fresh batteries, as well.

- An **infrared** cordless mouse needs a clean line of sight between the mouse and its receiving unit. (That clean line of sight is probably the only clean spot on your desk.) Your mouse starts acting up as soon as you set a book or some junk mail on that clean spot. Move the book or throw away the junk mail, and the mouse will probably go back to normal.
- **Radio-controlled** cordless mice aren't as picky about that clean line-of-sight stuff, so messy desks don't cause problems. However, make sure that the mouse and the receiving unit are level with each other. If the receiver is on the floor or up on top of the file cabinet, the receiver may not pick up your mouse's radio signals as well.

- Keep any cordless mouse within about five feet of its receiver. And if your mouse keeps calling those expensive 900 "chat" numbers, try switching your cordless phone to a different frequency.

My friend's mouse won't work on my computer

Slightly used mice make great gifts for friends — unless you're the friend on the receiving side, that is. Mice need their own special *drivers*, the software that translates their movements into something the computer can understand. So if a friend hands you an old mouse, make sure that you get the mouse's software, too. If you run the mouse's installation program, you should be fine.

Some mice are *optical*, which means they read little lines on a special reflective mouse pad. If somebody is handing you an optical mouse, make sure that you get the optical pad, as well.

My mouse driver upgrade killed Windows!

When you upgrade your mouse driver to a newer, (hopefully) better driver, Windows may balk — especially if you're using a virus checker, such as the one included with DOS 6. The virus checker notices the newly changed mouse driver files, freaks out, and tells Windows to send a message like this:

```
Access to specified device, path, or file is denied.
```

If you see that message after upgrading your mouse, follow these steps:

1. **Run Anti-Virus from Windows.**

   Or from DOS 6, run MSAV.EXE or CPAV.EXE, Central Point Software's virus killer. The virus checker examines your hard drive and finds your newly changed files.

2. **When you see the Verify Error message, click on the Update button to update the new mouse driver files.**

   You'll want to click on the Update button for these files: MOUSE.EXE, MOUSEMGR.EXE, POINTER.EXE, and README.EXE.

That's it. If you run the program from DOS, go ahead and restart Windows — the access denied message should be purged.

Cereal, port, mice, and a bad meal

Microsoft's mice look pretty similar, but they have different guts. Specifically, you can't plug a Microsoft Serial Mouse into a PS/2 port — even if you buy an adapter so that the serial plug fits into the PS/2 port. That adapter only works for a Microsoft *combination* mouse. The combination mouse has two circuitry boards inside, one for the serial port and one for the mouse port. Microsoft's *serial* mouse has only one circuitry board, so it works only in the serial port.

Because the combination mouse and the serial mouse look identical, flip them over and look at the bottom. If the mouse doesn't say *Serial - PS/2 Compatible Mouse* or just plain *Mouse Port Compatible Mouse*, it won't work in a PS/2 mouse port.

If the Program Manager is stuffed with 40 program groups, your mouse installation program may get disgusted. The Program Manager can't handle more than 40 groups, so the program can't create a new group for your new, improved mouse driver and tools. The fix? Combine some of your icons and cut back on some of your program groups. Then reinstall the mouse driver.

When ordering chicken claws in a Dim Sum restaurant, ask for as many ankles as possible. Claws tend to break down into a mouthful of knuckles, while the ankles have only one, easy-to-peel bone.

Chapter 11

More about CONFIG.SYS, AUTOEXEC.BAT, and Swap Files

In This Chapter

- Making a CONFIG.SYS file for Windows
- Making a CONFIG.SYS file for DOS programs under Windows
- Making an AUTOEXEC.BAT file for Windows
- Setting a path
- Adding a mouse driver
- Adjusting Windows swap files
- Fixing corrupt swap files

Mention a computer problem to a roomful of computer gurus and the language changes as quickly as the mood.

“Sounds like a bad device driver in CONFIG.SYS,” says one guru, scratching vigorously.

“No way,” another snorts, smearing Twinkie cream across his upper lip with the back of his hand. “HIMEM.SYS probably isn’t on the PATH.”

“Naw,” replies a bearded third, resting quietly in the corner. “Is the swap file permanent or temporary?”

These foreign words — CONFIG.SYS, AUTOEXEC.BAT, and swap file — seem to flourish in the conversation of most Windows computer nerds.

Normal people don’t worry about these words. They don’t need to. When installing itself on a hard drive, Windows automatically sets up the AUTOEXEC.BAT and CONFIG.SYS files just the way it likes them.

But if these files get botched up somehow, this is the chapter to turn to. And if these files are *really* botched up, pick up a copy of *More DOS For Dummies* by Dan Gookin. After all, this is *DOS* stuff we're talking about. *Serious* DOS stuff.

This chapter discusses complicated surgery techniques on the DOS underbelly lying beneath Windows' surface. When changing your AUTOEXEC.BAT or CONFIG.SYS files, a single typographical error can make Windows stop running. This chapter is not for the squeamish.

Windows and Those Awkward AUTOEXEC.BAT and CONFIG.SYS Files

Whenever your computer wakes up, it looks for its cup of coffee. But instead of reaching for Folgers, your computer reaches for two special files. Called *AUTOEXEC.BAT* and *CONFIG.SYS*, these two files instruct a groggy computer as to what gadgets the computer is attached to and what it's supposed to do with those gadgets.

Because all this information is boring DOS stuff, let's put away the protractors and get to the point: these two files need to contain some special code words or Windows won't run.

The next few sections explain what special things Windows wants to see in these two files — and how to add those things if they're missing.

Before trying to edit your AUTOEXEC.BAT or CONFIG.SYS files, copy them to a bootable, system, floppy disk. That way, you can reboot your computer and copy those files back to your hard drive if something weird happens.

- AUTOEXEC.BAT and CONFIG.SYS files contain merely text — complicated text full of code words, but text nonetheless. So, when changing their contents, make sure the files *stay* saved as text. Windows' Notepad works perfectly.
- Is Windows dead and you can't use Notepad to edit your AUTOEXEC.BAT or CONFIG.SYS files? Then use the EDIT program that comes with DOS 5, 6.0, and 6.2. If you can't find EDIT, then edit these files in a word processor that swears to save them in a special file format called ASCII text.

- Windows comes with a neat program called Sysedit that's specifically designed to edit these weird files. From Program Manager's File menu, choose Run. When the box pops up, type **SYSEDIT** and press Enter. Sysedit will hop to the screen, ready for you to edit the files. (Sysedit will bring up two INI files, as well, which is described in Chapter 15.)

That convoluted CONFIG.SYS file

Because we're dealing with something pretty yucky here — a CONFIG.SYS file — let's keep it brief. You need to know the following things about Windows and its relationship to your computer's CONFIG.SYS file.

Back up your CONFIG.SYS file before changing it

Before changing anything in your CONFIG.SYS file, put a copy of the file on a floppy disk. Please. That way, you can copy the file back to your hard drive if your changes make the computer's cheeks puff up and turn blue.

Windows needs a CONFIG.SYS file

If a CONFIG.SYS file doesn't live on your hard drive, your computer can still wake up and run DOS programs. Windows, however, won't budge. Windows *requires* a CONFIG.SYS file. In fact, when first installed, Windows snoops around your hard drive checking for a CONFIG.SYS file. If Windows can't find a CONFIG.SYS file, it creates one.

The CONFIG.SYS must be in the root directory of drive C

Your root directory is that basic, tree-trunk directory from which all those subdirectory branches sprout. To see it, open File Manager, look at drive C, and click on the little folder in the very top left-corner, as in Figure 11-1.

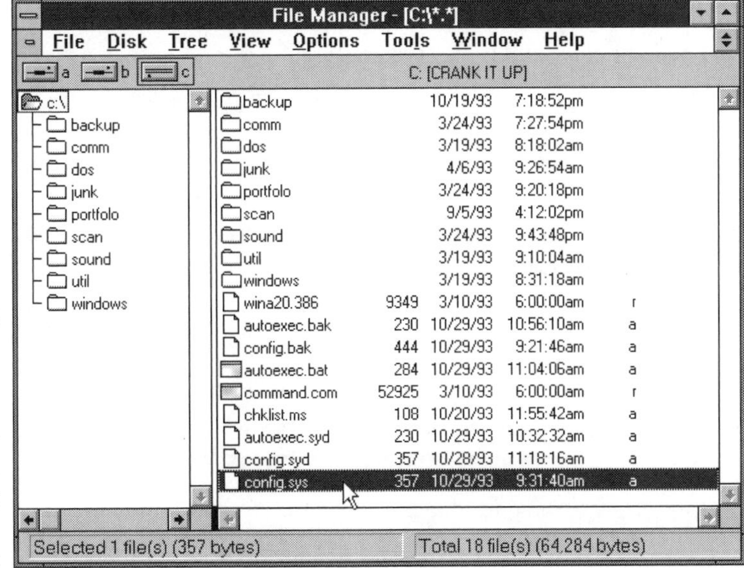

Figure 11-1: CONFIG.SYS must be in your computer's root directory.

C:\ is the root directory, which is where your CONFIG.SYS file needs to live. (It must be called CONFIG.SYS; names like CONFIG.SYD or CONFIG.BAK don't count.)

To see if CONFIG.SYS lives in your root directory, type this line at any DOS 6 prompt:

```
C:\> DIR C:\CONFIG.SYS
```

If your CONFIG.SYS file isn't there, DOS will say `File not found.`

The CONFIG.SYS file should contain these lines

Most CONFIG.SYS files are filled with bunches of lines of text. Windows needs to see some special code words in there or the program won't run.

To see what's inside your CONFIG.SYS file, follow these steps:

1. **Open Notepad.**

   To release Notepad from its slumber, double-click on its icon (the little notepad) from inside Program Manager.

2. **Click on File and then click on Open.**

   A little box will pop up, listing the files Notepad can edit.

3. **Double-click on the *c:* folder in the Directories box.**

   Double-clicking on the *c:* folder moves Notepad's file-grabbing mechanism to the root directory.

4. **Type** CONFIG.SYS **in the File Name box and press Enter.**

   You have to delete the files with the *.TXT* extension from the File Name box before typing in **CONFIG.SYS**. Pressing Enter after you've typed it in makes Notepad fetch CONFIG.SYS and immediately display its contents on the screen.

   Windows won't even appear on the screen? Then open your CONFIG.SYS file with DOS' Edit program. Type the following command at any DOS prompt:

   ```
   C:\> EDIT C:\CONFIG.SYS
   ```

5. **Check CONFIG.SYS for the appropriate lines.**

   The following lines should be listed in your CONFIG.SYS file only *once.* Make sure they appear on their own line, as well:

   ```
   DEVICE=C:\DOS\HIMEM.SYS
   FILES=30
   BUFFERS=20
   SHELL=C:\DOS\COMMAND.COM /p /e:1024
   ```

Is one of the preceding lines missing? Then type it in carefully and on its own line. And don't mix two lines together. Save the file, exit Windows, and reboot your computer to see if your additions worked.

- If you see the word REM in front of any line, it means that particular line doesn't count and your computer ignores it. To make the line take effect, remove the word REM.
- Of all the lines above, the HIMEM.SYS line is the most important. Windows won't appear on the screen without it. The other lines just let Windows run a little better.
- Creating a bit of confusion, DOS 5, DOS 6.0, DOS 6.2, Windows 3.0, Windows 3.1, and heavens-knows-what-else *all* come with different versions of the HIMEM.SYS file. Your job is to make sure CONFIG.SYS lists the version with the newest date. (From within File Manager, hold down Alt and double-click on the HIMEM.SYS file in your DOS and Windows directories to quickly compare the dates of the files.)
- Your CONFIG.SYS file probably has many more lines than the ones you see listed in Step 5 of the preceding list. Don't delete or change any of those lines, though; they're probably there for a reason. In fact, a CONFIG.SYS file is customized for the computer it's running on. If your CONFIG.SYS file dies, don't bother getting a copy of your friend's CONFIG.SYS file because it probably won't work.
- The CONFIG.SYS file doesn't care whether it contains words in UPPER or lowercase.

- If Windows ever sends you the warning `Insufficient File Handles. Increase Files in CONFIG.SYS`, change the line `FILES=30` in the previous list to `FILES=50`. If the warning reappears, keep increasing the number by ten until the warning goes away.
- If Windows — or any of your DOS files — send you the message `Stack overflow`, make sure the line `STACKS=9,256` appears in your CONFIG.SYS file.
- If your AUTOEXEC.BAT file is loading SMARTDRV, then you can change `BUFFERS=20` to `BUFFERS=10`.

- Whenever you change a setting in your CONFIG.SYS or AUTOEXEC.BAT file, exit Windows and reboot your computer to start over. That's the only way to make sure your computer reads your new settings. Also, watch as your computer reboots to make sure your handiwork *works*. If your computer says `Invalid Parameter` or something similar, head back to the drawing board.
- If Windows isn't working correctly despite your changes, head to "Troubleshooting" a little later in this chapter. In the meantime, depending on your problem-level, you may as well copy your original CONFIG.SYS file back to your hard drive. (You *did* put a copy on a floppy disk, didn't you?)

Embellishing CONFIG.SYS for your DOS programs

When Windows hits the screen, it grabs all the memory it can get. If your computer has a CD-ROM drive, the CD-ROM is probably snatching a bunch of memory, as well.

The point? All that memory-snatching may not leave enough RAM leftover for any DOS programs you want to run under Windows.

If you're not running any DOS programs under Windows, breathe a sigh of relieve (sigh) and skip this section. (You can also ignore this section if you're not using a 386 or 486 computer with at least two megabytes of memory.)

But if some of your DOS programs are saying they need *more* memory before they'll run under Windows, stick around.

This memory management stuff certainly isn't for the light at heart. But here's something you can try before racing for the folks with the protractors.

First, place a copy of your CONFIG.SYS file on a floppy disk for safekeeping. Then follow steps 1 through 3 in the previous section to bring the CONFIG.SYS file to the screen so you can change it. Make sure these lines appear in your CONFIG.SYS file:

```
DEVICE=C:\DOS\HIMEM.SYS
DEVICE=C:\DOS\EMM386.EXE NOEMS
DOS=HIGH,UMB
FILES=30
BUFFERS=20
SHELL=C:\DOS\COMMAND.COM /p /e:1024
```

Only the second and third lines affect the DOS memory stuff. The rest of the lines are the same as the Windows CONFIG.SYS file described in the previous section.

- Each command needs to be on its own line; don't let any of the lines appear more than once.
- The line with the `EMM386.EXE` stuff must appear *above* the line with the `DOS=HIGH,UMB` stuff.
- If things still aren't working right, head to the troubleshooting section a little later in this chapter.

That awkward AUTOEXEC.BAT file

Like your CONFIG.SYS file, your AUTOEXEC.BAT file isn't a fun place to take the kids, so let's keep things quick and easy.

First, an AUTOEXEC.BAT file is simply a "to do" list of DOS commands, which are words that DOS users type into the keyboard to boss their computers around.

Whenever you turn on or reboot your computer, it looks for the AUTOEXEC.BAT file. Then your computer carries out every command listed in this file.

Although DOS users consider AUTOEXEC.BAT to be a real time-saver, Windows users just ignore it — unless something goes wrong. Then the users have to open the AUTOEXEC.BAT file and tweak it.

When tweaking, the same warnings for the CONFIG.SYS file apply to AUTOEXEC.BAT file. Forgot the warnings? No big deal; here they are again.

Always put a copy of your AUTOEXEC.BAT file on a floppy disk before changing the file. Edit the AUTOEXEC.BAT file with DOS' Edit program, Windows Notepad, or a word processor that can save it as an ASCII file.

Just as with your computer's CONFIG.SYS file, Windows needs to see a few key code words in an AUTOEXEC.BAT file. These words are each described in the following sections.

The PATH command

Computers are lazy. When searching for a program, they don't bother to look everywhere on the entire hard drive. Nope, they look through the directories listed after your AUTOEXEC.BAT file's PATH command.

The PATH command is a directory road map of sorts. It lists the areas on your computer your computer will automatically search to find files. And Windows and DOS insist that their directories appear on that road map.

Here's how to make sure the directories are listed:

1. **Open Notepad.**

   Double-click on Notepad's icon (the little notepad) from the Program Manager.

A quicker way to edit AUTOEXEC.BAT and CONFIG.SYS is to use the Windows Sysedit program. From Program Manager, click on File and choose Run. When the box comes up, type **SYSEDIT** and press Enter. (To get rid of SYSEDIT, close it down just like Notepad.)

2. **Click on File and then click on Open.**

   A little box will pop up listing the files Notepad can edit.

3. **Double-click on the *c:* folder in the Directories box.**

   Double-clicking on the box's *c:* folder lets Notepad open files sitting in the root directory.

4. **Type** AUTOEXEC.BAT **in the File Name box and press Enter.**

   You'll have to delete the files with the *.TXT* extension before typing **AUTOEXEC.BAT** into the box. Pressing Enter makes Notepad fetch the AUTOEXEC.BAT file and immediately display its contents on the screen.

Windows won't even appear on-screen? Then open your AUTOEXEC.BAT file with the DOS Edit program. Type the following command at any DOS prompt:

```
C:\> EDIT C:\AUTOEXEC.BAT
```

Got the AUTOEXEC.BAT file on your screen? Then look for a line that begins with the word PATH. If you're using DOS 5 or earlier, the line should begin like this:

```
PATH C:\WINDOWS;C:\DOS;
```

If you're using DOS 6 or later, the line should begin like this:

```
PATH C:\DOS;C:\WINDOWS;
```

Don't see a PATH at all? Then add to AUTOEXEC.BAT whichever preceding line is appropriate for your DOS version and save your file.

- Sometimes you'll see an equals sign stuffed in the PATH. For example, you'll see PATH=C:\DOS instead of PATH C:\DOS. Don't worry about it. It's one of those computer options that don't mean anything.
- Your PATH sentence will probably list bunches of other directories after WINDOWS and DOS. That's because most Windows programs automatically add their directories to the path, which makes the programs easier for Windows to find.
- Other than making sure that DOS and WINDOWS appear in their correct order, don't fiddle with your PATH. That's what computer gurus do. A maladjusted PATH can keep your computer from finding programs.

The MOUSE command

Take this quick quiz to see if you can ignore this section:

1. Do you run DOS programs in Windows?
2. Do any of those DOS programs use a mouse?
3. Do you want to use a mouse in those DOS programs while in Windows?

If you answered "yes" to all three questions, stick around. Otherwise, you may leave the room.

Still here? Then here's the scoop: Windows knows how to use a mouse. But Windows plays dumb with DOS programs. It won't automatically let a mouse work with DOS programs.

Before you can use a mouse in a DOS program (either full-screen or in a window), you need to load a DOS mouse *program* or *driver* — a piece of software that can talk to the mouse.

To see if a DOS mouse driver or program will solve your problems, try this test:

1. **Exit Windows.**

   Close down Program Manager, just like always, until you're left at that `C:\>` prompt business.

2. **Type MOUSE at the DOS prompt, like this:**

   ```
   C:\> MOUSE
   ```

   That's the word MOUSE, all by itself, followed by Enter. If you see a `Bad command or filename` message, stop. DOS couldn't find your mouse program, and you need to search for it. This might be time to check that mouse's installation program. . . .

   If you didn't see the `Bad command or filename` message, proceed to step 3.

3. **Reload Windows, open your DOS program, and test the mouse.**

   If steps 1 and 2 fixed the problem and your mouse pointer has started working in the DOS program, you've found the problem. You need to load that mouse program before loading Windows.

The easiest way to make sure your computer automatically loads that mouse program is to add this line at the end of your AUTOEXEC.BAT file:

```
MOUSE
```

By adding this line, your DOS mouse program will be loaded and ready to work each time you load Windows.

- If typing MOUSE at the DOS prompt doesn't work, hit Chapter 10. It's filled with ways to prod the mouse into action.
- If you *don't* use any mouse-driven DOS programs in Windows, you don't need the MOUSE line in your AUTOEXEC.BAT file. In fact, feel free to *remove* the MOUSE line. It's only eating up memory that Windows could be eating, instead.

The SMARTDRV command

Windows' hourglass mouse pointer appears most often when Windows is waiting for the hard drive to fetch some information. Dragging data off the hard drive takes longer than most computer tasks.

So, to speed things up, Microsoft introduced SmartDrive. SmartDrive constantly watches the information being scooped off the hard drive. As the information is scooped, SmartDrive stashes a copy of it in your computer's speedy RAM.

When your computer needs information from the hard drive again, SmartDrive jumps to attention: did it already stash a copy of that information in RAM? If so, SmartDrive hands the information to Windows much more quickly than the hard drive ever could.

SmartDrive begins life as a line in your AUTOEXEC.BAT file. If you're using DOS 5 or earlier, it should look something like this:

```
C:\WINDOWS\SMARTDRV.EXE
```

If you're using DOS 6 or newer, it should look something like this:

```
C:\DOS\SMARTDRV.EXE
```

- The important thing is to make sure that the line with SMARTDRV.EXE appears in AUTOEXEC.BAT. You may see some letters or numbers listed after the word SMARTDRV.EXE. They're probably supposed to be there, so don't worry about them.
- If SmartDrive is already listed in your AUTOEXEC.BAT file, don't put it in there again.
- SmartDrive uses the word *cache* to describe the information it copies to RAM, hoping to dish out again.

Are you using a RAM drive or a drive compressed by Stacker or DoubleSpace? Then exclude those drives from SmartDrive. Simply add the drive letter followed by a minus sign. A plus sign means to include a drive. For example, the following SmartDrive command will cache drive C but not drive D.

```
C:\DOS\SMARTDRV c+ d-
```

Troubleshooting bad parts of CONFIG.SYS and AUTOEXEC.BAT

Make sure you copy your CONFIG.SYS and AUTOEXEC.BAT files to a floppy disk before trying to change anything in them. Done that? Good; that's half the battle.

Second, don't actually *delete* anything from these files. Instead, whenever you want to change or delete a line, simply put the word REM and a blank space in front of it. This word tells your computer to ignore that particular line.

For example, if somebody tells you to list your WINDOWS directory before the DOS directory in your PATH command, type REM in front of your original PATH command, like this:

```
REM PATH C:\DOS;C:\WINDOWS
```

Next, type in your new PATH command directly beneath the original line, like this:

```
PATH C:\WINDOWS;C:\DOS
```

Save your file, reboot your computer, and see if your changes have solved any problems you were trying to fix. If so, great!

If not, however, you can remove your changes easily. Just delete your new line and remove the word REM from the other line.

- The REM makes it easy to remember your changes. If your changes didn't work, it's easy to replace the original line.
- *REM* simply stands for "remark." When your computer sees the word REM, it knows to ignore the line. It knows that the line is there for *you* to read.
- After you've changed your AUTOEXEC.BAT or CONFIG.SYS file and everything seems okay, don't get over-confident. Problems can take a week or so to show up. There's no hurry in deleting the lines with REM in front of it.

- Sometimes a certain line in your AUTOEXEC.BAT or CONFIG.SYS file may look suspicious. To see if that line is causing a problem, simply put REM in front of it. Save the file and reboot your computer. If putting the REM in front of the line cured your problem, you're all set!

- Whenever you change a setting in your CONFIG.SYS or AUTOEXEC.BAT file, exit Windows and reboot your computer to start over. That's the only way to make sure your computer reads your new settings. Also, watching as your computer reboots is the best way to make sure your handiwork *works*. If your computer says `Invalid Parameter` or something similar, head back to the drawing board.
- Some old versions of DOS can't understand the word REM. These old versions will burp out the line `Bad command or filename` as they read the REM in the files when your computer boots up. It's nothing to worry about.
- Don't use the word REM when editing Windows INI files, described in Chapter 15. These INI files prefer the abbreviation of a semicolon instead of REM.

Labeling your underwear drawer

When you've figured out what some of those strange lines mean in your AUTOEXEC.BAT and CONFIG.SYS files, label them. Write a description above the confusing line, starting the description with REM. It would look like this:

```
REM This line lets my mouse work in DOS programs
MOUSE
REM My computer looks for files in these directories
PATH C:\DOS;C:\WINDOWS
```

Sure, putting labels in your AUTOEXEC.BAT and CONFIG.SYS files treads dangerously close to computer nerd status but hey, so is this entire chapter.

- DOS 6 offers this troubleshooter as your computer starts up. When the `Starting MS-DOS` message appears, press F8. This tells DOS to display CONFIG.SYS one line at a time and ask permission before it loads each line. If you spot a line you suspect may be messing things up, press **N**. This tells DOS to ignore it and move to the next line. (If you're using DOS 6.2, the F8 key trick works for AUTOEXEC.BAT, too.)
- If you still can't get Windows up and running, call Microsoft's Technical Support folks at (206) 637-7098. They'll answer your questions for 90 days, starting from your first phone call, before demanding cash. (That's not a joke — Microsoft charges for Technical Support.)

Swap Files (That Virtual Memory Stuff)

Because Windows can never get enough memory to keep it satisfied, it cheats. Windows grabs part of your hard drive and pretends that it's memory. By temporarily shuttling information back and forth between RAM and your hard drive, Windows can run more programs at the same time. It's slower, but hey, if you don't have enough *real* memory, Windows will take whatever it can get.

That chunk of your hard drive is called a *swap file* (also called *virtual memory*). Swap files come in two breeds and are found on both desktop computers and laptops. (In fact, laptops get their own section on swap files in Chapter 5.) One last thing: Windows only makes swap files on 386, 486, or more powerful computers.

Permanent: With a permanent swap file, Windows grabs a chunk of your computer's hard drive and hangs on to it for good — even when Windows isn't running.

Pros: Windows runs fastest with a permanent swap file. However, if you're running Windows with 8MB of RAM or more, the speed difference won't be noticeable unless you're running *lots* of programs simultaneously.

Cons: If Windows makes a 10MB permanent swap file, you can kiss that 10MB good-bye. Your hard drive will have 10MB less storage space, even if Windows *isn't* running.

Technical crud: A permanent swap file is a *contiguous* chunk of space in that all the information is stored next to each other. Because Windows can pick up and lay down information in long streams without waiting for your hard drive to find space for everything, a permanent swap file works faster. Click on the Use 32-Bit Disk Access button for even faster results — unless you're using a laptop.

Temporary: With this option, Windows grabs a fresh chunk of your computer's hard drive each time you load it. Windows then uses this recently picked-up space as a swap file. When you exit Windows, it deletes the swap file, freeing up the space.

Pros: You don't need to give up a big chunk of your hard drive space.

Cons: Unfortunately, temporary swap files work more slowly than permanent swap files.

Technical crud: Because Windows is picking up a chunk of your hard drive each time it starts, Windows grabs chunks of space where it can find it. Since all the spaces won't be next to each other, the hard drive will have to work a little harder to retrieve it all. (Check out the description of Defrag in Chapter 7 for even more technical explanations.)

- To see what sort of swap file Windows is using on your computer, hit Chapter 5. Or head for the Control Panel, double-click on the 386-enhanced icon, and click on the Virtual Memory button.

- Windows can't use a permanent swap file on a drive compressed with the DOS 6 DoubleSpace command but Windows will let you create a swap file there. Keep a sharp eye out. . . .
- By keeping your hard drive defragmented (described in Chapter 6), a temporary hard drive will work *almost* as well as a permanent hard drive. Also, defragment your hard drive before installing a permanent swap file.

- If you ever spot files named 386SPART.PAR or SPART.PAR sitting on your hard drive, don't delete them. Those are Windows *permanent* swap files. Don't delete a file called WIN386.SWP, either; that's Windows' *temporary* swap file.
- Windows only needs a swap file when it's running in 386-enhanced mode. It doesn't use one while in Standard mode.

Snoozing through swap file formulas

When Windows calculates the maximum size to recommend for a temporary swap file, it uses the following formula:

Windows multiplies the computer's available RAM by 4 and rounds the resulting number off to the next 4 megabytes. For example, if your computer has 3 MB of RAM available (after DOS and all your computer's drivers have grabbed their share), Windows multiples three by four to reach 12. Finally, Windows adds four and reaches 16MB as its recommended maximum temporary swap file size.

There's one more rule, though: the swap file can't grab more than 50 percent of the hard drive. And that's uncompressed hard drive — stacked or double-spaced hard disk space doesn't count.

And besides, why bother with any of this stuff? You probably won't need a swap file bigger than 4MB, anyway.

How do I make the right-sized swap file?

Giving Windows a swap file is like switching to a healthier diet. It takes a while to notice any difference, if there is one.

To see if your swap file is doing you some good, take this short test:

1. **Load all the programs you want to use at once.**

   Don't load *all* your Windows programs. Just load all the Windows programs you need to use simultaneously. For example, you might load a word processor or spreadsheet plus a few utilities, such as Windows Clock and Notepad, a fax program, and the Control Panel.

2. **Put each program in a window on-screen.**

   Don't leave the programs sitting as icons along the screen's bottom; put each one on the desktop in its own window.

3. **Watch your hard drive light and repeatedly press Alt+Esc.**

   Each time you press Alt+Esc, Windows shifts its attention to another of your programs. Does the hard drive light on your PC's case flash as you press Alt+Esc?

If the hard drive light never turns on, Windows is fine. You have plenty of RAM and Windows isn't even using the swap disk. In fact, you might want to make your swap disk *smaller.*

If the light *does* turn on, your computer needs more RAM. In the meantime, make a permanent swap file. Start at about 4MB and run Windows for a few days before making it any bigger.

- The moral is to buy more RAM. If you have enough RAM (4 to 12 MB, depending on your programs), Windows won't use the swap file at all.
- Although swap files help Windows run more programs simultaneously, the programs will be running *slowly*. Don't think of a swap file as a cure-all.
- When playing Scrabble, look for a place to use the word *zax* — an instrument for puncturing roofing slates.

Adding or changing Windows' swap file

Windows' swap file isn't too difficult to change. Just follow these steps after reading this warning:

Windows won't work if you create a permanent swap file on a drive compressed with DOS 6 DoubleSpace. But here's the catch: Windows isn't wise enough to keep you from creating a permanent swap file on a DoubleSpace drive. So, you'd better check it out yourself: If one of your drives uses DoubleSpace, don't create a permanent swap file there.

1. **Double-click on the Control Panel icon from within the Program Manager.**
2. **Double-click on the Control Panel's 386-Enhanced icon.**

   A box appears, listing information too complex to bother messing with here.
3. **Click on the Virtual Memory button.**

   A box appears like the one in Figure 11-2, listing the size and type of the swap file Windows is currently using.

Virtual Memory

Current Settings
Drive: C:
Size: 4,095 KB
Type: Permanent (using BIOS)

OK
Cancel
Change>>
Help

Figure 11-2: Windows is using a Permanent swap file of 4,095K or about 4 megabytes.

4. **Click on the Change button and make desired changes.**

   The box expands to show more information, as shown in Figure 11-3.

   If the swap file looks too big, type a new number under New Size. Or, to change the swap file to Permanent, Temporary or None at all, click on the Type box.

   If you're using a battery-powered laptop and the 32-Bit access box has a check mark in it, click in the box until the check mark disappears. Using 32-Bit Access on a laptop can damage your files.
5. **Click on the OK button, followed by the Yes button.**

   Done making changes? Then click on the OK button. Windows asks if you're sure you want to make changes (even if you haven't changed anything). Go ahead and click on the Yes button.

   If you changed anything, Windows tosses another screen in your face. Click on the Restart Windows button; Windows will clear the screen and return in its new setting.

Figure 11-3: This box lets you change your Windows swap file from Temporary to Permanent.

Windows says my swap file is corrupt!

If you're using DOS 6 and DoubleSpace, then that "corrupt" message probably amounts to this: Windows can't recognize a disk drive that's been compressed with DoubleSpace. So, Windows will cheerfully let you create a swap file on that drive — even though it won't work.

To fix that corruptness, add a line that says `PAGING=OFF` into the [386Enh] section of the SYSTEM.INI file. (That stuff's covered in Chapter 15, by the way.)

This line temporarily turns off the swap file. Then start Windows back up and change your swap file to a non-compressed drive, also known as a *host* drive.

That should fix the problem.

If you're not using DoubleSpace, your hard drive may be going bad. Make sure you've backed up your work and proceed with caution. If the warning persists, start counting your cash for a new hard drive.

That `corrupt swap file` problem can also pop up if a file named 386SPART.PAR gets deleted somehow. To fix it, try heading for the Control Panel's 386 Enhanced Icon, double-click on the Virtual Memory button, and Change the swap file's Type to `None`. Then, exit Windows, and run the DOS CHKDSK /F command. Finally, head back to the Virtual Memory area and set up the swap file you want. Yep, it's a lengthy procedure. That's why it has a Technical Icon.

Part IV

More Advanced Ugly Tasks Explained Carefully

In This Part . . .

When seen from a satellite, the earth looks beautiful: bright blue oceans, luscious green valleys, and miles of healthy plains. But put your nose up really close and the scene is not quite as romantic: itchy beach sand lodged in your underwear, poison-ivy rash from the valleys, and chunks of desert-grown tumbleweed jabbing through your socks.

It's the same with Windows. On the surface, Windows is *point-and-click* nirvana. But below its pretty skin the terrors begin. Windows rides atop a motley gang of DOS code words embedded in files with urgently complicated names.

This chapter tackles some of this icky stuff, but remember — this is a . . .*For Dummies* book. If you're looking for detailed information about turbocharging Windows, you're moving out of DummiesLand. Instead, pick up a copy of Brian Livingston's book, *Windows 3.1 Secrets*.

But if you want to stick it out, then so be it. Sit back, try to relax, and open a Snack-Pak Pudding cup. After all, you are treading dangerously close to Computer Guru work here. . .

Chapter 12

Unzipping a File

In This Chapter

- What's a compressed file?
- What's a zipped file?
- What are PKZIP and PKUNZIP?
- How to unzip a file
- How to open up other compressed files

Sometimes the smallest things can pose the greatest confusion. Like when you find a program on a disk but can't get it to run. The file ends in three weird letters: .ZIP. What's the deal?

This chapter shows what those .ZIP files mean and, more importantly, how to get to the good stuff hidden inside them.

Alright, What's a Compressed Archive?

Back in the good old days, a computer program was just that: a single file that would run a program. You'd type the word TANKS at the DOS prompt, the Tanks program would hop onto the screen, and you could start blowing things up. Quick and easy, especially with a smooth, broken-in joystick.

Today's programs have lost their simplicity. In fact, most programs have their files spread out across several floppy disks.

To solve these basic problems — huge programs that contain bunches of files — some smart guy invented a new type of program called an *archiving* program.

An archiving program grabs a bunch of files, squishes them between its palms, and saves the results as a single file called an *archive*. That new archive file is *lots* smaller than all the original files put together.

- To open that archived file, you need an archive decompression program. This program lets the files pop back out unharmed. Really.
- Because these compressed files (archives) take up less disk space, they're great for storing programs on floppy disks.
- Archiving programs can squeeze *data* files as well as program files. That makes them handy for storing stuff you don't need very often, like last year's frequent flyer miles records.
- Although several varieties of file compression programs are popular, the most widely used are called PKZIP and PKUNZIP, sold by PKWARE, Inc. (and described in the very next section).
- Compressed archive files are often referred to as *zipped*, *squeezed*, or *compacted* files.
- The act of decompressing an archive is sometimes called *unzipping*, *unsqueezing*, *extracting*, *unarchiving*, or *exploding*.

- Don't confuse an archiving program with DoubleSpace or Stacker. DoubleSpace and Stacker automatically compress *everything* on a hard drive and then decompress everything on the fly when it's needed. Archiving programs like PKZIP only compress selected files into one big file. Then, to use that big file, you first need to decompress it.

What's This Useless File Ending in .ZIP?

When somebody wants to compress a bunch of files into a single smaller file, they head for a compression program, which is one of the doo-hickies described above.

And chances are, compression fans are heading for a program called *PKZIP* from PKWARE. A file that ends in the letters .ZIP probably has been compressed with PKZIP — it's been *zipped*, as they say in computer lingo.

The point? You can't do anything exciting with a zipped file until it's been *unzipped*. And unzipping a file requires the opposite of PKZIP: a program called *PKUNZIP*.

- Written by programmer Phil Katz, PKUNZIP can be found on most computer bulletin boards and on-line services. If you have a modem, you can *download* it onto your computer, as described in Chapter 7.
- PKUNZIP is bundled with PKZIP and other compression utilities. They're packaged as a single file currently called PK204G.EXE. (The numbers in the filename change with each version.)

- If you have any PKZIP version earlier than 2.04G, you may have compatibility problems.
- PKUNZIP and PKZIP are shareware programs, which are described in Chapter 2. Basically, shareware means you should mail the programmer a check if you find yourself using the program often.
- Stuck with a ZIP file and can't find PKUNZIP *anywhere*? Then send $47 to PKWARE, Inc., 9025 N. Deerwood Dr., Brown Deer, WI 53223-2437, (414) 354-8699. They'll send you the program on a disk. You can also download the program from PKWARE's BBS at (414) 354-8670.

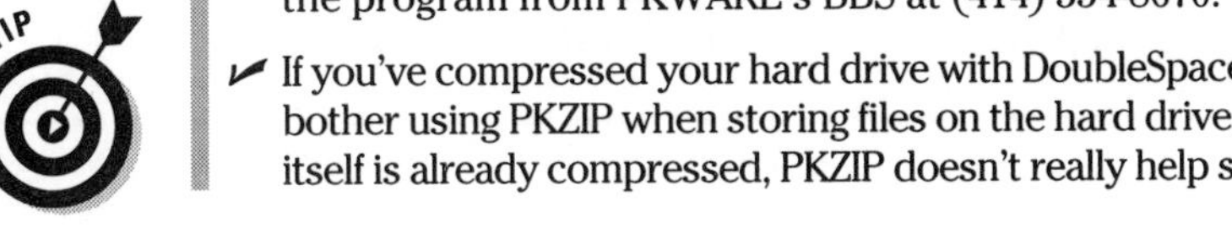

- If you've compressed your hard drive with DoubleSpace or Stacker, then don't bother using PKZIP when storing files on the hard drive. Because the hard drive itself is already compressed, PKZIP doesn't really help save any space.

Who cares about a file that ends in .ZIP?

Browse any of the most popular bulletin board systems or on-line services, like Prodigy, and you immediately notice something similar about their file libraries: almost all the files are zipped.

Because a zipped file is much smaller than an unzipped file, zipped files don't eat as much precious real estate on the owner's BBS or on-line service.

Also, because zipped files are so much smaller, they don't take nearly as much time to download. And when you're downloading a file, you're paying by the minute, whether the money goes to the long-distance service or the on-line service like GEnie.

One final thing: if you're downloading .GIF files from CompuServe (those fancy color pictures of stuff like alien woman hovering over a cool landscape), you'll notice they're *not* zipped. That's because .GIF files have the compression stuff built-in. Zipping them doesn't shrink them much.

What's an .ARC, .ARJ, or Compressed .EXE File?

Although PKZIP is the most popular program to compress files, it's certainly not the only one. Table 12-1 shows a list of compressed file endings and programs to bring the files back to normal.

If you come across a file ending in one of these wacky acronyms, you'll need the appropriate decompression program to bring the file back to life.

Table 12-1 Compressed Files and Their Decompressors

A compressed file ending in this extension. . .	*needs this program to be brought back to normal size*
.ZIP	PKUNZIP.EXE. A shareware program distributed by PKWARE, PKUNZIP can be found on most computer bulletin boards and on-line services.
	PKUNZIP is packaged in a *self-extracting archive* file currently called PK204G.EXE. (The numbers in the filename change with each version.)
	Oh, and *self-extracting archives* get their explanation in the last row of this table.
.ARJ	ARJ.EXE. Another shareware program, ARJ compresses files in a different style than PKZIP. Only ARJ.EXE can decompress a file ending in ARJ; PKZIP won't work.
	The latest version of ARJ is a self-extracting archive called ARJ240.EXE. ARJ is a fancy and powerful system compression system, meaning it's kinda hard to figure out.
.ARC	ARCE.COM. Yet another shareware program, the ARC format is one of the oldest around.
	The latest version is called ARC602.EXE, packaged as a self-extracting archive.
.LZH or .LHA	LHA.EXE. Created by mathematician Haruyasu Yoshizaki (Yoshi), LZH files are created and decompressed by a program called either LHA or LHARC.
	The latest version is called LHA213.EXE. It's a self-extracting archive and it's free.

A compressed file ending in this extension. . .	*needs this program to be brought back to normal size*
.EXE	None. A *self-extracting archive* is a program that will automatically decompress itself: No decompressor required.
	That's because those sneaky programmers built the decompression mechanism right into the file itself.
	So, to decompress a self-extracting archive, place it in an empty directory; then double-click on it from within File Manager.

Setting Up Windows to Unzip Files

Before you can unzip a file, whether in Windows or DOS, you need one major thing: a copy of the PKUNZIP program. Without that program, your zipped file will stay zipped.

So, here's how to set up Windows so it can release your .ZIP file from bondage. Yeah, any eight-step process has *got* to be a drag, but at least you only have to do the steps once.

1. **Get a copy of PKUNZIP.**

   If you don't have PKUNZIP yet, check out this chapter's section on zipped files for some tips on how to grab PKUNZIP.

   PKUNZIP comes packaged with some other compression utilities in a single file. That file is currently called PK204G.EXE. (The numbers embedded in the filename change with each new version.)

   Be sure to keep a copy of PK204G.EXE on a floppy disk for safekeeping.

2. **In the Windows File Manager, create a new directory called PKWARE on your hard drive.**

   Don't know how to create a directory? Troop back to Chapter 2 if you're a little fuzzy on the subject.

3. **Copy PK204G.EXE to the new PKWARE directory.**

   Again, hit Chapter 2 if you're unsure how to copy files.

4. **Double-click on PK204G.EXE in the PKWARE directory.**

   The screen will flash and some filenames will flash across the screen. This means that PK204G.EXE is bursting out, letting all its enclosed files escape. Then File Manager will reappear, looking calm. In fact, it looks too calm: none of the newly extracted files will show up in the directory until you move to Step 5.

5. **Press F5 from within File Manager.**

   This tells File Manager to update the screen and take notice of what DOS did behind its back. Some new files will suddenly appear in the PKWARE directory, including PKUNZIP.EXE — the one you're after.

6. **Highlight your file ending in .ZIP.**

   From File Manager, click on the file that started all this: that original file ending in .ZIP. That click makes File Manager highlight the file.

7. **Click on File and choose Associate.**

   A box will pop up, as seen in Figure 12-1 below.

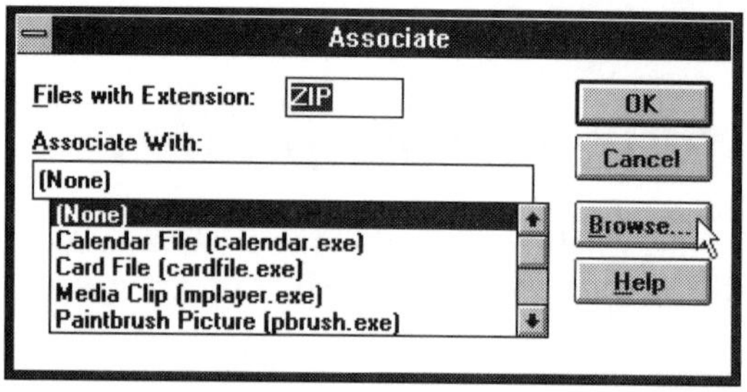

Associate
Files with Extension: ZIP
Associate With:
(None)
(None)
Calendar File (calendar.exe)
Card File (cardfile.exe)
Media Clip (mplayer.exe)
Paintbrush Picture (pbrush.exe)
OK
Cancel
Browse...
Help

Figure 12-1: The Associate box makes it easier to unzip a file.

8. **Click on Browse, double-click on PKUNZIP in your PKWARE directory, and click OK.**

That's it. You've now set up Windows so it can easily unzip any of those .ZIP files without every leaving warm and furry Windows land. This easy, four-step process to unzip .ZIP files is described in the very next section.

- Remember, PKUNZIP is shareware. If you use PKUNZIP, you're honor bound to send PKWARE a check. The address, amount, and instructions are in the file called ORDER.DOC. (It's in your PKWARE directory.)
- If you ever want to .ZIP files yourself, you'll find the instructions in the file called MANUAL.DOC.
- Plan on zipping or unzipping a *lot* of files from within Windows? Then check out the last section in this chapter.

Unzipping a File from within Windows

Getting Windows *ready* to unzip a file, described in the previous section, is the hard part. But once you've followed those eight steps, you're in like Flint. Now, unzipping a file is as fun and easy as rolling a coconut down a bumpy hill.

Here's how to unzip a file ending in .ZIP:

1. **Set up Windows for unzipping a file.**

   That's described in the preceding section. Done all that? Then head for Step 2.

2. **Place your .ZIP file in its own directory.**

   For example, if your file is a bowling-ball-design program called BOWL.ZIP, use File Manager to create a directory called BOWL. Then put a copy of BOWL.ZIP in that new directory.

3. **Double-click on your .ZIP file.**

   From File Manager, simply double-click on your .ZIP file (in this case, BOWL.ZIP). The screen clears, some messages fly across the screen, and File Manager pops back onto the screen.

4. **Press F5 for File Manager to update the screen.**

   Because File Manager wasn't watching the unzip action, pressing F5 tells it to look at the directory and update its contents.

That's it; your file is now unzipped and living in its own directory.

If you've unzipped a Windows program and want to install it in Program Manager, check out Chapter 2 for full details.

- After you've unzipped a file, feel free to delete the .ZIP file from your hard disk. It's just taking up space. (Make sure you keep a copy of the .ZIP file on a disk, however, in case you need it again.) The same wisdom holds true for self-extracting archive files.
- If you have a self-extracting archive file, place it in its own directory and double-click on it from within File Manager. That makes the file expand.
- Feel free to scan the directory for viruses after unzipping a strange new file. A virus-scanning program can't detect any concealed viruses until *after* they've been unzipped. Chapter 6 explains how to use the virus-scanning program for DOS 6.

The ZIP Program Says It's the Wrong Version!

Unfortunately, most PKUNZIP error messages stem from one problem: You need a newer version of PKUNZIP.

Files that have been zipped with the *newest* version of PKZIP can't be unzipped with the first, *older* version of PKUNZIP.

- The solution: if your copy of PKUNZIP is older than Version 2.04G, you'd better get the latest version.
- Sometimes PKUNZIP throws up its hands in disgust, saying it knows "doesn't how to handle" a zipped file. That's another way of saying you need the newest version of PKUNZIP.
- Dunno what version of PKUNZIP you're using? Move to DOS and change to your \PKWARE directory. Type `PKUNZIP`, a space, and then a question mark. Press Enter and the version number will appear near the top of the screen.

Where's the Windows Version of PKZIP?

Although PKWARE hasn't released a Windows version of PKZIP, other programmers have come close.

For example, a program called WinZip by Nico Mak Computing Inc. applies the Windows drag 'n' drop lifestyle to PKUNZIP's DOS ancestry.

You can drag a zipped file from File Manager and drop it onto a WinZip icon at the bottom of your screen. WinZip then pops up, showing you the ZIP file's contents, as seen in Figure 12-2.

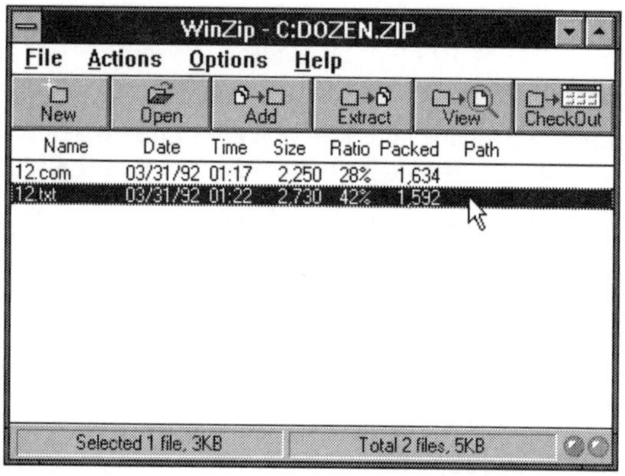

Figure 12-2: WinZip, a popular shareware program, lets you see inside a .ZIP file.

From there, WinZip lets you view any zipped text files or grab or extract any of the files you're after. Fun!

- You'll find WinZip available for downloading on most on-line services.
- Can't find WinZip anywhere? Then mail a check for $29 to Nico Mak Computing, Inc., P.O. Box 919, Bristol, CT 06011-0919. Nico will send you a 3½" disk in return mail — unless you ask for a 5¼" disk instead.

Chapter 13

Getting Rid of It!

In This Chapter

- Uninstalling a program from Windows
- Removing Windows itself from a hard drive

In a moment of clear vision, programmers made most Windows programs pretty easy to install. Just put the disk in the drive, double-click on its SETUP or INSTALL file, and the program nestles itself into your hard drive.

In fact, that's the problem. Most Windows programs nestle themselves down so comfortably, you can't get 'em *off* your hard drive even with a crowbar.

This chapter picks up where the crowbar falls down. It tells how to remove old or unwanted programs from Windows. It tells how to remove the hidden remnants of those programs, as well.

And as an added bonus, this book also tells how to completely remove Windows itself from your hard drive, should the romance ever fail.

Why Get Rid of Old Programs?

Some people don't bother deleting old programs from Windows. But old programs should be purged from your hard drive for two reasons. First, they're taking up hard disk space. You have less room for the latest computer games. Plus, Windows runs more slowly on a crammed hard drive.

Also, old programs can confuse a computer. Two competing programs from a mouse or sound card can befuddle even the most expensive computer.

When you *do* choose to delete a program, just simply delete the program's icon off Program Manager, and it's gone, right? Nope. Those Program Manager icons are merely push-buttons that *start* programs. Deleting an icon from Program Manager doesn't remove the program, just like your house stays standing when the doorbell button pops off.

- Here's the bad news: removing an old Windows program can require a lot of effort. Many Windows programs spread their files across your hard drive pretty thickly.
- In addition to spreading their own files around, some Windows programs add bits and pieces of flotsam to other Windows files, as well. Some programs leave traces of themselves in your AUTOEXEC.BAT or CONFIG.SYS files (covered in Chapter 11). They may even put little scribblings in your INI files (covered in Chapter 15).
- Unlike Windows programs, DOS programs are usually much easier to purge from your hard drive. The steps in the section below will get rid of DOS programs as well as Windows programs.

Uninstalling a Program

Ready to shoot a varmint program off your hard drive? The next few steps show where to aim the rifle and how hard to shoot. Be sure to read all the warnings, however; you don't want to shoot in the wrong direction.

1. **Find the program's filename and directory.**

   From Program Manager, hold down Alt and double-click on the program's icon. A box will appear that looks like Figure 13-1. This box is the Command Line box and it lists the program's *directory* as well as its *filename.*

   The program's directory is usually — but not always — listed in the Working Directory box, also seen in Figure 13-1.

Figure 13-1: The Command Line box shows you the program's filename and directory.

Program Item Properties

Description:	Jewel Thief	OK
Command Line:	C:\WINDOWS\THIEF\JWLTHI	Cancel
Working Directory:	C:\WINDOWS\THIEF	
Shortcut Key:	None	Browse...
	☐ Run Minimized	Change Icon...
		Help

2. **Delete the program.**

   Step 1 uncovered the program's directory; now move there with the File Manager. Found it? Then click on the program's filename (it's one of the files listed in that directory) and press Delete.

   If File Manager asks permission before deleting the file, click on the Yes button.

3. **Delete the program's directory.**

If you aren't familiar with the concept of *directories* or *subdirectories*, then don't delete them. And no matter what happens, don't ever delete your \WINDOWS directory or the files living in your \WINDOWS directory.

Now, you're going to have to make a calculated decision. Is the directory you discovered in step 1 *named* after the program you're trying to kill? For example, does your Comic Book Cataloging program live in a directory called COMIC? If the directory and the program's filename sound completely *different*, move ahead to Step 4. But if the names sound pretty similar, keep reading.

When a directory and program share a name, it usually means two things. First, the program probably *created* that directory. Also, the directory is probably full of the program's supporting files — files you should get rid of.

If you're *sure* that all the files in that directory belong to your purged program, delete the directory and all the files living in it. How, you ask? From within the File Manager, click on the program's directory and press Delete. If File Manager asks permission before deleting the directory, click on the Yes to All button.

This wipes away the program files, the program's directory, and any directories living beneath the program.

If you discover that you've deleted the *wrong* files and you have DOS 6, head for Chapter 6. The Undelete program that comes with DOS 6 can retrieve your deleted files if you act quickly.

4. **Remove its icon from the Program Manager.**

From within the Program Manager, click on the icon of the program you're sick of and press Delete. Windows will ask if you're sure you want to "delete that item." (Windows thinks icons are items.)

If you're sure, click the Yes button. You're almost done.

5. **Remove its .INI references.**

Most of the time, steps 1 through 4 will do the job. The program will be completely wiped off your hard drive.

Some programs leave a few remnants. For example, head for your \WINDOWS directory and look for a file named similarly to your program — but that ends in the letters .INI. Found one? Delete it.

Then, if you want to remove *all* traces, head for Chapter 15 and remove any program remnants appearing in your WIN.INI file. Make sure your program isn't listed after the words RUN and LOAD, which are the two lines near the top of the WIN.INI file.

When Windows starts up, sometimes it will complain about not being able to find your newly deleted file. If so, head for step 5 in the preceding list. You need to remove your program's name from behind the RUN or LOAD lines in the WIN.INI file.

Even after all this uninstall hassle, bits and pieces of the program may still linger on the hard drive, cluttering up the place. Some programs toss files into your Windows directory when they're installed but the programs don't tell you. There's simply no way of knowing which files belong to which program.

Chapter 16 holds a few clues as to what file does what.

There's Got to Be a Simpler Way to Uninstall Programs!

And there *is* a simpler way. Some frustrated technogeeks at MicroHelp wrote a program that puts Windows under a magnifying glass. MicroHelp's Uninstaller, seen in Figure 13-2, can identify any left-over program remnants and pluck them off your hard drive.

Uninstaller can find and delete duplicate files, clean up .INI files, remove unused screen drivers, and simply purge a hard drive of Windows' dirt.

For more information about Uninstaller, check your local software store or contact MicroHelp, Inc., 4359 Shallowford Industrial Parkway, Marietta, GA 30066; (800) 922-3383.

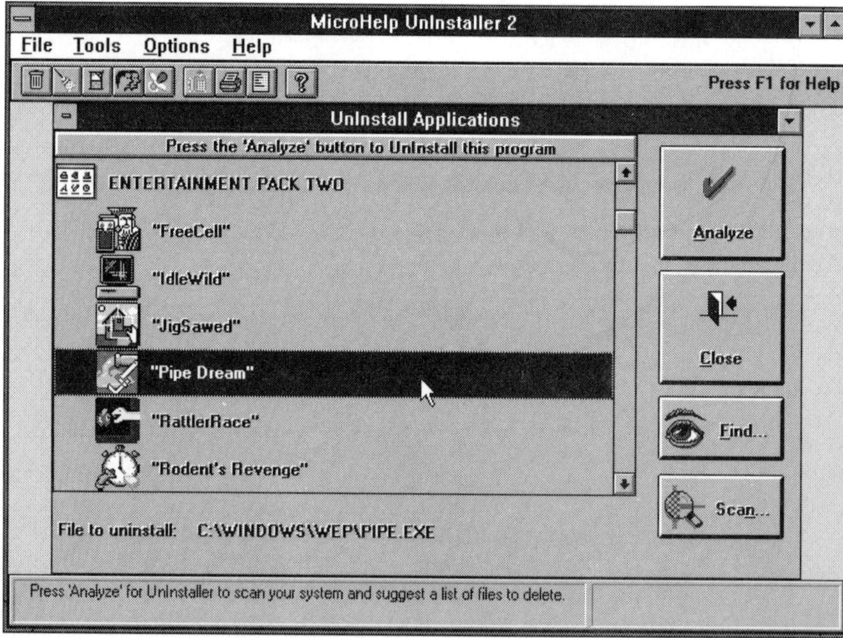

Figure 13-2: MicroHelp's Uninstaller can rip unwanted Windows programs off your hard drive and clean up their mess.

Installing a Program the Right Way

Chapter 2 shows how to install programs in Windows, but now's the time to repeat something: when installing a new program, create a new directory for it and dump the new files in there.

As you can see from this chapter, this simple step makes the program a *lot* easier to get rid of later if you decide that it really sucks.

Getting Rid of Windows Itself

Tired of Windows' happy *point-and-click* lifestyle? Want to wipe Windows *completely* off your hard drive? Then follow the bouncing steps below to remove all the Windows remnants.

1. **From within Windows, delete its permanent swap file.**

   Windows may be hanging onto a chunk of your hard drive, grabbing gobs of megabytes of space. Unless you physically pry Windows' hands off those megabytes, Windows will hang onto them, even after it's been deleted from your hard drive.

   If you have a *temporary* swap file, you're fine; skip this step. But if you have a *permanent* swap file or don't know *what* kind of swap file you have, here's what to do:

   Head for the Control Panel and double-click on the 386 Enhanced icon. When the 386 Enhanced box appears, click on the Virtual Memory button.

   When the Virtual Memory box appears, look at the line that says Type. Does Type say *Permanent* or *Temporary*? If it says Temporary, collect three points and move ahead to step 2. If it says Permanent, click on the Change button.

   When the Virtual Memory box opens up a little wider, click on the Type box and choose None from the drop-down menu. Click the OK button and click the Yes button when Windows asks if you're sure.

   Finally, click on the Continue button. Whew.

   And if all these instructions sound as confusing as a Christmas Tree Instruction Manual, head for Chapter 11. That's where swap files get a full treatment.

2. **Exit Program Manager.**

   Close down Program Manager for the last time. Sniff.

   If you have any special files that you've saved in your Windows directory or any of its subdirectories, now's the time to copy them to a floppy disk for safekeeping.

3. **Delete the Windows references from your AUTOEXEC.BAT file.**

   Never edited AUTOEXEC.BAT file before? Then hit Chapter 11 for the lowdown. If you're familiar with the basic surgical procedure, all you have to do is open your AUTOEXEC.BAT file with DOS 5's EDIT program (or any other program that can save an ASCII file). If you spot the word WIN sitting on a line by itself, delete it.

   You'll want to remove the C:\WINDOWS directory from that long line of directories listed after your PATH command, too.

4. **Change your CONFIG.SYS file.**

   Because you're going back to DOS, you may want to customize your CONFIG.SYS file for your DOS programs. And for that, you may want to pick up a copy of *More DOS For Dummies* by Dan Gookin.

5. **Delete all of Windows' directories.**

   Using DOS 6? Then type this command at your DOS prompt:

```
C:\> DELTREE WINDOWS
```

   This command deletes your Windows directory as well as any subdirectories beneath it.

   The DELTREE command removes the \WINDOWS directory *and* any directory lying beneath it. Because that's where most Windows programs live, this means DELTREE will probably be deleting most of your Windows programs. Before getting rid of Windows, make sure you've copied any of your important files to a floppy disk for safekeeping.

   If you're not using DOS 6, then type the following command in your Windows directory and all its subdirectories (yes, that's a lot of moving around):

```
C:\>\WINDOWS\DEL *.*
```

   Then remove each of your empty Windows subdirectories by using the DOS RD command. For example, to remove your now-empty WINDOWS directory, type this at the DOS prompt:

```
C:\> RD WINDOWS
```

   Before you can remove your Windows directory, however, you first have to remove all its subdirectories. See, you can't delete a subdirectory until all of *that* subdirectory's subdirectories have been removed.

   Welcome back to DOS!

Some DOS utilities like Lotus Magellan or XTree Gold can quickly delete a directory and all its underlying directories. This can save your fingers from typing a *lot* of RD and CD commands.

Once you've completely removed Windows, you're back to DOS and its world of unfriendly DOS commands. That's why a lot of people buy utilities like XTree Gold.

If you change your mind and want to reinstall Windows, grab your original Windows floppy disks. Put Disk 1 in drive A and type **A:SETUP** at your DOS prompt. Follow the instructions, and Windows will once again settle down comfortably onto your hard drive, without any lingering resentment.

Chapter 14

Creating a .PIF File for a New DOS Program

In This Chapter

- Understanding .PIFs
- Deciding when a .PIF is necessary
- Writing your own .PIFs
- Filling out the PIF Editor

The word *.PIF* sounds like a dainty sneeze, suppressed politely in a crowded elevator. But .PIFs carry a *lot* more impact on your computer. They're a sneaky way to fool cranky old DOS programs into running under Windows.

Unfortunately, .PIFs come faster in crowded elevators than in Windows. To create a .PIF, Windows makes you fill out a form uglier than a health insurance claim.

That ugly form requires the Windows PIF Editor, a wretched bastion of unfriendliness. This chapter points out which parts of the PIF form you can safely ignore and which parts you'll need to play with in order to convince a reluctant DOS program to run under Windows.

What's a .PIF?

Windows is supposed to run flashy new *Windows* programs. But some Windows users can't give up their favorite DOS programs of yesteryear.

Luckily, most DOS programs work just fine under Windows. If the program *doesn't* work, however, Windows makes you fill out a complicated form called a *.PIF*, which stand for: Program Information File.

Like a chart hanging on a hospital bed, the .PIF contains special instructions for Windows on how to treat that DOS program.

- Because Windows has grown so popular, many new DOS programs come packaged with a .PIF, free of charge. Check your DOS program's directory for a file ending in the letters .PIF. If you find one, you're safe.
- A program's .PIF usually sounds just like the program, but ends with the letters .PIF. For example, a .PIF for your FLATTER.EXE program would be called FLATTER.PIF.
- To load your DOS program from File Manager, double-click on its *.PIF*, not the program. For example, to load FLATTER.EXE, double-click on FLATTER.PIF — not FLATTER.EXE.
- Or, if your DOS program has an icon in the Program Manager, that icon should refer to the program's .PIF. For example, the icon for your Flatter program should refer to FLATTER.PIF, not FLATTER.EXE.
- Don't know whether your Program Manager's icon refers to a DOS program's .PIF or its filename? While holding down Alt in Program Manager, double-click on the DOS program's icon. If the DOS program has a .PIF, the .PIF should be listed in the Command Line box.

- Windows can automatically create a .PIF for the most popular DOS programs. Double-click on the Windows Setup icon in Program Manager, and choose Set Up Applications from the Options menu. Follow the instructions, and Windows sniffs out any programs on your hard drive and automatically creates .PIFs for any DOS programs it recognizes.

Do I Really Need a .PIF?

Most DOS programs aren't picky enough to require a .PIF. To find out whether your DOS program needs a .PIF, take this simple test:

Try to run the DOS program from within Windows.

If your program runs fine, you're safe. Ignore this chapter and concentrate on more important things, like whether it's time to switch to whole wheat English muffins. If your DOS program didn't run — or it ran kinda funny — stick around; this chapter might help out.

- .PIFs can fine-tune a DOS program's performance. For example, a .PIF can make a DOS programs start up in a window rather than filling the whole screen. (Be forewarned, however: Some DOS programs refuse to be squeezed into a window — even with the most powerful .PIF.)

- When Windows can't find a .PIF for your DOS program, it uses a .PIF called _DEFAULT.PIF. That .PIF lives in your \WINDOWS directory. If you want a change to affect *all* your DOS programs, but don't want to write a .PIF for each of them, just make your change to the _DEFAULT.PIF file.

Using PIF Editor

In order to confuse twice as many people, Microsoft lets Windows run in two different modes: *Standard* mode or *386 Enhanced* mode.

To carry on the confusion, Windows PIF Editor uses two different forms, one for each mode.

But here's some good news: The PIF Editor automatically checks to see what mode Windows is using; then it brings up the right form. No head scratching here.

So, unless you're a mode switcher (and if you are, you'll know it) just fill out the form the PIF Editor brings to the screen. That will be the right one.

- The PIF Editor is a breeze to use. Simply fill out the form: To turn an option on, click in its little box. An X appears inside the box to indicate that the option is turned on. Click in the box again to turn that option off.
- So where's the hard part? Deciding which boxes to click in. Because the .PIF Editor is designed to handle rough DOS problems, it forces you to play arbitrator among the ugliest DOS disputes: memory access, video modes and equally unfriendly geek turf. A .PIF is loaded with bizarre terms like *Optional Parameters* and *High Graphics*.

Feel free to skip this *Mode* stuff

The PIF Editor has two basic flavors. One part governs how a DOS program should be treated when running in Windows *Standard* mode. The second part covers how the DOS program should be treated when running in Windows *386 Enhanced* mode.

The two modes mainly govern the way Windows deals with memory.

Standard mode: This mode lets Windows run on 286 computers, as well as 386 or 486 computers with less than 2 megabytes of memory. As a side-effect, though, Windows Standard mode won't let a DOS program run in its own window. DOS programs must fill the entire screen while Windows waits in the background.

386 Enhanced mode: Designed for 386 or 486 computers with more than 2MB of memory, this mode lets DOS programs run in their own little windows — even bunches of little windows at the same time. Also, 386 Enhanced mode lets Windows create *Virtual Memory* by using a permanent *swap file*, a particularly odious subject covered in Chapter 11.

To see what mode Windows is using, click on Mode from the PIF Editor top menu. A menu drops down and lists both modes; you're using the one with the check mark next to it.

If you're like most people, you'll only be using Windows in one mode. And, because the PIF Editor always opens the correct form for the mode Windows currently uses, you won't have to worry about any of this stuff. Just fill out the form PIF Editor dishes up, and you're done.

- When stumped by something in PIF Editor, click in the box that has you dangling by the toes. Then press F1. When you choose the confusing box and then press F1, Windows dredges up helpful information pertaining to that particular box.

Editing or Creating a .PIF

This section tackles the options the PIF Editor tosses at you when Windows runs in *386 Enhanced* mode. The *Standard* mode stuff is covered right afterward.

The forms for the two modes are pretty much the same, however. In fact, most of the Standard mode options are listed right here, in the 386 Enhanced section.

And keep your chin up: You don't need to fill out the *entire* form to create a successful .PIF. In fact, only a few sections are mandatory — although the PIF Editor doesn't tell you that.

So, this book does. You'll find the words *Mandatory* and *Ignorable* next to each option's description below.

When creating your .PIF, fill out the *Mandatory* parts first; then save your .PIF and see whether the DOS program runs. If the program still needs some tweaking, open the .PIF back up and start fiddling with the parts marked *Ignorable*.

Good luck.

When testing a newly created .PIF from File Manager, be sure to double-click on the .PIF itself — not the program's file name.

Here's how to create a .PIF file:

1. **Grab your DOS program's box and manual.**

   The fine print on the box and manual can offer clues about what that program needs.

2. **Double-click on the PIF Editor from Program Manager.**

   PIF Editor

   The PIF Editor's icon looks like the luggage tags that litter the cargo bays of airliners. Still can't find the icon? Then click on the Program Manager's File button, choose, Run, and type `PIFEDIT` into the box. Press Enter, and the PIF Editor hops to the screen.

3. **Fill out the form.**

   If you're running Windows in 386 Enhanced Mode, the PIF Editor will look like Figure 14-1.

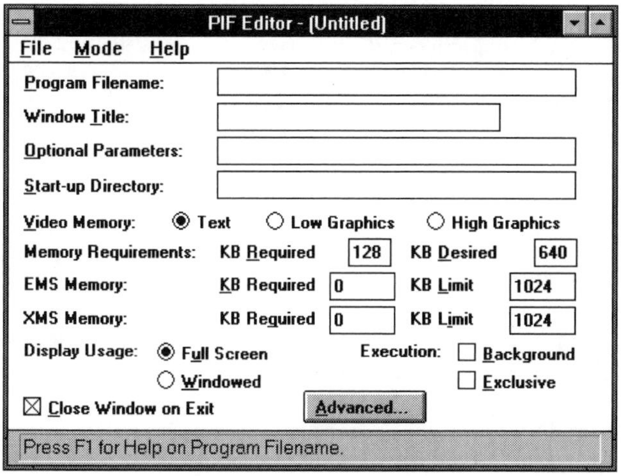

Figure 14-1: The PIF Editor for 386 Enhanced mode looks like this.

If you're running Windows in Standard mode, the PIF Editor will look like Figure 14-2.

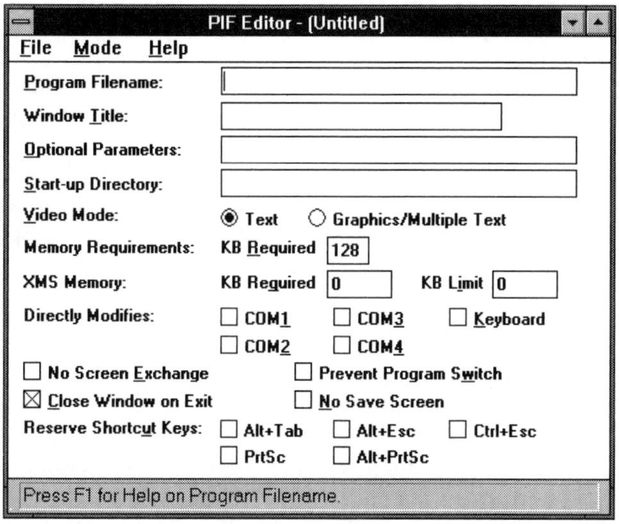

Figure 14-2: The PIF Editor for Standard mode looks like this.

PIF Editor automatically opens the right form, so start filling it out. Each option is described below.

The stuff you *have* to fiddle with is marked *Mandatory*. The boxes you can ignore say *Ignorable*.

Program Filename: *Mandatory*. Simply type in the name and path of your DOS program. Unlike Program Manager, there's no convenient point-and-click Browse button, so everything's done by hand. For example, to list the TASSLE program living in the \SHOE directory on drive C, you'd type `C:\SHOE\TASSLE.EXE` into the box.

Window Title: *Ignorable*. Want a name to appear along the top in the DOS windows' title bar? Then type a name here. (In Standard mode, this name appears under the DOS program's icon when the DOS program is minimized.) Or, don't type anything: Windows uses the program's file name as its title.

If you use a title, keep it short; otherwise, the icon's title will overlap with the other icon's titles in Program Manager.

Optional Parameters: *Ignorable*. Ever typed `TANKS 2` at a DOS prompt, telling your TANKS program to load up in *two-player* mode? That "2" is called a *parameter*. If you want to feed any parameters to your DOS program as it loads, type them here. Or, type in a `?` (a question mark) and Windows asks you for parameters each time it's about to load the program.

Start-up Directory: *Ignorable*. When you open a file from within your DOS program, what directory's files do you prefer to see listed? For your convenience, type that directory's name here. (If the program later gives you trouble with *Associations*, which are described in Chapter 19, head there and leave this space blank.) If you don't type anything, Windows simply uses the program's own directory as its Start-up Directory.

Video Memory: *Mandatory*. If your DOS program uses only text, choose Text. If you're stuck with an old CGA or Hercules monitor, choose Low Graphics. If you're using VGA or EGA graphics, choose High Graphics.

First, try Text. If the program doesn't work, change it to High Graphics.

Memory Requirements: Both of these sections are usually ignorable; they refer to *conventional* memory, the mainstay of DOS programs:

> **KB Required:** *Ignorable*. But if Windows says there isn't enough memory to run your DOS program, keep adding 128 to the KB Required box until the program works right. For example, start with 128; then increase it to 256, 384, 512, or 640.
>
> **KB Desired:** *Ignorable*. Leave the KB Desired box at 640. (Unless you want to be a computer guru, whereupon you can keep shaving the number *downward* by 128 until the program stops working. Then use the *lowest* number that still lets the DOS program run. That can free up a little bit of memory, if you're severely strapped for RAM.)

EMS Memory: *Usually ignorable.* Some expensive DOS programs use *expanded memory*, which is known as EMS. Check the side of your DOS program's box; unless the program claims to use expanded memory, leave this at 0. If it *does* want EMS, then type the required amount in the KB Required box. To keep the program from grabbing *all* the memory, type a limit in the KB Limit box. If the DOS program *still* gives you memory problems, ask a computer guru for a passport to the world of *DOS memory management* programs.

XMS Memory: *Ignorable.* Some DOS programs like EMS memory, but a few others like *XMS*, also called *extended memory.* The same rules apply here as for EMS. If your DOS program needs extended memory — and very few will — type the amount in the KB Required box. Then, add a limit in the KB Limit box.

To give a DOS program *all* the EMS or XMS memory that Windows can supply, put the number –1 (negative one) in the KB Limit box.

Display Usage: *Mandatory*, but it's an easy choice between these two options:

> **Full Screen:** Choose this option, and the DOS program fills the entire screen when it loads. Most graphics-heavy DOS programs (games or paint programs) run best when they fill the screen.
>
> **Windowed:** To try and cajole a DOS program into running in a window, choose this option. Many DOS games and graphics-intensive programs won't run in a window, however, or will run very slowly.

> While running a DOS program in a window, press Alt-Spacebar and choose Settings from the menu. That lets you change these settings on-the-fly if they look goofy.

Execution: These two options are usually ignorable.

> **Background:** *Ignorable.* When a DOS program sits beneath another window, it's usually resting comfortably. If you'd prefer that the program keeps *working* — sorting that database or sending a fax — choose this option.
>
> **Exclusive:** *Ignorable.* Choose this to give your DOS program *complete* control of your computer — until you turn the program into an icon or shift it into a window.

Close Window on Exit: *Ignorable.* An X in this box tells the DOS program to take its window along with it when it exits the screen. If there's no X, the DOS window stays put and shows a lonely DOS prompt.

Advanced: A click on the .PIF Editor's Advanced button brings up a host of largely ignorable options, all designed to make the most cantankerous DOS program happy.

> **Multitasking Options:** *Ignorable.* If Windows is juggling more than one program, the .PIF editor lets you decide how much time to devote to each program. Or, you could simply blow off these "fine-tuning performance" issues.

Background Priority: Is your DOS program *doing* something when it's sitting beneath a stack of windows? If it's doing something useful — downloading a file, or generating a spectacular fractal — feel free to increase this number. (Windows ignores this setting unless you've turned on the Background option under Execution, described above.)

Foreground Priority: To give a DOS program *all* of your computer's attention, choose the Exclusive option listed under Execution, as described above. But to give the program just a *little* more attention, try increasing this number to 300. If that's not enough, you can keep increasing this number up to a limit of 10,000.

Detect Idle Time: An X in this box means Windows keeps a lazy eye on the program. If the program doesn't seem to be doing anything, Windows automatically begins to ignore it and shifts resources to programs that definitely *are* doing things. Only turn this off if your DOS program isn't working well in the background.

Memory Options: *Largely ignorable.* Each option is described below:

EMS Memory Locked: Choose this, and Windows won't swap the program's EMS Memory to the swap file. Leave it off unless the program crashes.

XMS Memory Locked: Same as above. Leave it off unless the program crashes without it.

Lock Application Memory: This works just like the "locks" described above. Leave it off unless the program crashes without it.

Uses High Memory Area: This option should be On unless the program crashes with it on. Should only be turned off for old programs.

Display Options: Ignorable, and described below for further ignoring.

Monitor ports: Keep the Text, Low Graphics, and High Graphics options all turned off unless you're using an EGA monitor. If the screen looks funny, turn on each option and test them, one at a time, until the screen's fixed.

Emulate Text Mode: Leave this one selected unless the screen looks funny.

Retain Video Memory: Some DOS programs work in Text mode but occasionally switch to high-resolution graphics: A word processor might switch to page preview, for example. Windows hands over some extra memory needed for the page preview but steals the memory back when the word processor switches back to text mode. Therefore, the word processor won't have that memory on hand if it wants to switch to page preview again. To keep that video memory with the DOS program, select this option. Whew. Pretty thorough, this .PIF business, eh?

Other options: *Largely ignorable*, and described below:

> **Allow Fast Paste:** Keep checked unless your DOS program erupts in a cacophony of beeps or missing characters when you paste text into it from Windows clipboard. That slows down the clipboard's pasting speed, so the DOS program can absorb it.
>
> **Reserve Shortcut Keys:** Some DOS programs want to use the same keys that Windows uses, causing big fights. For example, when you press Ctrl+Esc, are you talking to the DOS program or signaling Windows to bring up the Task List? This option lets you turn off certain Windows shortcut keys so the DOS application can use them, instead.
>
> **Application Shortcut Key:** If you're a shortcut fanatic, and want your DOS program to leap to the top of the windows pile at the touch of two keys, enter those keys here. (The combination must start with an Alt or a Ctrl; if your choice is illegal, Windows won't let it appear in the box.) Otherwise, don't bother. First, Windows has too many shortcut keys already; second, the shortcut key only works if the DOS program's already running; and third, pressing Ctrl+Esc can do pretty much the same thing.

- There aren't any hard and fast rules for making .PIFs. In fact, a .PIF that works great one day, might choke the next day.
- That's because a DOS program's performance depends on its what it's currently doing, as well as what all the other programs are currently doing. That's a fancy way of saying you'll probably have to fiddle around a lot before your .PIFs will work right.
- Don't be afraid of goofing up when making a .PIF; Windows offers some leeway when it comes to DOS programs. Windows won't freak if your DOS program suddenly switches video *modes*, even if you didn't give it permission in your .PIF. Windows just figures you made a mis- take, and it gently switches video modes to let the DOS program run.
- If your DOS program does *work* in the background — it doesn't just sit there, waiting for you to come back and use it — be sure to check the Background option under Execution. If you're still having problems, head for the Advanced area, and remove the X from the Detect Idle Time box.

- The simplest way to avoid .PIFs is to buy a Windows version of your DOS program.

Standard Mode Settings

Can't find your PIF Editor's setting described above? Then you're probably running Windows in Standard mode, so PIF Editor opened the Standard mode form.

Most of the Standard mode's settings are the same as the ones described above. The rest are described below:

Video Mode: *Ignorable.* Leave it set on Text. If the screen looks weird when you switch back to the DOS program from Windows, choose the Graphics/Multiple Text option.

Directly Modifies: *Ignorable.* Don't select any of these COM options unless you're using a modem or fax program; then, select the COM port your modem or fax wants to use. Choose the Keyboard option on the odd chance your program needs direct control of the keyboard — and can't handle everything flowing through Windows master control.

No Screen Exchange: *Ignorable.* Do you ever press the PrtScr (sometimes labeled PrintScreen) key to copy the DOS program's screen to Windows' clipboard? Then *don't* select this box. If you never copy the DOS program's screen to the clipboard, then select this option; it might help if you're always running out of memory.

Prevent Program Switch: *Ignorable.* Normally, Windows lets you switch back and forth between programs by pressing Alt+Enter, Ctrl+Esc, or a few other key combinations. To deactivate *all* of them, click in this box. It's handy for DOS programs that can't be disturbed. (To switch back to Windows, exit the DOS program.)

No Save Screen: *Ignorable.* This has nothing to do with Windows' screen saver. When you switch away from a DOS program while in Standard mode, Windows takes a picture of the screen. Then, when you switch back to your DOS program, Windows displays that picture so everything looks normal. If your DOS program can update its screen by itself (which is rare), click here to save a little bit of memory.

- Just like the 386 Enhanced mode settings, the Standard mode settings are almost all ignorable.
- Most of them are designed to save little bits of memory, here and there. So, if Windows isn't complaining about *insufficient memory*, don't bother fiddling with them. If Windows *is* complaining, buy more memory; otherwise, you might have to spend an hour or so fiddling with your DOS .PIFs.

Ouch! I Messed Up My .PIF!

Windows makes .PIFs for any DOS programs it recognizes, as described in this chapter's first section. But if you change one of those Windows-created .PIFs and it doesn't work anymore, make Windows bring back the original one.

Double-click on the Program Manager's Windows Setup icon and select Set Up Applications from the Options menu.

When Windows finds your DOS program again, it will create a new .PIF and overwrite the one you've changed. Whew!

Chapter 15

Editing an Icky .INI File

In This Chapter

- Understanding the role of an .INI file
- Knowing when to edit an .INI file
- Identifying the right .INI file
- Editing an .INI file
- Changing WIN.INI and SYSTEM.INI files

Windows doesn't have sticky notes to keep track of details — like when somebody changes their desktop's color scheme from Rugby to Tweed.

So, Windows scrawls those details into a file called WIN..INI. Similarly, if a computer's guts get changed around — if your computer gets a new video card, for example — Windows stashes a few lines of code words into a file in SYSTEM.INI.

Handwriting is hard to read on sticky notes, but it's even *harder* to figure out what Windows writes into its WIN.INI and SYSTEM.INI files. This chapter translates some of Windows' wackier words into English.

Be careful, however: Losing a sticky note might result in a missed lunch date. Losing a Windows .INI file just might make Windows forget to show up on-screen. Don't change anything around "just to see if something cool happens."

What's an .INI File?

Windows comes in one package. But it's supposed to run on *millions* of different computers. And each of those computers are set up *slightly* differently. Some use Blotzo Brand floppy drives, others use is Blitzo.

To keep track of which computer it's running on, Windows writes the computer's personality traits into several *.INI* files.

Pronounced like the opposite of an *outtie* (the belly-button kind), an .INI file contains a bunch of text code words describing a computer's innards.

When Windows loads itself, it first reads its .INI files. When Windows knows what sort of computer it's running on, it knows how it's supposed to behave.

- The letters *.INI* are short for *.INItialization*. So, an .INI file always ends in the letters *.INI*. And those tidbits of information excite *very few people*.
- Because everybody's computer uses slightly different parts, everybody's .INI files are slightly different. If Windows doesn't work on your computer, copying your friend's .INI files onto your hard drive won't fix it.
- Windows creates its own .INI files when it's first installed. Then, Windows updates its .INI files to record any changes on your computer. It's all automatic.
- The two most important ones are called WIN.INI and SYSTEM.INI. Both files get their due in an upcoming section.

Why Bother Fiddling with an .INI File?

There's no earth-shattering reason, actually. In fact, there are more reasons *not* to change around an .INI file.

- Windows adds and subtracts the appropriate stuff to its .INI files *automatically*.
- Because Windows does all its .INI work automatically and behind the scenes, you'll probably never have to fiddle with an .INI file — unless Windows goofs one up, and you need to fix it yourself.
- Some people tweak their .INI files to fine-tine Windows performance, just like some people constantly adjust the spark-plug gaps on their El Caminos.
- Nonetheless, some people can't resist the urge to tinker with their .INIs — especially when they discover that simple changes to an .INI file can help them cheat on MineSweeper's Best Times high scores. (That trick's described in an upcoming section.)
- Also, some Windows programs will toss a message on-screen, ordering their hapless users to change a PIF setting. For example, some games say things like "`Set DMABUFFERSIZE=64 in SYSTEM..INI (386ENH) Section`. (That bit of rudeness is covered in an upcoming section.)

- Just like working under a car's hood, changing or editing an .INI file can be very dangerous. Don't change anything in an .INI file unless you're sure you know what you're doing. And be sure to keep a copy of your .INI files on floppy disk for safekeeping before editing them.

What .INI File Does What?

When you first install Windows, it places a few .INI files into your \WINDOWS directory; and it places another .INI file in your Windows \SYSTEM directory. Other Windows programs toss their own .INI files into the mix, as well.

If you change a program's option — change its color, for example — the program will probably write that information automatically into its .INI file. (That keeps you from having to mess with the .INI file.) Table 15-1 shows some of Windows' most popular .INI files, and what they're supposed to do.

Table 15-1 Popular .INI files

This .INI file . . .	*lets this program . . .*	*remember this . . .*
CLOCK.INI	Windows Clock	Its font, last screen position, and options you've chosen like *digital* or *analog*.
CONTROL.INI	Control Panel	Available color schemes and available drivers; screen saver options, and information on any new icons tossed in by other programs.
DOSAPP.INI	Your DOS programs	Each program's last location on the screen, and the size of its chosen fonts.
MPLAYER.INI	Media Player	The sound/video gadgets hooked up to your computer and their various options.
MSD.INI	Microsoft Diagnostics	Vital portions of your WIN.INI and SYSTEM.INI files and a few other goodies.
PROGMAN.INI	Program Manager	Names of your Group windows, their location within Program Manager, and any chosen options.
SOL.INI	Solitaire	Any chosen options, including the picture you've chosen to appear on the card's back.
SYSTEM.INI	Windows	Vital sound and video card information, and even *more* complicated hardware stuff.
WIN.INI	Windows	Selected options for your desktop and other Windows choices. Options for third-party Windows programs often appear here, as well.

(continued)

Table 15-1 *(continued)*

This .INI file . . .	*lets this program . . .*	*remember this . . .*
WINFILE.INI	File Manager	Selected options (like whether it should *ask* before deleting a file), as well as options other programs have added to the menu. DOS 6, for example, adds a Tools option for launching the Backup and Anti-Virus programs.
WINMINE.INI	MineSweeper	High scores, difficulty levels, colors, size, number of mines, and other explosive trivia.

- Don't worry if some of these .INI files aren't on your hard drive. For example, if you've never played MineSweeper, you won't have a WINMINE.INI file.
- There won't be a WINMINE.INI FILE until a winning game of Minesweeper has been played and you've exited from the game.
- Similarly, don't worry if you find even *more* .INI files lurking on your hard drive. Many Windows programs create their own .INI files to track important stuff.
- A program's .INI file usually sounds like its name but ends in the letters .INI. For example, the .INI file for DRINKME.EXE will probably be called DRINKME.INI.

How to Change an .INI File

Changing or editing an .INI file is *dangerous*. A single typo can keep Windows from loading on your screen. Before changing an .INI file, make sure you've saved a copy to a floppy disk for safekeeping.

Still here? Then here's the scoop. An .INI file is a plain ol' text file full of code words. To edit an .INI file, use Notepad.

Here's how to edit MineSweeper's .INI file to cheat on your High Scores. Gasp!

1. **Make a backup copy of your WINMINE..INI file.**

   Table 15-1 shows that WINMINE.INI is the .INI file for MineSweeper. Before editing it, however, copy WINMINE.INI to a floppy disk for safekeeping.

2. **From File Manager, double-click on the WINMINE..INI file.**

   Double-clicking on an .INI file in File Manager always loads it into Notepad and opens it on-screen, as seen in Figure 15-1.

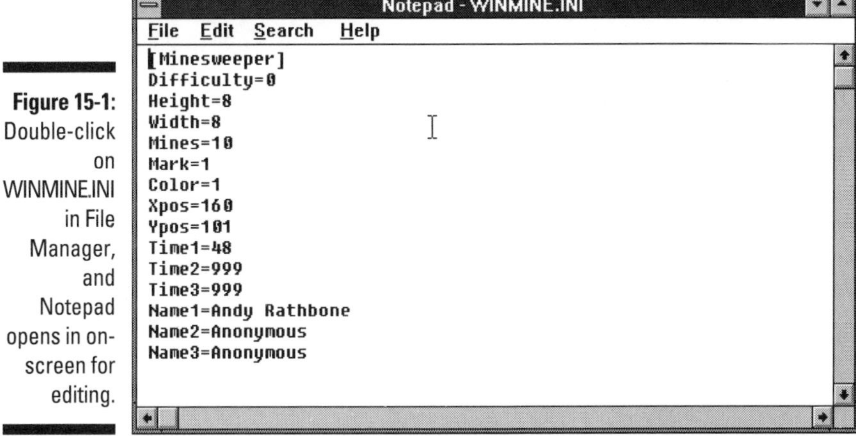

Figure 15-1: Double-click on WINMINE.INI in File Manager, and Notepad opens in on-screen for editing.

3. Find the lines starting with the words Time1 and Name1.

See how MineSweeper lists three times and three names at the bottom? Those are the three best times, and the names of the players. My best time is listed as 48 seconds. (You can stop laughing now.)

4. Add your own name and time to those lines.

Here's the trick: Change the name listed after `Name1` to your own name (or the name of a friend or book publisher).

Simply remove the old name (if there is one) from after the `Name1` line, and type the new name in its place. Make sure there's no space before or after the = sign.

Then, do the same thing for the `Time1` line by typing in the number of seconds. Don't use 0, because that's too obvious you're cheating. Type in the number 1, for example, and the WINMINE.INI file will look like Figure 15-2.

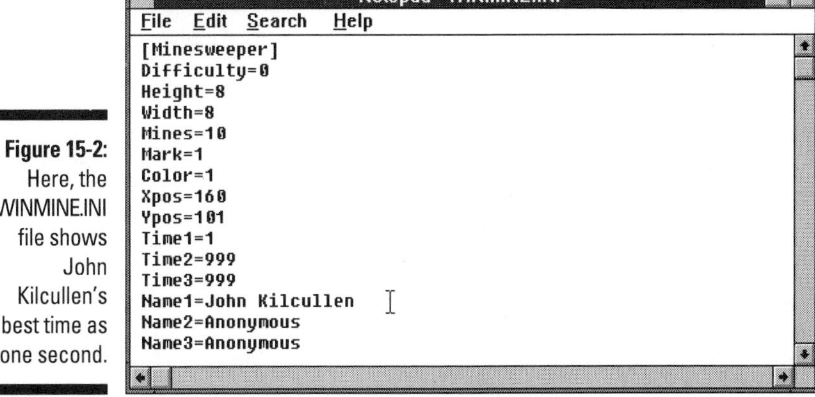

Figure 15-2: Here, the WINMINE.INI file shows John Kilcullen's best time as one second.

5. **Save your file and exit.**

   Exit Notepad the way you always do — an .INI file is a text file, like any other.

6. **Check MineSweeper's best times.**

   Call up MineSweeper, and click on Best Times from its Game menu.

Sure enough, as seen in Figure 15-3, John Kilcullen's best time (he's the president of IDG Books) is now one second. Quick fingers!

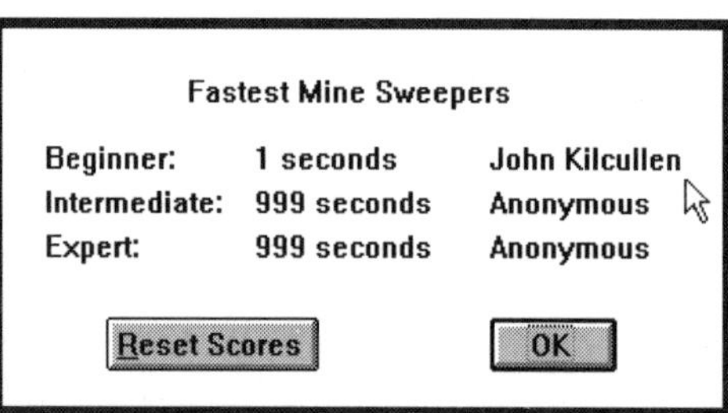

Figure 15-3: By editing the WINMINE.INI file, you can change your high scores to *any* name and number.

- These same techniques will edit any .INI file. Just be sure to make a backup copy, in case something goes wrong. And be sure to use Notepad. Write saves the file in its own weird format, which causes large dogs to rain from the heavens.
- If a DOS program tells you to do something obnoxious like `Set DMABUFFERSIZE=64 in SYSTEM.INI [386ENH] Section`, do just that: Open your SYSTEM..INI file, find the part marked [386ENH], and look for a line starting `DMABUFFERSIZE`. It it's there, make sure it says `DMABUFFERSIZE=64` or change the number if it says something else. If it's not there, then type that particular bit of gibberish, `DMABUFFERSIZE=64`, onto its own line beneath the [386ENH] section.

- Add the line `Sound=3` to the bottom of the WINMINE.INI file. That tells MineSweeper to make beeping sounds whenever a mine blows ups. The beeps will come out of the PC's speaker — no need for a sound card.
- Like the "sound" tip above, editing .INI files comes down to one thing: Knowing what secret options to change. The rest of this chapter explains some of the most common .INI options to change.

- Want Solitaire to switch to a different card background each time you play? Then make sure this line *doesn't* appear in your SOL..INI file: `Back`=number. Solitaire assigns a different number to each card back, and stores your choice in its SOL.INI file. But if there's no `Back`= line in its SOL.INI file, Solitaire will choose a card back at random.
- Before doing any heavy-duty .INI editing, be sure to read the tips that follow.

Quick .INI editing tips

- Text in INI files can appear in either upper *or* lowercase. Unlike English teachers, Windows doesn't care. (There's one exception: the word COM must always be uppercase.)
- Most of the time, it's easy to tell how to turn an option *on* or *off*. If a line ends in *On*, change it to *Off*. If it says *Yes*, change it to *No*. If it says *True*, change it to *False*. Here's the weird one: If it says *1*, then changing it to *0* will turn it off.
- Make sure that there's no space either before or after the equals sign. For example, the line Confusion=Off would work, whereas the line Confusion= Off might make things even *more* confusing.
- Only use Notepad to edit an .INI file.
- Only make one change at a time. That way you'll know which of your changes goofed things up.

.INI boredom, divided into sections

Windows INI files are all *very* meticulous about their structure, as described below.

Sections: Windows INI files contain lots of lines of text. To keep things orderly, the lines are separated into different sections. Each section starts with a *heading* — a word enclosed in brackets. For example, all the lines relating to an .INI file's *Frenzy* section would appear under the heading *Frenzy* in brackets, like this:

```
[Frenzy]
```

Lines or entries: Beneath each heading, you'll find one or more lines. Each line — also called an *entry* or *item* — tells Windows how to behave. Each line ends with an *equals sign* followed by numbers or words (usually *yes, no, on, off, 0, 1, true* or *false*). The stuff after the equals sign tells Windows what to *do* with that particular line.

For example, a line could say *CoolSwitch=1*. That line, when appearing in WIN.INI's [Windows] section, tells Windows to activate the Alt+Tab key combination. If the line said *CoolSwitch=0*, then pressing Alt+Tab doesn't open the fancy windows.

Remarks: Finally, some lines in an .INI file begin with a *semicolon*. Windows ignores those lines; they're meant for humans to read. In the WINMINE.INI file shown in an earlier section, for example, you could add these two lines to remember what's going on.

```
;This turns on the sound.

Sound=3
```

A semicolon in an .INI file is like a REM in an AUTOEXEC.BAT or CONFIG.SYS file: It helps you remember any changes you've made, why you've made them, and what lines should be removed if your changes make poor Windows croak like a dying frog. (Unless you *wanted* Windows to croak like a dying frog.)

That Scary WIN.INI File

Your WIN.INI file lives in your \WINDOWS directory, and it tracks how Windows should behave on your computer — what color scheme it should display, for example, or what wallpaper you've chosen.

Normally, there's no reason to fiddle with WIN.INI. To change your wallpaper, for example, use Control Panel. The Control Panel would then store your wallpaper selection in the WIN.INI file.

Changing your wallpaper by editing your WIN.INI file makes as much sense as buying heavy-duty oven mitts, and then pulling the chicken out of the oven with your bare hands.

Nonetheless, some of WIN.INI's settings can *only* be changed by your bare hands. You'll find some of those settings listed in Table 15-2 following.

- Windows SysEdit program works well for editing WIN.INI and SYSTEM.INI files. From the Program Manager's menu, click on File, choose Run, type `SYSEDIT`, and press Enter. The SysEdit program opens, which contains your WIN.INI, SYSTEM.INI, AUTOEXEC.BAT, and CONFIG.SYS files. When you change a file and save it, SysEdit automatically saves a backup copy of the changed file, which ends in .SYD.

- After changing a program's .INI file, restart that program to make your changes take effect. After editing WIN.INI or SYSTEM.INI, for example, restart Windows to see if your changes work.

Table 15-2 What's Inside That WIN.INI File?

Section	*Setting*	*What this stuff means*
[windows]	load=	When Windows starts up, it automatically loads the programs listed on this line — even if those program's icons aren't in Program Manager's StartUp group window. For example, to make Clock load automatically as an icon whenever Windows loads, change the line to this: `load=clock.exe` (Or, you could just put Clock in your Startup group.)
	run=	Same as above, but the listed programs load themselves into an open *window* — not as an icon at the screen's bottom.

Section	Setting	What this stuff means
	Programs=com exe bat pif	Usually, Windows assumes that files ending in .COM, .EXE, .BAT, or .PIF are *programs*. Double-click on them in File Manager, and they'll run. (Some people prefer a double-click on a .BAT file to bring up Notepad, however, so they remove .BAT from the list. Then they *associate* .BAT with Notepad using File Manager.)
	DoubleClickHeight=	Usually, the mouse must remain stationary during a double-click. If you have shaky hands, add this line; it lets your mouse move a few pixels upward in the midst of a double-click: `DoubleClickHeight=10` Remove the line to deactivate it.
	DoubleClickWidth=	Same as above, but this line lets your mouse stray a few pixels *sideways*.
	MouseTrails=	Ever played with the Mouse Trails option in the Control Panel? This trivial line controls how many mouse pointers (between 1 and 7) show up in the trail. To change the trails' size to 3, the line should read like this: `MouseTrails=3`
[Terminal]	Port=	Here's where Terminal writes down what COM port it thinks it should use. If Terminal is remembering the wrong COM port, change it to the right-numbered port, like in the example below: `Port=COM2`
[Desktop]	IconVerticalSpacing=	Control Panel's Spacing option controls how closely icons sit next to each other on your desktop and in Program Manager. Add this line to change the icons vertical spacing: The space between two *rows* of icons. (You might have to experiment; Windows automatically chooses different spacings for different fonts.)

(continued)

Table 15-2 *(continued)*

Section	Setting	What this stuff means
[Windows Help]	JumpColor= IfJumpColor= IfPopUpColor= PopUpColor=	Windows built-in help system uses light green *jump words*. A double-click on a jump word opens more information about that word. In WIN.INI, these four lines are followed by three numbers that determine the *color* of those jump words. If the lines aren't there, feel free to type them in yourself. (Chapter 5 has more information on this stuff.)

That SYSTEM.INI File

Although the WIN..INI file mostly controls cosmetic changes, the SYSTEM.INI file controls Windows physical health — how it should interact with your computer's innards, such as its hard drive, CPU, cards, and other vital organs.

That means there's a lot more at stake when changing things around. One typographical error, and Windows might try to connect your computer's esophagus to its aorta.

Table 15-3 shows a few areas in the SYSTEM.INI file you might need to change. But, hey: Make a backup copy and be *careful*.

Table 15-3 SYSTEM.INI Settings

The Section	Its Settings	What this stuff means
[boot]	shell=progman.exe	Usually, Program Manager is Windows *shell*. The shell is the program that loads along with Windows and, when closed, takes Windows down with it. If you *despise* Program Manager and want File Manager to work in its place, change it to this line: `shell=winfile.exe`
	mouse.drv=mouse.drv	Using a Microsoft mouse? Then this exact line should appear in the [boot] section of SYSTEM.INI.

The Section	*Its Settings*	*What this stuff means*
[NonWindowsApp]	DisablePositionSave=	When you exit a DOS program from its window, Windows normally remembers the window's position, as well as the font you used. If you'd prefer Windows to not remember that information, change it to this line: `DisablePositionSave=1`
[386Enh]	AllVMsExclusive=	Some folks want their DOS programs to have *complete* control of the computer. If you want all DOS programs to run in *exclusive, full-screen* mode, no matter what their PIF's say, make sure the line says this: `AllVMsExclusive=True`
	FileSysChange=off	Getting tired of pressing F5 to update the File Manager's screen whenever a DOS program changes a file? Then add this line: `FileSysChange=On` The problem? This slows Windows down considerably.

- For even more detailed SYSTEM.INI info, use Write to load SYSINI.WRI. (It's in your \WINDOWS directory.) Microsoft's packed it with much-too-detailed information on what does what.
- If something *awful* happens and Windows won't load, exit to DOS, move to your Windows directory, and type `Setup`. A DOS program appears and lets you change some of Windows' options. If it freezes while loading, use `Setup /i`.

- Dying to edit your SYSTEM.INI files? Then you've passed Dummy level. Check out Brian Livingston's *Windows 3.1 Secrets* for graduate work.

Purging an .INI File of Dead-Programs' Clutter

Like kids leaving socks draped over doorknobs, Windows programs tend to leave their clutter lying in Windows .INI files. The programs add lines to the .INI file when they're installed, but then don't *remove* those lines when they're uninstalled (as described in Chapter 13).

The WIN.INI file receives the most abuse. After you've installed and un-installed a few programs, you'll still find references to those programs living in the WIN.INI file.

Before deleting anything from a WIN.INI file, make sure you've made a backup copy of the file.

Getting rid of those remnants is as easy as pulling socks off a doorknob. Simply open the WIN.INI file, as described in the sections above, and delete the old lines, as shown in the steps below.

1. **Find the WIN.INI references to the old program.**

   When looking through your WIN.INI file, for example, you might spot references to your recently deleted program that had recipes for healthier potato chips. Look for the Yam Frying program's header. It will be in brackets, probably looking something like this:

   ```
   [YamFry]
   Healthy=True
   PalmOil=False
   OliveOil=True
   ```

2. **Delete the lines below that program's header.**

   Delete all the lines that appearing after the [YamFry] header but before the following header. Make sure you don't delete any other program's headers — the ones appearing below the [YamFry] header.

3. **Delete the program's header.**

   After you delete the YamFry program's lines, delete the [YamFry] header itself.

4. **Save the .INI file.**

   That's it; you're through housecleaning.

- References to deleted programs don't really hurt anything. Your WIN.INI file will still work, even if it's full of dozens of lines relating to deleted programs.
- However, some people don't like seeing clutter in those files. It makes them more difficult to read.
- Also, Windows chokes if its WIN.INI file ever grows larger than 32K. Usually only desktop publishers have trouble with this limit, because their WIN.INI file is stuffed with font names.

Chapter 16

Are These Files Important?

In This Chapter

- Getting rid of unnecessary files
- Knowing which programs create which files
- Running Windows with the fewest number of files

After about a year or so, that familiar ring of keys comes to life and begins burrowing a hole through a pants pocket. The solution, quite simply, is to get rid of some of the keys.

But which keys? What's this key for? The old apartment? The coffee machine cabinet in the *old* office? Did this key work on the *old* bike lock? Does this key open *anything*?

This chapter shows how to separate the important Windows files from all the junk Windows files living on your hard drive. You'll discover which of those suspicious-looking Windows files are important and which ones can be peeled off and tossed aside.

What's This File For?

Although computers may seem like bundles of geekisms, they're *organized* bundles of geekisms.

For example, most Windows programs tack three letters onto every file they create. Whenever Cardfile saves information in a file, that file's name ends in the letters .CRD. Called an *extension*, those three letters serve as a file's thumbprint: They identify which culprit created which file.

Table 16-1 identifies some of the most common file extensions you may spot on your hard drive, as well as their creators.

Table 16-1 Who Dunnit? Which Programs Use Which Extension?

Files ending like this. . .	*usually do this*
.386	These help Windows work with virtual memory — swap files — when running in *386 Enhanced* mode. (See Chapter 11.)
.2GR	Short for *grabber*, this helps Windows display text and graphics when running in *Standard* mode, both on a 286 and 386 computer.
.3GR	Same as above, but for the Enhanced mode reserved for 386, 486, and more powerful computers.
.AVI	Contain movies in a special format, playable through Media Player after it's been upgraded by Microsoft's Video for Windows (see Chapter 3). (You don't need any special hardware to view the movies, but movie *makers* usually need expensive *video grabbing* cards.)
.BAT	Short for *batch* files, these contain lists of DOS commands, including commands to load DOS programs. (Rarely used in Windows.)
.BMP	Short for *bitmap*, these contain pictures or illustrations, usually created by Paintbrush.
.CAL	Short for calendar, these contain appointments created by Calendar.
.CBT	Short for *Computer Based Training*, these usually contain tutorials for Microsoft software like Excel and Word for Windows.
.COM	Short for *command*, these almost always contain DOS programs.
.CRD	Short for *card*, these contain the names and addresses created by Cardfile.
.DAT	Short for *data*, these contain information for programs to look at. They're similar to a .INI file, but don't use any predictable format for storing stuff. (See .INI.)
.DLL	Short for *Dynamic Link Library*, these are like mini-programs. Other programs often peek at these .DLL files for help when they're working.
.DOC	Short for *document*, these usually contain text stored by a word processor. Microsoft Word saves files ending in .DOC, for example. Unfortunately, a .DOC file from one word processor won't always work on another word processor.
.DRV	Short for *driver*, these files help Windows talk to parts of your computer like its keyboard, monitor, and various internal gadgetry.

Files ending like this...	*usually do this*
.EPS	Short for *Encapsulated PostScript* file, these contain information to be printed on *PostScript* printers. PostScript is a special format for expensive printers to read and print information created by expensive PostScript-compatible programs.
.EXE	Short for *executable*, these contain programs. Almost *all* Windows programs end in .EXE; most DOS programs do, too.
.FLI	These files contain animation — high-tech cartoon/movies — often made with programs by a company called Autodesk. They're not compatible with .AVI, so you can't watch 'em in Media Player. (See .AVI.)
.FON	A font that's not *TrueType* compatible. (See .TTF and .FOT.) Windows uses these fonts mostly for its menus, error messages, and other "system" information.
.FOT	Part of a TrueType font. When combined with a similarly named file ending in .TTF, the pair make up a TrueType font. (See .TTF.)
.GIF	Short for *Graphic Interchange File*, these contain pictures stored in a space-saving format invented by modem hounds on CompuServe. Paintbrush can't view .GIFs, although several shareware Windows programs can.
.GRP	Short for *group*, these files let Program Manager remember which icons belong in which of its groups.
.HLP	Short for *help*, these contain the helpful information that pops up when you press F1 or choose Help from a program's menu.
.ICO	Short for *icon*, these contain — you guessed it — icons. (See Chapter 3.)
.INF	Short for *information*, these usually contain text for programs, not humans. Programs often grab information from .INF files when they're first installed. For example, a file called OEMSETUP.INF often lives on a program's floppy disk; Windows looks at the OEMSETUP.INF file for help when installing that program's drivers and other special goodies. (See .INI files.)
.INI	Short for *initialization*, these files contain code-filled text for programs to use, usually so they can remember any special options a user has chosen. Unlike .INF files, described above, humans can fiddle with an .INI file's content to make programs work better — or worse. (See Chapter 15.)

(continued)

Table 16-1 Who Dunnit? Which Programs Use Which Extension?

Files ending like this...	*usually do this*
.JPG	Short for *JPEG*, these contain pictures, similar to files ending in .GIF, .BMP, and .PCX. Paintbrush can't view them, but several shareware viewers can. (See Chapter 7.)
.MID	Short for *MIDI*, these files tell sound cards or synthesizers to play musical notes in a certain order. If everything goes right, the musical notes will sound like a pretty song. (See Chapter 3.)
.MPG	Short for *MPEG*, these are just like .JPG files except they contain movies. Nope, Media Player can't view them, but some other Windows programs can.
.MS	For police-keeping reasons, the DOS 6 program, Anti-Virus, often puts a file named CHKLIST.MS in every directory on your hard drive. (Don't delete these files, or Anti-Virus won't work as well.)
.OVR	Short for overlay, these are chunks of bigger programs. Sometimes the .OVR files share the same name as their main program, but don't count on it.
.PCX	These contain pictures viewable in Paintbrush. In fact, Paintbrush can save .BMP files as .PCX files, saving considerable hard disk space. (Convert them back to .BMP files before trying to use them as wallpaper, though.)
.PIF	Short for *Program Information File*, these contain special instructions for Windows to treat DOS programs. (See Chapter 14.)
.REC	Short for *Recorder*, these contain macros — stored groups of keystrokes — created by Windows Recorder.
.RLE	Short for *Run Length Encoded*, these contain pictures. Although these pictures can't be viewed in Paintbrush, they can still be used as wallpaper: Just type their names into the File box under the Wallpaper section of Windows Desktop. (See Chapter 3.)
.RTF	Short for *Rich Text Format*, these contain ASCII text with special codes. The codes let different brands of word processors swap files without losing groovy stuff like margins or italics. (Not used by Notepad or Write, but used by Microsoft Word for Windows.)
.SCR	Short for *screen*, these files contain a screen saver program. Copy a .SCR file to your Windows directory, and it will appear on the Screen Saver menu in Control Panel's Desktop area. (Chapter 3 offers much more elaborate instructions.)

Files ending like this...	*usually do this*
.SYD	Changed a file in Windows SysEdit program? Then that's where this file came from: This is the original version of the file you changed. (See Chapter 11.)
.SYS	Short for *system*, these contain information designed for your computer or its programs — not for humans. (See Chapter 11 for CONFIG.SYS). Also, SYS is a DOS command for making floppy disks *bootable*. (See *More DOS For Dummies*.)
.TMP	Short for *temporary*. Some Windows programs stash occasional notes in a file, but forget to erase the file when they're done. Those leftover files will end in .TMP. Feel free to delete them if *you're sure Windows isn't running in the background*.
.TRM	Short for *terminal*, these files save phone numbers and special modem settings so Terminal knows how to call another computer.
.TTF	Short for *TrueType Font*. When combined with a similarly named file ending in .FOT, the pair make up a TrueType font. (See .FOT.)
.TXT	Short for *text*, these files almost always contain plain old text, often created by Notepad.
.WAV	Short for *waveform* audio, these simply contain recorded sounds. Both Media Player and Sound Recorder let you listen to .WAV files.
.WPD	Short for *Windows PostScript Driver*, these files help Windows talk to those expensive PostScript printers.
.WRI	Short for *Write*, these contain text created in — yep — the Write word processor.
.ZIP	These contain a file — or several files — compressed into one smaller file. (See Chapter 12.)

Find any identifiable file extensions on your own hard drive? Jot them down here for further reference. (Finally — you're *allowed* to write in books.)

- Unfortunately, these file extensions aren't *always* a sure identifier; some programs cheat. For example, some plain old text files will end in the letters .DOC — not .TXT.
- Most of the file extensions listed in Table 16-1 are *associated* with the program that created them. That means when you double-click on that file's name in File Manager, the program that created the file will bring it to the screen. A double-click on a file named YUMMY.WRI, for example, makes Write pop to the screen, holding YUMMY.WRI in its belly.
- Although Table 16-1 lists most of the extensions you'll come across when using Windows, feel free to write down any others you discover in the space above. Many of your own programs are using their own special code words when saving files.

What Are Those Sneaky Hidden Files?

Many of the files on your computer's hard drive are for your computer to play with — not you.

So, to keep their computer-oriented files out of your way, some programs will stash them in hidden places. By flipping a mysterious little switch built-in to the file, programs can make files invisible: Their name won't appear in File Manager, nor will they show up in any menus.

Most hidden files are hidden for a reason: Deleting them can make your computer stop working or work strangely. Don't delete hidden files without serious reason, and even then, chew your lower lip cautiously before pushing the Del key.

Table 16-2 shows a few of the Sneaky Hidden Files you might stumble across in the dark.

Table 16-2 Under Rare Circumstances, You May Encounter These Hidden Files

These hidden files...	*do this*
IBMBIO.COM and IBMDOS or IO.SYS and MSDOS.SYS	These files, hidden in your computer's *root directory,* contain most of the life that's in DOS.
386SPART.PAR	If Windows grabs part of your hard drive for a Permanent swap file, this is the swap file. (See Chapter 11.)
A hidden directory called \SENTRY	If you turn on the Undelete program's Delete Sentry option, it creates this directory. Later, when you delete a file, it gets stuffed into this hidden directory. (Chapter 6 explains the whys and what fors.)

These hidden files...	*do this*
Identified any other hidden files? Feel free to write their names and identities in the places below.	

- Ever wiped an unidentifiable smudge from the coffee table? Well, that's why hidden files are hidden: To keep people from spotting them and deleting them, thinking they're as useless as a smudge.
- For the most part, hidden files stay hidden. But File Manager lets you spot them, if you're sneaky. Click on View from File Manager's menu, choose By File Type, and make sure there's an X in the Show Hidden/System Files box.
- When the novelty of seeing hidden files wears off, remove the X from the Show Hidden/System Files box. There's not much point in looking at them, anyway.

- When your computer hides a file by flipping the file's "hidden" switch, computer nerds say the computer has changed that file's *attribute*.

Purging the Unnecessary Files

Windows comes with slightly more than three trillion files, all poured onto your hard drive. After a few months, that number increases exponentially. But which files can you wipe off your hard drive without making everything tumble down?

The next few sections contain tips on what files you're allowed to get rid of. But first, a warning: Don't delete any of these files while Windows is running.

Removing Any Leftover Temporary Files

While it's humming away, Windows creates some files for its own use. Then, when you shut Windows down for the day, Windows is supposed to delete those *temporary* files. Unfortunately, it sometimes forgets.

So, when you've exited Windows, start purging those temporary files yourself. First, delete any files ending with the letters .TMP and starting with the weird @td character. For example, the file @tdWRI042C.TMP is something Write created, but forgot to erase when it was done with it.

Also, delete the file WIN386.SWP from your WINDOWS directory only if it's there when Windows *isn't running*. (That's the temporary swap file Windows forgot to delete; it's covered more in Chapter 11.)

- To be on the safe side, don't delete any files with the current day's date. Wait a couple of days — just to make sure they don't contain anything important.
- Windows often stuffs its temporary files in your \DOS directory; you might find some deletable remnants there.
- Also, check your hard drive for a \TEMP directory; sometimes Windows stashes its junky leftovers in there.

Dumping Windows Files to Save Hard Disk Space

Believe it or not, Windows doesn't have to eat up massive chunks of your hard drive space. Windows can run in less than 3MB of hard drive space. It won't be able to do anything fancy, but hey, 3MB is 3MB.

To start pruning, run through the following steps in the next few sections. They describe just about limb of Windows you can cut off — and still be able to run a Windows program. Feel free to pick and choose what parts you want to delete; some folks can't bear to prune Solitaire, for example.

- Before pruning, think for awhile about the parts of Windows you've been relying on and the parts you haven't touched.
- If you're packing Windows onto a laptop, for example, you probably won't need Paintbrush. Nor will you need a printer driver. Who prints while on the road?
- A laptop doesn't *really* need screen savers, either. And Solitaire is hard to play with a trackball — dump it.
- Finally, make sure you keep your Windows installation disks handy — the disks that came in the box. You might decide later you want to copy some Windows files back onto your hard drive.
- If you're hard up for hard drive space, the next few sections have tips on what to delete.

Dumping unneeded Windows programs

Do you really *need* Cardfile and Calendar? By deleting those two programs — along with their help files — you've just freed up almost 200KB. Windows makes it easy to pry off any other unnecessary accessories. Just follow the next few steps.

Windows Setup

1. **From the Program Manager, double-click on the Windows Setup icon.**

2. **From the Options menu, choose Add/Remove Windows Components (see Figure 16-1).**

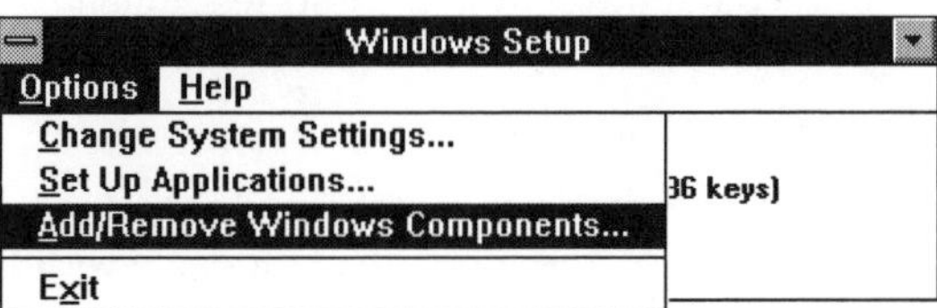

Figure 16-1: The Windows Setup Options menu.

A big new window will pop up, as seen in Figure 16-2.

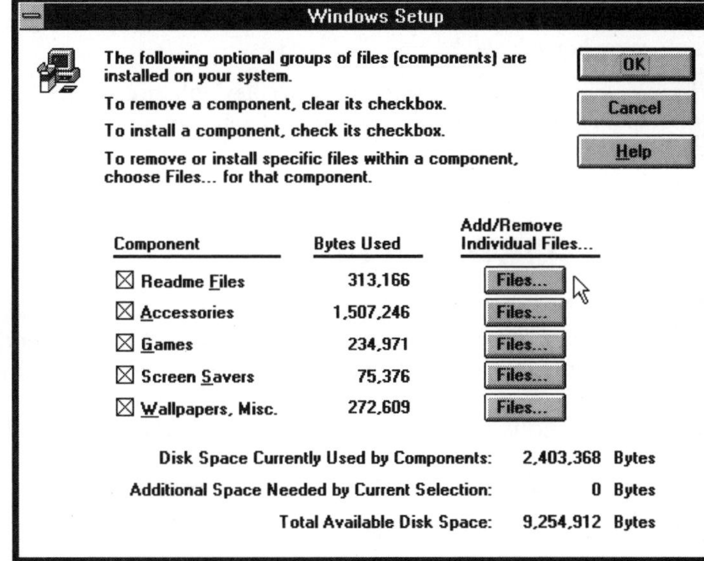

Figure 16-2: Windows Setup lets you delete Windows programs as well as set them up.

3. Pick and choose what to remove.

Here, it's up to you. For example, Microsoft packs a bunch of boring instructions — information on networks, printers, and other computer organs — into text files, and then slips the files onto your hard drive. Engineers call the files *Readme* files in the hopes people might read them.

To make Windows remove all those boring Readme files from your hard drive (clearing up more than 300KB of space), click in the Readme Files checkbox to remove the X.

Or, click on the Files button next to it: A list of all the Readme files will appear so that you can choose to remove only the *most* boring.

Follow the same steps to weed out unwanted Accessories (Calendar, Object Packager, Recorder, or others), Games (Minesweeper and Solitaire), Screen Savers, and Wallpaper.

- If you tell Windows Setup to remove *everything* you've just saved yourself 2.5MB of hard drive space. Sure, the programs that came with Windows will be gone. But you can still run other Windows programs — the ones you've bought at the store.
- Don't be scared of deleting too much, either. It's easy to put all that stuff back by running Windows Setup program again. Click in those same checkboxes you cleared earlier. Then, grab your Windows installation disks, follow the instructions, and Windows will copy the programs back onto your hard drive.

- To save a little space and *still* be able to play Solitaire, delete Solitaire's Help file. That frees up 14K of space, and you probably remember how to play Solitaire, anyway.

Dumping unwanted drivers

Windows uses bunches of *drivers* — pieces of software that let it talk to different kinds of printers, sound cards, and other gizmos. But if you're not using those gizmos anymore, their drivers are useless; here's how to get rid of them.

Control Panel

1. From the Program Manager, double-click on the Control Panel icon.

2. Double-click on the Control Panel's Drivers icon.

A box full of driver names opens.

3. **Click on the name of a driver you don't use.**
4. **Click the Remove button.**

   Windows asks whether you're *sure* you'd like to remove that driver. If you are sure, click the Yes button. Windows makes some erasing noises then say it needs to restart.

5. **Click the Restart Now button.**

   Windows clears the screen then hops back on — this time, without the driver you've removed.

Still have some more drivers to get rid of? Then start back at Step 1 and keep going.

Dumping unwanted printer drivers

If you've set up Windows to work with several different printers — and you're not using some of those printers anymore — then you can save space by removing those printer's *drivers*.

Printer drivers don't take up much space, but hey, sometimes every kilobyte counts. Use these steps to get rid of them:

Control Panel

1. **Double-click on Windows Control Panel icon.**
2. **Double-click on the Printers icon.**

   A list of installed printers will rise to the screen, as shown in Figure 16-3.

Figure 16-3: Removing drivers listed under Installed Printers can save some hard disk space.

3. **Click on any unused printers in the Installed Printers box.**

   Windows highlights the name of the printer you've chosen.

4. **Click the Remove button**

   Windows asks whether you're *sure* you'd like to remove that printer. Are you? Then click Yes.

That's it. If something's goofed, then follow the same steps to put a printer back on. This time, however, choose the Add button instead of the Remove button.

Dumping unwanted fonts

At first, fonts are fun, wacky ways to turn boring letters into weird arty things.

After a while, though, the fun can wear thin. Too many fonts can clog up the hard drive something fierce. Plus, they make Windows take longer when loading.

Here's how to dump the fonts you've grown sick of. For example, you can remove your Happy-Holiday-Card fonts in January and reinstall them next December.

Control Panel

1. **Double-click on Windows Control Panel.**

2. **Double-click on the Fonts icon.**

   A new boxful of fonts will appear, like the one in Figure 16-4.

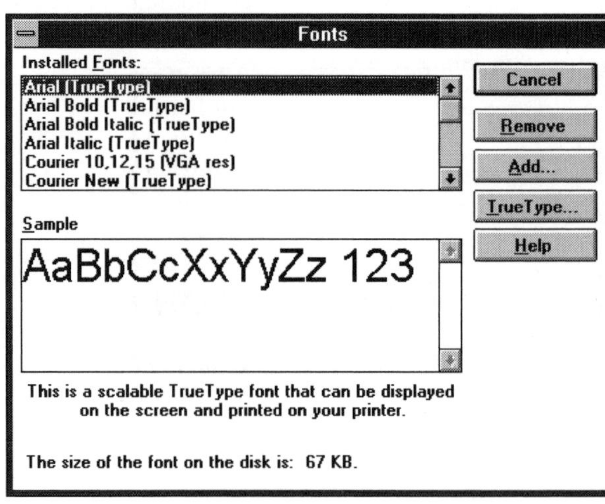

Figure 16-4: This box lets you remove or add Windows fonts — those fun ways to display letters.

3. **Click on any fonts you don't use.**

   Whenever you click on a font, Windows lets you see what it looks like, as seen in Figure 16-4.

   In fact, once you've found the fonts you're sick of, hold down Ctrl while clicking on the names of *all* of the unwanted fonts. Windows won't show you what the fonts look like anymore — you've clicked on too many. But Windows will remove all the fonts you've clicked on when you move to Step 4.

4. **Click the Remove button.**

   A new box will pop up, as shown in Figure 16-5.

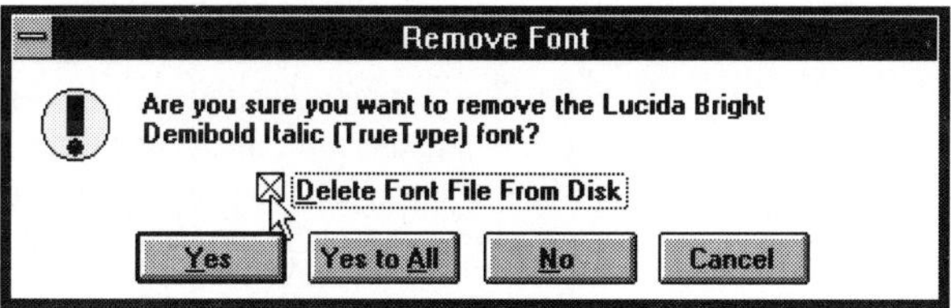

Figure 16-5: Click in the Delete Font File from Disk box to remove the fonts from the hard drive.

5. **Click the Delete Font File from Disk box; then click Yes to All.**

   Here's the trick: Before clicking the Yes button, click in the Delete Font File from Disk box. If there's no X in that box, Windows simply removes the fonts from the menu — not the hard drive. And that won't save any hard drive space at all.

   Clicked in the box? Then click the Yes to All button. The screen will twitch, and Windows will delete the fonts from your hard drive. You're done.

If you've found some cool replacement fonts — or deleted the wrong ones — Chapter 3 shows how to put them on your hard drive.

Removing other Windows remnants

The steps listed in the sections above will shave off most of Windows extraneous organs. A few files will still remain, however. Table 16-3 shows some of what's left, and what the files do.

Table 16-3 Whodunnit? These Windows Files Do These Things

What it is	*What it does*
CLIPBRD.EXE, CLIPBRD.HLP	Clipboard Viewer and its help file. This program lets you view what's on the clipboard. If you delete it, the clipboard will still work. You just won't be able to see the stuff you've pasted onto it.
CONTROL.HLP	Control Panel's Help file. This contains all that helpful information that pops up in Control Panel.
MSD.EXE	Microsoft Diagnostics. A program that provides boring technical information about your computer.
MSD.INI	A file where MSD keeps track of various options.
PIFEDIT.EXE	PIF Editor. This program creates and edits PIFs — the files that help Windows run DOS programs. If you delete this program, your existing PIFs will still work; you just won't be able to make new ones or change old ones. (See Chapter 14.)
PRINTMAN.EXE	Print Manager. A program that lets Windows print stuff in the background. Delete this file, and Windows will freeze up until it's done printing.
SETUP.HLP	The help file for Windows' Setup program. This file contains all the helpful information that pops up when you press F1 in Windows Setup program.
SYSEDIT.EXE	System Edit. A technically oriented program for editing WIN.INI, SYSTEM.INI, AUTOEXEC.BAT, and CONFIG.SYS files.
TASKMAN.EXE	Task List. The handy little "window juggling" program that pops up when you press Ctrl+Esc.
WINHELP.EXE	Windows Help program. Delete this, and *none* of your Windows programs will have help screens. (Last resort measure)
WRITE.EXE, WRITE.HLP	Windows Write program and its help file.

- Be sure and think twice before deleting any of the files described in this chapter. Also, don't delete all of these files at once — prune them gradually. That way you'll know which files to replace if you find yourself missing something vital.

- Some programs come with chunky tutorial programs. When you know how to use a program, feel free to dump its tutorials. For example, tutorials for Microsoft's programs (such as Word for Windows and Excel) usually live in files that end in the letters .CBT.
- If you want to strip Windows to its bare bones — a shell of a beast with little power — then buy Microsoft's Windows Resource Kit. It describes all the files you can remove to bring Windows down to 2.6MB — almost enough to fit on your digital watch.

Part V
More Shortcuts and Tips Galore

"YES, I THINK IT'S AN ERROR MESSAGE."

In This Part . . .

After a few years of driving a city's streets, a cabbie knows all the shortcuts: Which sidestreets will bypass freeway traffic, what hours the airport is clogged, and when the train station is a better market for quick fares.

Grizzled cabbies usually don't like to share their secrets; their livelihood's at stake. But Windows users? You can't *stop* them from talking about shortcuts.

Put two Windows users together, and you'll not only hear about secret places to click, you'll hear about what key to depress *while* you're clicking.

Toss in a few tips on how to cheat at Solitaire and Minesweeper, and you've got an idea of what you'll find in this part of the book.

Chapter 17

A Grab Bag of Tricks

In This Chapter

- Tiling Windows in different ways
- Reading the Character Map
- Starting programs just the right way
- Making pages print with numbers or titles
- Scrounging up more memory
- Cheating at Solitaire and Minesweeper
- Highlighting text

The programmers who created Windows tried to make things easy. For example, it's relatively simple to open a file in most Windows programs.

But after the programmers finished putting things on the menus, they started hiding some secret stuff in the cracks.

This chapter yanks the secret stuff out of the cracks and puts it on the coffee table for easy viewing.

Making Windows Tile Vertical — Not Horizontal

When too many windows start cluttering the screen, many folks reach for the Tile button: They double-click on an uncovered part of the screen (or press Ctrl+Esc) to bring up the Task List. Then, they click on the Tile button.

Presto! Windows grabs all the open windows and neatly tiles them across the screen.

If only two windows are open, Windows puts them side by side: one window on the left, and the other on the right. And that's the problem. If one of your windows is a word processor, that cuts off half your sentences.

So, here's the trick to make Windows tile its windows one *above* the other:

- To make windows tile horizontally instead of vertically, hold Shift while clicking the Task List's Tile button.
- File Manager, under its Window menu, can also Tile windows across its screen: It stacks windows across the screen from top to bottom. Hold down Shift while choosing Tile, and File Manager reverses itself: It tiles the windows *vertically* instead of horizontally.
- The Shift key does sneaky things with some other Windows programs. If you're feeling sneaky too, hold down Shift while choosing other menu items in Windows. If something unexpectedly wrong happens, press Ctrl+Z. That usually reverses what happened.

Character Map

Windows Character Map lets you add accented characters to funky foreign words like à votre santé. But when Character Map comes to the screen, all the letters and characters are small and hard to read.

Here's the trick, as shown in Figure 17-1.

- Hold down your mouse button while moving the pointer over the characters in Character map.
- By *holding down* the mouse button, a magnified view of the characters pops to the forefront for easy viewing.

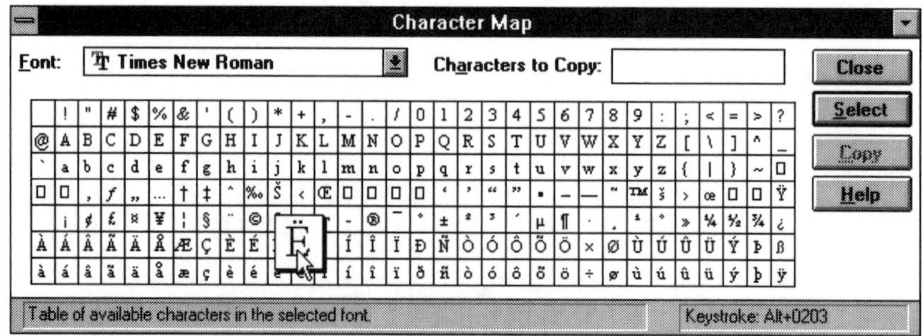

Figure 17-1: Hold down your mouse button while pointing at the characters in Character map to make them easier to see.

- Or, just click once on any of the characters. Then, when you move your arrow keys, a magnified view of the foreign characters will pop up wherever you move your arrow keys.

Make Windows Start Up — Just the Right Way

Face it, one of the most boring parts of computing is waiting for the computer to wake up in the morning and put Windows on-screen. Yawn.

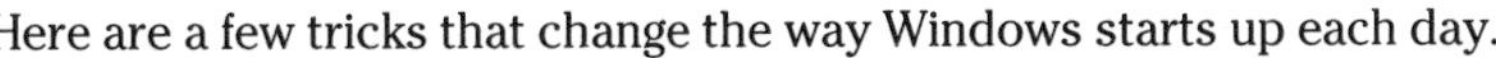

Here are a few tricks that change the way Windows starts up each day.

- Tired of typing `WIN` at the DOS prompt each morning? Then make the word `WIN` the last line of your AUTOEXEC.BAT file, which is a surprisingly easy process described in Chapter 11.

- Use the same Windows programs each day? Then hold down Ctrl and drag their icons into Program Manager's StartUp group window. When Windows starts for the day, it automatically loads any program with an icon in the StartUp group window.

- Organized the Program Manager so it's *just* right? Then hold down Shift and double-click on the box in its upper-left corner — yep, the box that usually closes Windows down. But holding down Shift tells Program Manager to *remember* the way it's currently set up. Then, to complete the process, disable the Save Settings on Exit option from Program Manager's Options menu.

Make Programs Print—Just the Right Way

Most Windows programs let you choose Page Setup from the File menu. That option lets you change how a page looks when it's printed. Should the page have numbers along the top or bottom, for example? Or should there be a title across the top of each page?

Unfortunately, none of the programs are very clear about how to add that stuff to a page. So, here's the trick:

By inserting special symbols into the Header and Footer boxes in most Page Setup areas, you can make the date, time, filename, page numbers, or personal text appear across the top or bottom of each of your printed pages.

Those special symbols — and what they do — appear in Table 17-1.

Table 17-1 Special Codes and Their Printing Effects

Adding this symbol to the Header or Footer box...	*adds this to the printed page*
&d	Current date
&p	Page numbers
&f	Filename
&l	Any text following this code will be started at the left margin
&r	Any text following this code will be started at the right margin
&c	Any text following this code will be centered between the margins
&t	Current time

Those Page Setup codes work with Cardfile, Notepad, Calendar, Paintbrush, and other third-party Windows programs.

Running Out of Memory?

No matter how much memory you've stuffed inside your computer, Windows always seems to want more. Here are a few tricks for fighting back.

- If Windows says it doesn't have enough memory to do something and you're sure that your computer *does* have enough memory, check your clipboard. If there's a big picture copied to the clipboard, delete it: That picture might be robbing Windows of the memory it needed to do something else.

- If you're using a lot of DOS programs, make .PIFs for them, as described in Chapter 14. Sometimes Windows will give too much memory to DOS programs; a .PIF can get some of that memory back.

Cheating at the Games

Cheating at games? Sure; there's no ethical problem here at all. Because Solitaire and Minesweeper are computer games, it's fair to use your computer against them. The next two sections tell how.

Sliding a fast one past Solitaire

Although Solitaire's a formidable opponent, you can turn the cards in your favor with a few tricks.

A few minutes after starting a game, for example, it's hard to remember whether or not Solitaire has already dealt you a specific card. Is there a King near the bottom of the pile? Here's how to peek.

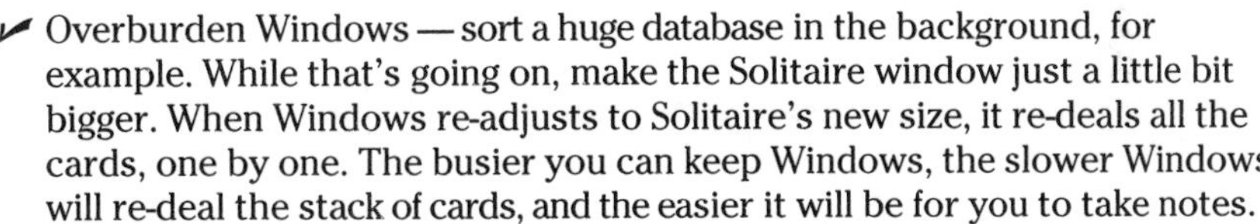

- Overburden Windows — sort a huge database in the background, for example. While that's going on, make the Solitaire window just a little bit bigger. When Windows re-adjusts to Solitaire's new size, it re-deals all the cards, one by one. The busier you can keep Windows, the slower Windows will re-deal the stack of cards, and the easier it will be for you to take notes.

- See a card that belongs on one of the four stacks above? Just double-click on it; the card will automatically shoot up to the right spot, saving a little time. In fact, double-click on each card Solitaire deals you; that way you won't miss any possible moves.

- When you're drawing cards three at a time, sometimes you need that *second* card. To make Windows give it to you, try this: Hold down Ctrl+Alt+Shift and click on the deck. Solitaire will start dealing out the cards one by one instead of three at a time.

- Bats' wings aren't flapping anymore? Sun not sticking out its tongue? Card not sliding in and out of the sleeve? Then switch Solitaire back into Timed Game mode by choosing Options from the Game menu. That starts up all the animation on the card's backs. (The sun and the sleeve only act up once every thirty seconds, though, so be patient.)

Blowing past Minesweeper's rules

Some people love Minesweeper: A logical game of clicking on little boxes, looking at their numbers, and deducing the sites of the hidden bombs.

Others think it's boring as all get-out.

Both parties will enjoy this trick, though. Sure, it's complete, utter cheating. But it's about time *we've* been able to cheat on the computers for a change, eh?

The whole idea behind Minesweeper is to avoid clicking on the boxes that contain explosive mines. Forget all that logical deduction stuff. Here's how to cheat:

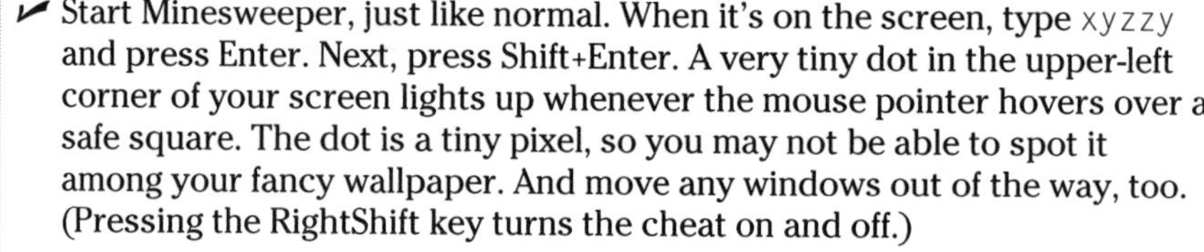

- Start Minesweeper, just like normal. When it's on the screen, type `xyzzy` and press Enter. Next, press Shift+Enter. A very tiny dot in the upper-left corner of your screen lights up whenever the mouse pointer hovers over a safe square. The dot is a tiny pixel, so you may not be able to spot it among your fancy wallpaper. And move any windows out of the way, too. (Pressing the RightShift key turns the cheat on and off.)

- To add sound to Minesweeper, add the line `Sound=3` to your WINMINE.INI file. Check out Chapter 15 for complete instructions as well as tips for cheating on your high scores.

Keeping Windows Safe from the Kids

Kids love to play with Windows. Something about pointing a mouse and clicking is, well, much more fun than babbling ol' Barney.

But how do you keep the kids from messing up your Program Manager, deleting any of its icons or program groups? Here's the trick:

Add the following lines to the tail end of the file called PROGMAN.INI in your Windows directory:

```
[restrictions]
NoFileMenu=1
EditLevel=4
```

Chapter 15 shows how to edit an INI file; it's simpler than it sounds.

The `NoFileMenu=1` line takes the word File — and all its powerful options — off the Program Manager's menu. That keeps the kids from using the menu's Delete option.

The `EditLevel=4` line keeps the kids from creating, deleting or renaming any of the groups or icons you've set up in Program Manager.

If something awful happens and they *do* mess up Program Manager something fierce, head to Chapter 21 for tips on restoring sanity.

Highlighting Text Quickly

I don't know why this trick works, but here goes:

When highlighting a bunch of text in Notepad and moving the pointer from the bottom toward the top, wiggle your mouse around above Notepad's window. That speeds up the marking process.

That trick works when highlighting information in other Windows programs, too. Weird.

Plugging It In Right Side Up

This tip doesn't have *that* much to do with Windows, so it's slipped in here unannounced toward the end, free of charge.

After your computer's up and running, with all the cables plugged into the right places, put a dot of correction fluid on the top of each cable's plug. That makes it easier to plug the cables back in right-side up when they fall out.

Chapter 18

Speedy Menu Shortcuts

In This Chapter

- Drag-and-drop shortcuts
- Quick-clicking tips
- Choosing items quickly from a list
- Replacing highlighted text

Before you can do just about *anything* in Windows, you need to click on a menu.

So, the quicker you can click, the quicker you can breeze through Windows and move on to the more important things in life.

This chapter shows some of the best quick click tips.

Moving through Menus Quickly

When choosing something from a Windows menu, people usually follow the most logical course:

1. Click on the option along the program's top, and watch as the little menu falls down.
2. Then, click on the desired item from the little menu.

That's two clicks: the first one brings down the menu, and the second chooses the item from the menu. However, you can reduce your finger action to a *single* click:

When you click somewhere to open a menu, *keep holding down your mouse button*. When the menu drops down, slide the mouse pointer until it rests over the item you want. Then *release* the mouse button to choose that item.

That simple trick turns a two-click operation into a single-click, cutting your click work in half.

Press the First Letter of an Item in a List

Windows often presents a menu with a zillion options. In fact, some menus have too many options to fit on-screen at the same time. So, to scroll up or down the list of options, people usually click on little arrows, as seen in Figure 18-1.

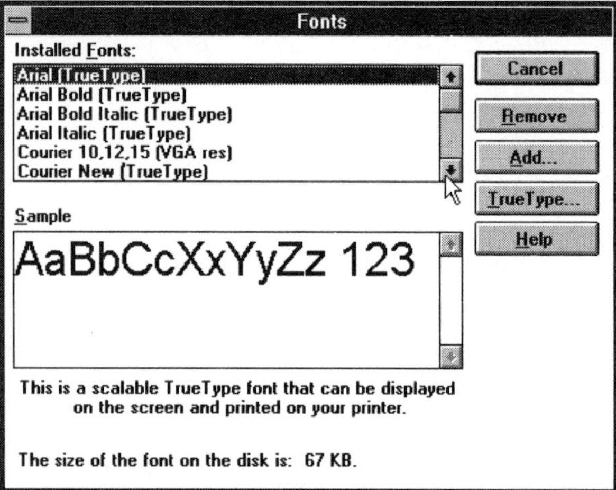

Figure 18-1: Clicking on the up- or down-pointing arrows can take too much time in a long list.

To reach an item in the bottom of the list, you could press PgDn several times, or click on the scroll bars a couple times. But here's a faster way:

When Windows lists too many items to fit on-screen at once, press the first letter of the item you want; Windows immediately jumps to that item's place in the list.

For example, Figure 18-1 lists all the fonts installed on the computer. To immediately jump to the Wingdings font, for example, press the letter W. Windows immediately shows you the fonts beginning with W. Slick, huh?

Secret Places to Click

Much of Windows consists of aiming carefully with the mouse and clicking the mouse button — pointing and clicking on an menu to choose something, for example. Or, clicking in a box to put an X inside it.

But here's a secret, welcomed by those with big fingers: You don't have to aim carefully with your mouse. The next few sections show some *sloppy* places to click that work just as well.

Clicking on an icon's title

Most people learn one thing about Windows right away: double-click on a program's icon to load it from Program Manager or to call it up from the bottom of the screen. But why bother aiming for the icon? There's an easier way, as shown in Figure 18-2.

Instead of double-clicking on an icon, double-click on the icon's *title*, instead. Both the icon and its title do the same thing, and at higher resolutions, the title's often much easier to spot than the icon itself.

Figure 18-2: Double-clicking on an icon's title works just as well.

Skipping past downward-pointing arrows

Some menus come packaged inside little boxes. And they're hidden. To make the menu drop down, you need to click on the little downward-pointing arrow next to the box. But you don't need to be overly precise, as shown in Figure 18-3.

Instead of aiming directly for the downward-pointing arrow next to a box, click inside the box itself. A click inside the box also makes the menu drop down, and it's easier to aim at than the arrow.

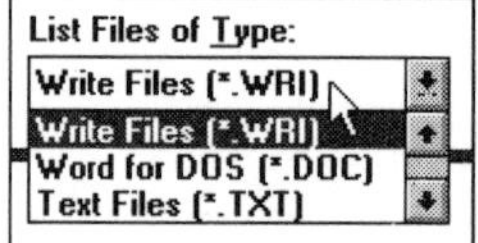

Figure 18-3: Clicking on the box itself makes the menu drop down.

Avoiding tiny checkboxes and circles

Some menus make you click inside a tiny circle or checkbox to change an option. For example, to change your wallpaper from Tiled to Centered, you're supposed to click in the tiny box next to Center, as seen in Figure 18-4. Or are you?

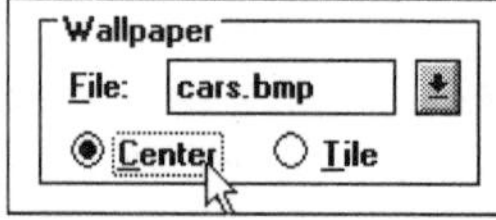

Figure 18-4: Click on the *word* Center — it's easier to aim at.

Instead of clicking on the tiny box next to an item, click on the name of the item itself. That chooses the item, just as if you'd clicked inside the tiny box.

Replacing highlighted text

To replace text in a word processor, the usual course is to highlight the text, press the Del key, and type in the new text. But there's a quicker way.

After highlighting some text you'd like to replace, immediately begin typing in replacement text. Your first keystroke will delete the highlighted text, just as if you'd pressed Del.

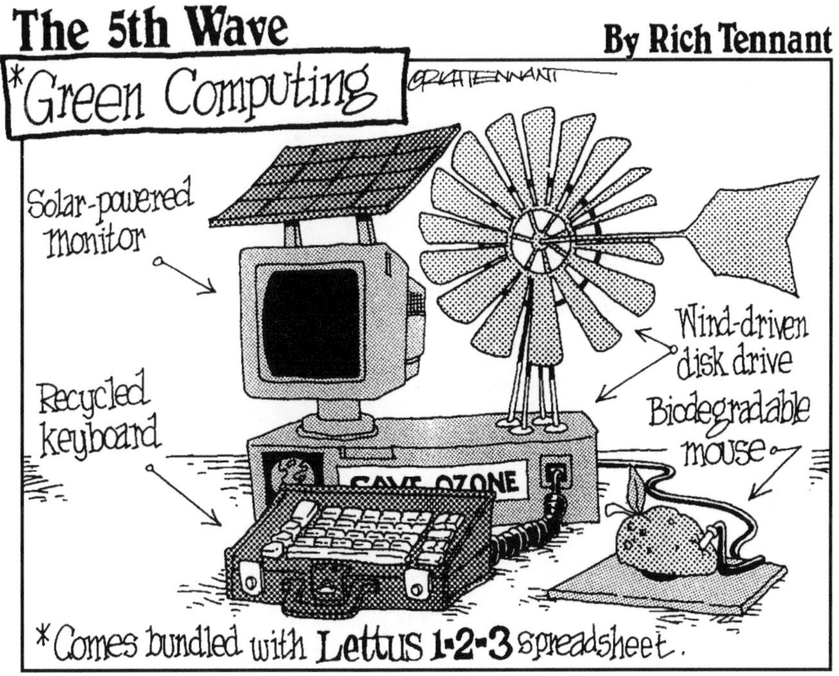
The 5th Wave
By Rich Tennant
*Green Computing
Solar-powered monitor
Wind-driven disk drive
Recycled keyboard
Biodegradable mouse
SAVE OZONE
*Comes bundled with Lettus 1-2-3 spreadsheet.

Chapter 19

File Manager Tips

In This Chapter

- Saving your File Manager's current setup
- Selecting files in File Manager
- Viewing drives and directories
- Moving and copying several files to other directories
- Making File Manager easier to read

File Manager's probably the most raggedy part of Windows. It's the hole in the comfortable Windows blanket, letting the cold air of DOS blow in.

Windows For Dummies covers the File Manager basics, so you won't find that stuff in this chapter. Instead, you'll find tips and shortcuts for pointing and clicking your way through File Manager's baffling catacombs of icons, menus, and filenames.

Saving Your File Manager's Current Setup

Sometimes, File Manager is simply a mess. Its windows often overlap, making it hard to find things. Plus, File Manager sometimes shows *bunches* of views of the same disk drive. Which view is the real one?

Frankly, File Manager sometimes just doesn't *look* right. So, after you've spent a few minutes organizing File Manager so it looks just *so*, try this trick:

- While holding down Shift, double-click on the box in File Manager's upper-left corner — the box that usually closes File Manager down. Holding down Shift while double-clicking tells File Manager to *remember* the way it's currently set up. The next time you load File Manager, it will look the same as it does now.

- To complete the trick, make sure there's no check mark next to the Save Settings on Exit option from File Manager's Options menu. That way, File Manager remembers its current layout only when *you* tell it to.
- That same Shift+double-click trick works for Program Manager, too, by the way.

Selecting Files and Directories in File Manager

If File Manager's on-screen, you're most likely looking for some files or directories to click on. Table 19-1 shows some shortcuts for grabbing bunches of 'em, quickly.

Table 19-1 Shortcuts for Selecting Files in File Manager

To grab these . . .	*do this*
A single file or directory	Click on it.
Several files or directories	Hold down Ctrl and click on them.
Several files or directories sitting next to each other	Click on the first file, hold Shift, and click on the last file.
All the files or directories in a window	Press /.
None of the files or directories in a window	Press \.
A file or directory beginning with a specific letter	Press that specific letter.
Several files or directories without using a mouse	Press Shift+F8. Then press your arrow keys to move to different files or directories, and press the spacebar to select them.

Uh, How Big Is This File?

When it comes out of the box, File Manager doesn't volunteer much information about your files. It merely lists their names which run down a list in alphabetical order.

And that's fine, when you're first starting out with Windows. But after awhile, you need to know *more*: How big is that file? Is this file *older* than that file?

This tip lets you see all the gory information about a file.

- While holding down Alt, double-click on a file's name in File Manager. A box opens on-screen and reveals the file's size, path, the date it was last saved, and its *attributes*: technical information about the file's various technical switches.
- The preceding tip lets you *change* the attributes of a file or directory, as well. For example, you could make a hidden directory to stash your most secret stuff.
- Tired of poking through File Manager to find all your .BMP files? Then tell File Manager to sort your files by their *extensions*. Choose Sort by Type from File Manager's View menu. File Manager will then display all the BMP files near the top of its file list; all the .WRI files will be toward the end.

Where'd they go?

Got a sneaking suspicion that File Manager isn't showing you *all* the files in your directory? Head for the By File Type option under the View menu. Then, make sure that box looks just like the one in this figure.

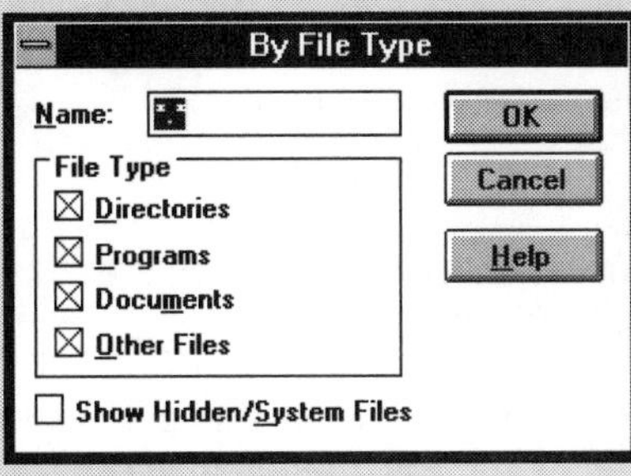

First, make sure *.* appears in the Name box. Then, make sure all the boxes listed under File Type have an X in them. (If a box doesn't have an X, click inside it; an X will appear.)

Also, make sure there *isn't* an X in the Show Hidden/System Files box. You don't need to see those types of files, anyway, as described in Chapter 16.

It Shows Three Views of the Same Directory!

File Manager's main job is to display the names of files and directories living on your hard drive. When you can see their names, you can play with them: copy them, rename them, or simply delete the ugly ones.

Unfortunately, File Manager sometimes goes overboard. It shows you the same view of the same drive or directory, over and over.

For example, Figure 19-1 shows a cluttered File Manager screen showing the same Windows directory three times.

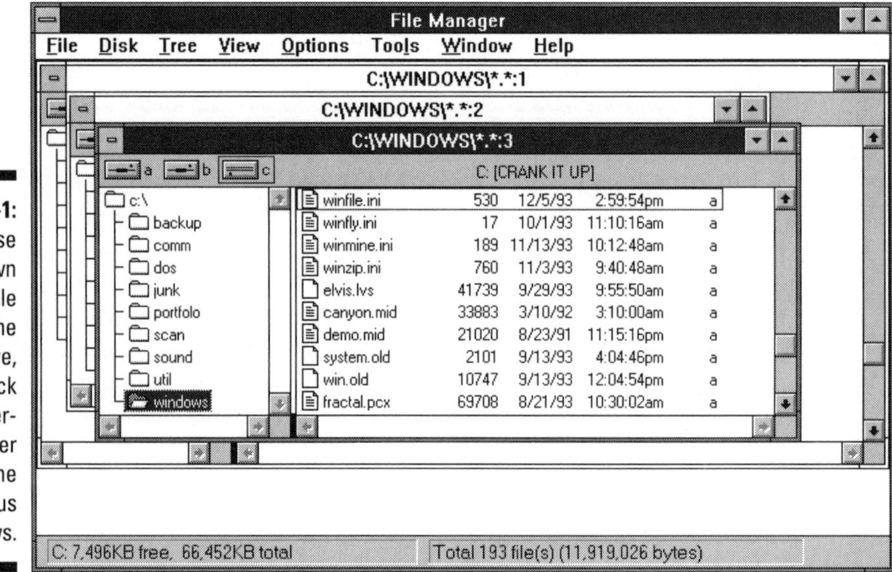

Figure 19-1: To close down multiple views of the same drive, double-click in the upper-left corner of the extraneous windows.

Other times, File Manager displays extra views of drives or directories, but they won't show up on-screen; they're hidden beneath the currently open window. Those renegade multiple views will show up if you click on File Manager's Window menu, as seen in Figure 19-2.

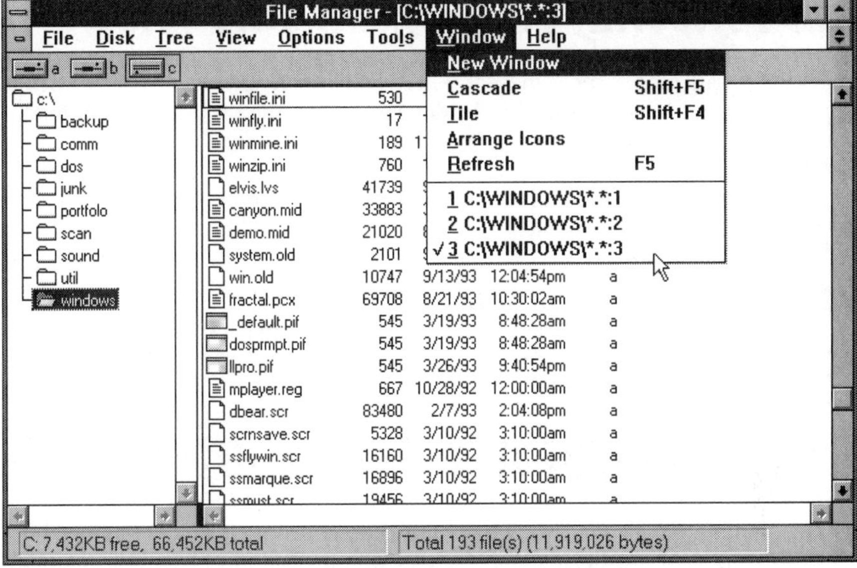

Figure 19-2: To see a list of you currently open windows, choose Window from File Manager's main menu.

Here are some tips to make File Manager knock off those multiple windows.

- Don't *double-click* on a drive's icon in File Manager unless you want a new window to leap to the screen, showing a view of that particular drive.
- To make a currently open window show the contents of a different drive, *single-click* on that drive's icon. That keeps other windows from popping up.
- To see how many windows File Manager is currently holding onto, click the Window option from its menu. A box will drop down, listing all the currently open windows.
- To make a single directory hop to the screen in its *own* new window, hold Shift and double-click on the directory's name.
- To make a window show a different drive, hold down Ctrl and press the letter of the drive. Pressing Ctrl+C, for example, makes the current window switch to a view of drive C.
- All this clicking and double-clicking stuff is terribly hard to remember, so don't worry if you can't figure it out, right off the bat.
- Even when File Manager shows you several views of the same drive, there's no harm done; it just makes File Manager seem more complicated than it really is.

Am I Moving or Copying This File?

Can't remember whether you're *moving* or *copying* a file as you drag it from window to window in File Manager? Then the tip below might help.

- As you begin dragging a file's little icon, look inside the icon. If it contains a plus sign, you're *copying* the file. If the icon doesn't have a plus sign, you're *moving* the file.
- If you're *copying* a file when you want to be *moving* it — or vice versa — then press and release Shift or Ctrl. One of these two keys will toggle File Manager. That toggles File Manager back and forth between copying or moving.

All the Letters Are Too Small!

File Manager's full of tiny words in tiny little rows and columns, but it doesn't have to be. In fact, File Manager will display your drive's file names and directories using any sized letters you want.

For example, the tip below can make File Manager's letters exceptionally large and easy to read on a groggy Monday morning.

- To change the way File Manager displays its words and letters, choose Font from the Options menu. File Manager will let you make the letters larger, smaller, or even boldfaced or italicized.
- To make File Manager return to displaying its *original* fonts, choose Font from the Options menu. Then choose the MS Sans Serif Font, and choose the Regular Font Style with a Size of 8. Finally, make sure an X appears in the Lowercase box.

Chapter 20

Program Manager Tips

In This Chapter

- Making Program Manager start right
- Shortening an icon's title
- Adding Control Panel's Desktop to Program Manager
- Fitting more icons on Program Manager
- Fixing Startup error messages

Program Manager, that ultimate elevator panel of buttons, lingers perpetually around the Windows desktop, carrying users from program to program.

This chapter shows what buttons to push to make that elevator move a little bit faster.

Program Manager Keeps Loading Itself as an Icon!

Whenever you start Windows, Program Manager hops to the screen, ready for action.

But sometimes Program Manager gets lazy: Instead of hopping up on the screen, it loads itself as an icon and simply sits there at the bottom of the screen.

That slows things down: Before you can get any work done, you have to double-click on Program Manager's icon, just to make it show itself.

It's not a deadly program, just an annoying one. But here's how to fix it.

- First, arrange Program Manager on the screen the way you'd like it to appear. Then, while holding Shift, double-click on the square in Program Manager's upper, left-hand corner — the place you normally double-click to shut down Windows. Program Manager will remember its current location and settings, and will look the same way the next time it comes to the screen.
- Be sure to disable the Save Settings on Exit option from Program Manager's Options menu. That way Program Manager will only save its current look when *you* want it to — by holding Shift while double-clicking in its top, left-hand corner, as if to shut it down.

How Can I Bypass My StartUp Group?

Place a program's icon into Program Manager's StartUp group window, and Program Manager will automatically load that program, each time you load Windows.

But what if you change your mind; you don't *want* those programs to pop up when you start Windows this morning? Easy solution.

When Windows starts to load, press and keep holding down Shift. That tells Program Manager not to load any of the programs listed in its StartUp Group window.

Changing an Icon's Title

Normally, there's not much reason to change an icon's title. But ever so often, an icon will push its title to the limit. For example, the title "Acme Cover Page Designer" is so long, it can cover up other icon's titles. The solution? Trim it with the tip below.

While in Program Manager, hold down Alt and double-click on the icon title you'd like to change. When the Program Item Properties box appears, type in a new, shorter title and press Enter.

Cramming More Icons into Program Manager

Sometimes, everything in Windows seems fast and automatic. For example, many brand new Windows programs will install themselves, create a new Program Group in Program Manager, and slip their own icon inside. How polite! And that new icon is easy to find, resting alone in its own huge group window.

But after you've added five or six more new Windows programs, the novelty wears off. In fact, with so many Program Groups lying around, it can be hard to find the program you want. You can combat the crowding in a couple of ways.

- Don't let each new program create its own Program Group. Instead, combine several programs into a single group, then delete their old Program Groups.

- To pack more icons into a Program Group, shrink the space between them. From the Control Panel's Desktop icon, head for the Icons box. Then change the number in the Spacing box from 75 to 65. Or, try different numbers until you find the spacing that looks best on your own desktop.
- For best results with closely packed icons, shorten the icon's titles, as described in the section above. That keeps them from overlapping.

Making Programs Start as Icons

If you don't want to use a program immediately, but want it to load from Program Manager and wait at the bottom of the screen as an icon, try this:

- When double-clicking on a program's icon in Program Manager, hold down Shift. That makes the program load as an icon at the bottom of the screen.
- Or, if you *always* want the program to load as an icon, hold down Alt while double-clicking on its icon in Program Manager. When the Program Item Properties box appears, click in the Run Minimized box.

Making Control Panel Open Sections Automatically

Some chores take a couple of steps. To change wallpaper, for example, you need to double-click on the Control Panel, then click on the Desktop icon before you can find the Wallpaper menu.

But here's how to make the Control Panel's Desktop area appear a lot faster, simply by double-clicking on an icon in Program Manager.

1. **Make a copy of the Control Panel icon in Program Manager.**

   First, point at the Control Panel icon. Then, while holding down Ctrl, drag the Control Panel to a new location in Program Manager. The mouse will *peel off* a new copy of the Control Panel icon.

2. **While holding down Alt, double-click on the new copy of the Control Panel icon.**

   The Program Item Properties box appears.

3. **In the Command line box, add a space and the word** `DESKTOP` **after the words** `C:\WINDOWS\CONTROL.EXE`.

   The Command line box should look like this:

   ```
   C:\WINDOWS\CONTROL.EXE DESKTOP
   ```

   (If Windows lives in a different directory on your own computer, you'll see your own Windows directory listed in the Command line box.)

4. **Change the Description to** `Desktop`.

   Delete the word `Control Panel` from the Description box, and type in `Desktop`.

5. **Click the OK button.**

You're through. Now, when you double-click on your new Control Panel icon, Control Panel will hop to the screen, just like before. But then Control Panel will *automatically* open its Desktop window, letting you change your wallpaper right away.

Then, when you close the Desktop window, Control Panel disappears, as well. Table 20-1 shows all the words, including DESKTOP, that will make Control Panel automatically open those special areas.

Table 20-1 Accessing Areas of the Control Panel

Adding these words . . .	*opens this area of the Control Panel after CONTROL.EXE*
COLOR	Different color scheme menu.
FONTS	Add or remove Windows fonts.
PORTS	Change the way Windows deals with your computer's COM ports.
MOUSE	Fine-tune the way Windows acts with your mouse.
DESKTOP	Change your wallpaper, screen savers, and other desktop options.
KEYBOARD	Controls the way keys repeat when you hold them down.
PRINTERS	Add or remove printers.
INTERNATIONAL	Lets Windows display currency and date in other culture's formats.
DATE/TIME	Change your computer's time or date.
MIDI MAPPER	Control how Windows plays MIDI music on your brand of sound card or synthesizer. (See Chapter 8.)
386 ENHANCED	Change Windows swap file.
DRIVERS	Add or remove drivers for things like sound cards or CD. ROM drives.
SOUND	Change which sounds are played for which Windows events.

Has a new Windows program added its *own* icon to Control Panel? Then add that icon's *title* after CONTROL.EXE in Program Manager, and Control Panel will automatically bring up that area, too.

Fixing That `Cannot find file specified in win.ini` Message

Sometimes Windows tosswa you a real headscratcher as it comes to the screen. It'll send a message like this:

```
Cannot find file specified in win.ini (or one of its components
Check to ensure the path and filename are correctand that all
required libraries are available.
```

Huh?

The solution's pretty easy, however. When Windows starts up, it looks inside a special file for instructions on what programs it should automatically heave onto the screen.

If Windows can't find a listed program, Windows heaves that "Cannot find file" error message onto the screen, instead.

That special file Windows peeks into is called WIN.INI, and it's described in Chapter 15. To stop the confusing error message? Look for the lines in WIN.INI beginning with the words `LOAD=` and `RUN=`. Both lines are near the top of the WIN.INI file.

Windows probably can't find a program mentioned in one of those two lines. Delete the reference to that program, and you'll also remove that head-scratching error message.

- That error message is harmless, just annoying.
- It usually appears after you've deleted a program that used to load itself that way. For example, if you delete Microsoft's Entertainment Pack #1 from your hard drive, the error message often starts popping up: The Entertainment Pack's screen saver used to load itself through the WIN.INI file.
- The message also appears if you've been moving directories around on your hard drive. Lazy ol' Windows doesn't bother updating WIN.INI about the move. So, when Windows tries to run a program listed in WIN.INI, the directory won't be there — so Windows sends out that merry error message.

Chapter 21

Whoops! Make It Go Back to the Other Way!

In This Chapter

- Undoing a mistake
- Restoring the original Program Manager
- Changing the name and company in the license box

Something gone horribly wrong in Windows? This chapter shows how to make Windows go back to the way it was when you first installed it. (And without having to re-install it, either.)

Undoing a Mistake

Whoops! Deleted the wrong paragraph? Entered the wrong information into a box? All is not lost.

As soon as you notice you've made a mistake, press Ctrl+Z or Alt+Backspace. Your Windows program will try to immediately undo whatever action you've just done.

Restoring Your First Program Manager Groups

Maybe the Velcro's gone bad. Some icons just seem to fall off the Program Manager and get lost.

Microsoft knew it would happen, though, so they added a fix. By following the steps below, all of Program Manager's original groups — and their original program icons — will come back to Program Manager.

1. **Select Run from the File menu in Program Manager.**
2. **Type SETUP /P in the Command line box and press Enter.**

   That's the word SETUP, a space, a forward slash, and the letter P. Then press Enter.

Program Manager will turn itself into an icon at the bottom of the screen, and your hard drive might make some churning noises. That's it; you're through.

- When you bring Program Manager back up to the screen, you'll find all your original Program Groups back on the screen again: Main, Accessories, and Games.
- All the original program icons — Calendar, Cardfile, Calculator, Clipboard Viewer, and the rest — should be back inside their normal groups.
- Do some of the restored icons look like little white boxes? That means the programs need to be re-installed onto your hard drive. Grab your Windows installation disks and head for Chapter 16. The section that says how to dump unwanted programs also says how to retrieve wanted programs.
- Are some of your Windows programs *still* missing? Then head for Windows Setup program, and choose Set Up Applications from its Options menu. Windows will root through your hard drive for every Windows program alive — and give you the option of putting their icons on Program Manager.

Changing Your Name and Company

Remember when you typed in your name and company name while installing Windows for the first time? Well, Windows remembers it. To see who Windows thinks you are, click on About Program Manager from the Program Manager's Help menu.

A box will pop up, and Windows will list the name and company you originally typed in.

But what if you change jobs? Or change names? Simply reinstalling Windows won't do the trick; Windows always sticks with the first name and company you've entered.

You could delete Windows from your hard drive and then re-install it, typing in the new information as you go. But there's a quicker way, described on the following page.

To update the name and company information, exit Windows for DOS. Then, find the file USER.EXE, living in your \WINDOWS\SYSTEM directory. Rename USER.EXE to USER.OLD. Insert Disk 1 of your Windows installation disks, and run the Setup program. Finally, follow the instructions and perform an "upgrade."

Windows will re-install itself, just like the first time. But this time, however, it will ask you to enter your name and company again.

Oh, and if something goes wrong? Then rename USER.OLD back to USER.EXE. At least that will get Windows on its feet again.

Chapter 22

The Secret Credits Screen

In This Chapter

- Hidden little doodads in Windows

When artists finish a painting, they place their names in the bottom corner. But when a programmer finishes a program, where does the name go? Many companies won't let their programmers stick their names on their programs.

So, since programmers are such a secretive, sneaky bunch, they often hide their names in the program itself. These hidden initials, sometimes called *easter eggs*, have been popping up for nearly 20 years.

Computer history buffs point back to the late 70s; back then savvy players of Atari's 2600 game console discovered a secret room with the programmer's initials hidden in the ADVENTURE game cartridge.

Today, programmers are hiding a lot more than their initials. Here are some of the goodies you'll uncover in Windows — as well as the secret keystrokes you'll need to discover them.

Uncovering the Hidden Credits in Windows 3.1

The folks at Microsoft certainly couldn't be stopped from hiding their names in Windows 3.1. Here's how to see their names:

1. **Hold down Ctrl+Shift throughout the next two steps.**
2. **Click on Program Manager's Help menu and choose About Program Manager.**

3. When the box pops up, double-click on the Windows icon.

The icon, seen in Figure 22-1, is in the box's upper-left corner.

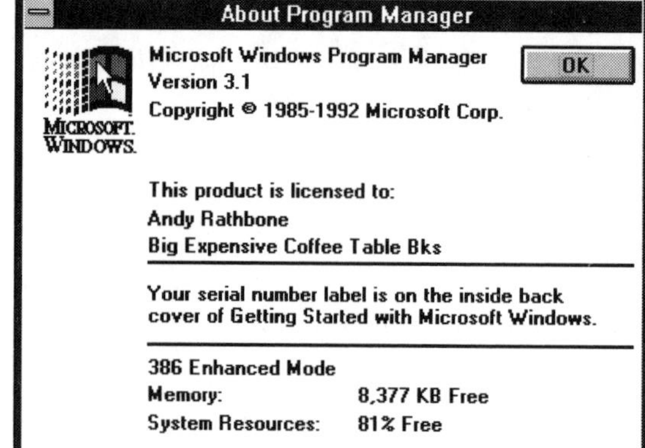

Figure 22-1: Double-click on this icon, in the upper-left corner.

4. Click OK.

5. Repeat Steps 2 through 4.

The Windows icon turns into a waving flag, as shown in Figure 22-2.

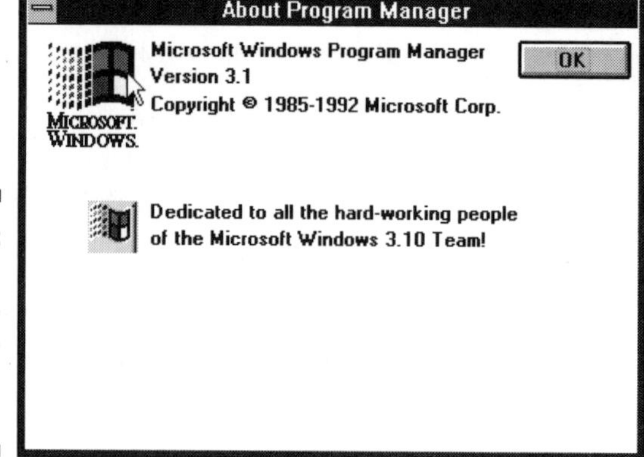

Figure 22-2: The Windows icon turns into a waving flag

6. Repeat Steps 2 through 4 again.

This time, you've hit it big time: The show begins, as seen in Figure 22-3.

- See the man pointing at the chalkboard? As you keep trying the trick, over and over, you'll spot four different guys.
- The guy with the glasses is Microsoft's CEO, Bill Gates.

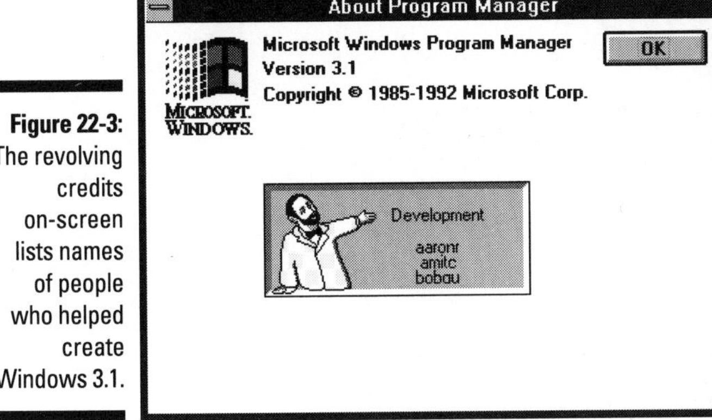

Figure 22-3: The revolving credits on-screen lists names of people who helped create Windows 3.1.

- The bald guy is Microsoft's Steve Ballmer.
- The bearded guy is Microsoft's Brad Silverberg.
- The bear is The Bear, Windows 3.1 team mascot.
- Another secret: When changing fonts in a DOS program's window (described in Chapter 5), you'll see the Bear listed as a program, BEAR.EXE, in the Selected Font preview window.
- Yet another secret: The credits screen isn't limited to Program Manager. It works in just about any program that comes with Windows: Cardfile, Calendar, Paintbrush, Clock, and others.

- Still using Windows 3.0? Then this fancy credits stuff won't work. But this trick will: While holding down F3, type `WIN3`. Then release F3 and press Backspace. Surprise — new wallpaper.

Index

• C •

• G •

• H •

• I •

• L •

• M •

• S •

• T •

• U •

• V •

• W •

Notes

DUMMIES PRESS

12/20/94

Title	Author	ISBN	Price
INTERNET / COMMUNICATIONS / NETWORKING			
CompuServe For Dummies™	by Wallace Wang	1-56884-181-7	$19.95 USA/$26.95 Canada
Modems For Dummies™, 2nd Edition	by Tina Rathbone	1-56884-223-6	$19.99 USA/$26.99 Canada
Modems For Dummies™	by Tina Rathbone	1-56884-001-2	$19.95 USA/$26.95 Canada
MORE Internet For Dummies™	by John R. Levine & Margaret Levine Young	1-56884-164-7	$19.95 USA/$26.95 Canada
NetWare For Dummies™	by Ed Tittel & Deni Connor	1-56884-003-9	$19.95 USA/$26.95 Canada
Networking For Dummies™	by Doug Lowe	1-56884-079-9	$19.95 USA/$26.95 Canada
ProComm Plus 2 For Windows For Dummies™	by Wallace Wang	1-56884-219-8	$19.99 USA/$26.99 Canada
The Internet For Dummies™, 2nd Edition	by John R. Levine & Carol Baroudi	1-56884-222-8	$19.99 USA/$26.99 Canada
The Internet For Macs For Dummies™	by Charles Seiter	1-56884-184-1	$19.95 USA/$26.95 Canada
MACINTOSH			
Macs For Dummies®	by David Pogue	1-56884-173-6	$19.95 USA/$26.95 Canada
Macintosh System 7.5 For Dummies™	by Bob LeVitus	1-56884-197-3	$19.95 USA/$26.95 Canada
MORE Macs For Dummies™	by David Pogue	1-56884-087-X	$19.95 USA/$26.95 Canada
PageMaker 5 For Macs For Dummies™	by Galen Gruman	1-56884-178-7	$19.95 USA/$26.95 Canada
QuarkXPress 3.3 For Dummies™	by Galen Gruman & Barbara Assadi	1-56884-217-1	$19.99 USA/$26.99 Canada
Upgrading and Fixing Macs For Dummies™	by Kearney Rietmann & Frank Higgins	1-56884-189-2	$19.95 USA/$26.95 Canada
MULTIMEDIA			
Multimedia & CD-ROMs For Dummies™, Interactive Multimedia Value Pack	by Andy Rathbone	1-56884-225-2	$29.95 USA/$39.95 Canada
Multimedia & CD-ROMs For Dummies™	by Andy Rathbone	1-56884-089-6	$19.95 USA/$26.95 Canada
OPERATING SYSTEMS / DOS			
MORE DOS For Dummies™	by Dan Gookin	1-56884-046-2	$19.95 USA/$26.95 Canada
S.O.S. For DOS™	by Katherine Murray	1-56884-043-8	$12.95 USA/$16.95 Canada
OS/2 For Dummies™	by Andy Rathbone	1-878058-76-2	$19.95 USA/$26.95 Canada
UNIX			
UNIX For Dummies™	by John R. Levine & Margaret Levine Young	1-878058-58-4	$19.95 USA/$26.95 Canada
WINDOWS			
S.O.S. For Windows™	by Katherine Murray	1-56884-045-4	$12.95 USA/$16.95 Canada
MORE Windows 3.1 For Dummies™, 3rd Edition	by Andy Rathbone	1-56884-240-6	$19.99 USA/$26.99 Canada
PCs / HARDWARE			
Illustrated Computer Dictionary For Dummies™	by Dan Gookin, Wally Wang, & Chris Van Buren	1-56884-004-7	$12.95 USA/$16.95 Canada
Upgrading and Fixing PCs For Dummies™	by Andy Rathbone	1-56884-002-0	$19.95 USA/$26.95 Canada
PRESENTATION / AUTOCAD			
AutoCAD For Dummies™	by Bud Smith	1-56884-191-4	$19.95 USA/$26.95 Canada
PowerPoint 4 For Windows For Dummies™	by Doug Lowe	1-56884-161-2	$16.95 USA/$22.95 Canada
PROGRAMMING			
Borland C++ For Dummies™	by Michael Hyman	1-56884-162-0	$19.95 USA/$26.95 Canada
"Borland's New Language Product" For Dummies™	by Neil Rubenking	1-56884-200-7	$19.95 USA/$26.95 Canada
C For Dummies™	by Dan Gookin	1-878058-78-9	$19.95 USA/$26.95 Canada
C++ For Dummies™	by Stephen R. Davis	1-56884-163-9	$19.95 USA/$26.95 Canada
Mac Programming For Dummies™	by Dan Parks Sydow	1-56884-173-6	$19.95 USA/$26.95 Canada
QBasic Programming For Dummies™	by Douglas Hergert	1-56884-093-4	$19.95 USA/$26.95 Canada
Visual Basic "X" For Dummies™, 2nd Edition	by Wallace Wang	1-56884-230-9	$19.99 USA/$26.99 Canada
Visual Basic 3 For Dummies™	by Wallace Wang	1-56884-076-4	$19.95 USA/$26.95 Canada
SPREADSHEET			
1-2-3 For Dummies™	by Greg Harvey	1-878058-60-6	$16.95 USA/$21.95 Canada
1-2-3 For Windows 5 For Dummies™, 2nd Edition	by John Walkenbach	1-56884-216-3	$16.95 USA/$21.95 Canada
1-2-3 For Windows For Dummies™	by John Walkenbach	1-56884-052-7	$16.95 USA/$21.95 Canada
Excel 5 For Macs For Dummies™	by Greg Harvey	1-56884-186-8	$19.95 USA/$26.95 Canada
Excel For Dummies™, 2nd Edition	by Greg Harvey	1-56884-050-0	$16.95 USA/$21.95 Canada
MORE Excel 5 For Windows For Dummies™	by Greg Harvey	1-56884-207-4	$19.95 USA/$26.95 Canada
Quattro Pro 6 For Windows For Dummies™	by John Walkenbach	1-56884-174-4	$19.95 USA/$26.95 Canada
Quattro Pro For DOS For Dummies™	by John Walkenbach	1-56884-023-3	$16.95 USA/$21.95 Canada
UTILITIES / VCRs & CAMCORDERS			
Norton Utilities 8 For Dummies™	by Beth Slick	1-56884-166-3	$19.95 USA/$26.95 Canada
VCRs & Camcorders For Dummies™	by Andy Rathbone & Gordon McComb	1-56884-229-5	$14.99 USA/$20.99 Canada
WORD PROCESSING			
Ami Pro For Dummies™	by Jim Meade	1-56884-049-7	$19.95 USA/$26.95 Canada
MORE Word For Windows 6 For Dummies™	by Doug Lowe	1-56884-165-5	$19.95 USA/$26.95 Canada
MORE WordPerfect 6 For Windows For Dummies™	by Margaret Levine Young & David C. Kay	1-56884-206-6	$19.95 USA/$26.95 Canada
MORE WordPerfect 6 For DOS For Dummies™	by Wallace Wang, edited by Dan Gookin	1-56884-047-0	$19.95 USA/$26.95 Canada
S.O.S. For WordPerfect™	by Katherine Murray	1-56884-053-5	$12.95 USA/$16.95 Canada
Word 6 For Macs For Dummies™	by Dan Gookin	1-56884-190-6	$19.95 USA/$26.95 Canada
Word For Windows 6 For Dummies™	by Dan Gookin	1-56884-075-6	$16.95 USA/$21.95 Canada
Word For Windows For Dummies™	by Dan Gookin	1-878058-86-X	$16.95 USA/$21.95 Canada
WordPerfect 6 For Dummies™	by Dan Gookin	1-878058-77-0	$16.95 USA/$21.95 Canada
WordPerfect For Dummies™	by Dan Gookin	1-878058-52-5	$16.95 USA/$21.95 Canada
WordPerfect For Windows For Dummies™	by Margaret Levine Young & David C. Kay	1-56884-032-2	$16.95 USA/$21.95 Canada

1/26/95

Fun, Fast, & Cheap!

CorelDRAW! 5 For Dummies™ Quick Reference
by Raymond E. Werner

ISBN: 1-56884-952-4
$9.99 USA/$12.99 Canada

Windows "X" For Dummies™ Quick Reference, 3rd Edition
by Greg Harvey

ISBN: 1-56884-964-8
$9.99 USA/$12.99 Canada

Word For Windows 6 For Dummies™ Quick Reference
by George Lynch

ISBN: 1-56884-095-0
$8.95 USA/$12.95 Canada

WordPerfect For DOS For Dummies™ Quick Reference
by Greg Harvey

ISBN: 1-56884-009-8
$8.95 USA/$11.95 Canada

Title	Author	ISBN	Price
DATABASE			
Access 2 For Dummies™ Quick Reference	by Stuart A. Stuple	1-56884-167-1	$8.95 USA/$11.95 Canada
dBASE 5 For DOS For Dummies™ Quick Reference	by Barry Sosinsky	1-56884-954-0	$9.99 USA/$12.99 Canada
dBASE 5 For Windows For Dummies™ Quick Reference	by Stuart J. Stuple	1-56884-953-2	$9.99 USA/$12.99 Canada
Paradox 5 For Windows For Dummies™ Quick Reference	by Scott Palmer	1-56884-960-5	$9.99 USA/$12.99 Canada
DESKTOP PUBLISHING / ILLUSTRATION/GRAPHICS			
Harvard Graphics 3 For Windows For Dummies™ Quick Reference	by Raymond E. Werner	1-56884-962-1	$9.99 USA/$12.99 Canada
FINANCE / PERSONAL FINANCE			
Quicken 4 For Windows For Dummies™ Quick Reference	by Stephen L. Nelson	1-56884-950-8	$9.95 USA/$12.95 Canada
GROUPWARE / INTEGRATED			
Microsoft Office 4 For Windows For Dummies™ Quick Reference	by Doug Lowe	1-56884-958-3	$9.99 USA/$12.99 Canada
Microsoft Works For Windows 3 For Dummies™ Quick Reference	by Michael Partington	1-56884-959-1	$9.99 USA/$12.99 Canada
INTERNET / COMMUNICATIONS / NETWORKING			
The Internet For Dummies™ Quick Reference	by John R. Levine	1-56884-168-X	$8.95 USA/$11.95 Canada
MACINTOSH			
Macintosh System 7.5 For Dummies™ Quick Reference	by Stuart J. Stuple	1-56884-956-7	$9.99 USA/$12.99 Canada
OPERATING SYSTEMS / DOS			
DOS For Dummies® Quick Reference	by Greg Harvey	1-56884-007-1	$8.95 USA/$11.95 Canada
UNIX			
UNIX For Dummies™ Quick Reference	by Margaret Levine Young & John R. Levine	1-56884-094-2	$8.95 USA/$11.95 Canada
WINDOWS			
Windows 3.1 For Dummies™ Quick Reference, 2nd Edition	by Greg Harvey	1-56884-951-6	$8.95 USA/$11.95 Canada
PRESENTATION / AUTOCAD			
AutoCAD For Dummies™ Quick Reference	by Ellen Finkelstein	1-56884-198-1	$9.95 USA/$12.95 Canada
SPREADSHEET			
1-2-3 For Dummies™ Quick Reference	by John Walkenbach	1-56884-027-6	$8.95 USA/$11.95 Canada
1-2-3 For Windows 5 For Dummies™ Quick Reference	by John Walkenbach	1-56884-957-5	$9.95 USA/$12.95 Canada
Excel For Windows For Dummies™ Quick Reference, 2nd Edition	by John Walkenbach	1-56884-096-9	$8.95 USA/$11.95 Canada
Quattro Pro 6 For Windows For Dummies™ Quick Reference	by Stuart A. Stuple	1-56884-172-8	$9.95 USA/$12.95 Canada
WORD PROCESSING			
Word For Windows 6 For Dummies™ Quick Reference	by George Lynch	1-56884-095-0	$8.95 USA/$11.95 Canada
WordPerfect For Windows For Dummies™ Quick Reference	by Greg Harvey	1-56884-039-X	$8.95 USA/$11.95 Canada

FOR MORE INFORMATION OR TO ORDER, PLEASE CALL ▸ 800. 762. 2974

For volume discounts & special orders please call Tony Real, Special Sales, at 415. 655. 3048

12/20/94

Order Center: **(800) 762-2974** *(8 a.m.–6 p.m., EST, weekdays)*

Quantity	ISBN	Title	Price	Total

Shipping & Handling Charges

	Description	First book	Each additional book	Total
Domestic	Normal	$4.50	$1.50	$
	Two Day Air	$8.50	$2.50	$
	Overnight	$18.00	$3.00	$
International	Surface	$8.00	$8.00	$
	Airmail	$16.00	$16.00	$
	DHL Air	$17.00	$17.00	$

*For large quantities call for shipping & handling charges.
**Prices are subject to change without notice.

Ship to:

Name ______________________

Company ______________________

Address ______________________

City/State/Zip ______________________

Daytime Phone ______________________

Payment: ☐ Check to IDG Books (US Funds Only)

☐ VISA ☐ MasterCard ☐ American Express

Card # ______________________ Expires __________

Signature ______________________

Subtotal __________

CA residents add applicable sales tax __________

IN, MA, and MD residents add 5% sales tax __________

IL residents add 6.25% sales tax __________

RI residents add 7% sales tax __________

TX residents add 8.25% sales tax __________

Shipping __________

Total __________

Please send this order form to:

IDG Books Worldwide
7260 Shadeland Station, Suite 100
Indianapolis, IN 46256

Allow up to 3 weeks for delivery.
Thank you!

IDG BOOKS WORLDWIDE REGISTRATION CARD

Title of this book: **MORE Windows For Dummies**

My overall rating of this book: ❑ Very good [1] ❑ Good [2] ❑ Satisfactory [3] ❑ Fair [4] ❑ Poor [5]

How I first heard about this book:

❑ Found in bookstore; name: [6] ❑ Book review: [7]

❑ Advertisement: [8] ❑ Catalog: [9]

❑ Word of mouth; heard about book from friend, co-worker, etc.: [10] ❑ Other: [11]

What I liked most about this book:

What I would change, add, delete, etc., in future editions of this book:

Other comments:

Number of computer books I purchase in a year: ❑ 1 [12] ❑ 2-5 [13] ❑ 6-10 [14] ❑ More than 10 [15]

I would characterize my computer skills as: ❑ Beginner [16] ❑ Intermediate [17] ❑ Advanced [18] ❑ Professional [19]

I use ❑ DOS [20] ❑ Windows [21] ❑ OS/2 [22] ❑ Unix [23] ❑ Macintosh [24] ❑ Other: [25] ________ (please specify)

I would be interested in new books on the following subjects:
(please check all that apply, and use the spaces provided to identify specific software)

❑ Word processing: [26] ❑ Spreadsheets: [27]

❑ Data bases: [28] ❑ Desktop publishing: [29]

❑ File Utilities: [30] ❑ Money management: [31]

❑ Networking: [32] ❑ Programming languages: [33]

❑ Other: [34]

I use a PC at (please check all that apply): ❑ home [35] ❑ work [36] ❑ school [37] ❑ other: [38] ________

The disks I prefer to use are ❑ 5.25 [39] ❑ 3.5 [40] ❑ other: [41] ________

I have a CD ROM: ❑ yes [42] ❑ no [43]

I plan to buy or upgrade computer hardware this year: ❑ yes [44] ❑ no [45]

I plan to buy or upgrade computer software this year: ❑ yes [46] ❑ no [47]

Name: Business title: [48] Type of Business: [49]

Address (❑ home [50] ❑ work [51]/Company name:)

Street/Suite#

City [52]/State [53]/Zipcode [54]: Country [55]

❑ **I liked this book!** You may quote me by name in future IDG Books Worldwide promotional materials.

My daytime phone number is ________

IDG BOOKS®
THE WORLD OF COMPUTER KNOWLEDGE

YES!

Please keep me informed about IDG's World of Computer Knowledge. Send me the latest IDG Books catalog.

NO POSTAGE NECESSARY IF MAILED IN THE UNITED STATES

BUSINESS REPLY MAIL

FIRST CLASS MAIL PERMIT NO. 2605 FOSTER CITY, CALIFORNIA

IDG Books Worldwide
919 E Hillsdale Blvd, STE 400
Foster City, CA 94404-9691